Stairway to Heaven

A Journey to the Summit of Mount Emei

SUNY series in Chinese Philosophy and Culture
Roger T. Ames, editor

Stairway to Heaven

A Journey to the Summit of Mount Emei

JAMES M. HARGETT

State University of New York Press

Cover image: "Buddha's Glory" on Mount Emei. Photograph by Liu Yong 劉勇.

Published by
State University of New York Press, Albany

Printed in the United States of America

For information, address State University of New York Press,
194 Washington Avenue, Suite 700, Albany, NY 12210-2384

Production by Judith Block
Marketing by Susan Petrie

Library of Congress Control Number
Hargett, James M. (James Morris),
       Stairway to heaven: a journey to the summit of Mount Emei / James M. Hargett.
       p.   cm.
       Includes bibliographical references and index.
       ISBN 0-7914-6681-7 (hardcover : alk. paper)—ISBN 978-0-7914-6682-7 (pbk. :
alk. paper)
    1. Buddhism—China—Emei Mountain. 2. Emei Mountain (China)—Religion.
I. Title: Journey to the summit of Mount Emei.   II. Title.
BQ649.O45H37 2006
294.3′435′095138—dc22

2005012106

ISBN-13 978-0-7914-6681-0 (hardcover : alk. paper)

10 9 8 7 6 5 4 3 2 1

To Professor Irving Yucheng Lo (1922–2005),
My Teacher

師恩難忘, 惠澤終生

Contents

Illustrations

Acknowledgments

This is a study about a famous mountain in southwest China called "Emei" (pronounced "Uh-may"; sometimes spelled "Omei"). Although few people in America and Europe have ever heard of Mount Emei, its reputation in East Asia is legendary. The landscape on Emei is spectacular and breathtaking, which is one reason that human activity on and around the mountain has been continuous for about the past three thousand years.

The Republican era scholar Zhao Xunbo 趙循伯, writing in his 1935 preface to the *Illustrated Talks on Mount Emei* (*Eshan tushuo*), remarks: "It is surely insufficient to portray in words the loveliness of Emei's scenery; unless one beholds it personally, he will not believe it." From the outset, a question related to Zhao Xunbo's observation has occupied my thoughts: how does one *write* about a natural phenomenon (in this case, a mountain) whose most apparent and striking quality is *visual*? At least a preliminary answer to this question is suggested by seventeenth-century scholar Luo Sen 羅森, who notes in his 1672 preface to the *Mount Emei Gazetteer*: "The beauty of landscape is enhanced and manifested by man; without travel there would be no way to discover its perfection; without writings there would be no way to reveal its wonders." In writing about the history and importance of Mount Emei in Chinese cultural history, I have sought above all else to explain how and why Emei earned and maintained the epithet "famous mountain." As we will see on the pages to follow, however, much of the mountain's fame is indeed related directly to its physical environment. If I can "reveal" some of the mountain's "wonders" and thereby help readers to discover at least some of its "perfection," then I shall feel gratified indeed.

During the research and writing of this book I received help and encouragement from many individuals. First and foremost, I acknowledge indebtedness to my mentor, Professor Irving Yucheng Lo (Luo Yuzheng

羅郁正; 1922–2005), to whom this book is dedicated. Whatever merit my study may have is due in large part to the training and encouragement I have received from Professor Lo. I also wish to express thanks to my colleagues in the Department of East Asian Studies at the University at Albany, State University of New York, especially Mark Blum, Anthony DeBlasi, Susanna Fessler, and Charles Hartman, who read through numerous draft versions of chapters and always had useful suggestions for improvement.

There are few scholars in the world who command detailed knowledge about Mount Emei and its long, complicated history. I am fortunate in that two of these experts, Justin O'Jack and Xiong Feng 熊鋒, played supportive and influential roles in the research and writing of this book. Justin often shared his vast knowledge of Emei with me and meticulously read through and commented on all of my chapters. Mr. Xiong Feng, Chief Historian at the Mount Emei Museum, always found time to accompany me on my climbs to the summit, and on numerous occasions helped to clarify problems or inconsistencies in the sources. I also thank Justin and Xiong Feng for preparing the two maps that appear in this book.

While preparing this study I received financial support from several institutions. Initial field work in China (1993) was undertaken with a grant from the Committee on Scholarly Communication with the People's Republic of China. Subsequent research and travel to Mount Emei was supported by two Faculty Research Awards from the University at Albany. A Fulbright-Hays Research Abroad Fellowship from the U.S. Department of Education made it possible for me spend the 2002–2003 academic year in China, where I completed most of my research and writing. To the many friends and colleagues at my host institution, Fudan University, especially Professors Chen Yinzhang 陳寅章 and Xu Yongming 徐永明 (now at Zhejiang University), I owe a tremendous debt of gratitude. Thanks also to the distinguished members of the Traditional China Seminar at Columbia University, who offered many useful comments about my Mount Emei project. I express special thanks to Professor Pei-yi Wu, for it was he who first suggested that I present my study of Emei shan through the travel writings of the twelfth-century writer and official Fan Chengda (1126–1193).

Much of chapter 2 appeared in an article titled "Li Bo (701–762) and Mount Emei," published in *Cahiers d'Extrême Asie* 8 (1995): 67–85. I am grateful to the editor of that journal, Dr. Hubert Durt, for allowing me to use material from the article in the present work. Some portions of chapter 2 were also presented at the conference "Mountains and Cultures of Landscape in China: Tang Dynasty, Five Dynasties Period, Song Dynasty," held at University of California, Santa Barbara, January 14–16, 1993. My specials thanks go to conference participants Terry F. Kleeman and Allan G. Grapard, who read and commented on my paper "Literary Visions of Mount Emei during the Tang and Song."

Other friends and colleagues who helped me along the way include Stephen D. Allee, Chi Ling 遲玲, Cong Zhiyuan 叢志遠 (who executed the beautiful calligraphy on the title page), Amy Goldman, Thomas H. Hahn, Ellen Johnston Laing, Li Cho-ying 李卓穎, Alexandra Xiaoying Li 李曉穎, Alfreda Murck, Denielle Nadeau, Jaclyn T. Stone, Wenjing Wang 王文靜, Zhang Cong 張聰, Zhang Jun 章君, and Zhenwei 鎮巍 (Jeffrey). Thanks also to Xia Tiqiang 夏體强, chairman of the Mount Emei Tourist Company, Ltd., and Chen Liqing 陳黎清, director of the Mount Emei Museum, both of whom hosted me during many visits to the mountain.

Of course, any errors that remain in this book are my responsibility alone.

James M. Hargett
Guilderland, New York
4 December 2004

Conventions

Buddhist/Sanskrit terms: Familiar Sanskrit words in English, such as sūtra, stūpa, and saṃgha, are not italicized. Sūtra titles and specialized Buddhist terms are usually given in Hanyu Pinyin; on first occurrence the Sanskrit version of the title or name, including diacritics, is also provided. With just a few exceptions, the names of Indian and Chinese Buddhist monks are given in Hanyu Pinyin.

Chinese characters: Chinese characters appear in the text and notes only when a special or technical term begs further clarification, or when an author/title is cited in the note that is not included in the selected bibliography. Chinese characters for all remaining names, official titles, places, terms, and so on, appear in the glossary-index.

Date Conversion: All original Chinese lunar calendar dates have been converted to Western dates based on the tables in *Liangqian nian Zhong-Xi li duizhao biao* 兩千年中西曆對照表 (*A Sino-Western Calendar for Two Thousand Years* (1940; rpt., Taibei: Guomin chubanshe, 1958).

Linear, Area, and Weight Measures: Song dynasty linear measures mentioned in this book are listed below. My main source for metric equivalents is Wenren Jun and James M. Hargett, "The Measures *Li* and *Mou* during the Song, Liao, and Jin Dynasties," *Bulletin of Sung-Yuan Studies* 21 (1989): 8–30.

LINEAR MEASURES

chi 尺: 1 *chi* ("foot") = 31.6 cm = 12.6 in

bu 步: 1 *bu* ("double-pace") = 5 *chi* = 158 cm = 6.3 ft

li 里: 1 *li* ("mile") = 360 *bu* = 568.9 m = 1,877.6 ft

ren 仞: 1 *ren* = 8 *chi* = 252.8 cm = 101.1 in = 8.4 ft

zhang 丈: 1 *zhang* = 10 *chi* = 316.1 cm = 126.4 in = 12.0 ft

Note: the last two measures on this list, *ren* and *zhang*, are often used with large numbers for hyperbolic effect, as in the line "A jade-white peak suddenly rises to a height of three thousand *zhang*!"

AREA MEASURES

mou 亩: 1 *mou* = 240 sq *bu* = 453.4 sq m = 1,373.9 sq ft

jian 間 ("room" or "bay"): *Jian* is a measure used for floor space in Chinese architecture, similar to the Japanese *tsubo* 坪. Oblong in shape, it varies in length and width.

WEIGHT AND CAPACITY MEASURES

dan 石 ("picul"): 1 *dan* = approx. 50 kg = 110 lbs

hu 斛 ("bushel"): 1 *hu* = 32.2 liters = 0.94 U.S. bushels

"Mount Emei": The Chinese characters for Mount Emei are usually written as 峨眉山 (Emei shan), though some authors prefer to write the name as 峨嵋山. I will use the first of these forms. Although in the past the name of the mountain was often spelled "Omei" in English, the more accepted spelling now is the Hanyu Pinyin version, which is "Emei."

Office and government agency titles: English translations for office and government agency titles generally follow those given in Charles O. Hucker, *A Dictionary of Official Titles in Imperial China*.

Orthography: Full-form or traditional Chinese characters (*fanti zi* 繁體字) will be used throughout this study.

Place names: The modern equivalents for Song dynasty place names are identified on first occurrence.

Romanization: This work follows the Hanyu Pinyin system of phonetic transliteration for Chinese names.

Song dynasty government administrative units: Song dynasty government administrative units are translated as follows:

lu 路: circuit

fu 府: municipality

zhou 州: county

xian 縣: town

jun 軍: command

zhen 鎮: market town

xiang 鄉: village

In order to distinguish the Song dynasty terms listed above from *modern* administrative names, such as *xian* 縣 and *shi* 市 ("city"), the latter will be written in italics (Emei *shi*, Baoxing *xian*, and so on).

Translations from the Chinese: With just one or two noted exceptions, all translations from the Chinese are mine.

CHAPTER 1

Introduction

I've come to understand that there's an interaction between people and environments that changes us, and I suppose it also changes the environment. Which is the actor and which is the reactor is not always clear.[1]
—Peter H. Hackett, M.D.

TEXT AND CONTEXT

Since first conceiving the idea to write a book about Mount Emei, I have been concerned about the context in which to present such a study. There are certainly enough primary and secondary sources available to produce a general history of the mountain organized along chronological or dynastic lines. I also considered adopting a framework that would present topically arranged chapters on key subjects critical in the development of the mountain's identity and role in Chinese culture. Examples might include individual essays on Mount Emei's rich Daoist immortal (*xian*) tradition, the later arrival and development of Buddhism on the mountain, and literary works written by famous visitors through the dynasties. While there is no denying that religious activity, especially Buddhism, is central to Mount Emei's growth as a cultural phenomenon in China, it is limiting to view Emei shan simply as a "famous Buddhist mountain." This is because religion represents just one part of the mountain's history and identity. I am more interested in looking at Emei in its greater complexity. But this approach presents a formidable challenge, for the full complexity I seek to define is an intricate and diverse picture and there are many factors that determine why and how Mount Emei functions as a "famous mountain." In other words, there are numerous ways in which Emei shan is understood.

Now, mindful of avoiding a plunge into what James Robson calls "the abyss of loose syncretism,"[2] I propose a methodological approach that includes scrutiny of, and yet at the same time is not limited to, religious traditions. Essentially, I view all of China's "famous mountains" as multifaceted phenomena of *human experience*. My main interest lies in examining Mount Emei's various properties of *place*, in particular, the special features of the mountain's remote location and the distinct physical, botanical, and meteorological characteristics that make it unique; *space*, that is, the relationships among various sites on Emei, both natural and man-made; and what I call *interaction*. This last category refers to the different ways in which humans have either reacted to and/or modified Mount Emei's place and space. Examples might include writing a poem, carving an inscription into a cliff-side wall, taking up residence in one of Emei shan's caves, building a monastery, or even hurling oneself off the summit in order to reach the arms of Buddha and achieve "instant nirvana." Without a doubt, Emei's remote location and unique environment have played decisive roles in what has happened there since humans first arrived thousands of years ago.

Of course, there are many reasons why particular persons might react to a given place and attempt to modify it to serve their own purposes. For instance, people of different occupations, religious interests, and educational backgrounds often brought their own understanding to Emei and thus responded to it differently. As we will see in later chapters, those persons who came to Emei tend to fall into certain groups with common interests and they reacted to and sometimes modified the mountain's place and space in ways that can be isolated and studied. Once this examination is complete, some assessment can be made of Mount Emei's role concerning sense of place in traditional China. The most practical way to undertake such an examination is to articulate and examine the various "imprints" of human activity that have been made there throughout the dynastic period. Although these phenomena appear in many forms, based on my readings and visits to the mountain I identify five that seem to be the most important and influential: (1) myths about the mountain's religious origins; (2) legends of Daoist immortals who are associated with Emei; (3) the arrival and development of Buddhism on the mountain; (4) the numerous poems, prose works, and inscriptions written about Emei through the dynasties; and (5) recent developments in the tourism industry there. These key imprints are all "present" on the mountain and affect its residents and visitors in one way or another. For instance, one cannot properly understand Buddhist activities on Emei shan without knowledge of its earlier Daoist immortal tradition; one cannot comprehend the miraculous "Precious Light" (Baoguang) on the summit without some knowledge of the mountain's physical geography; and one cannot visit Mount Emei today without being affected by the profound physical changes (roads, a cable car, ski slope, hotels, a museum, and so on) made by the government-run tourism industry now in operation there. These imprints will be examined on the pages that follow. My task is to elucidate how and why each of these imprints resulted from human interaction with Emei's place and space. I will also attempt to determine how and why they relate to each other. Ultimately, my goal is to define Mount Emei as a complex amalgam of distinct physical environment and diverse human experience.

Given my interest in presenting the "big picture" and in following a more "get-the-reader-involved" approach to examining Mount Emei, I propose that we take a journey to the mountain itself. In other words, rather than "talk at" readers about the mountain, most of whom have probably never visited Sichuan, I will attempt to lead readers on a "trip" to the mountain. Ideally, we should all gather at the Loyal-to-the-State Monastery (Baoguo si) in the foothills, and then begin our ascent on foot. Over the next two or three days, before finally reaching the summit, much of Emei's place and space would unfold before our eyes. We would also observe how people have interacted with the mountain in the past and how they continue to do so today. While this approach may be ideal, for logistical reasons it is not practical. I propose that we instead take a trip to the mountain vicariously through the writings of the twelfth-century writer and official Fan Chengda (1126–1193). Fan's travel diary and verse accounts of his climb to the summit of Mount Emei in 1177 still rank among the most detailed and informative descriptions of the mountain ever written. Through his eyes, words, and footsteps, along with background information, explanation, and commentary provided by me, we will discover and experience some of the ways in which the mountain has been "constructed" by diverse human experiences over the centuries.

On Studying Mountains

> mountain: *a natural elevation of the earth's surface, usually rising more or less abruptly from the surrounding level, and attaining an altitude which, relatively to adjacent elevations, is impressive or notable.*[3]
> —The Oxford English Dictionary

A fascinating area of inquiry that partly inspired the writing of this book concerns the different methodologies one can use to study mountains as cultural phenomena in China. There is no consensus on this issue in the scholarly community. Since I have already outlined the approach and context I will use to determine how Mount Emei's physical environment was understood and utilized in traditional China and how it continues to be modified today, it seems appropriate to now comment on previous studies about mountains in China and recent trends in the field. This background will help to illustrate how my approach differs from my predecessors.

In Western scholarship concerning mountain traditions in China, one frequently encounters the expression "sacred mountain(s)."[4] This is especially the case with reference to China's most famous group of peaks, the Wuyue, often translated as the "Five Sacred Mountains" or "Five Marchmounts"[5] (I will say more about the Wuyue later). The expression "sacred [Chinese] mountain(s)" originates in Western scholarship and has no precise counterpart in ancient or modern Chinese.[6] Presumably, scholars use this expression to demarcate certain "sacred" mountains in China from those that are not so "sacred." Mircea Eliade's term "profane" is even sometimes invoked when referring to "nonsacred" or "secular" space and mountains in China.[7] As a starting point, I would argue that the so-called separation between "sacred" and "profane" space has no place in scholarship about Chinese mountains because no such distinction exists in the Chinese context.[8] Mountains in China might be best described as multipurpose or multifunctional. That is to say, they serve many functions, some religious, some nonreligious, for a variety of people, oftentimes *simultaneously*. To cite just two examples, many hermits in the traditional period took up residence on Mount Emei because they thought it was an ideal place for meditation and study, while numerous businessmen today run hotels on the mountain simply to make money. It might also be mentioned that Buddhist monasteries on Emei and elsewhere, in addition to their religious interests and pursuits, have always engaged in business ventures of one sort or another, such as land ownership and management, operating industrial installations, managing financial transactions, providing lodging and meals to pilgrims, selling incense and candles, and so on.[9] Now, if someone decides to study one particular aspect of a mountain—for example, the development of Buddhism on Mount Emei—this is certainly a legitimate and potentially worthwhile endeavor. However, as I have already argued, to *define* Mount Emei solely as a "Buddhist mountain" is parochial and downright misleading. The development of Buddhism on the mountain is a central factor in its long history, but it is not the only one; there are many others. My "five imprints" represent the factors I regard as most important.

Scholars in China, on the other hand, have often lumped China's best-known mountains into one broad category, which they call "famous mountains" (*mingshan* 名山). This term is also problematic because it lacks precise definition. Virtually any mountain in China that has gained attention on just about any level can be declared *ming*, or "famous." Furthermore, ideas in China about which mountains were "famous" changed over time.[10] In other words, which peaks deserve the title *mingshan* would depend on the historical period we are talking about and the ideas about "famous mountains" circulating at that time. The gray area here is substantial. Therefore, use of *mingshan* as a critical term to enhance our understanding of the role of mountains in Chinese culture is limited. Having said that, there are still selected mountains in China that have consistently maintained their *ming* status over time. The Wuyue, mentioned earlier, certainly fit into this category, as does Emei shan.

Mount Emei was never part of the state-controlled Wuyue system. Yet, it has enjoyed an ever-increasing level of "famous" status from at least the Western Jin period (265–316) right up to today. We know about the mountain's long-standing reputation because it is confirmed in textual sources. The earliest of these is a reference in Zuo Si's (ca. 250–ca. 305) well-known literary composition "Shu Capital Rhapsody ("Shudu fu"). While delimiting the peripheral area around Chengdu, the ancient capital of Shu (or Sichuan), Zuo Si writes: "It adjoins the layered barriers of [Mount] Emei."[11] This line, probably written some time around the year 280,[12] is the earliest, reliable mention of Mount Emei in surviving written records.[13] Thereafter, we see a steady stream of literary references to the mountain that increase over time. The richest periods for written sources on the mountain—poems, inscriptions, travel diaries, local histories, and mountain gazetteers—are the Ming (1368–1644), Qing (1644–1911), and the early Republican (Minguo) eras. I will use these sources to help contextualize Fan Chengda's experience on the mountain in 1177 and Emei's subsequent development into modern times.

As far as my own research approach is concerned, I acknowledge the influence of two distinguished scholars whose work pioneered the study of mountains in China: Édouard Chavannes (1865–1918) and Edward H. Schafer (1913–1991). Chavannes' study of Mount Tai (Taishan) published in 1910 and titled *Le Tai chan: essai du monographie d'un culte chinois* consists largely of annotated translations of relevant historical texts, prayers, and stele inscriptions. Many of the source texts used for his study were gathered by Chavannes himself in the form of rubbings taken from inscriptions in temples on or near the mountain. Chavannes' main goal was to define the role of Taishan as it relates to the Wuyue system, popular beliefs, and especially religious rites. The varied content of *Le Tai chan* reveals that he did not view the historical development of the mountain as static. Instead, he saw a dynamic process over time that included local lore and a period of Buddhist influence. In other words, the role of Mount Tai in Chinese culture was a complex one that developed and changed over time. This is an important point that applies to all of China's *mingshan*: the way man viewed, interpreted, and used these peaks changed through the dynasties. One common paradigm related to change observed by many scholars is an initial period of Daoist-related activity followed by a later period of Buddhist influence.[14] The development of Daoism and Buddhism on Mount Emei follows this same pattern.

Edward H. Schafer's monograph *Mao Shan in T'ang Times* has also played an influential role on the methodological approach followed in this book. As was the case with *Le Tai chan*, Schafer has a particular, well-focused interest: Mount Mao (Maoshan; in modern Jiangsu) and its relation to a form of Daoism known by the same name that flourished among the upper classes of China between the fifth and tenth centuries. This persuasion of Daoism is also known as Shangqing, or "Supreme Clarity." In constructing the history of Daoist and alchemical traditions associated with Maoshan and the surrounding region, Schafer mines numerous texts, especially the verses of Tang poets. The author specially notes the importance of Tang poetry as a historical-geographical source. Rather than rely solely on Daoist works concerning Maoshan, Schafer consults a wide variety of texts, such as geographical treatises and gazetteers, many of which are not Daoist in orientation. One aspect of Schafer's methodology that influenced me is that in defining Maoshan's role as a "Daoist mountain" he carefully considers landscape and natural history, including the mountain's geological base, limestone caverns, and avian community; various structures, especially religious edifices, that dotted Maoshan's landscape in the Tang; and secular life and local industries in the area. Although Schafer's main interest is religious Daoism, readers of *Mao Shan in T'ang Times* get a full picture (as far as the sources will allow) of the physical features of the mountain, why it attracted human interest, and the results of that attention. This is what I will do with Mount Emei. The trails blazed by Chavannes and Schafer have defined the basic ingredients to my research approach: close attention to all primary sources available; presentation of selected, annotated translations; and the idea of viewing the development or evolution of the mountain and its relation with humans over time as a *dynamic* rather than a static process.

Over the last twenty years or so, the study of China's mountain traditions has burgeoned in the West, especially among scholars in the United States and Europe whose main research interest is traditional Chinese religion. One of the key issues to emerge from this body of work concerns methodology: is it productive and knowledge producing, some scholars ask, to follow the more "traditional" approach and study Chinese religion along strict sectarian and hence insulated lines? For instance, should researchers interested in one particular "Buddhist" mountain, such as Mount Wutai (Wutai shan) in Shanxi, limit their attention to only Buddhist-related texts, issues, and traditions? Should scholars concerned with a particular "Daoist" mountain, such as Mount Qingcheng (Qingcheng shan) in Sichuan, only pursue a Daoist-related research agenda? The late Anna Seidel (1938–1991) challenged this "traditional" approach, concluding it had led to the "particularly distressing gulf of mutual ignorance [that] separates Buddhist and Taoist studies."[15] One positive result of this debate has been the emergence, in the works of some scholars, of a methodological perspective that seeks to bridge the "distressing gulf of mutual ignorance" Seidel described more than a decade ago. Scholars following this interdisciplinary approach are now building bridges across traditional sectarian lines, primarily Buddhist and Daoist. In my view, there have been some excellent results to date and, assuming current publishing trends continue, we can expect to see more in the future.[16]

CRASHING CONTINENTS AND SALTY SEAS

Although the geology of Asia seems to present a chaotic jumble of land forms, much of the deformation of the surface, when viewed as a whole with the help of satellite photographs, seems to fall into a simple, coherent pattern attributable to a single cause: a geological collision between the Indian subcontinent and the rest of Eurasia.[17]

—Peter Molnar and Paul Tapponnier

In the early years of the twentieth century a few scientists, most notably the German meteorologist Alfred Wegener (1880–1930), suggested that the earth was once comprised of a single, massive, chunk of land, which later broke apart to form the major continents in the world today.[18] Although many experts were initially skeptical about Wegener's theory of "drifting continents," later discoveries confirmed his hypothesis. Today most geologists agree that the world's continents have indeed moved apart. This phenomenon has a special name: "plate tectonics." The idea of plate tectonics is simple: the earth's crust is made of up several rigid plates, comprised of both continents and oceans, all moving in different directions.

About forty-five million years ago, two of these continental "rafts," the Indian plate and the Eurasian plate, collided. The land along the impact zone was violently squeezed together, buckling and deforming the earth's crust. One major consequence of this crash of continents was the creation of the Himalayas, the highest mountains in the world. The crest of the Himalayas marks the precise collision line. Another result was the lifting of the Qinghai-Tibetan Plateau, which established the west-to-east river drainage pattern followed by China's major rivers. Even today China is still gradually pushed eastward to make room for India's continued "drift" northward. It is the pushing motion of this displacement that causes most of China's earthquakes.

In addition to creating the Himalayas and Qinghai-Tibetan Plateau, the collision between the Indian and Eurasian plates engendered widespread rifting, which in turn led to dramatic vertical uplift and subsistence. These upheavals were most intense in western China, closer to the impact zone and where the earth's crust was thickest (about 70 km/42 mi). This explains why the western part of the country is now higher than the eastern part. The elevated regions formed by this rifting process are today's mountains; those areas that subsided are today's basins and plains.

China's mountain systems are often classified according to their directional orientation, of which there are five general types: (1) west-to-east; (2) north-to-south; (3) north-to-east; (4) north-to-west; and (5) arc-shaped mountain chains. The first of these, mountain systems that run from west-to-east, are especially important because they mark key geographical boundaries in China. For instance, the Kunlun Mountain Range (Kunlun shanling) forms the dividing line between southern Xinjiang and the Qinghai-Tibetan Plateau. From the border of southern Xinjiang, the Kunlun Range then runs eastward into modern Qinghai province where it diverges to form the Bayan Har or Central Kunlun and Nanling chains. The second of these, the Nanling chain, extends southwest, where it forms the Min Mountains (Minshan) in northern Sichuan. This chain, in turn, continues on a southerly course and forms several smaller ranges, one of which is known as the Qionglai Mountain Range (Qionglai shanling). Mount Emei stands alone on the very southern fringe of this range.[19]

Before the crash of the Indian and Eurasian plates, the area now known as Sichuan, along with most of Southeast Asia, sat at the bottom of a huge, salty ocean. As a result of the great collision and later geological changes, this ancient sea vanished long ago. But remnants of its legacy, such as salt deposits, natural gas, and even marine fossils, remain deep within the bowels of Mount Emei. Access to the heart of the mountain is provided by caverns or grottoes (*dong* 洞). Emei's numerous grottoes, varying in size, are found at lower (about 650 m/2,132 ft), mid-mountain (about 1,700 m/5,576 ft), and higher elevations (about 2,100 m/6,888 ft).

In some traditional sources, these caves are collectively designated as Mount Emei's "grotto heaven" (*dongtian* 洞天). The word *tian* (or "heaven") in this expression refers to a counterworld or counteruniverse where Daoist adepts sometimes retreated to practice various meditation, visualization, and life-extending techniques.[20] It is not surprising, then, that Mount Emei's grottoes have long served as the setting for numerous ancient tales and as the home of some of its most famous and eccentric residents. Several of these legendary figures will be discussed in chapter 4.

SOURCE OF LIFE, ABODE OF GODS

All mountains, big and small, have gods and spirits.[21]
—Ge Hong (283–343)

China's first comprehensive dictionary, the *Shuowen jiezi* (or *Shuowen*), compiled by Xu Shen (ca. 55–ca.149) in 100 AD and presented by his son to the throne in 121, defines mountains as follows: "'Mountain' means propagate vital breath and disperse and give life to the myriad beings."[22] The significance of this definition cannot be overstated, for here, in what is China's most authoritative ancient dictionary, we are told that mountains propagate or exhale (*xuan* 宣) the very vital breath (*qi* 氣) of the universe, thereby dispersing and giving life (*sansheng* 散生) to the "myriad beings" (*wanwu* 萬物; that is, all living things). According to the *Shuowen jiezi*, then, mountains are the very source of life. Why would Xu Shen define mountains in such a way? At the outset we should note that rain, essential for human survival, came from the clouds that gathered above China's numerous peaks. Moreover, as in many other cultures throughout the world, because of their height mountains were viewed as points of contact between the human world and the heavens above. Related to this is the idea that mountains possess spiritual significance because they were believed to serve as the abodes of gods or spirits. This belief is confirmed in numerous ancient texts. As an example, consider the following passage from the *Record of Ritual* (*Liji*), one of the classic works of Confucianism. The extant version of this text probably dates from about the time of Xu Shen's dictionary: "Mountains and rivers are the means by which [the earth] plays host to ghosts and spirits."[23] Since mountains host spirits (*shen*), the Chinese believed they possessed spiritual power. This point plays an especially prominent role in the discussions that follow in subsequent chapters, for many people in traditional China believed that the divine or spiritual potency of mountains could, on special occasions and under the right circumstances, be tapped and used for the benefit of man.

That is not to say, however, that all mountains were thought to be allies of man. The line from the *Record of Rites* quoted in the previous paragraph mentioned that mountains also hosted ghosts (*gui*), which in China were never regarded as beneficial in human affairs. Indeed, some heights were viewed as potentially harmful to man and, at times, even deadly. As early as the fourth century, some observers still viewed mountains as what might be called "zones of terror."[24] The famous literary recluse Ge Hong (283–343), one of China's first advisers on mountain travel, offers a warning: "Most of those who are ignorant of the proper method for entering mountains will meet with misfortune and mishap."[25] To avoid such calamity, Ge Hong advised would-be mountain sojourners to take certain precautions. For instance, climbers should fast for seven days before their ascent, embark only during auspicious months of the year, and always wear certain talismans. Dangling a nine-inch mirror on one's back was believed to especially useful in warding off *mei*, or goblins.[26] The inspiration for Ge Hong's advice is twofold. First, he was concerned with visitors being unfamiliar with the strange sights, sounds, beasts, and vermin who inhabit mountain environs; and second, he was worried about human encounters with ghosts or goblins. This second point is significant in our discussion. While all mountains host spirits that serve as governing deities, not all of these are "proper spirits" (*zhengshen*). Some "lesser mountains" (*xiaoshan*) have noxious spirits and thus do not bring good fortune to man.

Ge Hong's advice and prescriptions tell us much about how man first came to understand mountains in China. In addition to their spiritual connections and attributes, mountains also have special or unusual *physical* features that inspire fear and reverence in human beings. Here I refer specifically to dramatic mountain topography, unfamiliar meteorological or geological phenomena, and strange beasts. Imagine a flatlander hearing the haunting roar of a tiger echo through one of Mount Emei's deep, mist-shrouded canyons for the first time. When man attempts to understand or deal with the fears inspired by such places, he reasonably concludes that mountains are the abode of spirits and gods. The presence of spirits and gods offers an immediate and convenient explanation for the unusual qualities of high-altitude environments: these are unique territories that host extraordinary beings. In turn, this explanation leads to other, related conclusions. For instance, since mountains are inhabited by "local" spirits, it seems they might act as intermediaries to even higher celestial beings. Here we find the explanation as to why so many people in traditional China, from emperor to commoner, often journeyed to mountains to offer sacrifices: mountains can serve as contact points between the mortal world and realms, powers, and beings that lie beyond.

Early in Chinese history, probably sometime during the late Zhou or early Han, a special group of peaks in China were selected by imperial authority to serve as official, state-sanctioned mountains.[27] These are the Wuyue, mentioned earlier. They include Mount Tai in Shandong, the "Eastern Yue"; Mount Hua (Huashan) in Shaanxi, the "Western Yue"; Mount Heng (Hengshan) in Shanxi, the "Northern Yue"; Mount Heng (Hengshan) in Hunan, the "Southern Yue"; and Mount Song (Songshan) in Henan, the "Central Yue." In 72 BC Emperor Xuan of the Western Han dynasty (r. 74–49 BC) formally institutionalized the Wuyue and ordered that state ritual ceremonies be performed there. Government officials were dispatched to these mountains, where state rituals would be carried out. Among the most significant of these was the *feng* and *shan* rituals performed at Mount Tai in Shandong. On some occasions, emperors personally attended and participated in these ceremonies.

The purposes of these sacrifices were many. The *feng* ritual, for instance, performed on the summit of Mount Tai, was designed so the emperor could express his thanks to Heaven for conferring upon him the mandate to rule. The *shan* ritual, on the other hand, carried out at the foot of Mount Tai, offered the emperor an opportunity to express his thanks to the Earth for a bountiful harvest. These rituals and the Wuyue came to be associated with the emperor's legitimate authority, sanctioned by Heaven, to rule. The various compass points marked out by the Wuyue signified the empire's four geographic regions and defined the cultural boundaries of China. When this happened, the Wuyue moved beyond their local reputations and assumed roles in a comprehensive, nationwide system of religious, social, and political beliefs. Of course, there was nothing sacred or historical about these mountains until humans started "altering" them by bestowing names, defining them as sites for official state ceremonies, and associating them with various symbolic qualities.[28] This is essentially what happened with all of China's so-called *mingshan*. They were first tagged, for specific reasons, with an assortment of titles or names. Over time they acquired various associations and qualities, determined in large part by location, physical geography, and especially the actions (or interactions) of humans there. It is the accumulated experience of these activities that defines a famous mountain's place within China's cultural cosmos.

AN EXTRAORDINARY PLACE

> *Mount Emei is so high—*
> *Its heights pierce the heavens!*[29]
>
> —Dagui (Ming dynasty Buddhist monk)

To most Western readers, the word "mountain" suggests a single mass of rock and earth prominently rising from the earth's surface. Humans have always found it necessary to give names to these conspicuous land forms, especially when they are first "discovered." Certainly one purpose of these designations is to establish an "identity" for reference purposes. For instance, it is much easier to say "Mount Whitney" than "the highest peak in the contiguous United States, located in Sequoia National Park in east-central California."

Since ancient times the Chinese have also customarily bestowed names on their mountains, and have done so for probably the same reason. It makes sense to use specific names to identify specific places. We must be mindful, however, that the Chinese do not always use these toponyms to identify *single*, prominent elevations of earth. In fact, on many occasions what appears to many Westerners as a single name is actually a collective term referring to a *number of* peaks within a defined area. Yellow Mountain (Huangshan) in Anhui province is a good example. Its surface area covers more than 150 sq km/93 sq mi and is dotted with seventy-two individual peaks, each with a separate name. In many ways, it resembles what Americans would think of as a national park. Mount Emei's physical layout follows this same general pattern.

The perimeter of the area usually identified as "Mount Emei" extends for more than 600 sq km/360 sq mi.[30] Four peaks within this zone traditionally comprised "Mount Emei." Although each of these mountains is known by a host of different names, most often they are simply called "Big Emei," "Second Emei," "Third Emei," and "Fourth Emei." Among these, Big Emei has received the most attention. There are many reasons that account for Big Emei's fame, but two stand out: first, it possesses some of the most sublime mountain landscape scenery in all China; and second, Big Emei's own trio of summits marks the three loftiest points on Mount Emei. The highest of these, standing at 3,099 m/10,167 ft above sea level, is called the "Ten Thousand Buddhas Summit" (Wanfo ding). Hereafter, unless otherwise noted, all references to "Mount Emei" will be to the Big Emei section of the mountain.

Geologists often discuss the chronology of the earth's development in terms of thirteen geological periods. The oldest rocks in the world date from the earliest of these intervals, the Precambrian, which goes back to about four billion years ago. After the Precambrian period (roughly, 570 million years ago), the earth developed through twelve additional geological periods. One prominent feature of Mount Emei's physical environment that makes it unique is that rock from ten of the thirteen known geological periods is found there. This brings tremendous visual diversity to the physical face of the mountain. The pinkish hue of the Emei's special blend of granite, prominent at lower levels, always attracts the attention of visitors, as do the rich beds of purple and green shale. A stratum of marine limestone measuring over 1,000 m/3,280 ft thick, deposited by the great Sichuan salty sea mentioned earlier, sits on top of this granite base. Aside from limestone, Mount Emei's rich deposits of dolomite and basalt also contribute to the ever-changing physical appearance of the mountain. As for the summit, it is sheathed by a layer of dark-red basaltic lava that in some places measures 350 m/1,148 ft thick. The entire mountain is formed by a large anticline, the eastern section of which has been eroded away by the flow of rivers. This is one reason that climbing trails have always approached the mountain from the east.[31] Experienced mountain travelers outside of China would probably not be impressed upon reading that Mount Emei's anticline rises to a height of just over 10,000 feet. There are certainly numerous peaks around the globe that reach much greater elevations. But the fact is, China's most famous mountains are not especially lofty. The main peak of Mount Tai stands 1,545 m/5,067 ft, while the highest of the Wuyue, Mount Hua in Shaanxi, measures 2,154 m/7,065 ft at its loftiest point. What distinguishes Emei shan from other mountains is its dramatic and breathtaking *verticality*. I use this term to refer to prominent, conspicuous local relief; specifically the marked elevation difference between the highest point on the mountain ("Ten Thousand Buddhas Summit") and the lowest point on the Sichuan plain far below. Consider the following: on a direct line, the distance from the base of the mountain to the summit is no more than 10 km/6.2 mi, yet the difference in elevation is 2,563 m/8,406 ft. The violent upward thrust that created Mount Emei pushed the earth's crust almost completely vertical. The steep and often serrated land forms that resulted from this uplifting, especially Mount Emei's soaring peaks and steep escarpments, some of which drop 2,000 m/6,560 ft to valleys below, all contribute to the *conspicuous* nature of the local relief around the mountain.

An inevitable result of such dramatic verticality is the creation of multiple climatic and biotic regions within the same mountain environment. On Mount Emei there are three such zones. The climate at the foot of the mountain, as well as that on the surrounding plain, is tropical, with an average year-round temperature of 17.2°C/63°F. At mid-altitudes, where forests are thick and streams bountiful, the temperature is much more comfortable. Not surprisingly, much of the human activity that has taken place on Emei through the dynasties has been concentrated in the mid-riff section of the mountain. On the summit, however, we encounter a frigid zone with an average annual temperature of only 3°C/37°F. During the blustery winter months it is not unusual for the temperature on the fog-shrouded summit, where it often snows, to drop well below freezing. The famous Song dynasty writer Su Shi (or Su Dongpo, 1037–1101) once described springtime visitors to Emei as follows: "Springtime winds blow day after day but snows never melt; / In the fifth month travelers look like frozen little ants."[32] Mount Emei's frigid, snow-blown summit is not a place that welcomes visitors. Rainfall is extremely heavy in all three climatic zones, especially between May and October. Rainfall on Mount Emei is heavier than any other place in China, averaging 264 days per year. Fog is even more common, averaging 323 days per year.[33]

Emei shan's three climatic zones host plant, tree, animal, and bird populations that vary as much as the mountain's temperatures. Space limitations prevent a thorough accounting of these ecosystems. Here I propose to follow the practice of most compilers of "mountain monographs" (*shanzhi*) in China and focus attention on Emei's more "unusual" flora and fauna, especially those specimens found nowhere else. I adopt this approach because it is precisely the unusual or extraordinary (*qi* 奇) features of the mountain, and here I am referring to *all aspects* of its physical environment, which attracted man to Emei shan in the first place. Virtually every human activity related to Emei undertaken throughout the dynasties was in some way a response to the *qi* qualities of its environment.

FLORA AND FAUNA

Following an examination, the giant panda was found to be a healthy female, a little over 3 meters in length, 67 cm in height, and weighing 75 kg.[34]
                                                —People's Daily (Overseas Edition)

The one visual aspect of Mount Emei that immediately captures the attention of visitors, especially as they approach the mountain and begin their ascent, is the thick, lush green color of its slopes. Many traditional poets have been inspired, at times even overwhelmed, by Mount Emei's "sea of green" (*canghai*). The source of this rich verdure is the dense forests that blanket about 85 percent of the mountain's surface. At lower altitudes (under 1,000 m/3,280 ft), cedar (*nan*), conifer (*shan*), and cypress (*bo*) are

especially plentiful. Of course, higher elevations can only welcome trees
able to survive the harsh climate there, such as the cliff mulberry (*yansang*)
and Buddha-summit holly (*foding qing*). One source reports that the
Buddha-summit holly grows only on the summit and bears greenish-blue
leaves that are especially shiny and brilliant.[35]

Against the backdrop of its "sea of green," Mount Emei hosts about
5,000 different species of flora. Bamboo thrives at lower and mid-
mountain elevations. Seed plants alone are represented by 242 different
families (*ke*), comprising more than 3,200 species (*zhong*). Among these
are 925 species found nowhere outside of China, 338 indigenous only to
Sichuan, and 107 that are unique to Mount Emei.[36] The mountain's flower-
bearing trees, such as the crabapple (*haitang*), woody lotus (*mulian*), and
cassia (*muxi*)—to name just three, have attracted considerable attention,
especially from poets. Emei's more than 60 varieties of azaleas (*dujuan*)
enjoy the greatest notoriety. The mountain's azaleas come in no less than
five different colors: yellow, white, purple, light red, and dark red, and are
prominently visible throughout much of the year, especially during the
peak visitor months. Many varieties remain in bloom from spring through
autumn. One of the rarest species of all, the "bright scales azalea" (*lianglin
dujuan*), grows only on the Golden Summit (Jinding).

Another botanical wonder, indigenous only to Mount Emei, is a
deciduous tree called the *gongtong*. Thriving at elevations around
1,450 m/4,756 ft, *gongtong* reach about 10–15 m/32–49 ft in height. In
May, when *gongtong* flowers first blossom, they are pale green. By summer,
when petals are in full bloom, they have already turned milky white. Many
visitors have remarked that these myriad dots of white that blanket Mount
Emei in July and August resemble flocks of doves perched on trees; hence
the *gongtong* is popularly called the "dove tree" (*gezi shu*).

Plants used for medicinal purposes (*yao*) are especially abundant,
which explains why the mountain is sometimes called a "natural herb
garden" (*ziran yaoyuan*). According to a report published in 1981, 1,655
varieties of such plants are known to flourish on the mountain.[37] This list
includes numerous famous medicinal plants such as Emei ginseng (*eshen*).
Two other plants have also received special attention. The first of these is
Gastrodia elata (*tianma*, or "heaven's hemp"), a plant whose tubers can help
expel all kinds of poisonous effluvia from the human body and whose roots
are considered to be an aphrodisiac. The second is *Coptis omeiensis* (*huang-
lian*, lit., "yellow links," sometimes called "golden thread" in English).
This Rauuculaceous plant is regarded as a panacea for many illnesses,
especially dysentery, and is highly prized in China and abroad. Some early
references to the mountain even speak of "immortal drugs" (*xianyao*)

produced from herbs gathered on Mount Emei. According to one report, Emperor Wu of the Han once dispatched special couriers to Mount Emei to locate these rare, life-extending plants.[38]

Emei shan is also populated with a diverse menagerie of rare and unusual critters. Two of its most fabulous inhabitants are mysterious yellow and white doglike creatures called *pixiu*, whose bark (*tuofo*) is said to sound something like "Amitābha Buddha" ("Amituofo"), and leopard cats (*baomao*), whose tracks are spotted on the summit every year. Curiously, though, the animal never appears to humans. Other members of Emei's animal community that are seen more regularly include antelope (*ling*), musk deer (*zhang*), and bears (*xiong*). As for primates on the mountain, the monkey contingent is perhaps deserving of special attention.

Although the Tang dynasty poet Cen Shen (715–770) once wrote of hearing cries of gibbons (*yuan*) at Mount Emei,[39] as far as I know there have never been any reports of any sizable gibbon population in existence on the mountain. On the other hand, Emei's macaque (*zanghou*; *Macaca thibetana*) are a familiar sight to visitors. The mountain's approximately 230 macaque constitute six separate groups or "tribes," each with its own "king" and territory. Most congregate on the northeastern slope of Emei at 1,260–2,100 m/3,936–6,888 ft elevation. Rather than forage for food, these intelligent primates rely on passing travelers for handouts. Some tribes, such as those that dwell near the Bathing Elephant Pool (Xixiang chi) and Encountering Immortals Monastery (Yuxian si), can at times be friendly and quite civil to wayfarers, while others, such as those living near Nine Elders Grotto (Jiulao dong) and the Huayan Summit (or Avataṃsaka Summit; Huayan ding), are much more aggressive, at times even blocking the road until the traveler produces a tasty snack (peanuts or corn kernels are recommended).[40]

Reports in the *Mount Emei Gazetteer* notwithstanding, bear sightings are rare. This has puzzled many observers, especially scientists concerned about China's diminishing giant panda (*da xiongmao*) population. Mount Emei's thick groves of bamboo, many of which are still far removed from human activity, would seem to provide an ideal environment for pandas. And yet, sightings of pandas or any other species of bear are now rare. In the fall of 1992, however, a dramatic discovery was revealed on the front page of many newspapers throughout China: a healthy, giant panda (a female) was spotted and captured on Mount Emei.

Mount Emei's avian community also boasts several distinguished members. Throughout the dynasties, these birds have been the subject of many poems. For instance, the colorful *tong*-flower phoenix (*tonghua feng*), so named because it supposedly only ate the flowers of a *tong* tree, inspired one of the earliest verses ever written about Mount Emei—a quatrain composed by the late Tang dynasty writer Ke You (dates uncertain):

Its multicolored feathery coat—a match for the phoenix!
Deep within clusters of flowers—it seems to not be there!
If a beautiful woman bought one of its feathers, she'd be inclined to take pity,
For when placed beside a golden hairpin, it weighs but a trifle.[41]

Another Emei bird that has achieved literary prominence is the silver pheasant (*baixian*). The coat of this magnificent creature is said to be as white as jade. This feature, along with the ripples of black across its back, its crown and beak of crimson, and vermilion claws, has attracted many writers, including the poet Li Bo (701–762). The renowned Tang writer was especially impressed with the bird's jade-white coat:

The silver pheasant, white as satin:
White snowflakes are shamed by its appearance.
It casts its image into pools of jade;
Prunes its feathers amid trees of gems.
At night it perches quietly under a frigid moon;
At dawn it struts casually over fallen petals.[42]

Finally, one other member Emei's avian population that deserves mention is known by an odd-sounding name: "Buddha-appearance bird" (*foxian niao*). Tradition says that two such creatures dwell near the Luminous Light Monastery (Guangxiang si) on the summit. Sporting shiny coats of kingfisher blue, they supposedly resemble the gray thrush (*huamei*).[43] When the "Precious Light" is about to appear on the summit, the twin "Buddha-appearance birds" announce its arrival with a call that sounds something like "Foxian! Foxian!" in Chinese. The corresponding English translation is "Buddha appears! Buddha appears!"

A GREAT GLOBE OF LIGHT

When the Light begins to appear, the monks toll a bell. And when pilgrims and the masses hear the bell they assemble in orderly fashion {along the edge of the cliff} and gaze downward, leaning against the railing.[44]
—Mount Emei Gazetteer

Aside from Emei's sublime landscapes, unusual "residents," and strange "products," there is yet another curious feature of the mountain that has attracted considerable attention throughout the dynasties and continues to fascinate visitors today. Without question, this phenomenon ranks as the mountain's most extraordinary physical trait. I refer to a spectacular "light show" that sometimes occurs on clear, windless afternoons, when bright rays of sunlight begin their downward slant over the Golden Summit. This marvel of nature has accumulated a host of names over the centuries, some of which are heavily laden with religious overtones. For now, I will refer to this phenomenon by one of its simpler names: "Precious Light."

We should perhaps first note that the "Precious Light" phenomenon is not unique to Emei shan. It has been observed on other peaks in China such as Mount Wawu (Wawu shan) in Sichuan (near Mount Emei), Mount Wutai in Shanxi, and even on Mount Tai in Shandong. Sightings have also been made in the Harz Mountains in central Germany, on Ben Nevis in Scotland (the highest peak in the British Isles), and even at the Grand Canyon. Nor is it an uncommon sight on Emei, appearing, on average, about seventy or eighty times a year. The most common Western name for this atmospheric wonder is "glory." While there is disagreement among scientists about the precise origin of this phenomenon, most would agree that three "ingredients" are necessary for an "appearance" to take place. First, precise meteorological conditions are required. It is essential that either raindrops, ice crystals, or snow flakes be present in the atmosphere; this explains why the "Precious Light" usually appears after a rain shower or snowfall. Second, the sun must be shining *behind* the would-be observer, at just the right angle to cast a shadow into the chasm below the Golden Summit. Lastly, a thick, flat cloud bank or heavy fog must be present and directly *below* the observer's position on the cliff edge, so as to "catch" the observer's shadow. The best place on the summit to view the "Precious Light" is appropriately called Observing-the-Light Terrace (Duguang tai). If an observer is standing on the terrace at just the right moment, and the direction of the sunlight above and behind him/her is shining down at just the right angle, an outline of that human figure's enlarged shadow will then be visible on the top of the clouds or fog bank. If weather conditions are especially ideal, several multicolored rings will form a rainbow-halo around the head of the observer's own shadow. Fan Chengda observed Mount Emei's "Precious Light" in 1177. Here is how he described it:

> Tūla-clouds again spread out below the cliff, gathered thickly, and mounted upward to within a few yards of the edge, where they abruptly halted. The cloud tops were as smooth as a jade floor. From time to time raindrops flew by. I looked down into the cliff's belly, and there was a great globe of light

lying outstretched on a flat cloud. The outer corona was in three rings, each of which had indigo, yellow, red, and green hues. In the very center of the globe was a hollow of concentrated brightness. Each of us onlookers saw our forms in the hollow and bright spot, without the slightest detail hidden, just as if we were looking in a mirror.[45]

I also once observed Mount Emei's "Precious Light." One sunny afternoon in April of 1993, several onlookers, positioned on the precipitous ledge that runs along the eastern side of the Golden Summit, suddenly began shouting: "Buddha appears! Buddha appears!" Rushing over to the Observing-the-Light Terrace, I looked down and saw "a great globe of light" shimmering on the clouds below. A reflection of my head was visible, as were my arms. Several monks who reside in monasteries on the summit came out later and informed us onlookers: "You are all blessed, for the 'Precious Light' only appears to a select few."

Looking back on my sighting of the Precious Light in 1993, and the experiences and knowledge I have gained from subsequent visits to the mountain, I have come to realize that nothing about Emei shan is ordinary. On the contrary, it seems extraordinary in almost every way.

CHAPTER 2

Land of Shu

Oh, how dangerous! Oh, how high!
The Road to Shu is hard,
Harder than climbing to the blue heavens![1]

—Li Bo (701–762)

THE ROAD TO SHU IS HARD

Sichuan is China's second largest province in land area. Comprising 487,000 sq km/301,940 sq mi, it is roughly the size of France. As for population, today it ranks third with 86.5 million people.[2] The heartland of the province comprises a fertile, low-lying basin. The alluvial farmland in this area, sustained by a warm, moist, central-tropical climate and extensive irrigation control, produces an abundance of food. Average annual rice yields, for instance, are estimated ten to fifteen times higher than elsewhere.[3] Lofty mountains and high plateaus girdle the province on all sides, forming an impressive physical barrier between Sichuan and lands beyond its borders. In particular, the lofty peaks and rugged passes in the north have long served as a daunting obstacle between Sichuan and the Central Plains (Zhongyuan)—the traditional cradle of Chinese civilization that extends along the Yellow River valley. When the Tang poet Li Bo sang "The Road to Shu (or Sichuan) Is Hard," he was not exaggerating. The first barrier is the rugged Qinling Mountains, next comes the Han River, and finally the formidable Daba Mountains. Traditionally, Sichuan is known by two alternate names: "Land of Heaven's Storehouse" (Tianfu zhi guo), which aptly implies the area's abundance, and "South of Sword Pass" (Jiannan), which suggests its inaccessibility.

Self-sufficiency in food supply and physical remoteness from the traditional center of Chinese civilization had a tremendous effect on

Sichuan's growth and development, especially in ancient times. Not until its annexation by the state of Qin in 316 BC did Sichuan come to be associated with what later (in 221 BC) became the unified Chinese empire.[4] Before the arrival of the Qin invaders, residents of the Central Plains regarded Sichuan as an ethnically different, marginal, strange, mysterious, and downright foreign land.

Although geographers cannot agree on the precise origin and meaning of the term "Sichuan" 四川 (lit., "Four Rivers" or "Four Streams"), there is consensus that its first textual appearance (referring to what we now regard as Sichuan) came relatively late in Chinese history, probably in the eleventh century.[5] In any case, it is not surprising that the character *chuan* 川 ("river" or "stream") appears in the place name for this part of China, for Sichuan hosts a vast network of navigable waterways. Because of the province's physical isolation from the rest of China, Sichuan's major rivers have long served as transportation channels to the outside world. The most important of these waterways is the Min. Running south from the lofty Min Mountains in northern Sichuan, the Min eventually joins with the Great River (or Yangzi) in modern Yibin City, and from there it was possible for river travelers to journey eastward all the way to Jiangnan, the fertile, scenic area "South of the [Yangzi] River." Fan Chengda's villa home at Rocky Lake (Shihu) stood on a hillside just south of Suzhou (modern Suzhou, Jiangsu), in the very heart of Jiangnan.

During the Warring States period (475–221 BC) the area we now call Sichuan was divided into two regions, Ba and Shu. Ba refers generally to the eastern part of Sichuan. Shu includes the city of Chengdu and the fertile plain that surrounds it, the Min River valley, Mount Emei, and various territories in western Sichuan. The term Shu 蜀 in Chinese functions both as a geographical reference (the place "Shu") and to a distinct people who once lived there and had their own recognizable ethnicity and culture.[6] Until about twenty years ago, with the exception of a few surviving textual references and genealogies on patriarchal founder figures, practically nothing was known about ancient Shu and its people. This situation changed dramatically in the 1980s with a series of remarkable archaeological finds made at Sanxing dui (lit., "Three Star Mounds")[7] in Guanghan county, just 40 km/25 mi northeast of Chengdu.[8] Information derived from these discoveries has provided valuable new insight into the early history of Shu and its people.

So far, the most important finds at Sanxing dui date from 1986, when two sacrificial pits were excavated. Using data culled from almost one thousand recovered artifacts, archeologists and historians have determined that Sanxing dui contains the ruins of an ancient, walled city that once served as the political, economic, and cultural center of Shu. From a historical standpoint, what is most noteworthy is the great antiquity and longevity of Sanxing dui culture: its four successive cultural stages extend from about 3,500 to 2,500 BC.[9] Prior to the Guanghan discoveries, the history of Sichuan was thought to be "only" about three thousand years old. Now it well exceeds four thousand years. Another fascinating result of the Sanxing dui finds is this: traditionally, historians and archaeologists saw only one place as the nuclear center of Chinese civilization—the Central Plains of the Yellow River valley, from which Chinese culture was thought to have diffused to outlying or peripheral regions. Knowledge derived from the Sanxing dui discoveries, however, supports the argument that there were *multiple* centers of traditional Chinese civilization, each with its own distinctive characteristics, which interacted with one another. Shu was one of these regions.[10] History is being rewritten, for it is now clear that the origins of Chinese civilization are multiple and that Shu and its people played a role in its formation and development.

The lengthy history of Shu culture and its role in the formation of the imperial Chinese empire notwithstanding, Sichuan still remained geographically isolated from the rest of China before 316 BC. Some seven or eight centuries earlier Shu armies had assisted the founders of the Zhou dynasty to vanquish their predecessor the Shang, most notably at the famous Battle of Muye in eleventh century BC, but by a few centuries later contact between the Shu and Zhou was already limited. Shu's isolation and absence from northern political and historical consciousness is perhaps most evident in the standard histories of the period, specifically the *Spring and Autumn* (*Chunqiu*), *Annals of Zuo* (*Zuozhuan*), and the *Conversations of the States* (*Guoyu*). These texts do not carry a single reference to Shu by name during the period from 722 to 481 BC.[11]

In 316 BC Qin armies set out over the famous "Stone Oxen Road" (Shiniu lu) across the Qinling and Daba Mountains and crossed into northern Sichuan.[12] Shu forces were no match for the invaders from the north, and Sichuan soon came under Qin control. With its sovereignty now lost and Qin annexation complete, a process of cultural integration followed over the next century. In effect, Shu was now a Qin colony. Qin dispatched legions of their faithful—soldiers, officials, engineers, craftsman, farmers— to Shu. Their mission was to integrate Shu culture and institutions with those of Qin. Ultimately, Qin sought to exploit Sichuan's land resources and favorable geographic position vis-à-vis other states that rivaled Qin power, especially Chu, a state that had held suzerainty over southern Ba since the fourth century BC. Over the next century, Chu and all other contender states eventually succumbed to the Qin war machine.

Following the annexation of Shu in the early fourth century BC, Qin initiated a series of public works projects. One of these was the governor-engineer Li Bing's (fl. ca. 250 BC) "Partition Mound" (Lidui), which created the Assembled River Weir (Dujiang yan) irrigation system. For the past two thousand years this ingenious irrigation project has helped to control drought and flooding on the vast Chengdu Plain, a fertile and densely populated area that occupies approximately 3,220 sq km/ 2,000 sq mi. Although this land was once agriculturally unproductive, being subject to droughts and floods, Li Bing's project transformed the original parcel of land into one of the richest farming regions in all China. Consisting of three major engineering works, the project made it possible to distribute the flow of the Min River and thereby control floods during the high-water season. Essentially, the Min is divided into two rivers by a channel ninety-nine feet wide that is cut through a hill. This is the so-called Partition Mound. One river is used to control flooding; the other for irrigation purposes. The irrigation and flood control system of the Chengdu Plain is still in use today. It is the oldest extant water conservancy project in China, and undoubtedly one of the greatest engineering operations ever undertaken anywhere.[13]

Another effort was the construction of a city from which Qin could manage its occupation. Built on the site of an earlier Shu settlement called Chengdu, and modeled on a smaller scale after the Qin capital at Xianyang, this square, walled fortress measured about 6 km/3.7 mi in circumference and had walls that stood approximately 25 m/82 ft high.[14] The city was divided into two parts—a larger area for officials and military personnel, and a smaller one for markets and shops. The name "Chengdu" literally means "become a [great] capital." Perhaps Kaiming IX, the Shu king who had moved his capital there before the Qin invasion, adopted this name because he had hopes that Chengdu would one day develop into a magnificent capital city.[15] If that was his wish, it certainly came true, for Chengdu has served, in one way or another, as the center or capital of Sichuan ever since.

Before turning our attention more closely to Chengdu, some additional comments concerning Shu's geographical isolation prior to the Qin annexation are necessary. My main intent is to demonstrate how Sichuan's remote location and limited contact with the rest of China affected the earliest-known ideas about Mount Emei. As is usually the case with early Shu history and culture, the textual sources we have to work with are limited in number.

The two most important extant textual sources on the ancient history of Shu are the *Basic Annals of the Shu Kings* (*Shuwang benji*), traditionally attributed to Yang Xiong, and the third chapter of Chang Qu's (fourth century) *Gazetteer on the Land South of {Mount} Hua* (*Huayang guozhi*), completed in 348. The former work says nothing about Mount Emei. Chang Qu's account, however, is useful for two reasons. First, it describes the history and legends of ancient Shu in some detail; and second, it specifically mentions Mount Emei by name. Although the *Huayang guo zhi* was completed after Zuo Si penned his "Shu Capital Rhapsody," Chang Qu's gazetteer is especially valuable to us because it cites a specific function Mount Emei played in the early history of Sichuan. The reference in question appears in a passage concerning an ancient Shu ruler named Duyu:

> The [heads] of the seven states [in Shu] were designated "kings"; Duyu was designated "Supreme Ruler." He styled himself "Wangdi" and changed his given name to Pubei. He regarded his accomplishments and virtues as superior to those of the various [other] kings. And so he took Bao-Ye [Pass] to serve as his front gate, Xionger and Lingguan as his back door, Yulei and Emei as his outer walls, Jiang, Qian, Mian, and Luo as his ponds and marshes, the Min Mountains as his pasture, and the lands in the south as his garden.[16]

According to Chang Qu, then, the boundaries of Duyu's domain stretched from the Bao-Ye Pass in the Qinling Mountains (in the north), all the way down to his "outer walls" at Yulei and Emei in the south. Whether or not these boundary markers are accurate need not concern us. A more important issue is the source of *Huayang guozhi* passage. Unfortunately, Chang Qu does not provide this information. We do know, however, that his chapter on Shu was based in part on sources from Sichuan still extant when the *Huayang guozhi* was compiled in the fourth century.[17] Now, assuming that Chang Qu's account of Duyu's domain is based on a reliable source— and I see no reason to suspect otherwise—then it is almost certain that Mount Emei was already well known during Duyu's reign and at some point had been designated one of the key barriers that delineated the boundaries of his kingdom. Although Duyu's reign dates are unknown, most estimates place him in power sometime between 1,000 and 500 BC. If this chronology is accurate, then Emei shan was already a prominent landmark in Shu during the middle or even early years of the Zhou dynasty.

Indirect and direct references to Emei are found in Zhang Hua's (232–300) *Monograph on the Investigation of Things* (*Bowu zhi*) and Li Daoyuan's (d. 527) *Commentary on the Waterways Classic* (*Shuijing zhu*), respectively. Zhang Hua's monograph, an important early source on myths in China, mentions a Mount Yamen (Yamen shan) in Shu, which probably was an early name for Mount Emei.[18] Li Daoyuan's geographical treatise makes several references to Emei, one of which is especially noteworthy because it offers the earliest explanation of the mountain's name: "[Although Mount Emei is] 1,000 *li* south of Chengdu, on clear, autumn days if you gaze at the mountain from afar, its two peaks seem to face one another like moth eyebrows."[19] In other words, the mountain's twin peaks resemble the arched, antennae of a silkworm moth (*e* 蛾), and so the name *emei* (蛾眉; lit., "silkworm-moth eyebrows") was adopted as the name for the mountain.[20] Many later writers enthusiastically drew on this fanciful image,[21] to the point where it became a cliché.

China's mytho-geographic masterpiece, the *Mountains and Seas Classic* (*Shanhai jing*), a composite work with sections dating from the Warring States, Han, and Jin, names over five hundred different mountains throughout China. It says nothing directly about Mount Emei, but only mentions the [Qiong]lai Mountain Range ([Qiong]lai shanling) in Sichuan, of which Emei is a part.[22]

Although our discussion of early textual references to Mount Emei has so far been brief, a pattern is beginning to emerge. Until the appearance of Zuo Si's rhapsody in 280, few people outside of Sichuan had ever heard of Emei shan. As already mentioned, its name does not appear in any of the standard Confucian histories on the Warring States period, and the sum total of all known references to the mountain up to the third century have already been discussed in this chapter. In the fourth century, Emei shan is mentioned in a letter written by the famous calligrapher Wang Xizhi (321–379; alt. 303–361), where he remarks: "In summer Mount Emei keeps its frost and hail."[23] But this reference was certainly inspired by what Wang had read about Mount Emei in some unnamed text, probably Zuo Si's "Shu Capital Rhapsody" or the later *fu* with the same title attributed to Yang Xiong. Wang Xizhi himself never visited Sichuan. As for Zuo Si, although his rhapsody plays a pivotal role in popularizing the name "Mount Emei" in Chinese literature, there is no evidence that Zuo Si himself ever traveled to Shu, let alone to Emei. Mount Emei's earliest reputation, then, especially outside of Sichuan, derived from second-hand *textual* sources. That is to say, readers heard or "learned about" the mountain from works such as the "Shu Capital Rhapsody" or descriptive comments made by influential writers such as Wang Xizhi. No one was reading first-hand accounts of visits to the mountain because none were available. This is no surprise, for Mount Emei stood isolated and far removed from virtually everywhere in China. Nor is it unexpected that Emei's earliest reputation was literary. Throughout the dynasties many "armchair" authors in China wrote about—and sometimes even painted—

mountains they had never seen or visited. What *is* important in the context of our discussion is that when influential writers like Wang Xizhi invoked the name Mount Emei it served to create or reinforce the notion that Emei shan was a distant, unusual, mysterious, and inaccessible place.

TANG AND SONG VISIONS

> *Throughout my whole life I've been fond of traveling to famous mountains.*[24]
>
> —Li Bo

We turn now to literary visions of Mount Emei during the Tang and Song periods. I use the word "vision" in two ways. The first type of vision derives from either the reputation of a place (transmitted from previous literary works or word-of-mouth) or from the author's imagination (places and events imagined in a dream or trance, or supernaturally revealed). The second type results from seeing something with the naked eye. Literary texts that carry this sort of vision include descriptions based on personal experiences. In other words, the author was an eyewitness to the scene or events described. All literary accounts of Mount Emei dating from the Tang and Song neatly fall into one of these categories. This is a simple distinction, to be sure, but a fundamental one that gives us a clear starting point. These visions are important because the Tang and Song periods mark critical stages in the development of Mount Emei's identity and reputation as a "famous mountain." The most basic and essential topoi associated with the mountain evolved in the Tang and Song and have influenced all subsequent writing about Emei shan, including the works of Fan Chengda.

We begin with the earliest surviving Chinese poem to mention Mount Emei, a verse attributed to the second emperor of the Tang dynasty, Li Shimin (Taizong; r. 626–649). His poem is titled "Passing into Autumn":

Summer's pipes—yesterday still had some ashes;[25]
Autumn's arrows—today stirred on the sun dial.
Mount Emei's peaks are first to emerge;
Lake Dongting's waves gradually rise.
Cassias whiten and emerge from hidden cliffs;
Mums yellow and bloom on River Ba's banks.
The passage of time is now so lamentable;
Nibbling on my brush, I write of matters subject to impalpable laws.[26]

Our main concern is the second couplet, where in neatly parallel lines the emperor describes the first signs of autumn on Mount Emei and Lake Dongting. These place names were familiar to Tang readers, so Li Shimin chose them to symbolize two of nature's most powerful physical entities: lofty mountains and great bodies of water. The irony, of course, is that even the most potent natural forces on earth cannot escape the passage of time (mentioned in the penultimate line). Note that Taizong's poem does not relate any sort of journey to Emei or Dongting. Rather, he evokes the names of these loci in order to suggest their power and vulnerability to seasonal change. Since Emei and Dongting are separated by a great distance (approximately 900 km/558 mi), this expanse adds spatial breadth to Li Shimin's lament, which in turn meshes nicely with his temporal images in the first and third couplets. Taizong's vision of Mount Emei, though brief, strengthens the force of that lament, but it is one based only on the mountain's reputation. What is most significant about the vision of Mount Emei in "Passing into Autumn," however, is that it marks the beginning of a literary fashion that would continue throughout the Tang and into the Song. The particulars of this trend will emerge as our discussion continues.

Now let us consider another early Tang verse, this one by the innovative poet Chen Ziang (661–702):

> Sitting in distant thought: how I yearn
> For my native Shu with its Mount Emei.
> I long to be with the Madman of Chu,
> Far, far away, meeting amid the white clouds.
> But these times! It grieves me they are not right;
> My tears have streamed down for oh, so long.
> In a dream I ascend to the grottoes on Mount Sui;
> In the south I gather mushrooms on Mount Wu.[27]

Here we find Chen Ziang in a moment of intense sadness. He grieves not only because the times "are not right," but also because official duties have forced him to leave his native Shu. At this point in our discussion, the second line of Chen Ziang's verse is noteworthy because, for him at least, Mount Emei represents Shu. Since Emei shan is arguably Sichuan's most notable landmark, this association comes as no surprise. Chen Ziang's distinction is that he was the first among many natives of Shu who would associate Mount Emei with "home." Thus, whenever the name of the mountain is mentioned in the works of these authors, it invariably sparks a host of associations, mostly nostalgic recollections of home and the strong desire to one day return there. In this verse, however, Chen Ziang sees

Emei beyond these general associations. Mention of the "Madman of Chu" and Mount Sui indicates that he had something more specific in mind.

Like many *mingshan* in China, the literary history of Mount Emei includes a rich repertoire of tales about "immortals" (*xian*).[28] One of these immortal figures—the Madman of Chu—is mentioned in Chen Ziang's poem. This is the same character who feigns madness and mocks Confucius in the *Lunyu* (or *Analects*).[29] According to some sources, after his famous encounter with Confucius, the Madman of Chu supposedly repaired to Emei shan, where he lived as a recluse for several centuries.[30] A rendezvous with the legendary immortal "amid the white clouds," which presumably refers to the puffy, white clouds that gather near Emei's lofty peaks, would provide Chen Ziang with immediate release from the troubled times in which he finds himself trapped. Moreover, the grottoes of Mount Sui[31] and life-extending "mushrooms" (*zhi*) on Mount Wu seem to offer the possibility that Chen Ziang might even join the ranks of Emei's paragons of immortality. This idea of "escape to" and "transformation on" Mount Emei will soon reappear in Tang literary history.

Among all traditional writers, the Tang poet Li Bo has the best-known affinity to Mount Emei.[32] This association in large part derives from two famous poems he wrote about the mountain, the first of which is "Song of Mount Emei's Moon":

> Mount Emei's moon—half round in autumn;
> Its image cast on the Pingqiang River flowing.
> Tonight, leaving Clear Creek for the Three Gorges,
> I think of you, unseen, heading down to Yuzhou.[33]

Equally celebrated is the often anthologized "Listening to Monk Jun from Shu Play His Zither":

> The Shu monk, clutching a Green Tracery zither,[34]
> Comes down from Mount Emei's peaks in the west.
> He lifts his hands to play for me,
> And I seem to hear whistling pines in myriad ravines.
> This traveler's heart is cleansed by flowing water;
> Those lingering tones pass into a frosty bell.[35]
> Before I know it, dusk falls on the emerald hills,
> And autumn clouds grow dark layer by layer.[36]

According to the folktale usually cited to explain the background of this poem, Monk Jun (or Guangjun) was a virtuoso *qin* (or zither) player who lived in a monastery on Mount Emei. Once, while visiting the mountain,

Li Bo heard him play and, impressed with the monk's musical skill, struck up a friendship with him. "Listening to Monk Jun from Shu Play His Zither" supposedly was written to commemorate this event and to praise the zither-playing talent of the Tang poet's newfound friend.

Aside from composing these verses, which are the most famous poems ever written about Mount Emei, we also know that Li Bo spent part of his youth living and traveling in Shu.[37] But more important, he is the first Chinese poet known to make more than a passing reference to Mount Emei in his works. Specifically, the name "Emei" appears nineteen times in thirteen of Li Bo's extant poems.[38] Since the Tang poet has left us more than one thousand verses, at first these numbers may not seem significant. I would argue, however, that these figures are indeed important because Li Bo had more to say about Emei shan than any other Tang poet. His Emei references are our most valuable Tang literary source on the mountain.

These references can be studied in a number of ways. For instance, one could explore how Li Bo's Emei poems relate to the numerous other verses about mountains in his collected works. Or, we might consider how Li Bo's references to Mount Emei correlate with his biography, especially to the poet's early years in Shu and the self-image he promoted as a native of the region. I would argue, however, that a more worthwhile approach is to organize his lines, couplets, and verses about Emei into thematic or topical categories. I propose this approach because a close reading of the poems reveals that Li Bo wrote about Emei shan from five discernible perspectives: (1) as a pristine, scenic environment; (2) as a distant, almost inaccessible retreat; (3) as his own, nostalgic home where he might return one day to "rest in idleness"; (4) as a place that has a special bond with the moon; and (5) as a land of immortals and other extraordinary beings, where humans might discover the secrets of longevity. One advantage of a thematic approach is that it gives us an immediate overview of those aspects of Mount Emei that most attracted Li Bo's attention. One possible disadvantage of this sort of compartmentalization, however, is that it might suggest that each of the poet's references to Emei is limited to only one of these perspectives. This is not the case. As we shall see shortly, it is common for *at least two* of these perspectives to be present in each of Li Bo's Emei poems.

The most immediately discernible of Li Bo's attitudes toward Emei is his admiration of the mountain's sublime visual wonders. The poet's esteem for Mount Emei's gorgeous scenery is detectable in virtually all of his verses that mention the mountain. At the same time, however, we should keep in mind that long, detailed descriptions of Emei's scenic

landmarks are conspicuously absent in Li Bo's poems. The poet never
concerns himself with depiction of fabulous waterfalls, secluded temples,
or unusual plant life. To do so would have detracted from other, more
central concerns of the Tang poet. A good example of how Li Bo relates
the majestic beauty of Emei to other interests is reflected in his "Song for
a Landscape Mural by Zhao Yan of Dangtu, the District Defender":

> Mount Emei emerges loftily in the far western heavens;
> Mount Luofu connects directly with the Southern Sea.
> The renowned artisan ponders how to wield his colored brush;
> Onward to mountains, speeding to seas—all unfolds before his eyes.
> 5 Brimming halls, empty blue skies, as if they could be swept;
> Red Rampart's roseate air, Cangwu's mists.
> Dongting and Xiao-Xiang, thoughts boundless and unbroken;
> Three Rivers and Seven Marshes, feelings flowing to and fro.
> Startled waves rush and gush to who knows where;
> 10 A solitary boat once gone loses its returning year.
> On a long journey it moves not, nor does it turn;
> Gliding along like riding the wind, it alights on the horizon.
> Heart beating, eyes fixed afar—such elation is hard to exhaust:
> But when can I reach the summits of the Three Mounts?
> 15 The western peak, lofty and lanky, spits out a flowing spring;
> Transverse boulders press against waters, waves and streams surge.
> The eastern cliff, piled in folds, hides the light fog;
> Deep forests, mixes of trees, skies rich and rolling.
> Here it is so dark and dim that day and night are lost;
> 20 Leaning on a bench, silently I listen to a soundless cicada.
> Below the tall pines feathered guests are arrayed;
> Sitting across from me without a word, the Nanchang Immortal.
> The Nanchang Immortal—Master Zhao,
> In his youth was a knowing and wise, blue-cloud scholar.
> 25 Government offices are idle, many guests are gathered,
> But they are all blurry, as in a painting.
> A five-colored mural: how could it adequately be prized?
> Perfected immortality could complete my body.
> If you wait for fame and fortune before dusting off and departing,
> 30 Then the peach blossoms of Wuling will laugh you to death![39]

It is noteworthy that in a poem dealing with a vast panorama of
well-known scenic sites scattered across the Chinese empire, including
Mount Luofu in Guangdong, Mount Red Rampart in Zhejiang, Mount
Cangwu in Hunan, and Lake Dongting, Mount Emei is mentioned in the
opening line. Since Li Bo's panorama does not appear to follow any logical,

geographical progression, it would not be unreasonable to assume that he regarded Emei as an exalted peak among China's many mountains. Yet here Emei's status is not based on physical beauty or size alone. For Li Bo, these are just two attributes of a *mingshan*. Like all Chinese poets he appreciated beautiful mountain environs. But he had other priorities. Paramount among these concerns is the view that some special *mingshan*, like Emei and Luofu, possess the power to affect certain metamorphoses or changes in human beings.

The idea that certain mountains can accomplish such feats is especially evident in the song honoring Zhao Yan and his mural. Note that the first twenty lines of the poem describe, in great detail, the scenic particulars of the painting. Mountains, especially Emei and Luofu, dominate this panorama. Ultimately, Li Bo's purpose in writing this verse is to praise the artistic talents of Zhao Yan. In lines 13 and 14, however, the Tang poet himself literally "enters the picture": "Heart beating, eyes fixed afar—such elation is hard to exhaust: / But when can I reach the summits of the Three Mounts?" It is precisely the poet's jubilation over the artist's fantastic vista that inspires the question about reaching "the summits of the Three Mounts," referring to the three immortal mountain-isles of Penglai, Fangzhang, and Yingzhou. Essentially, then, Li Bo is asking: "When shall I be able to join ranks with the 'feathered guests' (mentioned in line 21; this is another designation for *xian*), the 'Nanchang Immortal' (line 24; a reference to the painter of the mural, Zhao Yan, who was a native of Nanchang), and the extraordinary beings who reside on the Three Mounts?" Li Bo then answers his question in line 28: "Perfected immortality could complete my body."[40] In other words, if potent mountains like those depicted on Zhao Yan's colored mural were available to our Tang poet, then he too could "reach the summit of the Three Mounts" and become a *xian*. Li Bo viewed Emei as an "immortal mountain" (*xianshan*) and it is this quality that most inspired him to write about it.

Turning now to the second of Li Bo's Mount Emei perspectives, we observe that on several occasions he portrays the mountain as a distant, almost inaccessible retreat. We have already encountered this attitude in two of the poems introduced earlier, "Listening to Monk Jun Play His Zither" and "Song for a Landscape Mural by Zhao Yan of Dangtu, the District Defender." It will be recalled that in the first of these verses we were introduced to Monk Jun, who carried a special zither "Brought down from Emei's peaks in the west." Here, as well as in the poem about Zhao Yan's wall painting, Emei is depicted as a remote place situated at the western extremity of the empire. This is especially so in the mural verse, which locates the mountain in the *xiji tian*, or "far western heavens." We see this same quality in other Li Bo verses that mention Emei.[41] Many Tang writers, beginning with Li Shimin, were aware of Mount Emei's reputation as a remote and mysterious locale endowed with incredible scenic grandeur. Numerous poems from the period echo this reputation.

The third of Li Bo's attitudes toward Emei—that is, his view of the mountain as a place where he might one day return and comfortably retire—appears in verses on themes related to parting and separation. Here is one example, titled "In Jiangxi: Seeing Off a Friend to Mount Luofu":

> Cassia River divides the Five Ranges;
> Transverse Mountain faces Nine Doubts.
> Our native lands, faraway from Anxi;
> Drifting about—where do we go next?
> 5   A white sheen saddens the bright lake;
> An autumn islet shades the frigid contour of the land.
> Long ago our interest was the purple fragrance;
> Our brown-hair days have already passed.
> The emperor has allowed you to scatter and drift;
> 10 In cloudy ravines you hid like Chao and Yi.[42]
> Now you take leave for Mount Luofu,
> While I return to rest on Mount Emei.
> The broad road between us—ten thousand miles!
> Under a rosy moon we'll miss each other from afar.
> 15 If one seeks out the Madman of Chu,
> On rose-gem trees he'll find fragrant branches.[43]

Again we find Li Bo pairing Emei and Luofu, this time to emphasize the great distance that separates the poet and his friend bound for Jiangxi. What is different here, however, is the notion of Li Bo "returning" to Emei to "rest." This idea, which is not found in any other surviving Tang verse, echoes throughout several of Li Bo's Emei poems. Although we will never know all the nostalgic associations that Shu in general, and Emei in particular, had for Li Bo, sentiments expressed in the poems suggest that his fondness for Emei and desire to someday return there were triggered by recollections of past experiences. Presumably, these experiences date from the 720s, when the Tang poet lived and traveled in Shu. We might also speculate that, in the verse just considered at least, our poet regards his return to Emei as a "closing chapter" of his past as well as a "new beginning" for the future. Li Bo and his Jiangxi friend had once cultivated an interest in the "purple fragrance" (a reference to life-extending herbs), but now they have grown old (the "brown-hair days" of their youth have long since passed). To make matters worse, now they are physically separated.

And yet, despite the disappointment of this situation, Li Bo hints in the closing lines of his verse that each of them may eventually have a chance to experience the kind of physical metamorphosis that can take place at numinous *mingshan* like Emei and Luofu. The "fragrant branches" that each of them might find if he looks for the Madman of Chu offers such a promise.[44]

It is general knowledge that moon imagery is common in Li Bo's poetry. His four-verse sequence "Drinking Alone Beneath the Moon" ("Yuexia duzhuo"), in particular, has attracted the attention of numerous critics, some of whom have written at length about the poet's relation with and attitudes toward the moon.[45] Earlier in this chapter we looked briefly at Li Bo's famous "Song of Mount Emei's Moon." Here is another poem that treats the same theme, but in an expanded way. It is titled "Song of Mount Emei's Moon: For Yan, a Monk from Shu, on His Way to the Central Capital":

> When I was at the Three Gorges in Badong,
> I looked westward at the bright moon and recalled Emei.
> Rising above Emei, the moon shines on the iron-blue sea,
> Faithfully following men for ten thousand miles.
> 5   Before the Yellow Crane Tower, moonlight splendidly white;
> It is here where I suddenly spy the "guest" from Emei.
> Mount Emei's moon still sends you to me,
> But winds blow you westward to the streets of Chang'an.
> Chang'an's grand boulevards—as broad as the Nine Heavens;
> 10   Mount Emei's moon—shining brightly on Qinchuan.
> In the capital you'll inherit the Golden Lion Throne;[46]
> With a white jade deer-whisk you'll discuss profound mysteries.
> I am like a floating cloud, though now detained in Wu-Yue,
> But you may chance upon the Sage-Master as you travel through the
>   vermilion pylons.
> 15   Once you've stirred your lofty name to fill the Emperor's Metropolis,
> On your return home we'll again enjoy Mount Emei's moon.[47]

The sentiments expressed in this verse are conventional, especially in parting or separation poems. Monk Yan is embarking on a long journey to the Central Capital (a reference to Fengxiang, which served as the provisional "Central Capital" of the Tang between 758 and 761), where he will "discuss profound mysteries" and "stir" (or establish) his "lofty name." Although Li Bo and Monk Yan are separated by a great distance, they still have a spatial bond in Mount Emei's glorious moon, which "follows men for ten thousand miles." This spatial link is further reinforced by Li Bo's memories of his days in Badong. The three-way bond between the two friends, Mount Emei, and Shu strengthens the sentiments of friendship on the one hand, and the hope of reunion on the other. That hope finds strong expression in the closing line of the poem, where Li Bo voices confidence that after Monk Yan "returns home" to Shu they can once again together enjoy Mount Emei's beautiful moonlight. This promise repeats Li Bo's earlier pledge to "return" to Shu at some later date in order to "rest" and look for "fragrant branches."

So far, we have discussed four of Li Bo's postures or attitudes toward Emei, all of which are triggered by admiration of the mountain's physical appearance, its mysterious and seemingly inaccessible location, and various nostalgic associations for Shu, as represented by Mount Emei. One could convincingly argue that these same factors could also be cited or used to help explain Li Bo's attitudes toward other mountains. The question posed earlier, then, still remains: If Emei is such a special mountain for Li Bo— and I contend this is the case—then what ultimately entitles the mountain to that status? The mountain's physical beauty, pristine remoteness, and nostalgic link to the poet's past can no doubt claim some credit. But there is still another crucial element in the poet's attitude toward Emei that begs attention and discussion. To find this key, we must look to the fifth and final of Li Bo's perspectives toward Mount Emei—the mountain as a dwelling place of immortals and other extraordinary beings.

Earlier we encountered a poem about Monk Jun, the virtuoso *qin* player whom Li Bo supposedly met on Mount Emei. Here is a similar work, titled "Presented to Monk Xingrong":

> In Liang there was one Tang Huixiu,
> Who often followed Bao Zhao in his travels.
> Mount Emei's Shi Huaiyi,
> Alone accounts for Master Chen's fame.
> 5 Surpassing and superior, two Men of the Way,
> Connected and joined, a phoenix and unicorn.
> Xingrong in turn now bravely goes forth;
> I know that he has the bones of a hero.
> Ruo of the Sea does not hide the black pearl;[48]
> 10 The Black Dragon spits out the bright moon.
> To the great sea ride an empty boat;
> Follow the waves and let yourself glide along.
> Write poems in the Sandalwood Gallery;
> Indulge in wine on Parrot Isle.[49]
> 15 Wait until I make my way to Eastern Yue,
> Where hand in hand we'll climb the White Tower.[50]

The "extraordinary people" in this verse appear in parallel allusions in the first and second couplets. Huixiu, mentioned in the opening line, was a Buddhist monk (Tang was his lay family name) and close friend of the famous Six Dynasties poet Bao Zhao (ca. 414–466).[51] Shi Huaiyi, also a Buddhist monk, reportedly once lived on Mount Emei. Although no biographical details about his life are available, we know that he was a close friend of the early Tang poet Chen Ziang (referred to here as "Master Chen").[52] Li Bo's argument in these opening lines is clear: each of these famous literary men, Bao Zhao and Chen Ziang, was associated with a "surpassing and superior" Buddhist monk, and these "Men of the Way" played pivotal roles in their careers (Huixiu's influence on Bao is implied here; Shi Huaiyi's responsibility for Chen Ziang's fame, however, is stated outright). Li Bo draws on these allusions in order to suggest that a similar relationship exists between Monk Xingrong and himself. Especially noteworthy is the fact that all of these personalities who Li Bo associates with Emei are remarkable in some way, like the "phoenix and unicorn."

The most significant group of beings whom Li Bo associates with Mount Emei are *xian*, or immortals. Why is it that our poet prefers to associate extraordinary beings, especially immortals, with Emei shan? An answer to this question is provided in the poem "Climbing Mount Emei":

> The State of Shu abounds in immortal mounts,
> But none can match the beauty of Mount Emei.
> Even if one climbs all around it and tries to have a look,
> How could he know of its scenic wonders?
> 5 Blue-green peaks unfold against the heavens;
> Colored patterns emerge as if from a painting.
> Rising lightly on the wind, I enjoy the purple auroras;
> Surely I've discovered the secrets of the damask satchel.
> Among the clouds, rose-gem flutes are sounded;
> 10 From atop boulders, jeweled zithers are played.
> For a lifetime I've had this secret desire;
> Happiness and joy are henceforth complete.
> A misty countenance now seems to cover my face;
> Dusty involvements are suddenly left behind.
> 15 If I chance upon the Master riding his goat,
> Then hand in hand we'll soar beyond the bright sun.[53]

For several reasons, this poem tells us the most about Li Bo's attitudes toward Mount Emei. Most significantly, in the opening couplet he defines Emei as a *xianshan*, or "immortal mount." Several of the verses discussed

earlier, where Li Bo pairs Emei with other well-known peaks (such as
Luofu) inhabited by extraordinary or immortal beings, have already suggested that this was one important way in which he viewed Mount Emei.
I would extend this argument even further and contend that *all* of the
poet's attitudes toward the mountain are related, directly or indirectly, to
Emei's status (in Li Bo's mind) as a *xianshan*. If I am correct about this,
then it becomes clear why Li Bo chose to write about the mountain's
"unusual" scenic wonders, its seemingly inaccessible location, its function
as a "bonding point" between humans and heavenly bodies (that is, the
moon), and especially Emei's role as a place where he might one day return
to rest. These are all key attributes and functions of *xianshan*.

Our discussion of "Climbing Mount Emei" must begin with the
following observation: Li Bo's verse is not concerned with describing a
physical ascent to the mountain's summit. Rather, it is written after a style
of poetry in China known as "traveling to the lands of immortals" (*youxian*)
and, in following the conventions of that style, relates a visionary or
spiritual ascent to a heightened state of mind. Mount Emei functions as
the vehicle for this voyage because, as Shu's premier "immortal mount,"
it is endowed with the power to make such a trip possible in the first
place.

The description in lines 5 and 6 of Mount Emei's appearance in the
distance, which portrays the mountain's contours and color patterns in
attractive but general terms, follows Li Bo's customary practice of never
actually scanning the face of the mountain. The poet's concern here is to
relate how the mountain stimulates and helps him to realize his own
visionary quest. This experience begins abruptly in line 7, where attention
suddenly shifts from Emei's colorful, distant outlines to Li Bo himself,
who declares that he is now "rising lightly on the wind" (*lingran* 泠然).
Presumably, it is the appearance of the mountain that has rarefied him and
thus stimulated his ascent. The term *lingran* has its *locus classicus* in the
Zhuangzi, where it is used to describe the skill with which the Daoist
thinker Liezi rode the wind.[54] My translation "rising lightly on the wind"
is based on a gloss by Li Zhouhan (n.d.), the Tang commentator to the
Wenxuan, who describes *lingran* as "*qingju mao*" 輕舉貌 (lit., "the appearance of rising lightly").[55]

The power of extraordinary mountains like Emei shan to transform
mortal beings into *xian* has now been exercised. An immediate, visual
result of this new situation is the presence of "purple auroras" which served
to transport *xian* through ethereal realms.[56] Having now spied these air-
borne rafts, Li Bo confidently proclaims that he has indeed "discovered the
secrets of the damask satchel." A similar purse was once used by Emperor

Wu of the Han to store esoteric texts conferred on him by the mythical Daoist divinity Queen Mother of the West (Xi wangmu).[57] Because of this attribution, the term "damask satchel" has come to symbolize secret, arcane teachings. In the context of Li Bo's "Climbing Mount Emei," access to documents in the satchel allows the poet to immediately gain the "secrets" or "techniques" of immortality. And, without further comment or elaboration, the poet immediately takes advantage of his newfound knowledge to rise loftily into the clouds. Only after an impromptu concert high above the mountain does Li Bo descend to Emei, where the musical performance continues. The sonorous fanfares and fairy melodies produced by flutes and zithers are a fitting testimonial to the Tang poet's miraculous transformation. But rather than close his verse on this climax, Li Bo continues for six more lines. The proclamation in lines 11 and 12 ("For a lifetime I've had this secret desire; / Happiness and joy are henceforth complete.") is practically standard fare in traditional Chinese verses about earthly beings achieving immortality, as is the report in the next couplet concerning the "misty countenance" that now covers the poet's face and his emancipation from "dusty involvements" in the "world of men." Also predictable is the allusion in the ultimate couplet: "the Master riding his goat" refers to the Zhou dynasty woodcutter Ge You, who is one of Mount Emei's most famous *xian*. By promising to "soar" with Ge You through the universe, Li Bo has in effect proclaimed himself to be the newest member of Emei's pantheon of Daoist immortals.[58]

What about Li Bo's contemporaries? Do their works reveal similar visions of Mount Emei? Li's good friend, the great poet Du Fu (712–770), arrived in Chengdu in 759 and lived there for the next seven years. References to Mount Emei in Du Fu's poetry, however, are scant. For reasons that are not clear, he never visited the mountain. Aside from a few passing references that identify Emei shan as Shu's major landmark and a place that hosts immortals,[59] Du Fu's verses say next to nothing about Mount Emei.

A major eighth-century literary figure whose name is often mentioned in conjunction with Mount Emei is the poet Cen Shen (715–770). Cen served as chief administrative officer of Jiazhou (modern Leshan) in the mid-760s. This marks the first time that a major Tang writer lived and worked in close proximity to Emei shan. When we search through Cen Shen's *oeuvre* for a first-hand account of a trip to Emei shan, however, we are disappointed. Instead, we find only general descriptions, such as the following:

> Mount Emei's mists, blue and fresh,
> Bathed last night by an autumn rain.

Sharp and clear, the peak-top trees,
Stuck topsy-turvy in an autumn river bottom.[60]

Cen Shen had immediate access to some of the most beautiful mountain scenery in China, and yet he apparently never ventured beyond the
eastern foot of the mountain. Why? Could his apparent reluctance to
explore Emei be related to the fact that Li Bo and Du Fu never got there
either? Perhaps, but we will probably never know for sure. There is simply
not enough historical information available on Mount Emei during the
Tang to draw any conclusions. Among the few scattered references that
have survived, only one gives a clue that might help to solve our mystery.
This appears in Yue Shi's (930–1007) well-known administrative-
geographical work *Records Encompassing the Universe from the Taiping [Reign]*
(*Taiping huanyu ji*): "In the third year of the Qianyuan reign of Tang (760),
the Lao revolted. [The town seat] was then moved to the east of Emei
Abbey. This is where the town is managed today."[61] Revolts by the
Lao 獠, an aboriginal people who lived on or near Mount Emei,[62] must
have been a serious problem if the local seat of government had to be
moved eastward (that is, away from the mountain). Other sources
attest to the serious danger in the area. Cen Shen, for instance, although
appointed prefect of Jiazhou in 765, was delayed one year in taking up
the post because of a local revolt. And, in 768 when Cen resigned from
his post and was heading home to Henan, his route was cut off by yet
another insurrection. He eventually retreated to Chengdu, where he
died in 770.

There seems to be little doubt, then, that the area around Mount
Emei was a downright dangerous place in the mid-eighth century. This
being the case, were prospective visitors such as Du Fu, Cen Shen, and
others scared off by the threat of danger from local aborigines? Based on
the brief report in the *Taiping huanyu ji*, this could very well have been
the case, at least in the mid-760s. It seems unlikely, however, that local
unrest would have kept visitors away throughout the *entire* Tang dynasty,
a period of almost three hundred years. Since no written work describing
the slopes or summit of Mount Emei survives from the Tang, it seems
reasonable to assume that there were other reasons that kept potential
climbers and sightseers away. The gazetteers say nothing about this matter,
but we do find a hint in a poem by Sikong Shu (d. ca. 790) titled "Sent
to Refined Master Zhang on His Return to Mount Emei":

Grand Unity, Celestial Altar, west of the Celestial Pillar—
Dangling bindweeds make a curtain, boulders make ladders.

First you'll climb to numinous environs where the blue empyrean is
   unsurpassed;
Below you'll spy the world of men where the bright sun droops low.
Pine-tree tones, ten thousand notes, harmonize with pipes and chimes;
Cinnabar-red light, five colors, mix with rainbows and reflections.
Once you enter the mountain in spring, you'll look but find no paths:
Only birds crying out in mists deep and water brimming in torrents.[63]

   Although Emei shan is not mentioned by name in the body of this
poem, the title suggests that Sikong Shu is describing the scene that
Master Zhang will find on his return to the mountain. The first line sets
the stage for the description that follows. Refined Master Zhang is a *daoshi*,
or Daoist "Gentleman of the Way." At his "Celestial Altar" (Tiantan), sited
west of the Celestial Pillar (Tianzhu), he probably practices various health,
diet, and meditation routines in his search for the "Grand Unity" (Taiyi)
or "Way" (Dao) of Laozi. Of special interest is the reference in line 2 to
"boulders making ladders" and the comment in line 7 about "looking but
finding no paths." A fascinating question and one that none of the sources
tackle is this: just how accessible were the middle and upper environs of
Mount Emei during the Tang? Were trails available to Li Bo, Cen Shen,
and their contemporaries? In an indirect way, Sikong Shu provides some
answers to these questions. First, there must have been some paths in place,
at least at lower elevations. If not, then how could Refined Master Zhang,
various Buddhist monks, and other Tang residents of the mountain, who
are described in the sources, ascend to their monasteries, abbeys, or hermitage sites? While I do not have a definitive answer to this question, I suspect
that the great difficulties one always faces when attempting an ascent of
Mount Emei on foot were a major factor. Even today, with convenient trails
from the foot of the mountain to the summit, it is a long and difficult
climb measuring about thirty miles in length. Weather conditions can
change in an instant and, depending on the season, rain can fall for days
on end. Throughout a good portion of the year the temperature on the
Golden Summit is frigid, and snow is common during the winter months.
The steepest places on the mountain now have stone steps. Monks and
adepts climbing in the Tang period probably negotiated boulders that
served as "ladders." Fan Chengda confirms in the *Diary of a Boat Trip to
Wu (Wuchuan lu)* that there were no stone steps in place above the mid-riff
of the mountain in 1177, and that the climb to the summit was extremely
difficult and dangerous.[64] Wild animals may have also posed a threat.[65]
We will probably never know why the Tang period failed to produce one,
single eyewitness description of an ascent. We can only be sure of one
thing: the poets stayed away from Mount Emei.

As for the remaining lines of Sikong Shu's poem, this is the closest
Tang description we have of a firsthand account of the mountain. Since
Sikong once served under a military commissioner in central and western
Shu, it would not be unreasonable to speculate that the description in his
poem may have been based on an earlier personal visit to Emei. Of course,
a conversation with his Daoist friend may also have provided enough
information to fashion a verse. In any case, Sikong Shu has left us a work
written for an acquaintance about to return to the mountain. We do not
know the identity of "Zhang" mentioned in the title, but clearly Sikong
Shu deemed him worthy of the epithet "Refined Master" (Lianshi). This
term is also used in a number of Tang poems that refer to "Gentlemen of
the Way" associated with Mount Emei.[66] Works that mention "Refined
Masters" and "Gentleman of the Way" often include Daoist terms (like
"Celestial Altar") that are strongly reminiscent of the diction we saw
earlier in Li Bo's "Climbing Mount Emei."[67] What is new is that such
terminology is now appearing much more frequently. This strongly suggests that there was a Daoist presence on the mountain in the Tang.

At the same time, we also encounter many Tang verses that mention
Buddhist monks and Buddhist activities associated with Emei. Poems such
as Li Bo's "Listening to Monk Jun from Shu Play His Zither" and Cao
Song's (tenth century) "Sent to a Monk Traveling to Shu for the Summer"[68]
appear with increasing frequency. By the late Tang we even begin to find
poems written by monks themselves.[69]

A final development of the late Tang concerns the alleged first reports
in Chinese literature of a nocturnal phenomenon on Emei known as
shengdeng, or "sage lamps." Our next selection, a quatrain written by Xue
Neng (jinshi 846), who served as prefect of Jiazhou during the Xiantong
reign period (860–874), is heralded in all the Mount Emei histories and
gazetteers as the "first reported sighting" of shengdeng on the mountain:

> Dashing and darting in the void—the fading and fainting lights;
> I sit and watch deluded mists turn crystal clear and lucid.
> One should know that when the fire goes out smoke is useless;
> Throughout the night I chat beside a railing with a monk.[70]

There has been much debate among scholars as to the possible origin(s) of
the "sage lamps" on Mount Emei.[71] For our purposes, what is most noteworthy is that late Tang writers like Xue Neng and others are now reporting observations, made either by themselves or told to them by others,[72]
of specific meteorological phenomena on Mount Emei. This development,
I would argue, is related to the increased references to Refined Masters,

Gentleman of the Way, and Buddhist figures discussed earlier. That is to say, contacts in the mid- and late Tang between persons directly associated with the mountain and their various acquaintances (many of whom were literate men without a direct connection to Emei) resulted in the increased production of written descriptions and reports based on firsthand knowledge (or access to such information) about the mountain. Some of these accounts, such as Xue Neng's quatrain about the sage lamps, reveal new visions of Emei shan. The most important result of these increased contacts and new visions is that Mount Emei's reputation is continuing to grow and expand.

In poems dating from the early years of the Song Dynasty we encounter—for the first time—works that mention specific, historical sites on Mount Emei. The earliest such work is Fan Zhen's (1007–1089) quatrain "First Hall" (Chudian). Fan Zhen was a native of Chengdu and served in a number of government posts during the reigns of the emperors Renzong, Yingzong, and Shenzong. He probably visited Emei in 1075, after his return to Sichuan from Luoyang.

> I move onward toward Mount Emei's highest peak;
> Who knows how many thousand layers of crags and cliffs?
> A mountain monk smiles as he tells the story of Master Pu;
> It was here where the white deer once left its tracks.[73]

Of special interest is the first line of Fan Zhen's quatrain, which specifically mentions "moving onward to Emei's highest peak." Here, for the first time in Chinese literature, we have what seems to be a report of an ascent toward the summit. Unfortunately, Fan's account offers few details. The portrait of Mount Emei that emerges in his poem, however, is completely different from those in earlier verses. Fan Zhen's vision is charged with motion—the poet himself is moving up the mountain—and with a few scenic details (the crags and cliffs mentioned in line 2). Fan Zhen's extant writings tell us nothing more about his experiences on Emei. We are not even sure if he ever reached the summit. But the eleventh century produced numerous other famous writers who (like Fan Zhen) were natives of Shu, including the Song dynasty's best-known man of letters—Su Shi (or Su Dongpo). Perhaps his works might provide a more detailed account of a visit to the mountain? This would seem likely, for Su Shi not only was a native of Shu, but his home in Meishan town was only about forty miles from the foot of Mount Emei.

As incredible as it may seem, there is no indication in Su Shi's extant writings that he ever visited Mount Emei. In his poetry, however, he mentions the mountain on numerous occasions. Many of these are conventional references patterned after the Li Bo visions described earlier, especially as they relate to immortals and the moon[74] or the idea that Mount Emei represents "home." It certainly comes as no surprise that Su's long career on the "official road"—sometimes described as "three exiles and ten posts"—inspired longing to return to Meishan. For Li Bo, Mount Emei represented Shu, which in turn meant "home"; for Su Shi there was no intermediate level for "Shu"—Mount Emei *was* home. In fact, on many occasions, Su specifically pairs the word "home" (*jia*) with the name of the mountain. For example, in one verse Su Shi mentions that "My home is north of Mount Emei,"[75] while in another he refers to "My Emei home ten thousand miles away."[76] His association of home with Emei shan was no doubt inspired by the short distance from Meishan to the mountain. That Mount Emei is the most prominent *mingshan* in Shu only served to strengthen this association. It is also interesting to note that the origin of the name of the county in which his family lived, Mei, was adopted directly from the character *mei* 眉 in "Mount Emei."[77] Thus, for Su Shi the very name "Emei" inspired feelings of home. This explains why most references to the mountain in Su's poetry are related in one way or another to the general theme of "return."

Among Su Shi's works that mention Mount Emei, the one verse that perhaps expresses the greatest emotional intensity is "Fahui Monastery's 'Blue Expanse Gallery' ":

Spring comes to my homeland, but no date yet for my return;
Others say autumn is sad, but spring is sadder still.
Already I'm drifting across flat lakes, thinking of glittering brocade,
Now I gaze at this blue expanse and recall Emei.[78]

Su Shi's nostalgic recollections of home seem genuine, as does his intense desire to one day return there. The image of Mount Emei provides a prominent, physical focal point for those feelings. The mountain's role in this grand theme of "return," however, is limited to visions already established by Li Bo. All Northern Song writers who mention Mount Emei in their works follow these same conventions. Evidently, no major literary figure of the period had an opportunity to climb to the summit of Emei shan and record his experiences there.

CHAPTER 3

A Journey of Ten Thousand Miles

{Chengdu} is the junction of all land and water routes,
Which converge here from the six directions.
It is a place where bountiful luxuriance thrives,
The most prosperous and flourishing area of the empire.[1]

—Zuo Si

BROCADE CITY

When Fan Chengda arrived in Chengdu in the summer of 1175 to assume his new official post, the city already had a history of about fifteen hundred years. Since its founding around the fourth century BC, Chengdu has served as the cultural, commercial, and transportation center of southwest China. In Han times, the city hosted about half a million residents, and was second in population only to Chang'an.[2] Some of the richest families in the empire lived there, and at times during the Han, and later in the Tang, its size and splendor even rivaled the imperial capital. The one product that is perhaps most associated with Chengdu is silk brocade or damask (*jin*). A government Brocade Officer (Jinguan) was said to have resided in the city to oversee the collection of the choicest damask, which was then forwarded to the capital. Hence, very early on in its history Chengdu acquired the nickname "Brocade Officer City" (Jinguan cheng), which later was shortened to "Brocade City" (Jincheng).

Several themes run throughout the historical and literary sources that chronicle the history of the Chengdu. First, and perhaps most important, the area surrounding the city—specifically, the Chengdu Plain and peripheral mountainous areas—is extremely rich in natural resources, especially iron ore, copper, gold, silver, precious stones, cinnabar, salt, timber, fish, wild game, and various plants and trees. Abundant mulberry and lac trees provided the necessary raw materials for the city's famous silk and lacquer industries.[3] Chengdu was the heart of Shu's abundance, and this attracted the attention of its neighbors, especially tribes in the non-Chinese border regions to the south and west. In times of peace, trade would flourish between Shu and these areas. In times of "barbarian" strength and unrest, however, tribes eager to exploit its resources sometimes pillaged the city.

As described by Zuo Si in his "Shu Capital Rhapsody," during the Han and Three Kingdoms period (220–265), Chengdu was a city of extravagant palaces, elaborate pavilions, lofty towers, stately homes, and bustling markets. The abundance of natural resources in close proximity to the city stimulated and supported business enterprises and industries. Tremendous profits were made, especially in the salt and iron trade, by both private entrepreneurs and the Han government. Iron and steel was used to craft high-demand products such as swords, knives, farm implements, and cooking utensils. Since the Sichuan Basin is one of the few inland areas in China where salt deposits are plentiful, the production and trade of salt also flourished. Moreover, the brine pits of Shu yielded an abundance of natural gas, which is still being tapped today. By Han times, then, Chengdu was already a bustling commercial and manufacturing hub. Many of its entrepreneurs, trading mainly with non-Chinese neighbors to the west, made fortunes by swapping tea, cloth, and handicrafts in exchange for horses and slaves.

Chengdu's geographic location on the western frontier of China meant that it could enjoy steady contacts with Central Asia, India, southeast China, and Vietnam via overland trails and river routes.[4] As early as the Warring States and Han periods, trade plied along the Great River and its tributaries was vigorous and sustained. In the second century BC, the Han envoy to the Western Regions, Zhang Qian (fl. ca 125 BC), reported seeing "Shu cloth" (Shubu) in Bactria (Daxia; roughly, the northern part of modern Afghanistan).[5] Despite the general physical isolation of Sichuan from the rest of China, Chengdu was still close enough to Chang'an and Luoyang to have limited commercial contact with those cities during periods of peace. But these contacts were limited, and so Shu remained essentially isolated.

The long period from the fall of the Han in 221 to the reunification of the empire by the Sui in 589—the so-called Period of Disunion—was a time of chaos, suffering, and great instability throughout most of China. After the disintegration of the Han, the empire quickly divided into what is known as the Three Kingdoms (Sanguo) period. One of these kingdoms, called Shu, was based in Chengdu. Its chief military strategist and political leader, Zhuge Liang (181–234), is mentioned by Fan Chengda in the opening lines of the *Diary of a Boat Trip to Wu*. By 280, however, all three kingdoms had already fallen to a new power, the Western Jin (265–317). But the Western Jin soon collapsed and what followed was a long succession of contending political powers and independent kingdoms. One of these states, the Eastern Jin (317–420), attacked and destroyed Chengdu in the fourth century. At times during the Period of Disunion, Shu functioned as an independent kingdom, but more often than not it was under the nominal control of some larger and more powerful state.[6] One key development in this period related to Mount Emei concerns the prolonged drought, famine, and warfare in Sichuan and the mountainous region in southern Shaanxi—the area often called Hanzhong. The result was that tens of thousands of refugees swarmed into the Sichuan Basin in search of food and relief from military hostilities. Some of these people probably settled in areas near Emei shan. Yet despite this influx of immigrants into the region, the overall population of Shu decreased sharply during the tumultuous years between the Han and Jin. Without a doubt, warfare and famine took a heavy toll on the people of Sichuan during the Period of Disunion. I shall have more to say about refugee and population issues in chapter 4.

The task of rebuilding Chengdu began in the Sui and continued in the Tang. Soon Chengdu once again became one of the greatest cities in the empire. Although the city flourished, frontier unrest resulting from failed Tang expansionist maneuvers against non-Chinese people to the south and west led to great instability in southwest China. Two formidable military powers, the Tibetans in the west, and the Nanzhao Kingdom in the south, threatened Shu almost constantly during the Tang. Nanzhao actually attacked Chengdu in 829, and after a six-week battle most of the city was laid to waste. By the late ninth century, Tang troops had driven off the invaders, and Chengdu was essentially rebuilt once again. Under the direction of Gao Pian (d. 887), the city was enlarged and expanded southward to about four times its original size. The new outer wall measured some forty *li* in circumference. The precarious military situation vis-à-vis its hostile neighbors notwithstanding, Chengdu continued to develop and expand. The many sites and splendors of the city are celebrated time and again in Tang poetry. Here is just one example, a quatrain from Zhang Ji (ca. 776–ca. 829) titled "Song of Chengdu" ("Chengdu qu"):

> Brocade River just off to the west, its misty waters green;
> Fresh rain now on the mountain, the lichee fruits ripen.
> By Myriad Mile Bridge, oh so many taverns!
> I wonder which one this traveler will choose to spend the night?[7]

Surviving descriptions of the city, which at the end of the Northern Song had more than five hundred thousand residents,[8] often celebrate Chengdu's botanic wonders and note the presence of numerous gardens and scenic areas, through which the Min River and other waterways carried commercial and passenger boat traffic. In the 1170s, when Fan Chengda and Lu You served as officials in Chengdu, Sichuan continued to thrive, though in isolation far away from the exile capital in Lin'an. Much of the poetry they composed there celebrates the picturesque beauty of the city.[9]

In the twelfth century numerous historical sites were scattered in and around Chengdu. Among the more famous of these were the Shrine for Zhuge Liang (Zhuge gong ci), the Grave of Wang Jian (Wang Jian mu; also known as Yongling), the Black Sheep Palace (Qingyang gong), Du Fu's Thatched Cottage (Du Fu caotang), Myriad Mile Bridge (Wanli qiao), and the Great Compassion Monastery (Daci si; the city's largest Buddhist temple), to name just a few. Large-scale fairs were held every month, each on a different theme: January for traditional-style Chinese lanterns, February for flowers, March for silkworms, April for brocade embroidery, May for hand fans, June for incense, and so on. During the Song, Chengdu comprised five commercial districts, as well as a public market where farmers and craftsmen from outside the city could sell their goods. Night markets also were popular.

In addition to its beautiful silk brocade, Chengdu is also known for its paper manufacturing and printing industries, which thrived during the Tang and Song. The earliest known example of woodblock printing in the world, now housed in the British Museum, is an almanac printed in Chengdu in 220 AD. During the Song, Chengdu was one of three major printing centers in China. The fine quality paper produced in the city was also employed to print imperial decrees and edicts, as well as books for the Imperial Library. The earliest use of paper currency in China also took place in Chengdu, during the Northern Song, which greatly spurred the development of commerce in the region.

THE JOURNEY BEGINS

We now make a rather abrupt transition from the historical narrative of Mount Emei and Tang and Song visions of the mountain, presented in the previous chapter, and the brief historical sketch of Chengdu, which introduced this chapter, to the pages of Fan Chengda's *Diary of a Boat Trip to Wu*. In other words, it is time to set off on our journey. In the remaining portion of this and the following chapter I will present translations from Fan's travel journal; specifically, entries from the day Fan departed Chengdu (27 June) to the day he arrived in Jia county near Mount Emei (13 July). Commentary and explanation will accompany the translations. I will not present all of Fan's diary entries, but rather selected, representative samples. My aim here is to introduce readers to the form, content, and writing style used in the *Diary of a Boat Trip to Wu*, and to provide a description of Fan's travels in Sichuan before he reaches Jia county and begins his ascent of Mount Emei, described in chapter 5.

Our journey begins at the famous Joining River Pavilion (Hejiang ting), located on the banks of the Joining River (Hejiang) in the southeastern section of Chengdu. As was customary in traditional China, those about to embark on a long journey were feasted by friends bidding the traveler farewell. The site of Fan Chengda's banquet—the Joining River Pavilion—was built by the Tang official Wei Gao (*style* Chengwu; 745–805), who served as Intendant (Yin) of Chengdu in the 780s. During the Song dynasty the pavilion was an especially popular site for farewell parties. Fan Chengda clearly had thoughts of home as he departed Chengdu, for his very first comment in the *Diary of a Boat Trip to Wu* speaks of the luscious green countryside from Chengdu south to Xinjin town and how its forests and vistas reminded him of his home in Jiangnan:

> I, the Layman of Rocky Lake (Shihu jushi),[10] departed from Chengdu on the twenty-ninth or Wuchen day of the fifth lunar month, Dingyou year of the Chunxi reign period (27 June 1177). On this day we moored the boat below the Joining River Pavilion (Hejiang ting) at the minor, eastern outer wall. The Joining River (Hejiang) is a tributary of the Min River (Minjiang). From the Partition Mound in Yongkang {command}[11] it divides {and flows} into Chengdu and Peng and Shu commanderies,[12] and then rejoins {at the pavilion} here. The green countryside, level groves, misty waters, and clear vistas {from here} down to Xinjin {town}[13] are extremely similar to those in Jiangnan.[14]

Among the numerous varieties of flowers found in Chengdu, probably none was more appreciated and admired than the *meihua*, or "plum blossom."[15] Plum blossoms are especially prized because they bloom during the winter months, specifically in the final (or "La") lunar month, which roughly corresponds to January on the Western calendar.

> {The structure} above the pavilion is called the Fragrant and Flowery Tower (Fanghua lou). Numerous plum blossom {trees} are planted in front and in back of it. It is a customary practice to enjoy plum blossoms here during the La month.[16]

Myriad Mile Bridge, mentioned earlier in the quatrain by the Tang poet Zhang Ji, was one of Chengdu's famous "Seven Star Bridges" (Qixing qiao). It spanned the Brocade River (Jinjiang) just south of Chengdu, directly in front of the outer city wall. Rebuilt during the Qiande reign (963–968) of the Northern Song,[17] the wooden bridge sported bright vermilion railings. A pavilion stood on top, where sightseers could spy down and watch gaily decorated catamarans (*huafang*) cruising on the Brocade River. The area near the bridge was one of the most bustling places in town. An almost constant parade of travelers stopped and congregated thereabouts. Just west of the bridge is another famous landmark—the Tang poet Du Fu's famous "Thatched Cottage." Myriad Mile Bridge is best known as the place where the military commander Zhuge Liang once gave a farewell banquet to the Shu envoy Fei Yi (d. 235) on the occasion of the latter's diplomatic mission to the state of Wu. There were numerous markets, wine shops, and tea houses near the bridge, where singing girls and prostitutes would gather day and night. Showing his hometown pride, Fan Chengda boasts that the famous bridge was "actually fashioned for the benefit of natives of Wu."[18] Visits he made there while serving in Chengdu thus aroused nostalgia and thoughts of home.

> *Natives of Shu who journey to Wu all board their boats here.*[19] *To the west of the pavilion is Myriad Mile Bridge. When Zhuge Kongming (or Zhuge Liang) saw off Fei Yi on a diplomatic mission to Wu, he said: "Your journey of ten thousand miles begins here."*[20] *Because of this the bridge was later so named. Du Zimei's (or Du Fu's) poem says: "At the gate is moored a myriad-mile boat from Eastern Wu."*[21] *This bridge was actually fashioned for the benefit of natives of Wu. While {serving} in the commandery, I crossed it every time I came out to the eastern outer wall. Without fail, I was moved by it.*[22]

Although during his long journey home Fan Chengda made numerous side trips to historical and scenic sites along the way, in the next diary entry, before his journey south toward Mount Emei even begins, Fan heads off on a sightseeing excursion to various places *northwest* of Chengdu. Official duties likely prevented him from visiting this area during his two-year tenure as an official in Sichuan. Before heading out on his journey Fan dispatches his "family and provisions boat" (*nulei zhou*), which carried his wife, children, luggage, and supplies, downriver (south) to Pengshan town, Mei county, where he will join up with them later.

> *Sixth month, Jisi, or first day of the new moon (28 June): Dispatched the boat with my family and belongings down to Pengshan town (Pengshan xian), Mei county (Meizhou),*[23] *to moor. I rode {on horseback} alone around the city wall, passing by*

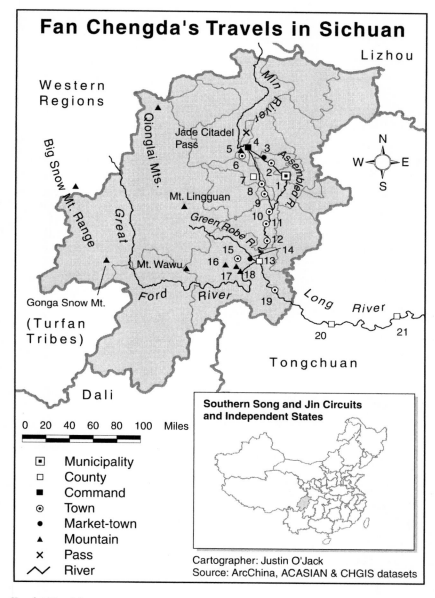

Map 3.1 Fan Chengda's Travels in Sichuan.

Fan Chengda's Travels in Sichuan

Lizhou

Western
Regions

Min River

Qionglai Mts.

Big Snow Mt. Range

Jade Citadel
Pass

Mt. Lingguan

Great

Green Robe R.

Assembled R.

N
W   E
S

Mt. Wawu

Gonga Snow Mt.

**(Turfan
Tribes)**

Ford   River

Long   River

Dali

Tongchuan

0 20 40 60 80 100 Miles

▣ Municipality
□ County
■ Command
⊙ Town
● Market-town
▲ Mountain
✕ Pass
〜 River

**Southern Song and Jin Circuits
and Independent States**

Cartographer: Justin O'Jack
Source: ArcChina, ACASIAN & CHGIS datasets

Key for Map 3.1

1. Chengdu municipality
2. Pi town
3. Ande Market-town
4. Yongkang command
5. Mount Qingcheng
6. Qingcheng town
7. Shu county

8. Jiangyuan town
9. Xinjin town
10. Pengshan town
11. Meishan town
12. Qingshen town
13. Jia county
14. Suji Market-town

15. Emei town
16. Mount Emei
17. Second Emei
18. Third Emei
19. Qianwei town
20. Xu county
21. Lu county

Map 3.1 Fan Chengda's Travels in Sichuan.

the eastern and northern gates.[24] *Next, I turned and headed west. As one travels west from the Attendant Esquire Causeway (Shilang ti),*[25] *on the road to the Min Mountains {Minshan},*[26] *the flowing channel rumbles and roars, clamoring as it quakes the surrounding countryside.*[27]

When Fan reaches Pi town,[28] northwest of Chengdu, he is greeted by numerous onlookers lining the road, all "properly dressed and gaily adorned" for the occasion of his visit. It was highly unusual, to say the least, for an official of Fan Chengda's high rank to journey to suburban towns. This explains why local residents in Pi town "clogged the thoroughfare" to watch him pass by.

Traveled fifty li *and reached Pi town. Onlookers clogged the road, all of whom were properly dressed and gaily adorned. Canopies faced one another {along the road}.*[29] *Presumably, a Regulation Marshal*[30] *has never traveled this road before. This was the case in all of the counties and towns west of here. The buildings in Pi district*[31] *are extremely stately. Home after home has running brooks and tall bamboos, but the residence of the Yang family is the grandest of all. The town orchard has huge bamboos in myriad number. A flowing stream cuts right through the middle. The thick halcyon-green hue {of the bamboos} seemed as if it was about to drip down.*[32]

Fan's journey continues toward the northwest, moving us closer to Li Bing's Partition Mound:

Gengwu day (29 June): Traveled twenty li *and stopped in the morning to rest at Ande market town {Ande zhen}. Traveled forty* li *and reached Yongkang command. Along the entire way the {Min} River divides and flows into various channels, all of which rumble like thunder and swirl like snow. Attractive fields filled my gaze. The line "fertile countryside below the Min Mountains" refers precisely to this spot.*[33] *The Exalted Virtue Temple (Chongde miao) is on a hill outside the west gate of the command wall.*[34] *This is the place where temple offerings of food are made to Li Bing, the Grand Protector (Taishou) of the Qin, and to his son.*[35]

Fan is now approaching one of the key sites on his trip northwest of Chengdu, Mount Qingcheng (Qingcheng shan), which stands southwest of modern Guan *xian*. It is so called because the contour of the mountain is said to resemble a city wall, and also because it is carpeted with luxuriant green vegetation the year round. Aside from its magnificent scenery, Mount Qingcheng is also famous as a Daoist center. According to tradition, Zhang Daoling, leader of the Way of the Celestial Master (Tianshi dao) movement in the second century (in chapter 4 we will consider this tradition in some detail), once preached there. "Western Barbarian Mountains" probably refers to the Qionglai Mountains, which lie to the west of Mount Qingcheng. In Song times this area was inhabited by various non-Chinese border peoples, known collectively as the Western Frontier-Tribes (Xirong; sometimes also called the Turfan/Tufan).

> *Xinwei day (30 June): On the opposite side of the River are the Min Mountains. The nearest of the Min Mountains is called Mount Qingcheng; the especially large peak {on Mount Qingcheng} is called Mount Damian (Damian shan). It turns out that everywhere behind Mount Damian are the Western Barbarian Mountains {Xirong shan}.*[36]

The next stop on Fan's itinerary is Jade Citadel Barrier, which is thirty *li* northwest of Yongkang, at the foot of a mountain from which it takes its name. This is the same "Jade Citadel" which, along with Mount Emei, functioned as one of the "outer walls" of Shu during the reign of the ancient king Duyu.

> *The west gate {of the command} is named Jade Citadel Barrier (Yulei guan). From the gate I made a small detour and climbed up to the Floating Clouds Pavilion (Fuyun ting), which was built by Li Fan, style Qingshu (1118–1178), when he served as Protector of the commandery.*[37] *He adopted the name {of the pavilion} from a line in a poem by Du Zimei: "Above Jade Citadel, floating clouds, ever changing, past and present."*[38] *The view from the pavilion is bold and surpassing. . . .*[39] *I emerged from Jade Citadel Barrier and climbed up the hill to pay a visit to the Exalted Virtue Temple.*[40] *The recently built gate tower in front of the temple is very imposing. It overlooks a great river known as the "Assembled River" (Dujiang). The source of the river is actually in the Western Barbarian {region}. It emerges {from that region} by means of streams and torrents in the Min Mountains that converge here. Thus, it is known as the Assembled River.*[41]

The hawser (or rope-suspension) bridge that Fan Chengda is about to cross, which will take us to Mount Qingcheng, is one of the most famous bridges in Chinese history. Located two *li* west of Yongkang, it is known variously as Pearl Estuary Bridge (Zhupu qiao), Hawser Bridge (Suoqiao), or simply Guan Town Bridge (Guanxian qiao).[42]

> *Just as I was about to reach {Mount} Qingcheng, I again crossed the Rope Bridge. The bridge measures 120 zhang in length and is divided into five spans (or sections). As for the breadth of the bridge, twelve ropes link and hold it together. Bamboo railings are installed on the bridge. Several tens of large timbers have been collected and erected in the sandy riverbed, where boulders are piled up to reinforce the base. Each group of several tens of timbers forms one span, which suspends the bridge in*

midair. When a strong wind blows, the bridge rises and undulates like a banner,
somewhat like the nets of a fisherman drying in the sun or the colored silks of a dyer
drying in the wind. Next I had to give up my sedan chair and step quickly {across
the bridge}. If you leisurely stroll across it, the bridge shakes and quakes, making
it impossible to stand still. All of my fellow travelers turned pale with fright.[43]

The next passage in Fan Chengda's diary is of particular interest because it mentions how "the present dynasty has exalted the sacrificial rites [performed at mountains]," while at the same time also noting that the Court sometimes confers special names or titles on mountains. Imperial patronage of mountains in traditional China was especially important to the leaders and residents of religious institutions on these peaks. In addition to special titles, which enhanced legitimacy and prestige, gifts and donations were also sometimes conferred, which at times could be quite extravagant (later we will see examples of this at Mount Emei). Such offerings and contributions provided resources, power, and influence to the religious institutions associated with a particular mountain. A good historical example of imperial patronage occurred in the Feifu Monastery (Feifu si) on Mount Qingcheng in the late seventh century. During the early years of the Tang dynasty, imperial interest and support concentrated mainly on mountains associated with Daoist religious traditions. The first Tang emperor, Gaozu (r. 618–626), even declared that Laozi, the patriarch of Daoism, was his ancestor. In the late seventh century, however, the religious tides changed. The ruling empress Wu Zetian (627?–705) developed a passionate interest in Buddhism. As a result, in the late seventh century Buddhist monks from the Feifu Temple, presumably with support from Chang'an, were able to assume control of the Eternal Way Abbey (Changdao guan; mentioned below) on Mount Qingcheng. During the reign of the Tang emperor Xuanzong, however, imperial tastes switched back to Daoism, and the adepts from the Eternal Way Abbey were able to regain control of their institution.[44]

Upon reaching Mount Qingcheng (described below), Fan Chengda spends the night at the Doyen Abbey, the mountain's foremost Daoist temple. The title "Doyen" (Zhangren), or more specifically "Doyen of the Five Cardinal Mounts" (Wuyue Zhangren) was supposedly conferred on the mountain by the Yellow Emperor (Huangdi), the mythical ancestor of all Chinese people. Ning Feng (or Ning Fengzi), once served as the Yellow Emperor's Master Potter (Taozheng). Legend has it that he later achieved immortality.[45] The other name mentioned in the next diary entry, Long Qiao, refers to an immortal who once resided on Mount Qingcheng. Like Ning Feng, Long Qiao also served as a Master Potter before becoming a *xian.* One source reports that the Yellow Emperor once came into posses-sion of a work titled the *Long Qiao Scripture* (*Long Qiao jing*), which helped him to "soar into the clouds."[46]

Traveled thirty li *and reached {Mount} Qingcheng. The {inscription above the} gate of the mountain reads: "Nine-Chambered Grotto Heaven of the Precious Immortals" (Baoxian jiushi dongtian). That night we stayed at the Doyen Abbey (Zhangren guan). The abbey is situated below the Doyen Peaks (Zhangren feng). The five peaks are pinnacled and pointy, like {those on} an ornamental screen. The abbey's terraces and halls extend all the way up to the belly of the cliff. Since the Tang {dynasty}, the Doyen has been styled "Doyen of the Five Cardinal Mounts, Realized Lord of Accumulated Merit and Determined Fate" (Wuyue Zhangren chufu dingming zhenjun). Historical records mention briefly that {the Doyen} was surnamed Ning, his given name was Feng, and that he was a contemporary of the Yellow Emperor. The {Yellow} Emperor studied with him and inquired about Long Qiao's art of flying and sauntering. The present dynasty has increasingly exalted the sacrificial rites {performed at mountains} and has bestowed palace names (or Daoist titles) upon both {Mount} Qian and {Mount} Lu.[47] This place alone is styled Doyen Abbey. Earlier, when disciples of the Doyen talked to me about the matter, on their behalf I submitted a request to the Court {that a new name be granted to the moun-tain}. . . .[48] {Mount Qingcheng} has thus been conferred the title "Palace of Assem-bled Felicity and Established Prosperity" (Huiqing jianfu gong). Just as I was about to pass into the mountain, an imperial missive just happened to arrive {formally announcing the mountain's new Daoist title}. So, we carried out the Jiao ceremony[49] in order to praise the emperor and express thanks for the favor He has shown us.*

In front of the Realized Lord Hall (Zhenjun dian) there is a large tower called Jade Splendor (Yuhua). Like a pheasant in flight, it coils and curls,[50] and is mag-nificent in design. On the four walls of the hall Sun Taigu painted thirty-two Immortal Realized {Ones}(Xianzhen {zhe}), who were subordinates of the Yellow Emperor.[51] The brush technique is matchless and marvelous; his tone and style are pure and effortless. This wall {painting} is preeminent in the Western counties (of Sichuan). There are numerous other ancient paintings along the two verandahs. Half of them are already flaking and falling down. Only the portraits of Zhangguo the Elder (fl. eighth cent.)[52] and Sun Simiao (581–682)[53] are undamaged.[54]

While at Mount Qingcheng Fan Chengda could never have anti-cipated the birthday surprise about to unfold before his eyes:

Renshen day (1 July): Moored at Mount Qingcheng.[55] Today is my birthday. In the spring of this year I became ill in the Minor City (Shaocheng)[56] and was near death. I barely survived. Because of this, I have come to a famous mountain to pray and offer sacrifice. During the night a Daoist adept came before the hall and performed the Pacing the Void (Buxu) ceremony.[57] Just as he was ascending the altar, a great flare of light appeared above the cliff behind the hall.[58] *Its color was a deep, fiery red and it encircled and surrounded the summit of the mountain. A moment later it disappeared. When my fellow travelers hastened over to observe it, the light was gone. Silently, I made a request to the Doyen: "Since this light has just come out for me, it should appear again so everyone can observe it together." The words had no sooner left my mouth when the light came out again. It separated and joined, whipped and whirled around, just like a revolving scripture {wheel}.*[59] *After the time it takes to eat a meal, it sank out of sight. The people at the abbey said that this peak did not always have a light, and that it had first appeared four years ago.*

Guiyou day (2 July): From the west {side} of the Doyen Abbey I ascended the mountain. Traveled five li *and reached the Supreme Clarity Palace (Shangqing gong),*[60] *on the summit of the mountain's loftiest peak. Its halls have been constructed {on the mountain} by inserting wooden frames into the rocky {cliff-side wall}.*[61] *I scanned the Doyen Peaks below, which are {like} a sheer, low-lying wall and nothing more. Several hundred peaks of the Min Mountains undulate beneath the railings like kingfisher-blue waves, while the contours of all the mountains lean eastward. One balcony stands directly opposite Mount Damian. If one goes up {the mountain road} sixty more* li, *there is a level and smooth area called "Lotus Flat" (Furong ping).*[62] *Daoists cultivate hemlock parsley there.*[63] *Without setting aside ten day's time, one cannot ascend to it. Moreover, one {must} pass through infidel territory where even the feathered robes*[64] *seldom venture. Like scintillate silver or polished jade, three peaks of the Snow Mountains (Xueshan)*[65] *charge out from behind {Mount} Damian. The Snow Mountains are in the Western Regions (Xiyu).*[66] *I do not know how many thousands of* li *distant they stand from here, but since I now see the mountains clearly, one can readily imagine their loftiness. A journey to the Supreme Clarity {Palace} truly offers a magnificent view of the world!*

On this night thousands of lights came out in the mountains all around us. These are referred to as "sage lamps." Although sage lamps appear in numerous places, those who have explained them cannot make a definite decision {about their origin}. Some say they are the glow of cinnabar drugs stored away by the ancients. Some say that the numina of herbaceous and woody plants has a glow. And still others say that they are made by dragon spirits and mountain demons. Most people believe {the lights} are fashioned and created by immortals and sages.[67]

"Sage lamps" (*shengdeng*), alternately called "spirit lamps" (*shendeng*), "devil fires" (*guihuo*), or "Buddha's lamp" (*Fodeng*), were described earlier by Fan Chengda as "great flares" (*daju*). In addition to the four possible origins of this phenomenon just mentioned by Fan Chengda, there is one other that is frequently cited in traditional Chinese texts. This explanation appears in the *Huainanzi*: "Long-standing blood turns into flitting fires."[68] The idea that concentrations of blood can, over a long period of time, generate *lin* 燐 (or "flitting fires" in my translation) is an old one in China, dating back to at least the Han period. Moreover, the term *lin*, or its expanded form *linhuo* 燐火, has been used by many commentators and scholars in China, both traditional and modern, to identify the "sage lamps."[69]

As Fan descends down Mount Qingcheng he provides additional information about the painter Sun Zhiwei (or Sun Taigu) and some specimens of the artist's work that graced the walls of the Long-Life Abbey (Changsheng guan). Here we can observe one hallmark quality of the *Wuchuan Lu* that makes it such a valuable text: detailed description and historical information that is unavailable elsewhere.

Jiaxu day (3 July): Descended five li *down the mountain and again reached the Doyen Abbey. Traveled twenty* li *and stopped for a morning rest at the Long-Life Abbey. This is the place where Fan Changsheng found the Way.[70] Sun Taigu's painting "Dragon, Tiger, and Two Lords"(Longhu erjun) is on the two walls outside the {abbey's} hall.[71] The brush style waves and sweeps; the clouds and mists soar and flow. One might say this is an especially fascinating example of Sun's brushwork. On a section of the wall one also finds Sun's painting "Wei River Dragon"(Weijiang long).[72] Tradition has it that Sun wished to paint a picture of a dragon but did not know what the true appearance of a dragon was like. {Just then} a man happened to pass by and said to him: "Do you, milord, wish to know the true appearance of a dragon?" Suddenly, the man changed his appearance and deformed and distorted himself {into a dragon}. Sun examined and scrutinized {the dragon} and succeeded in painting it. The story about Sun scrutinizing a subject for a little too long and consequently losing sight in one eye refers to this painting. During the Xuanhe reign period (1119–1126), the old wall {with the original painting} was selected to be taken to the capital city.[73] Just before it left here a Daoist adept summoned a famous painter to make a copy of it on a new wall. What survives today is the copy. That evening we spent the night at the Fan Clan Manor (Fanshi zhuangyuan).[74]*

Yihai day (4 July): Traveled fifteen li. *Then set out from Qingcheng town. . . .[75] Traveled forty-five* li. *That evening we spent the night at the Sage Buddha Cloister (Shengfo yuan) outside the wall of Shu county.[76]*

Bingzi day (5 July): Traveled twenty li *and stopped for a morning rest at the Zhou Family Compound (Zhoujia zhuang). Mr. Zhou's three huge mansions are lofty and smart, stately and clean. For the most part, this is a fertile land that has not seen war or fire for two hundred years.[77] The houses of the people living here seem like models, and evoke an atmosphere of continuous tranquility.[78]*

Fan Chengda has been on the road sightseeing for more than a week now, and yet we notice in the next diary entry that many of the friends who attended his farewell banquet at the Joining River Pavilion in Chengdu (ten days earlier) are still traveling with him. In fact, some of these well-wishers will remain with Fan after he departs Xinjin town and heads south toward Mount Emei. Although this practice of *songxing*, or "seeing off someone about to embark on a journey," may seem excessive by today's standards, in traditional China it was common. Not only did this custom provide an opportunity to express concern and respect for the departing traveler; at the same time it also served as an expression of the camaraderie one often sees in social relations, especially between members of the scholar-official class.

Dingchou day (6 July): Traveled thirty li *and stopped for a morning rest in Jiangyuan town. . . . Traveled forty* li *and spent the night in Xinjin town. The people from Chengdu, as well as the well-wishers from this commandery (or town), have gathered here to see me off. They have rented all the lodgings and cottages in the district. The people in the town consider this a major event.*[79]

Wuyin day (7 July): I was detained a day by well-wishers seeing me off. After the banquet, I sent them away, commanding each of them to return home. But five or six of them still remained.[80]

Jimao day (8 July): Heavy rain. . . . At the beginning of the chen *or fifth double-hour (7:00–9:00* AM*), we took a small boat down to Pengshan {town}. By the end of the* si, *or sixth double-hour (9:00–11:00* AM*), we had arrived there. I joined up with the boat carrying my family and belongings and we immediately untied our mooring lines. After the* wu, *or seventh double-hour (11:00* AM*–1:00* PM*), we reached the river outside the wall of Mei county, which in fact is the Transparent Glass River (Boli jiang).*[81] *In winter the river's color {is so clear that it} resembles transparent glass. But now in summer, as rains rage and waves swell, the entire river flows turbid yellow and that is all. On the banks of the river there is a small hill known as Frog Chin {Hill} (Mayi {shan}). The plains along the river are flat and distant, similar to those between Jiang{su} and Zhe{jiang}.*

Lotus flowers inside the county wall are particularly abundant, and there are ponds and pools everywhere. People in other {nearby} commanderies who cultivate lotus all buy their seeds in Mei. There are stone-paved streets throughout the city, which are most elegant and clean. They were built by the former Protector Wang Yangying, {style} Zhaozu (jinshi 1124; d. 1159).[82]

Gengchen day (9 July): The commandery seat in Mei {county} possesses an ancient hearth, which is located behind the Public Affairs Office (Tingshi). The Grand Protector[83] *does not dare reside there. He bars and locks the door, and offers sacrifices to the {spirit of the} hearth. I also heard there is a water urn in the {county's} Military Property Warehouse (Junzi ku) that is stuffed and stored with pebbles. On the first day of each month the Grand Protector sacrifices to it as well. He has been adding a container each of water and pebbles to the urn for who knows how many years, yet today it is still not full. Among the strange and false tales related to government offices, none can match those of the hearth and urn of Mei {county}.*[84]

Xinsi day (10 July): I invited the well-wishers to a feast in the Meishan Guesthouse (Meishan guan), where I bade my farewells. Although the lichee fruit season had already passed, there was still one lichee tree left in the commandery, the fruit of which seemed to be deep red in color. I had all the fruit picked in order to offer it to my guests. By chance, there were two plates of lichees left over in the guesthouse {after the feast}. After they sat overnight, I took a close look at them. Their green leaves and red fruits had a lustrous shine. I thus realized people customarily use reticulate baskets to hold and store lichees only because they want to expose them to the wind. But they fail to realize that if the fruit is moistened and dampened by rain and dew and toasted and dried by wind and sun, then overnight the color and fragrance are lost. As an experiment, I selected several hundred fruits, packed them into a large container, and then tightly sealed it. I dispatched a messenger to take the container to Chengdu for the purpose of presenting it to the two commissioners, Gao and Zhu. The messenger reached there in two nights. The two gentlemen (that is, Gao and Zhu) sent back a letter saying the aroma of wind and dew (that is, the fresh flavor of the lichees) seemed like that of newly picked fruit. I recorded this event in order to make it known to persons who are fond of such matters.[85]

Renwu day (11 July): Set out from Mei county. Traveled sixty li and by the wu *double-hour (11:00 AM–1:00 PM) reached Central Precipice (Zhongyan).*[86] *This place is known to have the most remarkable forests and springs in Western Chuan. Tradition has it this was the enlightenment site of the Fifth Luohan, Nuojuna,*[87] *and also as the place where the Compassionate Dame Dragon (Cilao long) resides.*

I climbed the riverbank and immediately found a mountain path. One half li down the path is the Calling Fish Tarn (Huanyu tan), the source of which emerges below the precipice. No one knows its depth. This serves as the cave dwelling of the {Compassionate Dame} Dragon. If you clap your hands by the banks of the tarn, schools of fish emerge from beneath the precipice. However, no one dares to sport with them. Two years ago, a retainer of the Supervising Inspector was bathing in the pool when a creature apparently pulled him under the cliff. The next day his corpse floated out onto the river.[88]

Jiashen day (13 July): I left the mountain early in the morning and reached the river landing, where I parted with the well-wishers, who were going home first. We cast off our boat, passed Qingyi,[89] *and then went through Hurang Gorge (Hurang xia).*[90] *From the old town of Pingqiang*[91] *we went on to reach Jia county*[92] *before sunset. From Mei county to Jia county it is 120 li. Central Precipice is halfway between them.*[93]

The abundance of forest lumber in Jia county, combined with several nearby waterways that provided convenient river transportation in almost every direction, stimulated a boat-building industry in the region that extends back to the Warring States period. When the Qin general Sima Cuo (fourth cent BC) threatened invasion of Chu, he boasted command of "myriad large junks" that could easily and quickly transport troops and supplies down the Min River (to invade Chu in the south).[94] These ships were constructed in Shu. No doubt, at least some of them were built with lumber harvested from the rich forests near Mount Emei. The boat-building industry in Jia continued to develop in the Han and subsequent periods,[95] and by Song times the county functioned as one of the major boat-building centers in Sichuan. In the twelfth century Jia and neighboring Xu county, in addition to producing craft for local use called "Shu Boats" (Shuzhou), also built "[Great] River boats" ([Chang]jiang chuan)— vessels designed specifically for travel on the Yangzi, or Great River.

In the next diary entry Fan Chengda mentions that his "Wu boat" had been specially built for him in Xu county, an administrative district just south of Jiazhou. He refers to the craft as a "warship" (*jian* 艦), and for good reason: a large, sturdy, dependable craft was needed to negotiate the treacherous rapids on the Yangzi, especially while passing through the unpredictable currents in the Three Gorges (Sanxia). The boat Lu You took from Zhejiang to Sichuan in 1170, which was owned and crewed by men from Jia county, had a capacity of sixteen hundred *hu*, and yet it was "tossed around like a leaf" on the Great River.[96] No further details are available about Fan's "warship," but it was probably similar to the Song dynasty craft excavated near Shanghai in 1978. This vessel measures about 9.35 m/30.66 ft in length, has a square-shaped bow, u-shaped hull, sculls, and a single mast (originally with sail).[97]

> Earlier, I had had our boat constructed in Xu {county}. When it was completed I had the boat taken upstream and moored in Jia {county}. It had been finished only a short time when I was summoned to Court. I {then} took a small boat from the Joining River {Pavilion} to here, where I boarded the new warship. We thereupon stowed our baggage and loaded up the seal and striker {funds} from the various commands.[98] As was customary, we remained here for a few days so that my traveling party could be thoroughly checked for engaging in the corrupt, tax evasion practices of private businessmen.[99]

> The hall on the flank of the traveler's guesthouse is called "Query the Moon Hall" (Wenyue tang).[100] Although it has been a long time since the hall was reno-vated, the moon actually does appear above its front eaves. Its name was not selected in vain.

> The county wall is made of heaps of large stones in order to provide protection from the rising and swirling waters {of the river}. The wall is low yet durable. The name tablet on the inner gate {leading to the county seat} reads: "Qianwei Commandery" (Qianwei jun), but this is not the former site of the Han commandery.

We are now in Jia county, about twenty-five miles from Mount Emei.

CHAPTER 4

Within Sight of Mount Emei

After Huan Wen destroyed Shu, the mountain passes were mostly deserted.
The Lao people then took the mountains and occupied the valleys, and mixed
and lived with others. Thus, Nan'an and the other towns were mostly uncul-
tivated and abandoned.[1]

—Ma Duanlin (1254–ca. 1325)

ADMINISTRATION AND IMMIGRATION

When Fan Chengda stepped off his boat in Jiazhou on July 14, 1177, he had reached the principal government administrative center near Emei. If the weather was favorable that day he probably saw the lofty peaks of Mount Emei rising in the distance, some twenty-five miles away. Jia county has a long and distinguished history. First, it was close to Emei shan and thus served as a dropping off point for visitors to the mountain. The customary itinerary for sightseers—overland from the Jia county seat to Emei town, and then from there to the base of the mountain, was easily accomplished in a few days. Second, Jia hosts some of most sublime and exquisite scenery in Shu. A section in the hand scroll *Panoramic Landscape—The Yang-tze Kiang*; see figure 4.1), which probably dates from the Southern Song, provides an overview of the superb landscape that extends from the Jia county seat (in the foreground) to Mount Emei (the dark bulk looming in the background). Next, three major rivers in Sichuan merge in Jia county; hence it has served, since at least the twelfth century, as a central point on a strategic river highway that links Sichuan with central and eastern China (note the dominant presence of the Min River in the hand scroll). And finally, the county hosts a magnificent, colossal statue of a sitting Buddha (the multilevel superstructure in the hand scroll, directly across the Min River from the county seat, supports

61

62

Figure 4.1 Detail of the hand scroll *Panoramic Landscape—The Yang-tze Kiang* (*Changjiang wanli tu* 長江萬里圖); anonymous; Southern Song (?). Ink on silk, 1654.0 × 43.7 cm (651 1/4 × 17 3/16in). Freer Gallery of Art, Smithsonian Institution, Washington, D.C.: Gift of Charles Lang Freer, F1911.168 sec.4.

the statue). Carved in the late eighth and early ninth centuries from the red granite cliffs of Traversing-the-Clouds Hill (Lingyun shan), it is the largest such icon in the world. The giant Buddha in Jiazhou, which still stands today, attests to the long presence of Buddhism in southwest Sichuan. Since Jia county is related closely to the evolution and development of Mount Emei, a general sketch of the county's administrative history, especially as it relates to the discussions to follow, will be useful.

The Qin unifiers organized their empire into administrative units called commanderies (*jun*). Among these, central Sichuan was designated "Shu commandery." We know of nineteen towns (*xian*) that fell under control of Shu commandery during the Qin, one of which—Nan'an—is associated with what later became Jia county. In 135, during the reign of Emperor Wu of the Han, Nan'an was reassigned to a new commandery called Qianwei. The territory under Qianwei's administrative control was immense,[2] and included most of what is now southern Sichuan, Zunyi (in modern Guizhou province), and even a portion of Yunnan. Mount Emei fell under the jurisdiction of Nan'an, which in turn was subordinate to Qianwei commandery.

Nan'an continued to function as a government administrative unit, without major changes, throughout the subsequent Three Kingdoms, Liu Song, Qi, and Liang dynasties (that is, from 221 to about 557). In 560, during the reign of Emperor Wu of the Northern Zhou (r. 560–578), a new town called Pingqiang, under the jurisdiction of Qianwei commandery, was created just east of Mount Emei. This marks the first time in history that a government administrative area (in this case, a *xian*, or town) was established in close proximity to the mountain. Just after the Sui reunification the toponym Pingqiang was dropped and a new name for the *xian* was coined. Henceforth it would be known as "Emei town."[3] During the Sui dynasty Emei town fell under the control of yet another commandery, Mei.[4] But Mei was abolished in the early Tang and a new county was created to take its place. This new county was called "Jia" 嘉 (lit., "elegant" or "beautiful").[5] In 1196 the county was elevated to municipality (*fu*) status and with this administrative change came a new, expanded name: "Jiading" 嘉定 (lit., "elegant permanence").[6] With just one interruption, this remained the official title of the municipality until 1914. The city that stands today on the site of old Jiading municipality is called "Leshan City."[7]

Who lived in Jia county throughout the many centuries before Fan Chengda's arrival in the summer 1177? How did they make a living? Did anyone actually reside on Mount Emei? If so, who? How does the history of the surrounding region up to the Southern Song relate to Mount Emei, if at all? The histories and gazetteers provide some general answers to these questions, but supply few details.

According to the *History of the Han* (*Hanshu*), Qianwei commandery comprised twelve *xian* during the Former (or Western) Han, with a total population of 489,486 people (*kou*).[8] Although we do not know how the population in Qianwei was distributed among its twelve *xian*, if we agree to work with average figures, the population of Nan'an was probably somewhere around 41,000 during the Former Han.[9] Figures for the subsequent Later (or Eastern) Han period indicate only a modest increase in population to around 45,000.[10] Given the hundreds of square miles under the town's administrative jurisdiction,[11] these figures indicate a sparse population in Nan'an during the Han dynasty.[12]

The key industries in Nan'an during the Han were salt and iron. We know this because the Han government posted a Salt Commissioner (Yanguan) and Iron Commissioner (Tieguan) in the town. There were only three such commissioners for each of these industries in all of Sichuan.[13] Most of Nan'an's residents probably lived either within or near its protective wall. The town was situated in an isolated and remote area of Sichuan; hence, its walls provided security and protection (the reasons for this need will become obvious in the discussion that follows). Local markets, which supplied food and other basic needs, stood inside or just beyond Nan'an's town rampart. As for Mount Emei, perhaps some tea growers, herb gatherers, or even hunters lived on the mountain during the Han or ventured there from time to time.[14] However, since most of Nan'an's population was concentrated at the town seat, it seems extremely unlikely that any significant number of people lived near or on Mount Emei during the Han. Having said that, at the same time we should note that archaeological discoveries in recent decades have confirmed that there were people in ancient times living on the fertile plain just below Mount Emei, where an abundant water supply supported agricultural activity.[15] In fact, excavated artifacts confirm that the general area around Mount Emei has a long history of cultural and economic development. For instance, a number of Eastern Han cliff tombs (*yanmu*) have been discovered in the region, yielding bronze vessels (*tongqi*) and silver coins (*wuzhu qian*) dating from the Ba-Shu era.[16] These objects suggest an advanced level of cultural development that extends back to the Warring States period or earlier.[17] While particulars about Qianwei's early history are still unknown, the limited archaeological record proves that there were indeed farmers living on the plains below Mount Emei well before the Qin annexation in 316 BC.

Who were these ancient people who lived near Mount Emei, tilling the flat, fertile lands between the Great Ford and Green Robe rivers, well before the Qin colonized Sichuan? Were their numbers significant? Did they manufacture any of the ancient bronze vessels, silver coins, and other implements discovered near Emei in recent decades? From what little information can be gathered from histories, gazetteers, and archaeological reports, the farmers who lived below the slopes of Emei shan in the Warring States period (and probably before) were a non-Shu (and non-Han) people of uncertain origin. These were *not* the people whose culture produced the bronzes and silver coins mentioned in the previous paragraph. Those artifacts are products of Shu culture. And, although the bronzes and other objects excavated from the cliff tombs suggest a high level of Shu cultural growth in the Qianwei region well before the arrival of the Qin, no additional details are available on the history and extent of that development. We do know, however, that many Qin (and later Han) immigrants arrived in Sichuan after the annexation in 316 BC.[18] These newcomers, some of whom settled in Qianwei and Nan'an, almost certainly lived and worked within or near the walls of these administrative centers. The farmers living and working on the plains below Mount Emei were a different stock of people, who had migrated to the area well before the Qin invasion. It is essential, then, to view the history of the Nan'an-Emei shan region—both before and after the Qin annexation—in terms of *two* resident populations: the Qin and Han immigrants who lived with and, over time, intermarried and merged with the local Shu people, and the farmers who dwelled below Mount Emei, well beyond Nan'an's protective walls.

According to a passage in the *Liji* (*Record of Ritual*), non-Han people who lived in the "Western Quarters" (Xifang) were called "Pei" 棘.[19] A check of the *Shuowen jiezi* dictionary reveals that the term Pei specifically denotes "the Manyi 蠻夷 people of Qianwei commandery."[20] The term Manyi is unabashedly condescending, referring to people who are wild, savage, or even barbarous. The modern scholar Zhou Cong is more complimentary, calling the Pei an "industrious, brave people who were active among the thorns and brambles, and who cleared the wastes and opened up the wilds." Moreover, Zhou convincingly identifies the Pei as the earliest aboriginal people (*tuzhu minzu*) to live in the general vicinity of Mount Emei.[21] Originally, the Pei were concentrated in the Yibin area in southern Sichuan, but later moved north to Emei and areas nearby. Many of the stone axes described earlier, dating from the Warring States era, were probably used by the Pei to "clear the wastes and open up the wilds" near Mount Emei. The numerous twin-shoulder stone hoes (*shuangjian shichu*) and stone spades (*shichan*) excavated near the mountain, also dating from the Warring States era or before, were likely used by the Pei as farming tools.[22] It seems likely, then, that at least some of the ancient farmers "of uncertain origin" who tilled the flatlands below Mount Emei were Pei people.

In addition to the Pei, there is evidence that other non-Chinese people also settled in the Nan'an region during the Qin and Han. The *Hanshu* biography of Sima Xiangru (ca. 180–117 BC) mentions that a road was opened to the western border regions, which "extended all the way to the Mo (or Great Ford) and Ruo (or Green Robe) rivers."[23] Thus, Mount Emei stood near the terminus of the main immigration route that brought Qin, Han, and non-Chinese settlers to southwestern Sichuan. Favorable climatic and agricultural conditions no doubt attracted some of these settlers. Among them were the nomadic Qiang 羌 people, who came south following the Min River valley. We know for sure that some Qiang were driven south into the Emei area after their defeat by the Han.[24] Ba people from eastern Sichuan also arrived and settled in the Qianwei region. Some of the lances (*mao*) and pikes (*ge*) excavated near Mount Emei dating from the Warring States period bear a distinct white tiger design that suggests pre-Qin contact with the Ba people.[25] It also seems likely that Yi people from Yunnan moved into the Emei area during the Qin and Han as well.[26]

The foregoing description of immigration activity in the Emei area might give the impression that Nan'an was a thriving, bustling town during the Qin and Han. This was not the case. As we have already seen, the population of Nan'an at this time was quite limited. Moreover, as far as we know, there was no significant economic development in the area during the roughly four centuries of Qin and Han rule. Nan'an was in the backwaters of Shu, far removed from virtually everywhere. The presence of non-Chinese people in the region, however, deserves close attention, for they play a major role in what happened (or, more accurately, what did *not* happen) in the Nan'an-Emei area during the centuries that followed the collapse of the Han dynasty in 221.

The period from the fall of the Han to the official founding of the Sui in 589 witnessed almost constant warfare, local unrest, great human suffering, and substantial refugee population shifts. Consider the following: the population of China at the end of the Former Han was about 59.6 million; at the end of the Later Han it was 56.5 million.[27] By the Eastern Jin period—specifically, the year 370—it had fallen to under 10 million.[28] Hence, although non-Chinese immigrants continued to arrive and settle in the Qianwei region during the period from the Qin-Han to the Jin, there could not have been any sizeable population influx to the area. The population of Nan'an was probably still very small during the Jin period.[29] What is important to note is that the Sichuan region was extremely volatile and unstable from 221 to 589 (altogether, 368 years). Again, the histories do not provide many details, especially about warfare or unrest that might have taken place in and around Qianwei. But in light of the turbulent times and dramatic fall in population (from about 50 million to under 10 million), very little, if any, development could have taken place in Qianwei and Nan'an before the Sui unification at the end of the sixth century.

During the Jin yet another non-Chinese people arrived in Sichuan. These were a mountain-dwelling people called the Lao 獠. According to one source, some 100,000 Lao people immigrated to Shu in the Jin period.[30] They settled throughout Sichuan, residing in twenty-eight towns within six counties; one of these counties was Qianwei.[31] Just how many Lao lived near or on Mount Emei is not known, but one text mentions that during the Jin, the area near Emei was "inundated by Lao."[32] The gazetteers repeatedly mention the "great calamity" caused by the Lao people and the "trouble" they made for local Chinese authorities.[33] Moreover, we also know that from the beginning of the Jin period (265) to the Western Wei (middle of the sixth century) the Lao in Qianwei led several local revolts. While the source of the Lao's discontent is never mentioned, the result is shocking. After their arrival, much of the land in Qianwei remained "uncultivated and abandoned" (*huangfei*) for about three hundred years,[34] presumably because of unstable conditions in the commandery. When one considers that Qianwei has some of the most fertile soil in all Sichuan, the presence and influence of the Lao in the region becomes even more significant. If we look at the various reports in the gazetteers, then, a general picture of Qianwei-Nan'an's early history emerges: outside the commandery and town walls there were very few people and, as a result, little or no agricultural activity. Thus, there was practically no tax base for the commandery and town governments, which in turn meant little or no funds were available for infrastructure (roads, water management, and so on) development. Beginning in the early Jin, the presence and actions of the Lao destabilized the region to the point where in the sixth century "most of the [commandery] was still uncultivated and abandoned."[35] We must be mindful, of course, that reports of "Lao uprisings" in Qianwei were written by Chinese historians, who viewed all non-Han people as inferior to themselves. Nevertheless, the preponderance of evidence concerning the Lao in Qianwei supports our earlier conclusion: little or no development of any kind could have taken place in Qianwei in general, and on Emei shan in particular, before the Sui dynasty.

WAY OF THE CELESTIAL MASTER

> *The primary concern of the priests of the Way of the Celestial Master is said to have been the curing of disease.*[36]
>
> —Michel Strickman

At the end of the second century there was organized Daoist religious activity in Sichuan. Qianwei and Nan'an were directly involved, and so this activity plays an important role in Mount Emei's early reputation as a "Daoist mountain." Since the Daoist tradition associated with the mountain claims much greater antiquity than the arrival of Buddhism, our reconstruction of the historical development of Mount Emei as an important place in China's religious geography will begin with Daoism.

One of the key figures in the early legends of Daoism in China is Zhang Ling, also known as Zhang Daoling. As mentioned in chapter 3, he is credited with founding a second-century religious movement in Sichuan known as the Way of the Celestial Master. With a strong following among the local population in Shu, including many non-Han people, Zhang Daoling became the first Celestial Master. A native of Jiangsu, Zhang reportedly lived in Sichuan from 126 to 144, where he studied, prepared texts to propagate his doctrine, and set up a religious center at Crane-Call Mountain (Heming shan), a peak in Western Shu. Precisely why Zhang Daoling traveled to Shu to engage in these activities is not clear. But he purportedly "found the Dao" on Crane Call Mountain and established his first religious community there.[37] Zhang's son, Zhang Heng (second cent), and grandson, Zhang Lu (second cent), both became Celestial Masters and thus carried on the family tradition. In the declining years of the Han dynasty Zhang Lu amassed a considerable amount of political power, which was partly based on his popularity as a religious leader with the local population in Sichuan. Although the information we have on Zhang Daoling and Zhang Heng is a mix of hagiography and history, by all reliable accounts Zhang Lu is the central figure in the founding and success of the Way of the Celestial Master.[38]

What was it about the teachings and practices of the Celestial Masters in Sichuan that appealed to the general population? At the risk of oversimplifying what is certainly a complex issue, practitioners skilled in Celestial Master ritual techniques provided special services to the local population that were probably not readily available elsewhere. For instance, Celestial Master adepts were trained to carry out ceremonies, on behalf of clients, during which they could "send up petitions" (*shangzhang*) to

Celestial Officials (Tianguan) for the purpose of curing illnesses and other maladies.[39] Practitioners could also provide believers with charms or talismans to ward off danger and calamity, or even promise them long life. On some occasions Celestial Master intermediaries might even conduct séances to establish communication with the dead, or perhaps offer someone a glimpse into the future. These faith-healing and other services appealed greatly to the general public and attracted many followers. We know this because the teachings of the Celestial Master later gained substantial popularity in both north China and the Jiangnan region. Given the unstable and uncertain political and military situation in Sichuan and the rest of China, especially after the fall of the Han, it is not difficult to understand why the teachings and practices of Celestial Masters attracted a large following.

Zhang Daoling is also credited with establishing an institution called "parishes" (zhi). In order to organize his followers in Shu, the first Celestial Master created a network of twenty-four parishes, each of which was headed by a libationer (jijiu) who managed various ritual activities and looked after the needs of local people. This supposedly took place in 143. All but one of these zhi was sited in Sichuan. Four parishes were located in the Qianwei and Nan'an areas. Eight additional "travel parishes" (youzhi) were added later, one of which was specifically designated the "Emei travel parish."[40] A stone stele erected in Yisu Village (Yisu xiang), Hongya town (near Emei), attests to the presence of Celestial Master activity in the general Nan'an-Emei region during the Han.[41] Tradition even attributes a text in three chapters (juan) to Zhang Daoling titled Records of the Supernatural and Extraordinary on Mount Emei (Emei shan shenyi ji).[42] If this tradition has any historical basis, it is possible that Zhang Daoling may have even once visited Emei shan.

At each parish altars made of earth (tutan) were erected in simple thatched structures (caowu).[43] These altars were used for worship and ritual purposes. Essentially, altars were power-conductor sites which, when accessed by a Daoist adept knowledgeable in such matters, could tap and transmit numinous power from the parish site. Presumably, then, the Emei Parish, which was either on the mountain itself or somewhere nearby, included an altar used for Daoist worship and sacrificial purposes, where adepts and knowledgeable practitioners drew on Mount Emei's numinous power. Once tapped, adepts could harness the mountain's energy to enhance their own qi, or vital breath, and thereby ascend high into the sky and rendezvous with other immortals. In his poem "Climbing Mount Emei" Li Bo intended exactly this sort of celestial meeting with the woodcarver-immortal Ge You.

Unfortunately, further details about Mount Emei's parish remain unknown. It seems quite likely that the five parishes in the general Qianwei-Emei area were still active during the Jin period. By the Tang, however, they were gone.[44] That is not to say, however, that departure of the Celestial Masters meant that Daoist influence and activity in the area subsided or ended.

ADEPTS AND ABBEYS

> *It doesn't matter if a mountain is lofty or not; if it has immortals, then it will be famous.*[45]
>
> —Liu Yuxi (772–842)

Traditional sources on Mount Emei, especially the gazetteers, contain numerous references to man-made structures built on the mountain through the dynasties. While many names are used to designate these buildings, most fall into two categories. The first is retreats associated with Daoism. These structures most often include the word *guan* 觀, or "[Daoist] abbey," in their name. The second category includes edifices associated with Buddhism, and these are usually denoted by the word *si* 寺 ("monastery") or *yuan* 院 ("cloister"). The identification and dating of these abbeys and monasteries is crucial in determining when organized religious activity first began on the mountain. The word "organized" is important here, for I will attempt to distinguish between individuals or sole practitioners who lived and engaged in some form of religious activity on the mountain, and organized communities of individuals, as might be found say, in a Buddhist temple complex. Although the gazetteers and modern secondary sources provide extensive lists of chronologically arranged *guan* and *si* and other structures associated with Daoism and Buddhism, the lack of reliable, corroborating primary sources written before the Southern Song makes accurate dating of these buildings extremely difficult. As we move back in history, to the Tang, Jin, and Han, dating becomes even more challenging, if not impossible. Moreover, two additional obstacles always seem to be present. First, reports about the earliest abbeys and monasteries on the mountain are irrevocably entwined with myth and hagiography. One example is the Master Pu legend, mentioned earlier.[46] A second obstacle is the religious bias of Hu Shian (1593–1663) and Jiang Chao (1623–1672), the compilers of Emei's two most detailed and influential gazetteers. The former was a follower of Daoism, while the latter was a devout Buddhist. Though both have their shortcomings and biases as scholars and gazetteer compilers, Jiang Chao is especially culpable. On some occasions he deliberately altered Daoist titles, quoted earlier in Hu Shian's *Yi elai*, to Buddhist names.[47] Clearly, then, in our attempt to discover when organized religious activity began on Emei, it is essential that we make every effort to divorce myth from history, fact from fabrication.

Source materials related to Mount Emei's Daoist tradition fall into three general categories, which are closely related. First are the reports and tales of immortals associated with the mountain. These connections are established mainly in a genre of writing called "biographies of immortals" (*xianzhuan*). A huge corpus of such works survives, the earliest extant collection of which—*Biographies of Immortals (Liexian zhuan)*—dates from the Han. With some of the later immortal biography collections on occasion it is possible to trace the source(s) of these accounts, but oftentimes this task is extremely difficult because the compiler did not work with original texts, but rather copies.[48] While biographical material in these collections is terse and can vary greatly in style, the common thread is commemoration of the feats and deeds of a *xian* and description of his exemplary status. Most of the immortal figures in these stories exist only in myths. Only a very few are historical persons who later allegedly became *xian*. The second type of Daoist source material appears in the form of references or biographies in official historical works (*zhengshi*), such as the dynastic histories, where myth is sometimes repeated and seemingly taken as history. The third and final variety is a collection of selected texts in the official *Daoist Canon (Daozang)*. These works are extremely important because they identity, define, and map Daoist territory, particularly on famous mountains.

Followers or practitioners of Daoism, or "Daoist adepts" (*daoshi*), sought to become a *xian* because to do so meant to reach the highest state of perfection. Adepts followed various regimens and employed different techniques in their pursuit of perfection, including drug therapies, dietary restrictions, sexual regimens, breathing practices, meditation, reading of talismans, and even yoga and gymnastic practices.[49] Theoretically, one could become a transcendent or immortal anywhere. Some places, however, were thought to be more suitable than other sites. Mountain environments were regarded as especially efficacious; in particular, mountains with grottoes (*dong*; that is, caves with water sources). As mentioned in chapter 1, Mount Emei has an abundance of watery caves, the best known of which is the Nine Elders Grotto (Jiulao dong). This cave complex still serves today as a site to worship Lü Dongbin (or Lü Yan), the sixth of the famous Eight Daoist Immortals.

Daoist adepts favored mountain retreats because they are secluded and removed from civilization. Mountains are also a source of herbs, mushrooms, and minerals (gold, mercury, realgar, and jade) used in alchemical preparations, and offered the prospect of encounters with immortals who reside there.[50] And, perhaps most important, mountains have numinous power which, as we have already seen, with the right practice and technique could be used to help one "soar up into clouds." Hence, for the Daoist adept, mountains were potentially a place of passage to a transcendent or immortal state of being. The grotto itself could also serve as a passageway or conduit, connecting with other Daoist or supernatural realms.[51] In many ways, then, the grotto is the very essence of the mountain and its power.

Many mountains in China have *xian* traditions, and Mount Emei is no exception. Emei shan's identity as a "Daoist mountain" is rooted in a collection of tales and references to various legendary and immortal figures, some of whom are quite well known, who supposedly either visited or lived on the mountain. Although a few of the stories mention historical figures, we should not be overly concerned about whether the exploits of Mount Emei's *xian* can be confirmed or collaborated in other texts. In the overwhelming majority of cases this simply cannot be done because no such evidence is available. A more fundamental and important question to keep in mind is this: what is the origin of these tales and how do they collectively function in the formulation of Emei shan as a "Daoist mountain"?

Emei's earliest immortal figure is the Sovereign of Celestial Perfection (Tianzhen huangren). The first report of his association with Mount Emei appears in Ge Hong's *The Master Who Embraces Simplicity*: "The Yellow Emperor . . . arrived at Emei shan, saw the Sovereign of Celestial Perfection in the Jade Hall, and inquired about the Way of the True One."[52] Numerous later texts repeat and refine the events of this momentous encounter, all noting the Yellow Emperor eventually "found the Way" on Mount Emei. An influential work in the *Daoist Canon* dating from the Song, *Seven Tablets in a Cloudy Satchel* (*Yunji qiqian*), even goes so far as to say: "Lingbao Scriptures (*Lingbao jing*) that survive today in fact were transmitted to Xuanyuan (that is, the Yellow Emperor) by the Sovereign of Celestial Perfection on Mount Emei."[53] In other words, the place of origin for the primary texts of Lingbao (or "Numinous Treasure"), one of the major schools of early medieval Daoism in China, was on Mount Emei. Perhaps not surprisingly, the scholar credited with defining the so-called Lingbao catalog of scriptures, Lu Xiujing (406–477), also has an Emei connection.[54]

The Yellow Emperor, the common ancestor of all Chinese people, has long been associated with longevity practices and famous Daoist mountains in China. It is no surprise, then, to find him mentioned in conjunction with early *xian* activity on Emei. But who was the Sovereign of Celestial Perfection and why is he associated with Mount Emei? We know that he was a "superior immortal" (*shangxian*; which contrasts with *dixian*, or immortals who live on earth), reputedly wrote commentaries to Daoist texts, and is credited with explaining basic Lingbao talismans to the Yellow Emperor. In another passage in the *Seven Tablets in a Cloudy Satchel* it appears that the Sovereign of Celestial Perfection is none other than Daoist patriarch Laozi himself: "Master Lao descended to Mount Emei and conferred the *Lingbao Scriptures* on the Yellow Emperor."[55] Although it is not clear why the Sovereign is associated with Mount Emei, the fact that early and influential Daoist works such as the *The Master Who Embraces Simplicity*, and many later texts, including the *Seven Tablets in a Cloudy Satchel*, mention his activities there in conjunction with figures like the Yellow Emperor and Laozi is noteworthy, for these accounts are repeated time and again in later Daoist and non-Daoist sources, even the dynastic histories.[56] Over time, these textual references collectively worked to establish and legitimize Emei as a "Daoist mountain," and this reputation eventually became an integral part of the mountain's image and identity in traditional China. In other words, these tales influenced how people thought and wrote about the mountain. It is no accident that Li Bo, who identified Emei as the premier "immortal mount" in Shu, once remarked: "Those after Xuan (the Yellow Emperor) who made inquiries about the Dao came to Emei."[57] Moreover, the Song emperor Taizong once wrote a commemorative piece of calligraphy for Emei that bore the following words: "The Place where Sovereign of Celestial Perfection Expounded on the Way."[58] And finally, there are physical sites on the mountain identified with specific *xian*. Just one example is the Ten Character Grotto (Shizi dong), where the Sovereign of Celestial Perfection supposedly conferred texts and discoursed on the Way.[59] This association or mapping process—correlating specific physical space on the mountain with events related to immortals—reinforces the legitimization process. As this practice is repeated with other immortals and their activities at specific sites, a "map" or "geography" of Daoist territory on the mountain is constructed and defined. This was a critical step in the process that culminated in Mount Emei becoming a full-fledged Daoist mountain.

The next significant development took place when the Tang authors Sima Chengzhen (647–735) and Du Guangting (850–933), both well-known Court Daoists, codified two sets of grotto-heavens throughout China. The expression *dongtian*, or grotto-heaven, specifically denotes "a Daoist grotto conceived as a heaven or paradise, and abode of supernatural beings."[60] Grotto-heavens, according to Du Guangting, are among the most important places in Daoist geography. The two sets of grotto-heavens described in his *Records of Grotto-heavens, Blessed Sites, Cardinal Mounts, Rivers, and Famous Mountains (Dongtian fudi yuedu mingshan ji)* are called "Ten Great Grotto-heavens" (Shi da dongtian) and "Thirty-six [Lesser] Grotto-heavens" (Sanshiliu [xiao] dongtian).[61] The precise relationship between the two sets is unknown. Nor is it clear how the thirty-six grottoes are "lesser" than the ten "greater" ones. In any case, Mount Emei is identified as one of the thirty-six lesser grottoes; specifically, the seventh. With this status came a special name: "Grotto-heaven of Vacuous Mounds and Grand Subtleties (Xuling taimiao dongtian)."[62] A "Perfected One" (Zhenren) named Tang Lan supposedly once supervised Emei shan as the seventh smaller grotto-heaven.[63] And, at least three different places on the mountain have been identified as the site of Emei's Grotto-heaven of Vacuous Mounds and Grand Subtleties.[64]

Mount Emei's community of immortals is extensive. In our previous discussion of literary visions of Mount Emei in Tang and Song poetry (chapter 3) we encountered two of these figures: Ge You, the woodcrafter with whom Li Bo hoped to soar through the universe, and the Madman of Chu (also known as Lu Tong or Lu Jieyu), with whom Chen Ziang longed to rendezvous "Far, far away, amid the white clouds." Both supposedly lived during the Zhou dynasty, making them Emei's first immortal figures. Ge You's brief biography in the *Liexian zhuan* reads as follows:

> Ge You was a native Qiang person. In the time of King Cheng of Zhou (r. 1115–1078 BC), he made wood carvings of goats and sold them. One day he came to Shu riding a goat. The nobles and aristocrats in Shu followed him all the way to Mount Sui. Mount Sui is southwest of Mount Emei. Those who followed him never returned. All found the immortal Way.[65]

This brief biographical notice is the earliest reference that connects Ge You to Emei (more specifically, to Mount Sui). It is typical of the biographies that link specific *xian* with the mountain. Sparing in biographical details, we only get a bare-bones account, noting the immortal's origin (Ge You was not a Chinese, but a Qiang), when he was active (the reign of King Cheng during the Zhou), personal characteristics (Ge was a bit eccentric), and notable deeds (he presumably transmitted the Way to others on Mount Sui). This same account is retold, in slightly different form, in many later anthologies, including *Records in Search of the Supernatural (Soushen ji)*, an influential collection of stories compiled around 300 AD.[66]

Lu Tong's biography in the *Liexian zhuan* is strikingly similar to that of Ge You. Mention of his Emei connection is brief: "He resided on Mount Emei in Shu; generation after generation of locals saw him there; he spent several centuries on the mountain."[67] Lu Tong's Emei link is recounted in numerous later collections, including *Biographies of Lofty Scholars* (*Gaoshi zhuan*).[68] Again, what is especially critical here is this process whereby a story or reference to particular *xian* associated with Mount Emei is repeated and retold in different collections and anthologies over time. Emei's reputation as a Daoist mountain was built, in large part, through this cumulative process of association. Speaking in general terms, the compilers of these collections and anthologies do not seem to be concerned about their sources. How did Liu Xiang (77–6 BC), editor of the *Liexian zhuan*, find out that Ge You traveled to Shu riding a goat? We will probably never know the answer to this question. Li Bo, who was extremely influential in helping to build Emei's reputation as an "immortal mount," probably never even considered the question.

The next best-known figure traditionally associated with Mount Emei is Sun Simiao (581–682), who is often identified as one of the fathers of Chinese medicine. A physician and pharmacologist, he is credited with compiling several texts related to alchemy, pharmacology, and medicine. The Song emperor Huizong, who himself had a great interest in Daoist pursuits, even canonized Sun the "Perfected One of Miraculous Response" (Miaoying zhenren). Strictly speaking, Sun Simiao does not fall into the category of immortals associated with Mount Emei because he is a well-known figure in Tang history. But since he reportedly lived for over one hundred years, Sun is often mentioned in conjunction with *xian* and perfected ones (*zhenren*) associated with the mountain. Sun Simiao's link to Mount Emei appears to originate in an influential Tang work by Duan Chengshi (d. 863) titled *Assorted Notes from Youyang* (*Youyang zazu*), which relates an incident in which the Tang emperor Xuanzong had a dream about Sun Simiao seeking realgar (*xionghuang*) on Mount Emei, after which the emperor dispatched ten catties (*jin*) of the drug to the summit.[69] From the content of this anecdote we see that by the eighth century Sun Simiao was already considered a member of Emei's pantheon of immortals. This connection was then repeated and embellished in many later works, and even in a couplet by Su Shi: "Since the gentleman's passing—five hundred years; / But still he remains in the western hills of Emei."[70]

Although it is certain that Sun Simiao visited Sichuan in his lifetime, probably more than once, there is no conclusive evidence that he ever reached Mount Emei in his travels.[71] But his work as a physician and pharmacologist, and interest in alchemy, certainly fits the "standard profile" of *xian* and recluses associated with Emei shan (Daoist interests, reclusive lifestyle, brewing elixirs in grottoes, and so on). The result is that Sun Simiao plays a prominent role in the legend and lore of Daoist recluses associated with Emei shan. Fan Chengda will tell us more about Sun in chapter 6.

Why was Mount Emei a suitable place to host myths about immortals? Why would Ge Hong and other authors identify the mountain as a site of immortal happenings? The mountain's early literary reputation, beginning with Zuo Si's late third-century rhapsody, certainly plays a role here. To most readers, including Ge Hong, the name "Mount Emei" conjured images and associations of a peak in the "Western Regions," far removed from the heartland of China. And, in fact, unlike many other *mingshan* and Daoist mounts in China, Mount Emei *was* situated in an extremely remote and isolated region. As we have seen, this sort of isolated environment was ideally suited to Daoist pursuits. Moreover, the mountain's space hosted virtually all the resources (plants, minerals, elaborate grottoes, and so on), needed by adepts to pursue and reach a state of perfection. Hence, Emei shan provided a perfect setting for tales of immortals. It is especially significant that stories about the Yellow Emperor and other illustrious figures associated with the mountain were in circulation already in the fourth century; specifically, in Ge Hong's influential work *The Master Who Embraces Simplicity*. These early tales are the foundation of Mount Emei's identity as a Daoist mountain.

In contrast to the various myths and stories of immortals just considered, historically there *were* adepts who actually practiced Daoism on Mount Emei. We know this because in Tang poetry there are references to several of these *daoshi* by name. "Refined Master Zhang," whom we met in chapter 3, is one of these adepts. But where did they live on the mountain? Were they mainly solitary practitioners or did they congregate in abbeys?

The earliest Daoist structure on Emei shan mentioned in the gazetteers is the Celestial Illumination Abbey (Qianming guan), which tradition says was erected in the Jin period.[72] The gazetteers do not provide details about its early history, except to say that adepts there were sometimes known to soar off as immortals. Another fanciful legend says that a python (*mangchong*) was once wreaking havoc near the temple, terrorizing the adepts. A clever Buddhist monk named Mingguo came along one day and managed to outwit and kill the snake. Moved by this heroic act, the resident Daoists in the abbey then "agreed" to convert the building into a Buddhist monastery. The result was the creation of the Central Peak Monastery (Zhongfeng si).[73] Finally, the *Mount Emei Gazetteer* reports that

during the Song period three "perfected ones" experienced "feathery transformations" (*yuhua*; that is, became immortals) at the original site of the
abbey.[74] Admittedly, in all likelihood these reports are more fantasy than
fact. Still, the Celestial Illumination Abbey-python tale is our earliest
reference to a Daoist structure on the mountain. Hu Shian mentions spot-
ting the old remains of a "Song Huang Abbey (Song-Huang guan), where
"in ancient times there was 'Hall of Daoist Chronicles' (Daoji tang) and
various centers (*guan*) and chambers (*shi*), comprising 350 rooms (*jian*)."[75]
Whether Hu's reference to "ancient times" predates the Tang dynasty is
not known. In fact, the history of Daoism on Emei shan before the Tang
is murky at best. Aside from the python story, I have found no other reference to Daoist activity of any sort dating from the Jin. If there were Daoist
adepts on the mountain before the Tang, in all likelihood they were solitary
practitioners.

As already mentioned, however, in the Tang there were certainly
Daoist adepts living on Mount Emei. In addition to Li Bo's friend
"Refined Master Zhang," we know of at least three other *daoshi* who made
their homes on Emei shan. One of these adepts is described in a poem
by Bao Rong (ninth cent) titled "Sent to Refined Master Yang of
Mount Emei":

> The Daoist adept at night recites the *Stamen Gem Classic*;
> White cranes spiraling downward are heard in fragrant mists.
> The night moves on, the *Classic* is exhausted, and he mounts the crane;
> Immortal winds stir and blow, the autumn is dark and gloomy.[76]

Again, we are not provided details about Refined Master Yang or his
activities on Emei. However, surviving references to other adepts who also
practiced on Emei confirm the presence of Daoist activity during the
Tang.[77] Whether these adepts lived on the main mountain or on Mount
Sui is not clear, but I strongly suspect that the latter served as home for
most Emei adepts during the Tang. Mount Sui has a long-standing reputation as a Daoist enclave that extends at least back until Li Bo's time, and
probably much earlier. Moreover, most references to Daoist sites and
abbeys in the *Mount Emei Gazetteer* are concentrated at Mount Sui. For
instance, Ge You supposedly resided in the Ge-the-Immortal Grotto
(Gexian dong) on Mount Sui and rode his goat thereabouts.[78] Since none
of the references to Daoist adepts found in Tang poetry mention association
with a particular abbey, my guess is that most were solitary practitioners,
living in grottoes or simple wood or thatched structures on Mount Sui.
Although it is well known that the Tang Court promoted Daoist

institutions at *mingshan*, especially the construction of abbeys, there is no evidence of *organized* Daoist religious activity on Mount Emei during the Tang. On the other hand, judging by the number of references in Tang poetry alone, Emei's *reputation* as a Daoist mountain reached its height during the Tang. Li Bo is the one writer most responsible for this development. By the Southern Song, however, the presence of Daoism had subsided on Mount Emei.

ŚĀKYAMUNI'S TEACHINGS COME TO SICHUAN

> *The religious doctrine and practices developed in Buddhist centers in northern and central China by figures such as Daoan and Huiyuan were transmitted to places like Chengdu by the dispersal of Buddhist monastic communities. Once Buddhist missionaries were established there, the region's relative stability, freedom from imperial constraint, and support from the local lay community fostered continued evolution of the Buddhist tradition.*[79]
>
> —Dorothy Wong

Sichuan's first contact with Buddhism probably dates from the Later Han. Some of China's earliest images of Buddha (*foxiang*)—fashioned during the second and third centuries—have been found in the southwestern part of the province.[80] Of special interest to us is a stone relief image in the first chamber of a cave-tomb complex discovered in 1940 at Mahao, located less than a mile from the Colossal Buddha in Jia county (modern Leshan). Richard Edwards, a University of Michigan art historian, visited the Mahao site in 1949 and 1950 and published the results of his findings in a two-part article that appeared some years later in *Artibis Asiae*.[81] Among the Mahao artifacts described by Edwards is a single figure carved in relief against a plain background on the tomb's stone lintel. The image appears in a sitting position, with its left hand grasping a portion of the gown, while the right hand is raised in a salutary manner.[82] The head is ringed by a halo. Edwards concluded the image was a depiction of a sitting Buddha and dated it to "the last half of the second century or early in the third.[83] Yu Weichao, a well-known authority on Buddhist iconography, dates the image specifically to the reigns of the Han emperors Huan (r. 146–168) and Ling (r. 168–189).[84] This identification and dating is quite significant, for most experts today believe the Mahao stone relief image is one of the earliest extant artistic representations of Buddha in China. Similar carvings have been found elsewhere in Sichuan, dating from about the same period, which suggests that "the use of the Buddha's image in tomb decoration might have been a widespread custom on the Sichuan plain, during the Eastern Han."[85] If this is the case, then Buddhism (the religion) and Buddhist art already had assumed important roles in Sichuan by the second century.[86]

By the second half of the fourth century Buddhist monks had already begun to engage in missionary work in Sichuan. Clergy first came to Shu, and ultimately to Mount Emei, for two reasons. First, they sought to establish monastic communities, where monks could follow a pious life-style of prayer and meditation; second, they sought to propagate the teachings of Śākyamuni to the masses. One important way to disseminate Buddha's teachings was to build monasteries where Buddhist religious ceremonies could be held, which not only would appeal to local lay supporters, but attract pilgrims as well. Pilgrims served an especially important and practical function for these institutions: their visits generated income, which usually came in the form of donations. We will return to this and related economic issues in chapter 7.

The spread of monasteries throughout China followed a general pattern: they first appeared in major cities, like Luoyang, from where they spread to counties and smaller administrative units, like Jiazhou, and ultimately to mountains, like Emei. Following this trend, the earliest monasteries in Sichuan were built in and around Chengdu. These include the Myriad Buddhas Monastery (Wanfo si), constructed during the Liang dynasty (502–557), which later became a major Buddhist art center; the Buddhist Peace Monastery (Fan'an si), built during the Sui; and the Great Compassion Monastery. This last structure, erected in 757, comprised a huge complex of some ninety-six cloisters, which included 8,542 galleries, halls (*dian*), reception rooms (*ting*), and private quarters (*fang*).[87] During the Tang at least fourteen other major temples were constructed in and around Chengdu, including the Brilliant Awareness Monastery (Zhaojue si) and the Mañjuśrī Cloister (Wenshu yuan).[88] Buddhism thrived in Chengdu during the Tang.

Huijiao's (497–544) *Biographies of Eminent Monks (Gaoseng zhuan)*, an important source on the early history of Buddhism in China, provides information on some twenty monks, both foreign and Chinese, who had associations with Sichuan between the fourth and mid-sixth centuries. Among them, there are three—Fahe (fourth cent), Huichi (337–412), and Daowang (d. 465)—whose missionary activities were instrumental in defining the character and early development of Buddhism in southwest China.[89] Huichi deserves especially close attention, for he is the most influential historical figure associated with early Buddhist activity in Sichuan. Huichi may also have been responsible for initiating the first temple-building project on Mount Emei.

Huichi was the younger brother of Huiyuan (334–416), the patriarch of Pure Land (Jingtu) Buddhism in China. Originally, the brothers were members of a Buddhist community in the city of Xiangyang (in modern Hubei) and disciples of the Dharma Master Daoan (312–385), a major figure in Chinese Buddhism during the fourth century. Huiyuan was Daoan's most brilliant disciple. When Xiangyang dispersed (Eastern Jin and Former Qin armies fought there about 379) the two brothers and their followers fled to Mount Lu in Jiangxi. Huiyuan spent the remainder of his life in seclusion there. According to tradition, Huiyuan and one-hundred and twenty-three followers founded the famous White Lotus Society (Bailian she) on Mount Lu. Their principal religious goal was rebirth in the Pure Land paradise of Amitābha Buddha. To attain this goal they practiced *nianfo*—repeatedly invoking the name "A-mi-tuo-fo" (or "Amitābha Buddha"). This practice, they believed, would not only help them to gain true understanding of the scriptures; it would also assist their rebirth in the blissful Pure Land.

Some of the ideas that Huiyuan developed, especially during his long residence at Mount Lu, significantly influenced the development of Buddhism in China. One of these ideas is his notion that affiliates religious pursuits with the natural world; specifically, scenic mountain environments like Mount Lu. That is to say, Huiyuan believed that appreciation of beautiful, pristine landscapes could inspire the devout to heightened levels of religious awareness and understanding.[90] Huichi and his older brother's followers continued to promote the same idea: the most fitting place to construct a monastery was on a mountain, preferably one in a remote location with a beautiful landscape. Not coincidentally, at about the same time Huiyuan and his supporters were advancing ideas about integrating spiritual life with the natural world there appeared in China a new or awakened interest in the beauty of natural landscapes. One tremendously important result of this trend was the appearance and later development in China of landscape poetry and art.[91]

Huichi eventually left Mount Lu to engage in missionary work. His *Gaoseng zhuan* biography, the most informative source on his life and religious interests, says the monk traveled to Shu in 399 because he had heard "Chengdu was fertile land with numerous people." Huichi's purpose in going there, we are told, was to "transmit [Buddha's teachings] and convert [the people].[92] After arriving in Chengdu, Huichi took up residence in the Dragon Pool Purification Hall (Longyuan jingshe), where he "transmitted scriptures and expounded on the dharma." The next line in his biography mentions Emei shan by name: "Huichi desired to behold and gaze upon Emei, and make a trip to the peaks of the Min [Mountains]."[93] Later in his *Gaoseng zhuan* biography Huichi is quoted as having even once remarked: "I've always desired to nestle in luminosity of the peaks on Emei."[94] The references cited here have led many scholars, both traditional and modern, to conclude that Huichi visited Emei in 399 in order to engage in missionary work; specifically, to build a monastery. Furthermore, we are told that he succeeded in this effort. The result, many historians believe, was construction of the Samantabhadra Monastery (Puxian si) on Mount Emei. Some years later, probably before 406, Huichi returned to Chengdu and remained there until his death in 412.[95]

Huichi's *Gaoseng zhuan* biography says nothing about him actually journeying to Emei. Since Huichi presumably spent thirteen years in Sichuan (399 to 412), and given his strong interest in scenic mountain environments and temple building, it seems reasonable to assume that at some point in his missionary work he would have paid a visit to Mount Emei. As we have seen, references in his biography indicate that he knew about the mountain and desired to journey there. Moreover, for reasons explained earlier, Emei probably seemed like an ideal place for missionary activity; specifically, construction of a monastery. But temple building requires resources to pay for materials and labor. Where did Huichi find such support? The sources do not say much about this, except that Huiyuan had a benefactor named Mao Qu (d. 405), who was a high government official in Sichuan.[96]

For the sake of argument, if we assume that Huichi visited Emei shan during his stay in Shu, we can be certain that he did not find a large Buddhist community already in place there. If Buddhist monks were living on the mountain in the early fifth century—and this is not confirmed in any source I know of—their number was probably very small. But if Huichi indeed reached Emei shan during his travels, what would he have done there? Here we can only speculate. My guess is that he would have organized monks already in residence on or near Emei and led them in some small-scale building activity. The result could very well have been construction of Mount Emei's first monastery. If this happened, the building would have been a simple structure, made of wood, with perhaps a few rooms with some locally crafted images of Buddhist deities on display. I doubt highly, however, that Huichi and his fellow monks dubbed the result of their construction effort the "Samantabhadra Monastery." Samantabhadra (Puxian in Chinese) is the name of an Indian Buddhist deity, whose association with Emei dates, at the very earliest, from the Tang.[97] It seems, then, that Huichi's "Samantabhadra Monastery" is a later invention, perhaps coined by Buddhists in the Tang or Song to support the idea that Emei was the residence of the bodhisattva Samantabhadra, and perhaps to help establish Huichi as the Founding Patriarch (Zushi) of Mount Emei. Although there is no historical evidence to confirm Huichi's visit to Mount Emei, references to other monks and monastery building in the gazetteers suggests there may have been a few Buddhist structures on the mountain in the Eastern Jin.[98] But to repeat my earlier point, these could only have been small, modest buildings. According to Fahe's *Gaoseng zhuan* biography, when he reached Sichuan in 365 "few people in Shu had ever heard of the Buddhadharma."[99] Thus, Buddhist activity could not have been widespread in Shu when Huichi arrived there in 399.

Information on the development of Buddhism on Mount Emei following Huichi's lifetime is sketchy. Accounts related to Emei from the Jin to the Sui focus on individual Buddhist monks who supposedly either visited or lived on the mountain. Among the more notable figures of this era is the Indian monk Baozhang. He is credited with building the Sagely Compassion Monastery (Shengci si) in Chengdu and the Numinous Cliff Monastery (Lingyan si) at the foot of Mount Emei.[100] During the Tang, Song, and Ming, the Numinous Cliff Monastery developed into one of the largest and most prosperous temples in Sichuan. Some scholars have argued unconvincingly that Baozhang's various monastery-building efforts were the result of patronage received from Emperor Wu (r. 503–549) of the Liang dynasty, who was a devout Buddhist.[101]

Other monks associated with the mountain before the Tang include Danran (sixth cent), who came to Emei from Jianye (modern Nanjing) and built a thatch hut near Central Peak Ridge (Zhongfeng ling), where he "recited sūtras by day and meditated by night."[102] An Indian monk said to have visited Emei in the Jin period is Apoduoluo, who is credited with building the Conjured City Monastery (Huacheng si), so named because the landscape where he built the temple was said to resemble a place in India called Huacheng, or Conjured City.[103] The roof of this building was made of wood, so it is also acquired the alternate name Tree Bark Hall (Mupi dian). The Tang poet Cao Song (tenth cent) wrote a poem that mentions this hall.[104] Fan Chengda, in fact, will stop to rest there during his ascent of the mountain.

One major reason why Buddhism expanded throughout China during the Tang was imperial patronage and support. Several Tang sovereigns—most notably Taizong (r. 626–649), Gaozong (r. 649–684), Wu Zetian (in power 690–705), Xuanzong, Wenzong (r. 827–840), and Xizong (r. 873–888)—all supported the religion in one way or another.[105] The one figure in the early Tang who played the most influential role in attracting Court attention to Buddhism was Xuanzang (596–664), the well-known Chinese pilgrim who traveled to India in the seventh century. In 645, when

Xuanzang returned home, Taizong received him in Luoyang with great fanfare. Afterward, the emperor made arrangements for the monk to carry on his translation work in the Magnanimous Prosperity Monastery (Hongfu si) in Chang'an. Some of the most renowned scholar-monks from around the country were assembled to assist him. Taizong even wrote a preface to one of Xuanzang's translations and, later in life, after many conversations with the monk, himself became a devout follower of the Indian religion. Taizong's son and eventual successor, Gaozong, also cultivated an interest in Buddhism and strongly supported Xuanzang's translation efforts by appointing several prominent Court scholars to his staff. Other major efforts by Gaozong in support of Buddhism include the construction in 648 of the Compassionate Grace Monastery (Cien si) in Chang'an. Then later, in 651, two years after he ascended the throne, the new emperor converted Chang'an's famous Jade Flower Palace (Yuhua gong) into a monastery.[106] As for the Empress Wu Zetian, she is well known for her support of Buddhist-related projects, especially the famous Dragon Gate (Longmen) cave complex outside Luoyang. One important event related to Mount Emei that took place during her rule was the retranslation of the *Huayan jing* (*Avataṃsaka-sūtra*) in the 690s, to which the empress herself contributed a preface. The *Huayan jing* is extremely important in the history of Mount Emei because it provides scriptural authority that identifies Samantabhadra as the resident bodhisattva of the mountain. We will discuss this issue in chapter 7.

As for Mount Emei, when we get to the Tang period, the sources supply more reliable details about Buddhist pursuits in and around the mountain. The main activity was temple building. The Sagely Longevity Monastery (Shengshou si; later renamed the Xipo si, or "Western Slope Monastery") was constructed just after the founding of the Tang, outside the western gate of Emei town.[107] This is the first Buddhist structure built in close proximity to the town. Monks and pilgrims would customarily stop there to burn incense, offer prayers, and spend the night before ascending the mountain.[108] As for monasteries constructed on the mountain during the Tang, the Black Stream Monastery deserves special mention. In the late ninth century a historical monk named Huitong lived on Mount Emei. Huitong was well known in Shu, and his fame spread all the way to Chang'an. The emperor Xizong, himself a supporter of Buddhism, commissioned the construction of the Black Stream Monastery. Moreover, the emperor wrote out, in his own calligraphy, a name plaque for the monastery that read: "Eternally Bright Lotus Depository Monastery (Yongming Huazang si). The new monastery received personal gifts from the emperor as well.[109] The significance of such imperial patronage cannot be overstated, for not only did it provide resources and enhance the reputation and credibility of Huitong's efforts on the mountain, it also probably helped him to attract additional support from local sources. Since Huitong is also credited with expanding four other monasteries on the mountain: Samantabhadra, Extended Prosperity (Yanfu), Central Peak (Zhongfeng), and Huayan Monastery (Avataṃsaka Monastery),[110] it seems likely that he found such support, perhaps from local officials or well-to-do families in the area.

Shi Huaiyi, a historical figure and well-known monk in Shu, is reported to have resided in the Samantabhadra Monastery during the Kaibao reign (713–742) of the Tang. He was good friends with the Tang poet Cui Hao (*jinshi* 723; d. 754), who supposedly once visited him there. Cui Hao left a poem in which he refers to Shi Huaiyi as a "Dharma Master" (Fashi) who "recited sūtras on Mount Emei."[111] And, as we saw earlier in chapter 2, Li Bo is also reported to have once stayed in the Samantabhadra Monastery, where he heard the monk Guangjun play his zither.

What did Shi Huaiyi and other Tang monks do on Emei? Were the monasteries on the mountain organized or coordinated in any way? Did pilgrims travel to Emei during the Tang? We can be sure that at least some temple building occurred during the Tang dynasty. We know this because there are historical monks (Shi Huaiyi, for instance) whose presence on the mountain is confirmed in Tang sources. Since there were monks and monasteries on the mountain, it seems reasonable to assume that there was some organized Buddhist religious activity present, such as ritual and prayer ceremonies. But from what little information is available, one certainly cannot conclude that Buddhism thrived on Emei during the Tang. Temple building seems to have been sporadic, and whatever organized religious ceremony or ritual took place was probably limited. The Song writer Shao Bo (d. 1158), who served as an official in both Mei and Ya counties (near Emei), mentions that none of the Buddhist shrines (*foci*) on Emei in the twelfth century had stone inscriptions dating from the Tang, which led him to suspect that Buddhism did not flourish on Emei until the Song."[112]

The construction of the Sagely Longevity Monastery (or Western Slope Monastery) outside the gates of Emei town is significant. If this temple dates, as the sources say, from the early Tang, this would indicate that pilgrims were already visiting Mount Emei as early as the seventh century. If this was the case, then certainly a trail (or trails) must have been in place to take these visitors to the various monasteries on the mountain. The ascent to the White Stream Monastery at mid-mountain was probably manageable for most able-bodied pilgrims, especially since

stone steps were in place by then. But hiking beyond there to higher elevations would have been extremely difficult and dangerous. As already mentioned, in the Southern Song there were no stone steps above the mid-riff
of the mountain.[113] Certainly some younger and more energetic monks or
pilgrims may have ascended to the Golden Summit during the Tang, but
it was not accessible to the general public, even in Fan Chengda's time.

A COLOSSAL BUDDHA

> *The greatest landscape in the world is in Shu; the greatest scenery in Shu is
> in Jia county.*[114]
>
> —Shao Bo (d. 1158)

Upon arriving in Jia county Fan Chengda immediately set off on a
sightseeing tour of local scenic and historic sites. Two of these places are
mentioned in the next diary entry. The Transversing-the-Clouds Monastery (Lingyun si) is Jia's first major Buddhist temple. It was built at the
beginning of the Kaiyuan reign of the Tang,[115] around the same time the
several large-scale monasteries described earlier were constructed in
Chengdu. Perched atop a hill of the same name, directly across the Min
River from the county seat, the monastery comprised several halls, galleries, and pavilions, many of which housed images of the Buddha, the
Goddess of Mercy (Guanyin), and Samantabhadra. The Transversing-the-
Clouds Monastery is best known because of its association with a giant
statue of a sitting or Maitreya Buddha (Milefo)—that is, the Benevolent
Buddha or Buddhist Messiah, which is carved out of the cliff right next
to it. Hence, an alternate name for the Traversing-the-Clouds Monastery
is the Great Buddha Monastery (Dafo si). Originally, each of the "nine
crests" mentioned by Fan Chengda below hosted a Buddhist monastery,
but after the ninth century only the Transversing-the-Clouds Monastery
remained.[116]

> *Yiyou day (14 July): Moored in Jia county. Crossed the river and went on an outing
> to Transversing-the-Clouds (Lingyun), which is situated on the riverbank opposite
> the county wall. The hill is not very high, but there are nine hilltops stretched out
> across it in a line. Thus, it is also known as Nine Crests (Jiuding). Formerly,
> it was known as Green Robe Hill (Qingyi shan). Green Robe is the spirit of
> Cancong.[117] {Jia} was formerly part of Pingqiang town. When that town was
> abolished, it then became part of Longyou {town}. I clambered up the stone steps and
> ascended to the Traversing-the-Clouds Monastery. On the monastery grounds is the
> Heavenly Peace Gallery (Tianning ge), which in fact is the site of the Colossal
> {Buddha} Statue. Jia county marks the confluence point of numerous rivers.*

*The Dao River (Daojiang), the Mo River (Moshui), and the Min River all join
below {Traversing-the-Clouds} Hill and then flow south down to Qianwei {town}.*[118]
*The Mo River joins with the Great Ford River (Dadu he) and courses here from
Ya county until it pounds directly into the mountain wall. Since the rushing torrent
is perilous and sinister, this is a place known to be most dangerous for boats.*[119]

Visitors to Jia county are immediately struck by the massive size of
the Maitreya Buddha. It stands 71 m/233 ft high, while the head alone
measures 14.7 m/48 ft from top to bottom. The ears extend 6.72 m/22 ft,
the nose measures 5.53 m/18 ft, and the eyes span 3.3 m/10 ft across. The
breadth of the Buddha's shoulders stretches 24 m/79 ft. The width of the
feet (just one) is a whopping 9 m/29 ft.[120] If these numbers fail to convey
the massive size and presence of the statue, then consider the following:
two adults could "fit" into one of the Buddha's ear cavities, while more
than one hundred persons could stand on just one of his feet, all at the
same time. It is, as Fan notes, the "largest image of Buddha in the
world."[121]

*During the Kaiyuan reign (713–742) of the Tang, the Buddhist Haitong began
chiseling away at the mountain, making it into an image of the Maitreya Buddha
in order to subdue the torrent. It stands 360 chi high. The crown of the head measures
ten zhang in circumference; the eyes are two zhang in width. Supported by a
thirteen-tiered superstructure from the top of its head down to its feet,*[122] *it is the
largest image of Buddha in the world. Its two ears are still made of wood. The
Buddha's feet are just a few double-paces from the river. Frightening waves rage
and howl, and rush and gush as they pass before it, making it impossible to stand
here and gaze straight ahead. Today these are called the Buddha Head Rapids
(Fotou tan). The Buddha Gallery (Foge) directly faces the Three-E{mei} peaks; on
the other three sides are remarkable mountains. Numerous rivers interlace and flow
between the mountains. This is the most beautiful view I have seen since coming from
the Western counties.*[123]

Earlier it was mentioned that initial Buddhist missionary work in
Sichuan, especially in Chengdu, was successful in part because of patronage
received from local benefactors and government officials. Haitong traveled
far and wide to raise the necessary funds to build the Colossal Buddha and
personally supervised the construction work, which began in 713. Several
sources report that when a corrupt local official attempted to extort some
of the funds earmarked for construction purposes, Haitong responded by
saying: "You can gouge out my own eyes, but you'll never get the money
for the construction of the Buddha!" The corrupt official became angry

Figure 4.2 The "Colossal Buddha." Photograph by the author.

and threatened: "Then let's see if I can rip out one your eyes!" Haitong then gouged out one of his own eyes and presented to the official on a plate. The official ran off in a panic, begging forgiveness.[124]

Haitong died before the Colossal Buddha was completed. Fortunately, two high-ranking government officials, Zhangqiu Jianxiong (eighth cent) and Wei Gao (745–805), both of whom had served as Military Commissioner (Jiedu shi) of Sichuan, decided to support the project and see it through to completion. The two officials together contributed 700,000 cash (*qian*) out of their own salaries toward the effort.[125] Wei Gao, himself a devout Buddhist, personally supervised the final stages of the project, completed in 803. In order to celebrate the occasion, Wei composed a commemorative essay in which he details the history and motivation behind the construction of the Buddhist monument. In his "Record" Wei Gao notes that Haitong's main purpose in carving the statue was to disperse and thus control the treacherous river currents of the Min, which crashed into the cliffs of Traversing-the-Clouds Hill (directly below the statue), making it an especially dangerous place for boat traffic. Moved by Haitong's compassion, Wei mustered the necessary labor and resources to complete the Colossal Buddha.

Our next stop is the Myriad Prospects Tower (Wanjing lou), another key Jia county landmark. The tower is visible in the section of the hand scroll reproduced in figure 4.1. Standing west of the county seat, the tower was built in the late Northern Song by Lü Youcheng (*style* Ziming), when he served as Administrator of the county.[126] Fan was so impressed with the scenic views from the tower that he commissioned a local artist to execute a painting of the scene so he could take it home with him.[127] The administrative term "Hanjia" refers to Jia county.

Bingxu day (15 July): Moored in Jia county. Went on an outing to the Myriad Prospects Tower, which is on top of a high mound next to the county wall. The surpassing scenic views from heights in Hanjia already have an outstanding reputation in the Western counties, but those seen from Myriad Prospects Tower are paramount in the entire commandery. The Great {Min} River, right before it, flows onward to course through Qianwei, Rong, and Lu,[128] where distant mountains are vague and dim, now visible and now gone, and where mists and clouds are boundless. To the right are aligned the Three Emei;[129] spanning on the left are the Nine Crests. The remaining mountains and rivers can be seen alternately emerging between them. The name "Myriad Prospects" is truly not an excessive boast. My poem should probably be titled "First Tower of the Southwest."[130]

CHAPTER 5

The Ascent

Every one or two miles of the upward journey brought us to a large temple erected in memory of some saint or deity of the Buddhist faith.[1]

—L. Newton Hayes

ON TO EMEI TOWN

Dinghai, Wuzi, Yichou, Gengyin, and Xinmao days (16–20 July): Leaving my family on the boat moored below the banks of Jia county, I rode alone toward Emei. . . . It is recorded in Buddhist texts that this is the place where the Bodhisattva Samantabhadra (Puxian dashi) makes his appearance and manifestation. I departed from the west gate of the commandery wall. Then crossed Swallow Ford (Yandu), where the river rushes and gushes and is very dangerous. . . . Crossed the ford and spent the night at Suji Market-town (Suji zhen).[2]

Following the customary itinerary of travelers heading to Mount Emei from Jia county, Fan Chengda now departs for Emei town, some 33 km/20 mi to the west. Those accompanying him include his younger brother Chengji and several friends, along with a staff of porters carrying Fan's bamboo sedan chair and trunks of personal belongings. The first landmark mentioned after leaving Jia—Swallow Ford (modern Xuhao), is 20 *li* west of the county. At Swallow Ford Fan Chengda crosses the Ya County River (or Green Robe River) and travels another 5 *li* to the Suji Market-town, where he spends the night. A "market town" (*zhen*) is an unwalled commercial gathering place, populated mainly by traders, where commodities are collected and redistributed. While passing through Suji Fan probably saw many local products for sale, such as tea, medicinal herbs, and silk.

As we accompany Fan Chengda toward Emei and then up its steep mountain trails, we will consider some of the poems he wrote to commemorate the visit. One of these verses, a quatrain titled "After Passing Swallow Ford, I Gazed at Great Emei, with Its White Mists of Storied Towers, Seemingly Plucked from Amid the Clusters of Clouds," describes Fan's first impression of seeing Emei's "thousand peaks" tower in the distance:

> Encircled by wastes, a thousand peaks, dimmed by summer sky;
> Big Emei's mists and vapors, all scattered and jumbled about.
> A jade-white peak suddenly rises to a height of three thousand *zhang*!
> This must be the tūla world of silvery, cotton clouds.[3]

This short poem presents a striking word picture of Mount Emei, as first seen after passing Swallow Ford. The "wastes" that encircle the mountain are the flat, fertile fields that stretch between Jia county and Emei town. Of particular interest to us is the reference to the "tūla world of silvery, cotton clouds," mentioned in the last line of Fan's poem. The term *douluo yun* 兜羅雲 (or *douluo mianyun* 兜羅綿雲) derives from the Sanskrit word tūla, and refers to a soft, white, cottonlike substance produced by a certain type of willow or poplar tree in India. Here, however, the term is used as a metaphor for the cottonlike clouds amassed above Mount Emei, which Fan imagines to form a "jade-white peak." Why would he choose tūla-clouds to describe his initial, visual impression of the mountain? Note that in the diary entry that opens this chapter, one of the first things Fan Chengda mentions as he observes Emei in the distance is that "Buddhist texts" identify the mountain as the place "where the Bodhisattva Samantabhadra makes his appearance and manifestation." It is here where we find the tūla-cloud connection: Buddhist tradition says that when Samantabhadra (or "Buddha's Glory" [Foguang 佛光]; this is the more popular name of the "Precious Light" described in chapter 1) appears on the summit of Emei, the Indian deity's image is revealed on a bed of tūla-clouds. At the very outset of his journey, then, even before reaching the foothills of the mountain, Fan Chengda reveals that he has more on his mind than just aesthetic appreciation of Emei's breathtaking scenery: he is preparing himself for a visit the abode of Samantabhadra, the mountain's resident bodhisattva. Fan surely knew about Buddha's Glory and, like all pilgrims, hoped to witness an "appearance and mani-festation" on the summit.

> *Renchen day (21 July): In the morning we set out from Suji {Market-town}. At the noon hour passed Fuwen Market-town (Fuwen zhen). Both of these market-towns are flourishing and prosperous, like a thriving town (xian). . . . Village women grouped together and observed us on the road. All of them were knitting hemp as*

they walked, and there was not one among them with idle hands. The local people tie artemisia (aihao) *to their gates, which produces smoke as it burns. They do this to scent and cleanse the foul {local} air, and to serve as a welcoming gesture {for visitors}. It was after the noon hour when we reached Emei town, where we spent the night.*[4]

When Fan Chengda visited Emei town in 1177, the population of the *xian* and its market towns and villages was probably over seventy thousand.[5] Contrary to Fan's reference (in the next poem, translated below) to Emei *xian* as a "hamlet," in the twelfth century the town was no poor backwater of Sichuan. On the contrary, recent bronze and ceramic discoveries dating from the Song indicate a sophisticated level of transportation, commercial, and tourist industries in the area, as well as the presence of some very wealthy families.[6] Most of the land within the town's jurisdiction, which includes Emei shan, is mountainous, heavily forested, and rich in minerals such as salt, coal, iron, phosphorus, and copper. Granite and basalt are especially plentiful, and have long supported mining and building material enterprises in the area. Fan Chengda's arrival understandably caused some commotion, for it was a rare occasion indeed when a former governor of Sichuan paid a personal visit to a rural *xian* like Emei. The poem translated below relates his impressions of the town. "Official banners," mentioned in the first line, were carried by Fan's porters and identified him as a high-ranking government officer:

The humble village still can't recognize official banners;
Chickens and dogs exclaim their joy, lanes and paths are noisy.
Old village women gather to watch, spinning thread as they walk;
Rustic old men bow to welcome us, then kneel and burn artemisia.
Streams are clear, soil is fertile, rice shoots are early;
The town's ancient woods are dense, knots in locust trees run high.
We pay respect to village scholars who come to offer praises,
And talk at length of the rare chance of meeting in such a hamlet.[7]

Later in this chapter, as we accompany Fan on his ascent of Mount Emei, attentive readers will notice that almost every place mentioned by him along the way is related in some way to Buddhism. What happened to the Daoist presence on the mountain, described earlier? Clearly, a major development concerning the religious orientation of Emei shan has taken place since our discussion of the Tang period in chapter 4. In order to understand how this transformation took place and why, we must look at the development of Buddhism during the Song, especially in Sichuan. Consider these numbers: in 1021 there were just over 20,000 registered

Daoist adepts (*daoshi*) and nuns (*nüguan*) in China. In that same year, however, the total number of Buddhist monks and nuns was 397,615.[8] The numbers for Sichuan in 1021 are also one-sided: Daoist adepts: 4,653; Buddhist monks and nuns: 56,221.[9] Moreover, according to one estimate, during the reign of the emperor Renzong, there were about 40,000 Buddhist monasteries throughout China.[10] Buddhism flourished in China during the Song dynasty, especially during the Northern Song, and it is no historical coincidence that Mount Emei became a "Buddhist mountain" at precisely the same time."[11] How did this happen? To answer this question we will first consider state and private patronage for Buddhism, especially during the early years of the Northern Song.

PATRONS IN THE CAPITAL, SUPPORTERS IN THE PROVINCES

Imperial patronage and its commemoration reflects a common conception of Buddhist monasteries as concentrations of spiritual power, whose cooperation facilitated the perpetuation of Song rule. By accruing merit in unceasing fashion through good works on behalf of the church, the ruling house amassed colossal stores of felicitous karmic wealth that enhanced its authority.[12]

—Mark Robert Halperin

Government support for Buddhism during the Song begins with its founding emperor, Taizu (r. 960–976), one of the few rulers in Chinese history to take the vows of a Buddhist layman. One of Taizu's first acts as emperor was to reverse the severe prohibitions against Buddhism promulgated during the Later Zhou (951–960).[13] At the same time, however, he instituted a number of policies aimed at limiting and thus controlling the influence of Buddhism on his political power. For instance, in the very first year of his reign Taizu promulgated a policy that said all monasteries destroyed by feat during the Later Zhou (specifically, up to the year 955), could not be rebuilt, while those still standing would be allowed to continue to operate. In 967 another new decision was announced: destroyed images of Buddha made of bronze could not be recast, nor could new ones be fashioned.[14] This policy was initiated because overzealous monks had earlier destroyed numerous iron farming tools in order to devise Buddhist images. Taizu regarded this activity as detrimental to agriculture, and instructed local officials to strictly enforce the new rule. Taizu's early policies toward Buddhism, then, essentially had two goals. First, he sought to restrict and control the size and influence of the Buddhist church so it could not adversely affect the political or economic order. And second, Taizu's early policies indicate that he did support a "rebirth" of Buddhism (for reasons to be explained below), but on his terms, which meant that the emperor would decide on the scope of the Buddhist community (saṃgha) and its influence in society.

Despite the restrictions on Buddhism imposed by Taizu, throughout his sixteen-year reign the emperor patronized the religion with increasing frequency. Not only did the emperor himself spend considerable time copying, reading, and chanting the *Jin'gang banruo jing* (*Vajracchedikā-sūtra*; often called the "*Diamond-sūtra*"); he also regularly attended ritual ceremonies held at major temples in Kaifeng. During a severe drought in the spring of 962, for instance, he traveled twice in one month to the Monastery of the State of Xiang (Xiangguo si) to pray for rain.[15] Three years later, in 965, Taizu ceremoniously welcomed the Buddhist pilgrim Daoyuan (tenth cent) to the capital, on the occasion of the monk's return from an eighteen-year pilgrimage to India. Based on his favorable conversations with Daoyuan, the following year Taizu commissioned a large group of monks to travel to India to "search for the dharma," each of whom received 30,000 cash (*qian*) for expenses.[16] This was the first time in Chinese history that an emperor personally organized and commissioned a major religious embassy to the "Western Regions." On numerous occasions throughout his reign Taizu also welcomed foreign monks to the capital and sponsored embassies staffed by Chinese monks to India. His greatest contribution to the Indian religion, however, was certainly the printing of the *Tripiṭaka*, completed in 983. This was a monumental event in the history of Buddhism in China. As already noted, Chengdu was one of China's major printing centers. The city was also well known for using carved and inked wood blocks to produce books with text and illustrations, especially religious tracts and almanacs. The *Buddhist Canon* required 130,000 separately carved blocks, making it the longest book ever printed in China.[17] Finally, and perhaps most important, Taizu was very much involved in Buddhist temple building and restoration efforts. To cite just one example, during the Kaibao reign (968–977) he rebuilt the reliquary-stūpa (*sheli ta*) of the Dragon Ascendancy Temple (Longxing si) in Tong county (modern Dali, Shaanxi), at considerable expense.[18]

In the early 980s, during the reign of Taizu's brother and successor, Taizong (r. 976–997), several Indian monks arrived in the capital bearing sūtras from their homeland. A Sūtra Translation Bureau (Yijing yuan), under central government control, was then established in Kaifeng in 982 to oversee the translation of these texts into Chinese. The following year the bureau's name was changed to Institute for Transmitting the Dharma (Chuanfa yuan) and a printing house was added. It was here that the finished woodblocks for the *Tripiṭaka*, carved earlier in Chengdu, were sent to produce the first printed Chinese version of the *Buddhist Canon*. The translations prepared by the institute were printed and disseminated throughout China.

Taizong's major efforts in support of Buddhism—the construction and restoration of temples and stūpas, the casting of images, the sponsoring of missions to India, the creation of a translation bureau in Kaifeng, and the printing of the *Buddhist Canon*—helped to attract many new followers to the faith. According to one source, during the first six or seven years of Taizong's reign the number of Buddhists in China increased by more than 170,000.[19] Many scholars interpret this development as a direct result of the emperor's personal support for the Indian religion. Like his brother before him, Taizong was especially active in lavish temple-building projects. He directly supported the construction of numerous monasteries, in both Kaifeng and in the provinces. For instance, in the capital he spent a considerable sum of money on the construction of a reliquary-stūpa at the Opened Treasure Monastery (Kaibao si), one of Kaifeng's most distinguished temple complexes.[20] The emperor himself personally deposited Buddhist relics in the temple's eleven-story stūpa. Another large-scale project was construction of the Enlightened Sage Chan Monastery (Kaisheng chansi), built in the capital to commemorate Taizong's own birthplace. It took six years (980–986) to complete the project. Despite his enthusiasm for temple building, Taizong still set limits on the number of monasteries to be restored and the maximum number of Buddhist priests and nuns allowed in China.[21] Thus, although Taizong made substantial efforts to support Buddhism during his reign, and viewed the teachings of Buddhism (and Daoism) as potentially beneficial to society and his own political power, at the same time he sought to control the religion so it could never pose a threat to the authority of the Song ruling house. Both Taizu and Taizong were keenly aware of the lessons to be learned from the experiences of emperor Wu of the Liang dynasty (r. 502–549), whose obsession with Buddhism led him to turn over much his governing powers to his followers and, on at least three occasions, "give himself over" to a monastery to serve as a menial. Taizu and Taizong were also mindful of events that occurred earlier in the mid-ninth century, when the growth and accumulated wealth of the Buddhist church shook the financial stability of the Tang empire, leading to widespread persecutions.[22]

Subsequent Northern Song emperors also appreciated Buddhism in various ways and made efforts to support it. Zhenzong (r. 997–1022), for instance, well known for his passionate interest in Daoism, was also actively involved in Buddhist temple restoration. In 1010 he ordered that seventy-two precept altars (*jietan*; novices took their vows at these sites) be constructed throughout China, seven of which were in Sichuan.[23] The following year the emperor dispatched three thousand taels of gold to Mount Emei in order to rebuild and expand the Samantabhadra Monastery (see below for additional details on this important event). Zhenzong's son and successor Renzong (r. 1022–1063), wrote a work titled "Essay on Śākyamuni" ("Shishi lun") in which he remarks: "[Buddhism] brings out the good in people; prevents evil in people. . . . If people aren't killing each other, then they will be humane. If they are not stealing, they will be honest. If they are not desirous, they will be trustworthy. If they are not reckless, they will be upright."[24] Renzong, who seems to have had a personal interest in Chan, saw the benefits of Buddhism in terms of Confucian values, such as humaneness, honesty, and trustworthiness. In other words, pious Buddhists will manifest behavior that is beneficial to society. Following the lead of his predecessors, however, Renzong imposed a limitation on the number of monks and nuns in society. At one point during his reign, when their ranks swelled, efforts were made to reduce the overall number by one-third.[25]

The development of Buddhism during the Song suffered a setback during the reign of Huizong. As is well known, Huizong's main religious interest was Daoism. He built a Daoist monastery within the precincts of the imperial palace, ordered the collection of Daoist scriptures, himself wrote a commentary to the *Laozi* (or *Daode jing*), established a Daoist Institute (Daoxue), and, in 1117, even sponsored a convention in Kaifeng attended by three thousand adepts. Huizong even went so far as to style himself the "Religious Prelate, Daoist Sovereign, and August Emperor" (Jiaozhu Daojun huangdi). At the same time, he was openly inimical toward Buddhism, which he regarded as a "barbarian religion" (*hujiao*) and harmful to Confucian rituals and ceremonies (*liyi*). One of his adept-advisors even placed Buddha under the supremacy of Daoism. Buddhism's place in Song society, however, was too firmly entrenched by the early twelfth century, and so removal or dismantling of the monastic system was probably not an option. Instead, in 1119 Huizong ordered reforms, the goal of which was Daoism's assimilation of Buddhism. Buddhist priests (*seng*) would hereafter be called "virtuous adepts" (*deshi*); practitioners (*xing*) would be called "virtuous acolytes" (*detong*); monasteries would be called "palaces" (*gong*); cloisters would now be called "abbeys" (*guan*).[26] Huizong's efforts to absorb Buddhism, however, were short-lived. By the end of 1120 all of his anti-Buddhism "reform" measures had been withdrawn.

The first emperor of the Southern Song, Gaozong, did not follow the anti-Buddhism policies of his father, Huizong, nor did he do anything to support Buddhism in any significant way. His policies were instead aimed at controlling the religion; specifically, the ranks of Buddhist monks, which in the early years of the Southern Song had swelled to about two hundred thousand, twenty times the number of Daoists.[27] One of Gaozong's chief concerns was agricultural: "Most fields today lie fallow. Yet those who eat (that is, Buddhist monks) but do not till the land still number two hundred thousand. If we supply more ordination certificates (*dudie*), then this would harm agriculture just for the sake of monks."[28] Gaozong's main control measure was a ban on issuing additional certificates, which assured no legal increase in the total number of monks and nuns. He also required that monasteries pay a special fee for each of their monks, which discouraged these institutions from adding clergy to their rolls. Gaozong's policies did not last long, however, for as the Southern Song's political position vis-à-vis its belligerent neighbors in the north (the Jin) became more strained, the government needed more funds for defense. Buddhist ordination certificates were soon sold once again.

Despite the many difficulties China had with its neighbors to the north and the relocation of the imperial Court to Hangzhou, Buddhism continued to develop during the remaining years of the Southern Song, though not on a level equal to that during the Northern Song. The major reason for the growth of Buddhism in the twelfth and thirteen centuries was continued imperial patronage of the religion.

Against this background of general imperial support (or, in some cases, tolerance) of Buddhism during the Song, we now turn to individual instances of direct imperial support to Mount Emei. Three points are especially important to keep in mind regarding patronage from Kaifeng. First, support often came in the form of gifts, which were either specific items bestowed upon the mountain, or cash "grants" designed to pay for imperially mandated projects, such as monastery construction, expansion, or renovation. Second, imperial gifts were not conferred on the mountain itself, but rather on particular institutions that represented it or on monks who lived there. In the case of Mount Emei, this was the White Stream Monastery. Since the Song dynasty this institution has functioned as the primary Buddhist temple on the mountain. And finally, imperial gift giving to Emei shan was inspired in the first place by its reputation and role as a Buddhist mountain; specifically, as the *daochang* of the bodhisattva Samantabhadra.

Emei shan and several monks associated with the mountain received substantial imperial patronage during the Northern Song, especially from the emperors Taizu, Taizong, and Renzong. What brought the mountain to the attention of these rulers and why would they continue to patronize it in such generous fashion? After the founding of the Song dynasty in 960, local officials in Jia county began submitting memorials to the throne

concerning Emei shan. It was not at all unusual for the central government
in Kaifeng to receive communications from officials in the provinces
concerning "famous mountains" in their jurisdictions. In fact, it will be
recalled that Fan Chengda himself once proffered just such a memorial,
requesting a new Daoist title for Mount Qingcheng. Another situation
that might inspire a local official to dispatch a memorial to the capital is
the occasion of an auspicious occurrence or sighting. Emperors and ministers were especially fond of hearing about such unusual events, for they
could be interpreted as an affirmation of benevolent and legitimate rule
or be understood to signal some special religious significance or event.

The sources on Mount Emei record one such sighting. This event took
place during the reign of Taizong and is chronicled in the *Fozu tongji*, an
important thirteenth-century source on the history of Buddhism in China:

> Wang Gun, Controller General of Jia county, submits the following memo-
> rial: "Recently I went to Mount Emei to supervise the casting operation
> at White Stream Monastery. [While there] I saw that Mount Wawu (Wawu
> shan) was able to change into the color of gold.[29] Therein was the gilded
> body-form of Samantabhadra, 1.6 *zhang* in length. At noon the following
> day two arhats (*luohan*) were [observed] floating along in meditation, passing
> into purple-colored clouds."[30]

Despite its brevity, Wang Gun's memorial, listed in the *Fozu tongji* under
events that took place in the year 980, is remarkable in several ways. At
the outset we learn that Wang served as a Controller General (Tongpan)
in Jia county. Officials holding this office were essentially overseers of the
chief administrator of a county, and could submit memorials concerning
local affairs without his knowledge. Wang Gun mentions that he was in
charge of (*tidian*) "the casting operation" at the White Stream Monastery.
The reference here is to the casting, in Chengdu in the 980s, of a huge
bronze statue of Samantabhadra.[31] Wang Gun apparently supervised the
installation (not the actual casting) of this image in the White Stream
Monastery, an important event that will be discussed in more detail later
in this chapter. The next line of the memorial mentions Mount Wawu, a
well-known peak in southwestern Sichuan, located approximately 42 km/
26 mi west of Mount Emei. Although the language in the Controller
General's memorial is terse, he seems to be saying that while visiting Emei
he saw a light phenomenon that seemingly turned the distant mountain
into "the color of gold." This remark is interesting because it is physically
impossible to see Mount Wawu from the White Stream Monastery, which
is on the *eastern* side of Emei, well *below* the mid-mountain point. Wang
Gun could only have spied Mount Wawu from the *western* side of the

Golden Summit, yet the Foguang he claims to have seen typically appears on the *eastern* edge of the mountain's pinnacle. The identity of the Controller General's "gold visage" is revealed in the phrase *zhangliu jinshen Puxian* 丈六金身普賢, or "gilded body-form of Samantabhadra, 1.6 *zhang* in length."[32] This unmistakably refers to Samantabhadra, who appears to most humans in a physical state called *huashen* 化身 (lit., "transformed body"). This is necessary because humans (who have not yet found the Dharma) could not see him otherwise. The statue of Samantabhadra in the White Stream Monastery is the "common" *huashen* manifestation of the Indian deity. Appearances of the bodhisattva on the summit, in the form of Buddha's Glory, are called *baoshen* 報身, or "the reward body." The idea here is that Samantabhadra will use the Foguang to manifest himself to those who are predestined to see him. In his memorial, then, Wang Gun is reporting a sighting of the bodhisattva. If Wang Gun actually saw an appearance of the Indian diety (in the form of Buddha's Glory) from the summit of Emei, I suspect this took place while he was gazing into the distance *toward* Mount Wawu in the west.[33] In other words, if he witnessed an appearance of the Foguang, it was probably Emei's Foguang.[34] In any event, for our purposes what is most important is the following. First, Wang Gun's memorial reports a sighting of Samantabhadra on Mount Emei. Second, the contents of his memorial must have caught the immediate attention of Court officials (and probably the emperor) in the capital, for it was precisely at this same time (980) that the emperor Taizong, through a series of mandates, began to confer lavish imperial patronage upon the White Stream Monastery. Was Wang Gun's memorial alone responsible for inspiring support for Mount Emei from Kaifeng? I doubt it. There very well could have been other reports sent to the capital concerning auspicious happenings observed on the mountain. No such reports, however, have survived. In any event, already by the early 980s, Mount Emei was officially sanctified by imperial authority as the site of Samantabhadra's "residence."[35] Nothing in the religious history of Emei shan is more important and influential than this single event.

Following is a brief outline, arranged chronologically, of activities related to imperial patronage of Mount Emei during the Northern Song:[36]

- 964: A large retinue of Buddhist monks is dispatched to India under imperial auspices to search for Buddhist relics and palm-leaf manuscripts.[37] The monk Jiye (see below), who is associated with Emei shan, participates in the mission.

- 966: Local officials in Jia county send memorials to the capital concerning "appearances" of Samantabhadra on Mount Emei. As a result,

Kaifeng dispatches the Palace Attendant Zhang Zhong (tenth cent) to the Samantabhadra Monastery to "adorn it with a Buddhist image" (zhuangyan foxiang).[38]

- 976: The monk Jiye returns from India and is granted an audience with Taizong, to whom he presents sūtras, relics, and other items acquired during his pilgrimage. The emperor enjoins him to select a mountain where he could practice his asceticism. Jiye selects Mount Emei. The retreat he builds there is later expanded and becomes the Ox Heart Monastery.[39]

- 980: Taizong dispatches the Palace Attendant Zhang Renzan to Chengdu to arrange for the casting of a bronze image of Samantabhadra, to be presented to the White Stream Monastery.[40]

- 980: Taizong orders the restoration of the "Five Temples of Emei": White Stream, Black Stream, Central Peak, Celestial Illumination, and Luminous Light.[41]

- 980: Taizong orders the casting of two bronze bells, one in Taiyuan (Shanxi), the other in Chengdu, to be presented to Mount Wutai and Mount Emei, respectively.[42]

- 987: An unnamed Palace Attendant travels to Emei to confer several imperial gifts to the White Stream Monastery. It is reported that on the day the gifts were presented, the "crowds" gathered on Emei shan saw Samantabhadra "riding through the sky on a purple cloud."[43]

- 989: The Inner Palace Attendant Xie Baoyi orders that the Chamberlain for Palace Buildings (Jiangzuo Jiang) travel to Emei shan and, by imperial command, take along three hundred taels of gold for the purpose of adorning the bronze image of Samantabhadra and to further renovate the White Stream Monastery. Moreover, a collection of imperially authored texts (yuzhi wenji) is presented to the temple.[44]

- 1011: Three-thousand taels of gold are dispatched to Emei for the purpose of expanding the White Stream Monastery.[45]

- 1012: The Emei monk Maozhen (fl. early eleventh cent.) is summoned to Court and awarded poems from the emperor for his prognostication skills.[46]

- 1062: The emperor Renzong confers various gifts, including lavishly decorated sūtras and a monk's raiment of red silk with purple embroidery, upon the White Stream Monastery. The raiment is embroidered with the emperor's calligraphy.[47]

• 1102–1106: The White Stream Monastery is presented with several cash pennants (*qianfan*) and red streamers (*hongchuang*).[48]

No less than three Northern Song emperors, Taizong, Zhenzong, and Renzong, presented calligraphy specimens to the White Stream Monastery. The prestige and honor of such attention—characters written in the emperor's own hand—was substantial, to say the least. As far as the development of Buddhism on Mount Emei is concerned, what is most important about Court gifts is not their monetary value. Such treasures carry tremendous symbolic and legitimizing power. This is especially the case when an emperor selects a particular mountain, like Emei, and then writes messages on pennants such as "Buddha's Dharma is enduring and exalted" and "The Dharma Wheel is forever turning" (see below). These pennants, no doubt displayed proudly in the White Stream Monastery, greatly enhanced Mount Emei's reputation and notoriety and, along with the other forms of imperial patronage describe earlier, helped to establish Emei as a preeminent Buddhist mountain in China.

What imperial motivation(s) lay behind such generous support? Although sources such as the *Fozu tongji* and *Song huiyao jigao* typically provide dates, facts, and figures concerning acts of patronage, rarely do we find even a hint about the *motivations* behind such gift giving. In the case of Mount Emei, we are fortunate to have a text that provides some preliminary answers to the question. Xu Xuan (916–991), a Hanlin Academician and one of the most distinguished scholars in the capital, was commanded to write a stone-tablet inscription to commemorate the restoration and expansion of the White Stream Monastery. For our purposes, the most informative part of Xu's inscription appears in the verse section, beginning with line 17:

> . . . .
> The barriers of Emei,
> For the Courts of various emperors,
> Has served as a stronghold, served as a garrison,
> 20   And nestles in perfection, dwells in the numinous.
> Samantabhadra halted there,
> But his glory lay dormant for a thousand years.
> Although we have never seen you,
> We now cast an image of your likeness.[49]
> 25   Relying on the sūtra teachings to guide us,
> Your divine brilliance has thus been fashioned.[50]

> The auspicious image—now manifest, now obscure;
> The globe of light—so swift and sudden![51]
> Myriad transformations traverse the peaks;
> 30 The Hundred Spirits fill the valleys.
>
> . . . .
>
> How wonderful is the august realm!
> Capable indeed are the two sages!
> An empire now united into one
> 45 Has received Heaven's brilliant mandate![52]
>
> . . . .

The opening line of this selection is inspired by Zuo Si's "Shu Capital Rhapsody," where the Han author speaks of "the layered barriers of Emei" south of Chengdu.[53] Here Xu Xuan acknowledges the mountain's role as a protective barrier that has faithfully served Duyu and other "various emperors" of ancient Shu as a "stronghold" and "garrison." The next several lines in Xu's verse establish an unmistakable connection between Emei shan and Samantabhadra, who chose to "halt" and establish his *daochang* on the mountain. Unfortunately, the bodhisattva's "glory" or "brilliance" (*yao*) has been dormant and hence unacknowledged for a thousand years.[54] But now, Xu Xuan contends, just as Samantabhadra's "divine brilliance" at last appears on Mount Emei (in the form of the statue), Song dynastic rule finally prevails in the empire. Especially interesting is the last four lines quoted here from Xu's poem. Rather than cite Buddhist sūtra references to confirm and legitimize Samantabhadra's residence on Emei (the usual approach), Xu Xuan instead draws upon the traditional Confucian idea of Tianming, or "Mandate of Heaven." In other words, Heaven has conferred its blessing on the "august realm" (or "territory"; *huangtu*) of the Song empire, and has done so by granting an "appearance" of Samantabhadra on Mount Emei (again, in the form of the statue). This, the author suggests, is precisely because of the "capable" rule administered by the "two sages" (*ersheng*), Taizu and Taizong. In other words, the world is now in proper order. This interpretation is of course intentionally designed to help legitimize the young dynasty and its monarchy. Thus, here we have a good example of how the Song ruling house used or manipulated religion (in this case, Buddhism) to support, strengthen, and legitimize its political power. Ultimately, perhaps the most important point of all is this: most Northern Song emperors supported Buddhism through various forms of patronage, such as bestowing prestigious titles on worthy monks, direct gift giving, land grants, and even tax exemptions. They did so in return for church backing of the monarchy and state. The monasteries, for their part, supported Song rule by praying to Buddha and asking that the dynasty receive blessings and longevity, holding ceremonies honoring imperial birthdays and death days, serving as a repository for calligraphy works penned by Song emperors, and providing humanitarian aid, welfare assistance, and disaster relief to needy persons. Clearly, the monasteries and central government both reaped benefit from this arrangement.

Turning now to patronage on the provincial and local levels, we begin by noting that after the consolidation of the Song dynasty in 960, many officials and landowners of the former Later Shu kingdom in Sichuan, in an effort to ingratiate themselves with the founding Song emperor Taizu—whom they knew supported Buddhism—donated lands to temples. One important result of this action was that several monasteries in Sichuan, especially in Chengdu, amassed immense land holdings and wealth. To cite just two examples, the Orthodox Dharma Monastery (Zhengfa si) controlled 8,546 *mou* of land in the Northern Song,[55] while the Great Compassion Monastery, constructed in the eighth century, by Song times comprised 96 cloisters and 8,524 rooms. This monastic complex was especially well known for its collection of paintings, which included the works of Wu Daozi (685?–758), Li Sheng (eighth cent), and Huang Quan (903–968), all famous artists. This expansion and development of monasteries in Chengdu during the Northern Song could only have had a favorable influence vis-à-vis the position and development of Buddhism in Jiazhou and on Mount Emei.

Although there certainly was substantial local patronage for Buddhist activities on Mount Emei throughout the traditional period, especially after the religion began to flourish on the mountain in the early years of the Northern Song, the gazetteers and histories are largely silent about such support. As far as I know, only one surviving source provides clues concerning patronage from Jia county, Emei town, and the surrounding areas. This source is not a printed text but a long inscription (in all, 61,600 Chinese characters) on a huge, bronze bell. One of the few surviving ancient artifacts on Emei, this massive bell—2.8 m/9.18 ft tall and weighing about 25,000 kg/55,250 pounds—was cast in 1534 and paid for with funds raised by a Chan monk named Biechuan (d. 1579). Originally, the bell was housed in the Sagely Accumulation Monastery (Shengji si), one of the largest temple complexes on the mountain during the Ming. It tolled melodiously each evening and supposedly could be heard both on the plains below and on the summit above. Today the "Sagely Accumulation Evening Bell" (Shengji wanzhong), though damaged in places, stands intact in an attractive pavilion positioned directly across from the Loyal-to-the-State Monastery.

In late July, 2003, accompanied by my good friend from the Mount Emei Museum, Mr. Xiong Feng, I inspected, recorded, and studied the inscriptions on the Sagely Accumulation Evening Bell. It carries two types of inscription: those originally cast on the bell in the sixteenth century and those inscribed sometime later. While it seems certain that Biechuan was directly involved in selecting the names to be cast on the bell, the provenance of the (later) inscribed names is less certain. There are about five hundred names on the bell, most of which are organized chronologically into groups arranged by dynasty. The name roster includes emperors, military and civil officials at the national, regional, and local levels, and a list of prominent writers, all of whom have some connection to Emei shan. No doubt, many of these men were patrons of the mountain. Others, like the famous calligrapher Wang Xizhi, only have a literary connection. Among the names originally cast on the bell, the earliest is that of emperors Wu (or Sima Yan, r. 265–290) and Hui (or Sima Zhong; r. 290–306) of the Western Jin dynasty. Were they patrons of Buddhism on Emei? Was emperor Hui in some way related to Huichi's activities in Shu around the turn of the fourth century? Unfortunately, neither Biechuan nor the standard sources provide answers to these questions. After inspecting the names on the bell, however, one fact became clear: Biechuan traced the origin(s) of Buddhism on Emei shan back to the Western Jin dynasty. This chronology tallies with information in the gazetteers and other primary sources on Mount Emei. That is to say, the origins of Buddhist activity on the mountain extend at least back to the Eastern Jin, and possibly even back to the Western Jin.

THE ASCENT

I submit that of all the mountains to be climbed in the whole world, none matches this one in danger and height.[56]

—Fan Chengda

Fan Chengda spent only one day in Emei town. After arriving there, he left the very next morning to begin his ascent of the mountain:

My chronic passion for mists and vapors needs no doctor;
This trip will truly be a time for rein-less roaming.
Detained at Supreme Clarity, overlooking Mount Damian,
Yet still I follow Li Bo and investigate Emei.
In the mountains, the law of causation now becomes familiar;
In the world, fame and fortune have always been folly.

I shall paint a picture, to hang on the wall after my homecoming,
So in later years I might still wander here in my dreams.[57]

From Fan's comments in lines 3 and 4 we learn that he was "detained" during his earlier sojourn to Mount Qingcheng (Supreme Clarity, it will be recalled, is the main Daoist abbey there)—meaning he spent too much time sightseeing and got behind schedule, yet now he still finds time to follow in Li Bo's footsteps and "investigate" Mount Emei. This deference to the Tang poet is to be expected because Li Bo is the first major poet in China to sing about Emei shan. Of more interest to us is the declaration in lines 5 and 6. The "law of causation" (*yuanfa*) is a Buddhist term that refers to three of the four fundamental dogmas of Buddhism; namely, that all is suffering, that suffering is intensified by desire, and that extinction of desire is practicable. Lines 5 and 6 of Fan Chengda's poem might thus be paraphrased: "I have now entered Mount Emei and, as a result, have become more aware of the fundamental laws of Buddhism; / I see now that my career as an official, seeking fortune and fame, is simply folly and nothing more." At this point in the journey, Fan is not renouncing his worldly ways; he is acknowledging Emei's Buddhist tradition, which the poet senses more and more as he draws closer to the mountain. Fan Chengda is reacting here, in very predictable ways, to the Buddhist space on Emei. Chinese writers who visit Buddhist mountains customarily pay deference to Buddhism by acknowledging their suffering in the "dusty net" and finding some sort of "enlightenment" in secluded, alpine environments. In Fan's case, acknowledgment of and deference to the mountain's Buddhist tradition is just a first step. As he climbs higher and higher, he will be affected in other, more dramatically religious ways.

Guisi day (22 July): Set out from Emei town. Leaving by the West Gate, I began my ascent of the mountain and passed the Benevolent Fortune (Cifu)[58] and Universal Security (Pu'an) cloisters, White Stream Manor (Baishui zhuang), and Shu Village Way-stop (Shucun dian). After twelve li came to Dragon Spirit Hall. From here on, mountain torrents ripped and roared; shady forests stood mighty and deep. Took a brief rest at Huayan Cloister.[59]

The trip from Emei town to the *shankou*, or "entranceway to the mountain," is not far—about four miles. Fan saw the two Buddhist cloisters, manor, and rest-stop mentioned in the last entry as he traveled the main road to the entranceway of the mountain. This is the same route modern travelers follow from Emei City to the base of the mountain. Today the road is lined with hotels, restaurants, and souvenir shops. A huge ornamental gate stands at the head of this road, adorned with characters written by the famous writer, poet, and historian Guo Moruo (1892–1978). The inscription on the top of the gate reads: "The Most Famous Mountain in the World" (Tianxia mingshan 天下名山).

The first important stop on Fan Chengda's itinerary is the Dragon Spirit Hall (Longshen tang). This was probably a modest-size structure during the Song. Later, however, a large temple complex called the Crouching Tiger Monastery (Fuhu si) was constructed in the hills just behind the hall. Nothing remains today of Dragon Spirit Hall, but the Crouching Tiger Monastery survives and still ranks as one of the most prominent monastic complexes on the mountain. It sits within a lush forest of green bamboo and lofty *nan* trees, where an almost deafening chorus of cicadas drones day and night. Luo Peak Retreat (Luofeng'an), located at the rear of the monastery, once served as the residence of the early Qing dynasty official Jiang Chao (1623–1672), and it was there where he compiled the *Mount Emei Gazetteer*, one of the primary sources on which this book is based. The area around the monastery was supposedly once infested by tigers; hence the name "Crouching Tiger." Another explanation of the name says it derives from the contours of the hills around the monastery, which supposedly resemble a recumbent tiger.[60]

The *shankou* is just a few minutes walk from Dragon Spirit Hall. After formally "entering the mountain" (*rushan*), Fan Chengda and his traveling party first headed north, through a deep valley with lush green vegetation and soaring cliff walls, then turned eastward, passing rushing torrents and thick forests until they reached the Huayan Cloister, where they took a brief rest.[61] This is still a popular route for mountain hikers. As Fan Chengda approached the monastery he probably saw a road marker that read: "70 *li* to the Golden Summit."[62] The Huayan Cloister, erected during the Tang and situated just below the Jade Maiden Peak (Yunü feng), is one of the oldest temples on Emei and is regarded as one of the "Six Great Ancient Monasteries on the Mountain" (Shanzhong liu da gusi).[63] In the Tang period the Chan Master Huitong changed its name to "Returning Clouds Gallery" (Guiyun ge). During the reign of the Song emperor Renzong, one of Emei's most distinguished monks, Maozhen (no relation to "Maozhen, the Venerated One," who we will meet very shortly) rebuilt the monastery. With the exception of a single, carved stone lion, nothing of the temple remains today.

Next we follow Fan Chengda eastward until he reaches what is reputedly one of Emei's most ancient institutions: Central Peak Cloister (Zhongfeng yuan; also known as Zhongfeng si, or Central Peak Monastery). This is the place where legend says the clever monk Mingguo slayed a python, convincing the Daoist residents to convert their Celestial Illumination Abbey into a monastery. Several immortals are said to have once lived in the vicinity of the Central Peak Monastery and in the nearby Three Immortals Grotto (Sanxian dong). For instance, "Shout-and-Response Retreat" (Huying an), built below a nearby peak of the same name, is where "Maozhen, the Venerated One"—a legendary Emei monk of the Sui-Tang period—occasionally traded shouts with his chess partner and good friend, the doctor-herbalist Sun Simiao.

> *Then crossed Green Bamboo Bridge (Qingzhu qiao), the turn-off to Emei's New Abbey (Emei xinguan),*[64] *Plum Tree Bank (Meishu ya), Double Dragon Hall (Lianglong tang),*[65] *and reached Central Peak Cloister (Zhongfeng yuan).*[66] *The cloister has a Samantabhadra Gallery (Puxian ge) wreathed by a circle of seventeen peaks.*[67] *It nestles against White Cliff Peak (Baiya feng). The highest of the peaks, rising prominently on the right, is called Shout-and-Response Peak (Huying feng). Below it is the Retreat of Maozhen the Venerated One (Maozhen zunzhe an)—a place rarely visited by man. Sun Simiao lived in seclusion on Mount Emei. When Maozhen was here he often shouted and responded back and forth with Sun Simiao from this spot, or so it is said.*[68]

The next stop on our itinerary is the Ox Heart Cloister (Niuxin yuan), which is also classified as one of the Six Great Ancient Monasteries of Emei shan. Huitong is credited with enlarging this temple in 877. The name "Ox Heart" was chosen by the Song dynasty monk Jiye (the same priest received by Taizong), who lived, preached, and translated sūtras at the monastery after his return from India in 976. He supposedly selected this name because there was a boulder nearby that resembled the heart of an ox. Tradition also says that the walls of the cloister were once graced with murals of arhats painted by the Tang artist Wu Daozi.[69] Over the centuries it has hosted many notable guests, including Sun Simiao, who practiced asceticism there. Twin Streams Bridge (Shuangxi qiao), just below Ox Heart Cloister, is also a famous landmark. As the name suggests, it comprises two bridges, each about 7 m/22.96 ft in length, which connect to a gallery in the middle. The bridges stand 10 m/32.8 ft high, and the thunderous sound of water from the White Stream and Black Stream (these are the "Twin Streams") plunging into the great ravine below is almost deafening. The bridge on the left (or north) was supposedly built when the Yellow Emperor visited Mount Emei; the bridge on the right (or south) looks today much as it did when Fan Chengda walked across it in the twelfth century. In the early Ming period the structure between the two bridges acquired the name Clear Tones Gallery (Qingyin ge). The area around the Clear Tones Gallery still offers some of the most breathtaking scenery on Mount Emei. Today several mountain trails merge here, so there is an almost constant parade of passing tourists.

> *Left the cloister and passed Camphor Tree (Zhangmu) and Ox Heart (Niuxin) ridges, as well as the turn-off to Ox Heart Cloister (Niuxin yuan). Next I reached the Twin Streams Bridge (Shuangxi qiao). The jumbled mountains here huddle together like standing screens. There are two mountains opposite one another, each of which produces a stream. Side by side they flow to the base of the bridge. Their rocky channels are several tens of zhang deep. With dark waters of a deep green hue, the soaring torrents spurt foamy snowcaps as they race beyond the bridges and then pass into a high thicket. Several tens of double-paces from there the two streams join and then plunge into a great ravine. The waters in the abyss, still and deep, clear and pure, disperse to form stream rapids. All the small stones in the rapids are either multicolored or have patterns of green on a white background. The pale yellow hue of the water complements the colors of the stones, making the rapids look like an outstretched piece of emerald-colored brocade. This scene is not something that could be captured in a sketch. When the sunlight of dawn shines on the water and rocks, a shimmering brilliance emits from the surface of the stream that reflects off the cliffs and ravines. Tradition says this is a "Minor Manifestation" of the bodhisattva (or Samantabhadra).*[70]

In the closing lines of this diary entry we again encounter the name of the mountain's protector, Samantabhadra. Fan is so taken aback by the magnificent scenery around Twin Streams Bridge and sonorous sound of water coursing through the area's colorful rocky streams, he calls the sight a "Minor Manifestation" (*xiaoxian*) of Samantabhadra.

After leaving the Clear Tones Gallery, Fan follows the trail in a northwesterly direction and continues his ascent. Having already traveled about 40 *li*/13 mi, we have reached Emei's most distinguished Buddhist institution—White Stream Samantabhadra Monastery (Baishui Puxian si). This is the same institution that received generous imperial patronage in the Northern Song dynasty, described earlier. The elevation here is 1,020 m/3,345 ft—just one-third the height of the mountain. Fan and his traveling companions have yet to reach the most difficult part of the climb.

> *From here I climbed some precipitous stone steps and passed the Bodhisattva Gallery (Pusa ge). On the road there was a sign that read: "Emei, the Greatest Mountain in the World." Then I reached the White Stream Samantabhadra Monastery. Every step along the way from the town to here is nothing but steep hillsides for more than forty* li. *Only now am I beginning to climb the foothills of the crested peaks.*[71]

White Stream is Mount Emei's oldest surviving Buddhist temple. Since the Song it also served as the central monastic complex on the mountain. The history of the temple, as we have already seen, possibly dates back to the late Eastern Jin period (ca. 420) and Huichi may have been responsible for its construction. In 887 Huitong enlarged the structure and renamed it White Stream Monastery. Then, in the early Northern Song, the monastery was expanded by Chan Master Maozhen and renamed White Stream Samantabhadra Monastery (Baishui Puxian si). And finally, during the Wanli reign (1573–1619) of the Ming dynasty, it acquired yet another name: Sagely Longevity Myriad Years Monastery (Shengshou Wannian si). Today it is known by an abbreviated version of that name: Wannian si, or "Myriad Years Monastery."

Among the very few, surviving ancient relics on Mount Emei, certainly the most spectacular in a visual sense is the bronze statue of Samantabhadra housed in the White Stream Monastery. The statue (mentioned earlier) was cast in sections in Chengdu and then transported to Emei by mule, where it was assembled. Samantabhadra is perched on a gilded, lotus throne, which sits atop a huge, six-tusked white elephant standing on four lotus blossoms (figure 5.1). When Fan Chengda saw the statue in 1177 it was probably still housed in the original "wooden hall" (*mudian*) built in the Northern Song. In 1601 to 1602, a square and beamless Brick Hall (Zhuandian) was erected to protect the statue (the previous structure had burned down the year before). Despite numerous devastating fires through the centuries (the most recent major one in 1946), and human attempts to destroy the statue (the Red Guards in the 1960s), Samantabhadra and his white elephant still stand majestically in the Myriad Years Monastery.

As far as the development of Buddhism on Mount Emei is concerned, the Samantabhadra statue carries tremendous religious significance. Above all else, the statue is *the* key physical focal point within the mountain's Buddhist religious space. Pilgrims still flock there daily to glimpse the colorfully painted statue of Puxian and his elephant, and offer prayers and donations. We should also note that the White Stream Monastery is located in a very accessible part of the mountain. That is to say, many, if not most, visitors can personally view Emei's most famous statue without making the difficult and perilous climb to the summit.[72] This surely attracted visitors and pilgrims who otherwise had no chance to "see" an "appearance" of the mountain's resident bodhisattva on the Golden Summit. At the same time, the magnificent sight of the bronze statue certainly must have inspired at least some to attempt a climb to the top of the mountain, where they might see a "live appearance" of Samantabhadra in the form of Buddha's Glory.

Figure 5.1 Statue of Samantabhadra in the White Stream (or Myriad Years)
Monastery. Photograph by the author.

The imperial gifts described in the next entry attest to the importance of the White Stream Monastery as Mount Emei's most distinguished
Buddhist institution during the Song. Some of these presents mentioned
here were still in the monastery in the late sixteenth century,[73] but today
are all lost.

> *Jiawu day (23 July): Spent the night at White Stream Monastery. It was raining*
> *heavily, so I could not ascend the mountain. Paid a visit to the bronze statue of the*
> *bodhisattva Samantabhadra. It was cast in Chengdu by imperial decree at the begin-*
> *ning of the dynasty. Among the gifts conferred to the monastery by the Courts of*

emperors Taizong, Zhenzong, and Renzong are more than one hundred books of impe-
rial authorship, a seven-jeweled headdress, a gemmy necklace of gold and pearls, a
monk's raiment, a gold-and-silver alms bowel, an incense storage case, joss sticks, a
fruit plate, bronze bell, drum, gong, stone chime, glazed tea saucer, and zhi *plant.*
There are also many other items conferred by the Empress during the Chongning reign

Fan Chengda's Mount Emei Itinerary

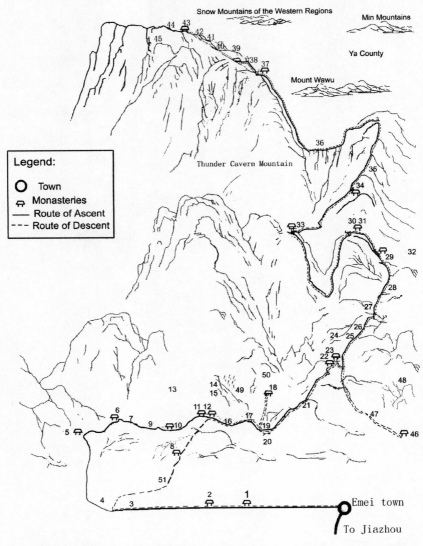

Map 5.1 Fan Chengda's Mount Emei Itinerary. Sketch map by Xiong Feng.

Key for Map 5.1

1. Benevolent Fortune Cloister
2. Universal Security Cloister
3. White Stream Manor
4. Shu Village Way-stop
5. Dragon Spirit Hall
6. Huayan Cloister
7. Green Bamboo Bridge
8. Emei's New Abbey
9. Plum Tree Bank
10. Double Dragon Hall
11. Central Peak Cloister
12. Samantabhadra Gallery
13. White Cliff Peak
14. Shout-and-Response Peak
15. Retreat of Maozhen, the Venerated One
16. Camphor Tree Ridge
17. Ox Heart Ridge
18. Ox Heart Cloister
19. Twin Streams Bridge
20. Precious Manifestation Stream
21. Bodhisattva Gallery
22. White Stream Samantabhadra Monastery
23. Three Thousand Iron Buddhas Hall
24. Brush-the-Heart Mountain
25. Thatched Pavilion Point
26. Small Stone Thunder

27. Greater and Lesser Deep Gullies
28. Camel Ridge
29. Clustered Bamboo Way-stop
30. Peak Gate
31. Arhat Way-stop
32. Greater and Lesser Supports
33. Illusory Joy and Delight
34. Tree Bark Village
35. Monkey's Ladder
36. Thunder Cavern Flat
37. New Way-stop
38. Eighty-four Switchbacks
39. Azalea Flat
40. Longing-for-the-Buddha Pavilion
41. Tender Grass Flat
42. Foot-washing Stream
43. Luminous Light Monastery
44. Heavenly Immortal Bridge
45. Luminous and Bright Cliff
46. Black Stream Monastery
47. Tiger Creek Bridge
48. Facing-the-Moon Peak
49. White Cloud Gorge
50. Azure Lotus Peak
51. Dragon Gate

Map 5.1 Continued

(1102–1107), such as pennants embroidered with gold coins and pennants woven with red silk. Among these treasures is a monk's raiment of red silk with purple embroidery conferred by the emperor Renzong. On it are proclamations written in the emperor's own hand that read: "'Buddha's Dharma is enduring and exalted'; 'The Dharma Wheel is forever turning'; 'May the Empire be mighty, the people secure, winds favorable, and rains opportune'; 'May spears and pikes be forever at rest'; 'May the people know peace and joy'; 'May sons and grandsons be abundant'; 'May all living beings reach to the opposite shore of salvation.' Recorded and signed by the emperor on the Hall of Prosperity and Peace (Funing dian) on the seventh day of the tenth month in the seventh year of the Jiayou reign (20 November 1062)."[74]

White Stream Monastery had its own library, called the Sūtra Depository (Jingzang). Judging from Fan Chengda's description below, the library—built by artisans dispatched from the capital—housed some magnificent texts printed in picture-book form.

Next I reached the monastery's Sūtra Depository, which is a treasure depository built by artisans from the Directorate of Manufacturing dispatched here by the imperial

Court. The front of the depository is a pylon. Smaller towers flank it on both sides. The gate-tower's nails and hinges are all made of jade-stone, and are extremely well crafted and amazingly extravagant. Tradition says they are modeled exactly after the style of the main gate in the National Capital. The sūtras here were produced in Chengdu. They use blue, heavy paper with characters written in liquid silver. At the head of each scroll is an illustration painted in liquid gold. Each illustration depicts the events in one scroll. A wheel sign and objects such as small bells and pestles are embroidered on the outside covers of the sūtras, as well as expressions such as "Peace in the Empire!" and "Long Live the Emperor!," which are placed amid patterns of dense flowers and elaborate foliage. Today one no longer sees this type of embroidery pattern.

Next we reached the Three Thousand Iron Buddhas Hall (Sanqian tiefo dian). Someone said Samantabhadra resides on this mountain, and that a company of three thousand disciples live with him. Thus, they fashioned these Buddhas.[75] The casting is very plain and simple. On this day I set out offerings and prayed to the bodhisattva (or Samantabhadra), begging for three days of fine, clear skies so I could climb the mountain.[76]

Until now, Fan Chengda and his traveling party have been ascending the mountain by climbing stone steps, just like modern hikers do today. In the Southern Song, however, these convenient steps ended at White Stream Monastery. Since much of the terrain above the monastery consists of steep trails that undulate over the spines of narrow, lofty peaks, in the twelfth century climbers at times had to crawl up the cliff-sides on ladders made of timbers. In fact, there are still trails like this on the mountain today, but they are closed to tourists. To say the least, it is a difficult climb. And there is still another 60 *li*/20 mi to go before reaching the summit. Fan Chengda would have never made it to the top of the mountain without the assistance of his crew of strong yeomen and "mountain lads," who on several occasions literally hoisted Fan and his sedan chair up the precipitous peaks. Despite the obvious dangers, Fan Chengda is still able to maintain a sense of humor. In one poem, describing how he felt as his sedan chair was being pulled up the ladders attached to the cliff-side, he jokingly remarks: "I am like a flopping fish being hoisted up on a long pole."[77] On another occasion he regards the difficulty of the climb as a potential rejuvenating force that might even restore the original black sheen to his hair!"[78]

Yiwei day (24 July): It was a clear, beautiful day and so I began my ascent to the upper peak. From here to the Luminous Light Monastery (Guangxiang si) and Seven Treasures Cliff (Qibao yan) on the peak's crest is another sixty li. The distance to there from the flat land in the town {below} is probably no less than one hundred li. No longer do we find any stone-step paths. Timbers have been cut and made into long ladders, which are fastened to the cliff wall. One ascends the mountain by crawling up them. I submit that of all the mountains to be climbed in the whole world, none matches this one in danger and height. As strong yeomen supported my sedan-chair in its forced ascent, thirty mountain lads drew it upward as they advanced pulling on a huge rope. My fellow travelers {also} made use of the "ladder sedan chair" on the mountain.[79]

While climbing up treacherous Brush-the-Heart Mountain (Dianxin shan; so called because your knees touch your heart and chest as you climb up it), Fan managed to compose a poem that also closes on a humorous note: "To travelers who yearn to tread these scenic paths, / Let us chant: 'The Road to Shu is Easy' "![80] Notice that there is now less frequent mention in the *WCL* of place and temple names. This is because the terrain on the final leg of the climb is extremely steep, and there are very few small mesas or flats (*ping*) along the way. The way-stops Fan mentions in the next entry were surely a welcome sight to travelers. Clustered Bamboo Way-stop (Cudian) is where Master Pu supposedly built Emei's first Buddhist monastery; later it became known as the "First Hall" (Chudian).

I left the White Stream Monastery through a side gate and then ascended to Brush-the-Heart Mountain. It is said to be so steep that it makes climbers' feet and knees touch their hearts and bosoms. Passed Thatch Pavilion Point (Maoting zui), Small Stone Thunder (Shizi lei), the Greater and Lesser Deep Gullies (Daxiao shenkang), Camel Ridge (Luotuo ling), and the Clustered Bamboo Way-stop (Cudian). Generally, when one speaks of a way-stop, they mean a one-room wooden structure along the trail. If there are travelers about to climb the mountain, monks at the monastery first dispatch men ahead to boil water at a way-stop so travelers can enjoy a hot meal when they get there.[81]

We are now at 2,430 m/7,970 ft elevation and approaching the summit. At this point there is a discernible change in attitude and orientation in Fan Chengda's Emei poems. As he moves ever closer to the summit, we hear much more about the experience he expects to have there. At the same time, Fan also reminds readers of what has now been left behind him. For instance, in one verse he remarks: "The high-flying swan has no companion, lonely flies the crane; / I look back at the dusty cage and chuckle in delight."[82] In another poem he confidently exclaims: "On the summit all will be quite unlike the dusty world."[83] And finally, referring to the "suffering masses" of the world, he laments: "On earth how pitiable are the uprooted tumbleweeds."[84]

The trail described in the next entry presents a series of inclines that are the most difficult and fearful part of the ascent. "Illusory Joy and Delight" (Cuo huanxi) is a well-known scenic spot on the mountain.

During the Song it was also called the "First Pleasure Pavilion" (Chuxi ting). Today it is called the Bathing Elephant Pool. This name derives from a nearby hexagon-shaped pool, where Samantabhadra supposedly once washed his elephant. The general area (elevation: 2,070 m/6,789 ft) around the Bathing Elephant Pool today serves as home for a tribe of macaque (monkeys) who invariably block the trail seeking food handouts from passing travelers, sometimes in a most aggressive manner. The Peak Gate (Fengmen) and Arhat Way-stop (Luohan dian) sit atop a slope just above the Bathing Elephant Pool, while the Greater and Lesser Supports (Daxiao Fuyu; "support" here probably refers to the ladders described earlier, used to scale the mountain) are perched above there. Tree Bark Village (Mupi li), also known as Tree Bark Hall (Mupi dian), is another notable landmark. This is where the Indian monk Apoduoluo supposedly once built his "Conjured City Monastery" (Huacheng si) during the Western Jin. Since the Ming period the temple on this site has been known as Greater Vehicle Monastery (Dacheng si). Perhaps the most dangerous section on this part of the mountain is Monkey's Ladder (Husun ti). According to the *Mount Emei Gazetteer*, an Indian priest known simply as the "Foreign Monk" (Huseng) once lived here. In order to assist climbers he constructed a "ladder" (*ti*) out of rocks and wood. This came to be known as the Foreign Monk's Ladder (Huseng ti). Because the pronunciation for the terms "foreign monk" (*Huseng*) and "monkey" (*husun*) are similar, the slope eventually became known as "Monkey's Ladder."[85]

The "breach" described in the next entry is in fact one of three ravine alleys along the flat trail above Thunder Grotto Flat (Leidong ping). One can look down these openings all the way to the valley floor several thousand feet below. It is not clear who (at this high elevation) might be praying for rain to the "divine dragon" at the "third grotto." Perhaps it was people from Tree Bark Village, mentioned in the next entry. Apparently, when useless items like dead pigs and worn-out shoes are cast down to the dragon, the creature becomes angry and produces wind and rain. Notice at the close of the next entry Fan mentions the source of the tūla-clouds, which support Samantabhadra when he makes an appearance at the summit.

Next I passed the Peak Gate, Arhat Way-stop, Greater and Lesser Supports, Illusory Joy and Delight, Tree Bark Village, Monkey's Ladder, and Thunder Grotto Flat. Generally, when one speaks of a flat, they mean a place where one can more or less find a foothold. As for Thunder Grotto {Flat}, the path here is on a steep cliff ten thousand ren high. There is a breach in the stone steps.[86] If you spy down through it into the murky, black depths, there appear to be grottoes. Tradition says that a divine dragon lives in a deep pool down there. In all, there are seventy-two grottoes.

If there is a drought, people pray for rain at the third grotto. At first, they cast down perfumes and silks. If the dragon does not respond with rain, they then cast down a dead pig and worn-out women's shoes, which are meant to irritate him. Often thunder and wind then suddenly burst forth. Most of the so-called tūla-cotton clouds above the Luminous and Bright Cliff (Guangming yan) on the peak's summit are produced in this cavern.[87]

In chapter 1 we discussed some of the unique and unusual plant life found on Mount Emei. Now, as we follow Fan Chengda to higher elevations where climatic conditions are distinctly different from those at mid-mountain and the plains below, we hear about one of Emei's most distinct and extraordinary flowers: the *dujuan*, or azalea. Fan Chengda refers to the flowers by their Buddhist name *suoluo* (Sanskrit: *Śāla*), because he associated the flower with a place on the trail called "Azalea Flat" (see the next diary entry), where they grow in great abundance. Mount Emei hosts about thirty varieties of azalea.[88] Some grow at lower altitudes, while others thrive near the summit. From early spring until late summer, there are *dujuan* in bloom somewhere on the mountain. Most, however, are concentrated in the area where Fan Chengda is now climbing; that is, between Illusory Joy and Delight (mentioned in the last entry; elevation 2,070 m/6,789 ft) and the Golden Summit (elevation: 3,077 m/10,092 ft).

We have now reached a section of the trail where it is so steep that travelers must serpentine back and forth in order to make progress in their ascent. During the Song dynasty this section of the mountain, at 2,540 m/8,331 ft, was called Eighty-Four Switchbacks (Bashisi pan); today it is known as the Three Great Turns (Sanda guai):

Passed New Way-stop (Xindian),[89] Eighty-Four Switchbacks, and Azalea Flat (Suoluo ping). As for the azalea tree, its frame and leaves are similar to those of the tobira shrub (haitong). They also resemble the red bayberry tree (yangmei). Their blossoms are red and white, and they bloom between spring and summer. {Such} azalea trees are found only on this mountain. I first saw them when we reached mid-mountain. But when you get here, they are everywhere. For the most part, the plants, trees, birds, and insects on Mount Emei are found nowhere else in the world. I certainly heard about this long ago. Today I personally verified it.[90]

Although summers in Sichuan are scorching, when travelers get above one thousand meters on Mount Emei the climate turns temperate and is thus quite comfortable. At higher elevations, especially near the summit, cloud cover and mist are common. The average daytime July temperature on the Golden Summit is about 12C/54F, but in summer it can—and does—sometimes snow.

I came here during the last month of summer.[91] A few days ago there was a heavy snowfall. The tree leaves are still marked with mottled patterns of snow. As for the extraordinary vegetation, examples would be the Eight Immortals (baxian), which here is deep purple, the Oxherd (qianniu), which here is several times the usual size, and the knotweed (liao), which here is pale green.[92] I heard that in springtime the extraordinary flowers are especially numerous. But in that season the mountain is cold, so few people are able to see them. As for the extraordinary plants and trees, their numbers are also beyond calculation. The mountain is high and windy. Trees do not grow well here. Their branches all droop down. Ancient mosses, like disheveled hair, hang loosely from treetops, drooping to the ground, several zhang *in length. There are, as well, stūpa pines (tasong) that resemble conifers (shan) in shape, but their needles are round and slender. They are also unable to grow tall. Layer upon layer, they turn and twist upward like a stūpa. When you get to the mountain's summit they are especially numerous. Furthermore, there are absolutely no birds here, probably because the mountain is so lofty they cannot fly up this high.[93]*

Fan Chengda has now reached his ultimate destination—the Luminous Light Monastery, yet another one of Emei's "Six Great Ancient Monasteries." Because of its position on the summit and association with Buddha's Glory, numerous ancient tales are associated with the structure. For instance, one tradition says that it was built by Master Pu during the Han dynasty, who named it Universal Light Hall (Puguang dian). The term *guangxiang*, here rendered into English as "luminous light," can refer to a Buddhist image (*foxiang*) or to Buddha's Glory. Both meanings relate to the Luminous Light Monastery, since images of Puxian were certainly on display inside the temple and the primary viewing spot for Buddha's Glory was almost right next to the temple (on the western side of the summit). No one knows for sure when the monastery acquired the name "luminous light,"[94] but certainly the primary referent in the name is Buddha's Glory. Near the monastery is another key site on the summit, the Beholding-the-Buddha Terrace (Dufo tai; also called the Light Emitting Terrace [Fangguang tai]). As the name suggests, this is where pilgrims congregate in hope of spying the mountain's bodhisattva.

Fan Chengda covered the last 60 *li*/20 mi in about twelve hours, which is excellent time, especially given the difficult conditions on the trail. After reaching the summit, Fan donned padded jackets, felt boots, and other cold-weather gear, but still "could not stop shivering and trembling" from the cold.

From Azalea Flat I went on to pass Longing-for-the-Buddha Pavilion (Sifo ting), Tender Grass Flat (Ruancao ping), and Foot-washing Stream (Xijiao xi). Then I reached my destination, the Luminous Light Monastery on the peak's summit. This monastery is also a wooden structure with several tens of rooms. No one was staying there. Inside there is a small hall dedicated to Samantabhadra. I began my ascent in the mao *double-hour (5:00–7:00* AM*). When I reached here it was already past the* shen *double-hour (3:00–5:00* PM*). At first, I wore my summer garments, but it gradually got colder as I climbed higher. When I reached the Eighty-Four Switch-backs, it quickly turned cold. By the time I got to the summit of the mountain, I had hastily put on two layers of wadded jackets, over which I added a fur cloak and a fur robe. This exhausted all the clothes stored in my trunks. I wrapped my head with a double-layered scarf and put on some felt boots. Still, I couldn't stop shivering and trembling. Then I burned some coals and sat stiffly as I pressed against the brazier.*[95]

The weather on the summit of Mount Emei can change in an instant. Without warning, a cloud bank can swiftly move in and blanket the summit with a sea of clouds; conversely, favorable winds can cleanse the mountain of mists and fog in just minutes, revealing an incredible scenic panorama in all directions. The unusual topography immediately surprises visitors. The summit of Emei shan is a big place. The distance from the Golden Summit south to the Ten-Thousand Buddhas Summit extends 4 km/2.48 mi. Although the terrain undulates in places, it is mostly flat, as if the top of the mountain had been sheared off by a giant razor. Everyone immediately notices the thinner air.

As we follow Fan Chengda's experiences on the Golden Summit, it will be useful to keep in mind that Fan's physical and emotional states, which are described in both his diary and poems, are influenced (or even conditioned) by high-altitude experience. Physical reactions are easy to spot. During the initial adjustment period there is pronounced discomfort from the cold (note how Fan huddled by the brazier in the last diary entry), which is often accompanied by headaches and insomnia. At the same time, however, many people—and Fan Chengda seems to be among them—at higher altitudes experience a heightened state of energy, lightness, and even euphoria. This is because cold often works as an antidepressant. Lower air pressure reduces the oxygen in the body, which results in heavier breathing and exhaling of carbon dioxide. Ultimately, the brain gets more oxygen, resulting in a more wakeful state and feeling of contentment. Such feelings are already detectable in Fan's poem "Seven Treasures Cliff" ("Qibao yan"). The railing mentioned in the last line was erected to prevent onlookers from falling off the cliff while observing Buddha's Glory:

> The sky seems like a blue-jade bowl,
> Overturned and covering a white-jade platter.
> Crystal-clear light dazzles me with brilliance;

Alone, I am positioned between clouds and sky!
5   Looking straight ahead, I cannot bear to gaze further;
I retreat a step and take a brief respite.
Aware only of the rushing flood of wind,
Bone and hairs stand on end, as if I am frozen.
With divine immortals hidden and out of sight,
10   How can one talk of the dusty mortal life?
My body is as light as a withered leaf;
My two arms extend like a bird in flight.
My fellow travelers reach to grab hold of my gown:
"Where are you going? When will you return?"
15   I tarry a while, write this poem and then depart:
How marvelous it is just leaning here against this railing![96]

CHAPTER 6

The Summit

The highest of the four Buddhist mountains is the western one, Emei shan. . . . There, among the mists that drift from peak to peak, Samantabhadra, the "All Good" Bodhisattva, rides on a white elephant, performing good works for the benefit of all living beings.[1]

—Edward Bernbaum

THE IMMORTAL SAGE APPEARS

On the peak's summit, the four seasons are like the depths of winter;
Fragrant flowers and fragrant grasses grow thick in the spring.
Mossy scars are newly sun-dried in the mid-summer snow;
Tree shapes are old and bent in thousand-year-old winds.
Cloudy forms turn into people and spread all over the world;
The sun's disk accompanies me as I pace the vacuous void.[2]
An unattached life has always offered transcendence and release;
On earth, how pitiable are the tragic, uprooted tumbleweeds.[3]

Although titled "Luminous Light Monastery," this poem has nothing to do with the famous temple of that name on the summit of Mount Emei. Instead, after reporting on some of the physical oddities he observed on the summit (snow in mid-summer, deformed trees, and so on), Fan Chengda uses the verse as a vehicle to reflect on his life and career. Now perched atop Emei shan, ten thousand feet above the "tumbleweed world" below, he discovers a "vacuous void" that provides—for the time being at least—"transcendence and release" from the humdrum routine of official life.

On the summit of the mountain there is a spring. If you boil rice in water from the spring it will not cook. It just disintegrates into something like fine sand.[4] *One cannot cook things in the icy, snowy juices of ten-thousand antiquities! I knew about this before, and so I had some water in an earthenware pot brought up from the lower reaches of the mountain, which was barely enough for myself.*[5]

119

Just behind Luminous Light Monastery is an area called "Luminous and Bright Cliff" (Guangming yan). This name refers to a large, rocky outcrop that extends along the eastern side of the summit, which is used for viewing purposes. Visitors fortunate enough to witness an appearance of Buddha's Glory usually do so from this section of Golden Summit. Other popular designations for the viewing area include Luminous Light Terrace (Guangxiang tai), Beholding-the-Buddha Terrace, and Suicide Cliff (Sheshen yan), the last of these names taken from zealous pilgrims who sometimes hurl themselves down the chasm in hopes of falling into the arms of Buddha.

The next three lines in Fan's travel diary are of particular interest because they mention the prominent Southern Song writer Wang Zhiwang (*style* Zhanshu; *jinshi* 1139), who once served as an official in Sichuan.[6] Although the precise year of Wang's visit to the summit of Mount Emei is unknown, clearly it predates Fan Chengda's ascent in 1177:

> *A short time later I braved the cold and climbed to the Heavenly Immortal Bridge (Tianxian qiao). Reached the Luminous and Bright Cliff. I burned incense in a small hall covered with a roof made of tree bark. Wang Zhanshu, the Vice Grand Councilor (Canzheng), once put tiles on the roof, but they were worn away by snow and frost. Without fail, the tiles crumble to pieces within a year. Later he changed the roof back to tree bark, which can last two or three years.*[7]

What is not mentioned here is the fact that Wang Zhiwang also witnessed an appearance of Buddha's Glory on the summit of Mount Emei. We know this because Wang's collected works include a long poem that describes, in detail, his observation of Emei's famous light phenomenon. This verse, titled "Fashioning a Long Poem in Twenty Rhymes on My Climb to the Summit of Big Emei and Seeing the Globe of Light, Buddha's Glory," has gone unnoticed in all previous scholarship on Mount Emei. The verse is extremely important because it is the first, detailed eyewitness report on Mount Emei's "Globe of Light" in Chinese letters. For this reason it deserves close scrutiny.

Wang's lengthy poem begins with a brief description of Emei's lofty heights, as seen in the distance from Myriad Prospects Tower in Jia county. The hill on which this tower stands is sometimes called "Lofty Standard" (Gaopiao):[8]

Emei stands lofty to the limit—its name manifest in the southwest;
Myriad Prospects Tower, majestic and dignified, plays host to all the
    Buddhas.

From Lofty Standard's celestial pillars, the eight tethers expand;[9]
On the mighty citadel, protector of earth, the Hundred Spirits gather.[10]

The next section of the poem provides details of Wang's ascent, which took place in late spring:

5   Rain clears after my arrival, clusters of peaks emerge;
    It's just the time of springtime warmth, in these twilight days of
        March.
    At higher elevations the freeze thaws, monks flock to the cliffs;
    Sojourning laymen come from afar, travelers fill the trail.
    Bamboo litters are pulled and hauled, for sixty *li* they march,[11]
10 Up the stairs and up the ladders, high and low, thirty thousand
        steps!
    In single file you climb and clamber, till all your strength is spent;
    Like a bird soaring to precipitous heights! Fear strikes your soul!
    Trudging across cliffs and banks—who knows how many twists and
        turns?
    I gaze to the limit across heaven and earth, as clouds meander and
        merge.

After reaching the summit, Wang first gazes north toward Chengdu (or "Brocade Village"), but can barely make out the city through the haze. Next he looks westward toward the Snow Mountains of Sichuan, so beautiful that they look like a winter scene painted on a standing ornamental screen:

15 I gaze toward Brocade Village in the distance: the well-bottom is
        murky;[12]
    Suddenly I notice the Snow Mountains, and mistake them for a painted
        screen.
    Secluded cliffs find some sunshine, rocks sparkle with color;
    Hidden grottoes make rumbling sounds, but the thunder harbors its
        anger.[13]
    Like melodious voices in the *Lengjia*, wondrous birds call out;[14]
20 A tūla-cloud downy world, where a divine dragon stands guard.
    In the vast ocean the tide returns, waves and billows turn calm;
    In indigo fields sunshine is warm, a foggy expanse spreads forth.

Now that tūla-clouds (or "waves and billows") have turned calm and blue sky (or "indigo fields") provides the necessary sunshine, conditions are favorable for an appearance of Buddha's Glory:

Extended rainbows suddenly release white tufts of light;[15]
From the inky reflection suddenly I see a mass of purple and gold.[16]
25   An arhat with a flying staff! The crowd gathers to look;[17]
The globe of light absorbs my body![18] I look back at my own
    reflection.

Samantabhadra is often described in Buddhist literature as riding an albino
elephant with six tusks:[19]

A six-tusked white elephant, shimmering in mid-air;
A fiery-red raven with three feet, submerged in hidden fog.[20]
Lustrous as a lapis lazuli vase, white as an autumn moon;
30   Pure as an udumbara flower embracing the morning dew.[21]
The auspicious realm joins and links with Mount Wawu;
Merging into a single world that seems reciprocal and connected.

We know that Wang Zhiwang remained on the summit of Emei until
evening, for in the next line he reports on sage lamps blazing in the nighttime sky. "Nine Crests" (Jiuding) probably refers to the nine hills that
comprise Traversing-the-Clouds Hill, upon which stands the Colossal
Buddha of Jia county.

Sage lamps from the Nine Crests pay homage in the night,[22]
Scattering about the thousand peaks, blazing to no end.
35   With mortal eyes I myself witness the convening of a Buddha
    Assembly,
With this common body I'm afraid to pursue the swift, immortal
    wind.[23]
I desire now to seek out Fu Yue, who straddles the Winnowing Basket
    and Tail,[24]
So there's no need for me to ask Junping about Dipper-Ox Ferry.[25]
So now I will push open the heavenly gates and ascend to the
    lofty orb:[26]
40   The mortal domain is so troubled and tormented—what's the point
    of staying around?[27]

Wang Zhiwang's poem provides information about Mount Emei in
Song times that is not available anywhere else. In line 7, for instance, Wang
mentions that monks on Mount Emei did not venture to the summit until
after the spring thaw, which indicates that priests lived at lower levels of
the mountain during the colder winter months and occupied temples on
the summit only during the summer. Mention of "stairs and ladders" in
line 10 tallies with Fan Chengda's earlier comment that at higher eleva-

tions travelers had to climb cliff-wall ladders in order to reach the summit. Given the paucity of information on pilgrim activity on Emei before the Qing dynasty, it is especially noteworthy that Wang Zhiwang says specifically in line 8 that novices and sightseers "filled the trail." This proves that there was pilgrim activity on Emei in the twelfth century.

Perhaps the most valuable section of Wang's verse is lines 23 to 32, where he describes his observation of Buddha's Glory. Many of the necessary key elements of an appearance are mentioned, such as tūla-clouds, the "white tufts" of light emerging from "long rainbows," Samantabhadra and his white elephant, and so on (we will hear much more about these details from Fan Chengda later). Finally, lines 31 and 32 mention that Emei's "auspicious realm" (that is, Samantabhadra's "appearance") links with Mount Wawu, rising in the distance, to form a "single world." Although Wang Zhiwang's description here is not as detailed as perhaps we might like, the general idea is clear: Buddha's Glory on Emei shan has a dynamic quality that allows the clouds and the "light" itself to move toward or away from the mountain. On the day of Wang Zhiwang's sighting, it moved away from Emei shan and seemed to "join and link" with Mount Wawu. Shafts of sunlight that sometimes dart through openings in tūla-clouds during "appearances" can also form "bridges" or shafts of "golden light" (sunlight), which could also extend toward Mount Wawu to the west. Fan Chengda's description below describes these same features. It seems quite possible, then, that the official Wang Gun's tenth-century sighting of a "gilded body-form of Samantabhadra," which he seems to identify as originating on Mount Wawu,[28] may in fact have been an "extension" of Emei's famous light phenomenon.

We now rejoin Fan Chengda on the summit:

Someone told me that "Buddha's Manifestation" (or "Buddha's Glory") only comes out during the wu *double-hour (11:00 AM–1:00 PM). Since it was already past the* shen *double-hour (3:00–5:00 PM), I thought it might be best to return to my lodgings and come back tomorrow. Just as I pondered my decision, clouds suddenly emerged from the gorge to the side and below the cliff, which is Thunder Grotto Mountain (Leidong shan). The clouds marched in columns like imperial honor guards. When they reached the cliff, the clouds halted for a short while. On top of the clouds there appeared a great globe of light with concentric coronas of various colors in several layers, positioned opposite from where I stood. In the middle was a watery, inky reflection that looked like the Immortal Sage (or Samantabhadra) riding an elephant.[29] After the time it takes to drink a cup of tea, the light disappeared. But off to the side appeared yet another light just like the first one. In an instant it too disappeared. In the clouds there were two shafts of golden light that shot across into the belly of the cliff. People also called this a "Minor Manifestation."*

At sunset all the cloud forms scattered. The mountains in the four directions fell silent. At the yi night watch (roughly, 10:00 PM) the lamps came out. They teemed everywhere below the cliff—tens of thousands of them filling my gaze. The night was so cold that I could not stay outside for very long.[30]

The "lamps" described in the closing lines of this entry are in fact the "sage lamps" or "Buddha lamps" described earlier by Fan Chengda and Wang Zhiwang. Presumably, these are the same type of phosphorescent lights Fan observed earlier on Mount Qingcheng. According to sightings and investigations made in China in the 1980s, Mount Emei's "sage lamps" have now been traced to three main sources: (1) concentrations of bacteria on tree leaves, which produce light when their moisture content reaches a certain level; (2) fireflies or flying glowworms (*yinghuo chong*); and (3) layers of phosphorous strata (*linyan ceng*; also called *linkuai yan*) on the valley floor below the eastern escarpment of the Golden Summit, which sometimes emit a glow.[31]

On clear days the panoramic view from the summit of Mount Emei is nothing short of spectacular. Mount Wawu stands to the west. One of the distant scenic wonders visible from the top of Emei shan is the Snow Mountains (Xueshan; also known as the Daxue shanmai, or Big Snow Mountain Range), which extend along a north-south axis through western Sichuan. The highest peak in this range is Gongga Snow Mountain (Gongga xueshan; 7,556 m/24,784 ft):

Bingshen day (25 July): Again I ascended to the cliff to view and gaze at the sights. Behind the cliff are the ten-thousand folds of the Min Mountains. Not far to the north is {Little} Mount Wawu ({Xiao} Wawu shan), which is in Ya county.[32] *Not far to the south is Big Wawu (Da Wawu), which is near Nanzhao.*[33] *In shape it looks just like a single tile-roofed house. On Little Mount Wawu there is also a luminous light called the Pratyeka-Buddha Manifestation (Bizhi foxian). Behind all these mountains are the Snow Mountains of the Western Regions. Their jagged and cragged peaks, which seem carved and pared, number upwards to a hundred. With the first light of day their snowy hue is piercing and bright, like glistening silver amid the dazzling and resplendent light of dawn. Since ancient times these snows have never melted. The mountains stretch and sweep into India and other alien lands, for who knows how many thousands of li. Gazing at them now, they seem spread out on a little tea table right before my eyes. This magnificent, surpassing view tops everything I have seen in my life.*[34]

As mentioned earlier, weather conditions on the summit can change in an instant. After Fan offers further prayers to Samantabhadra, Mount

Emei is suddenly engulfed by a dense fog, followed by a heavy downpour. As tūla-clouds gather and rise up from the great chasm below, one of the monks present announces that a "Great Manifestation" (Daxian) is about to take place. Samantabhadra is approaching again. . . .

I paid a second visit to the hall on the cliff and offered prayers. Suddenly a dense fog arose in the four directions, turning everything completely white. A monk said: "This is the Silvery World" (Yinse shijie). A short time later, there was a heavy downpour and the dense fog retreated. The monk said: "This is the rain that cleanses the cliff. Buddha is about to make a 'Great Manifestation'." Tūla-clouds again spread out below the cliff, gathered thickly, and mounted upward to within a few yards of the edge, where they abruptly halted. The cloud tops were as smooth as a jade floor. From time to time raindrops flew by. I looked down into the cliff's belly, and there was a great globe of light lying outstretched on a flat cloud. The outer corona was in three rings,[35] each of which had indigo, yellow, red, and green hues. In the very center of the globe was a hollow of concentrated brightness. Each of us onlookers saw our forms in the hollow and bright spot, without the slightest detail hidden, just as if we were looking in a mirror. If you raise a hand or move a foot, the reflection does likewise. And yet you will not see the reflection of the person standing right next to you. The monk said: "This is the Body-absorbing Light" (Sheshen guang). When the light disappeared, winds arose from the mountains in front and the clouds scurried about. In the wind and clouds there again appeared a huge, globular form of light. It spanned several mountains, exhausting every possible color and blending them into a beautiful array. The plants and trees on the peaks and ridges were so fresh and alluring, so gorgeous and striking, that you could not look at them directly.[36]

Samantabhadra's "Great Manifestation" complete, Fan Chengda now supplies an explanation for his readers:

When the clouds and fogs have scattered and only this light remains shining, people call it a "Clear-Sky Manifestation" (Qingxian). Ordinarily, when Buddha's Glory (Foguang) is about to appear it must first spread out some clouds—this is the so-called Tūla-Cloud World (Douluo mian shijie). The light-form depends on the clouds to make its appearance. If it does not depend on the clouds, it is called a "Clear-Sky Manifestation," which is extremely rare. In the time it takes to eat a meal, the light gradually moved off, traversing the mountains and heading off westward. When we looked back to the left, on Thunder Grotto Mountain another light appeared like the first one but a little smaller. After a short while, it too flew off beyond the mountains. When the light reached the level countryside, it made a special point of circling back into direct alignment with the cliff.[37] Its color and shape changed completely, turning into a golden bridge that somewhat resembled Suspended Rainbow Bridge on the Wu River.[38] But the ends of this bridge have purple clouds holding them up. In general, the cloud forms clear away between the wu *and* wei *double-hours (11:00 AM–3:00 PM). This is called "Closing the Cliff" (Shouyan). Only the "Golden Bridge Manifestation" (Jinqiao xian) waits until after the* you *double-hour (5:00–7:00 PM) before it disappears.*[39]

The highlight of Fan Chengda's experience on Mount Emei was certainly his observance of the "Great Manifestation." For the most part, his diary description of the phenomenon is objective and detailed. Fan's main intention is to carefully document details of the sighting so this information might be passed on to posterity. To discover how the experience affected him in a personal way we need to examine what might be called the "climax poem" of Fan Chengda's Emei experience. This long verse, in forty lines, is full of imagery related to Buddhism. The title of the poem is also lengthy: "On the Twenty-seventh Day of the Sixth Month in the Fourth Year of the Chunxi Reign, I Climbed to the Summit of Big Emei, Which Is Also Known as Superior Peak Mountain; Buddhist Texts Regard This As the Place Where the Bodhisattva Samantabhadra Dwells; For Consecutive Days Bright Visages and Great Manifestations [Have Appeared Here] and I Composed a Poem To Record the Event; Then Entrusted [the Monk] Yinlao to Engrave It on the Mountain, So It Might Serve as an Important Public Case." Unlike the graffiti commonly found on mountain rocks and walls in China (so-and-so was here on such-and-such date), Fan Chengda's poem is a carefully crafted literary composition designed with a specific goal in mind. As mentioned in the title, his immediate purpose was the make a record of his sighting of Buddha's Glory so that it might serve as a "public case" (*gong'an*; Japanese: *kōan*). The term *gong'an*, or "public case," originally referred to example case records illustrating good and bad legal decisions made by local government offices in China. Later, however, the term became common in Chan writings. During the Song dynasty, there were at least three types of *gong'an* employed in Chan-related texts. Here Fan Chengda is utilizing one of these three techniques, called *niangu* 拈古 (lit., "fitting together the ancient"). When using this approach one first relates or describes an important event, then reflects on the meaning or significance of the event that lies beyond the words that describe it. Here is how Fan Chengda describes—in verse—the "important event" he witnessed on the summit of Mount Emei:

> Superior Peak, oh so high! It rubs against the purple-azure sky;[40]
> A white deer guides me in my ascent to the Conjured City.
> The bodhisattva who lives on the mountain delights in my arrival;
> Tūla-clouds spread throughout his realm, offering a profusion of greetings.

5 A round luminescence, bright and resplendent, rests upon the clouds;
  Sparkling like the Seven Treasures, its majestic dignity assumes form.[41]
  Before one light is fully fixed, another light appears;
  In the center—an inky image, projecting itself at will.
  White tufts of clouds from the earth below pierce the jade-blue void,
10 Then scatter to illuminate stars and planets, startling even Devas and Nāgas.[42]
  Nighttime spirits become Buddhas—offerings are made ready for them as well;[43]
  They illuminate the world ever so brightly—a myriad number of lights![44]
  Tomorrow morning the Silvery World will become a blur of total whiteness;
  So close to it now—I'm dazed, muddled, and trembling from the chill.
15 Countenance of sky and hue of wastes quickly open up, and then hide away;
  Such dark and gloomy transformations grieve even the immortal spirits.
  Someone said the Six Perspicacities are about to make a Great Manifestation;[45]
  The mountain is bathed with a rush of rain as if from an overturned bowl.
  The sun's orb and layered colors[46] make their mark on the belly of the cliff:
20 They are neither mist nor fog nor pigments on a painting.
  Together with the Transformed One I am lodged in the very center;[47]
  In the mirror's reflection we see each other, face to face.
  A great globe of light suddenly wells up before the mountain:
  Like a lunar halo besieging the sun, it floats in the blue depths of the sky.
25 Forests and springs, plants and trees are all completely engulfed by it;
  This is none other than the Universal Light Radiance.
  Words and phrases from the Ocean Treasury are inadequate to praise it;[48]
  At the northern peak the Golden Bridge extends across once again.
  Our devout group stands fast for a long time, until the Buddhist miracle concludes;
30 Not a speck of dust rises up—the mountain falls silent and still.
  There has never been a dharma that can be preached or explained;

Let me ask: though you have ears, how would you hear it?

In three reincarnations I have maintained the same practices and vows;

And so, in an instant of consciousness a response to destiny has come forth.[49]

35 I've come on this journey to again confirm my mental ground;[50]

Now I don clothes with Mani pearls—so what else is there to seek?[51]

I have written this poem as a *gāthā* so it may serve as a public record,[52]

So those who come later will know of my experiences here.

Divine Perspicacity and the Buddha's teachings must be distinguished:

40 I have completely indulged myself in the hot bowl, yet spring thunder has nevertheless resounded.[53]

The opening lines of Fan's poem immediately set the stage for the observations and declarations that follow. Line 2 alludes to the legend of Master Pu who, it will be recalled, followed deer tracks to the summit of Emei where he observed a vision identified later as Samantabhadra. Mention of ascent to the "Conjured City" (Huacheng) suggests that Fan is expecting to reach a place where he might experience awakening or enlightenment.[54] This expectation is probably the result of the "profusion of greetings" our traveler receives from the tūla-clouds amassing below Emei's cliffs, sent by Samantabhadra, who "delights" in Fan's arrival. Lines 5 through 30, replete with Buddhist terminology and imagery, present a vivid poetic description of Buddha's Glory. Of particular interest are lines 21 and 22, where Fan finds himself "lodged" together with Samantabhadra—the "Transformed One" (Huaren; that is, a Buddha or Bodhisattva that has transformed himself into human form), in the very bullseye of Buddha's Glory.

The closing couplets (beginning with line 31) tell us much about the deep impression Fan Chengda's Emei experience made on his mind or "mental ground" (*xindi*). The author's observation of the mountain's physical wonders, climaxed by the "Great Manifestation," leads him to comment on his own religious practices and beliefs. Especially important is the declaration in lines 33 and 34: Fan claims that he has maintained the same practices and vows throughout the three previous reincarnations of his life. In other words, he has been a constant and faithful flower of Buddha's teachings. Fan further remarks that his piety has been rewarded with a "response" in the form of an "appearance" by Samantabhadra. The author's message here is clear: his sighting of the bodhisattva was no chance meeting, but a realization of destiny or fate (*yuan*).

The most fascinating part of this poem is the closing couplet. Here Fan Chengda makes an assessment of how his experience on Mount Emei ultimately affected him in a religious way. This is accomplished by means of an admonition (line 39) and a statement (line 40). To say the least, these lines are extremely difficult to understand. Although the poem under discussion has been translated into English on at least two other occasions, these renditions reflect an understanding or interpretation of Fan's final couplet that is different from my own.[55] What I find to be especially perplexing is the expression *rewan* (lit., "hot bowl") and how it relates to the other images in lines 39 and 40. A search through the *Taishō* and standard reference sources on Buddhist terminology provided a few clues about *rewan*, but no definitive answer concerning the meaning of the two lines in question.

If my assumption is correct about Fan employing the *niangu* technique described earlier, we can be reasonably sure that in the final lines of the poem the author is reflecting on the meaning of his encounter with Samantabhadra, but in a way that seeks to go beyond the words he used to describe that experience (earlier in the verse). I would argue that is also essential to keep in mind that in the final couplet Fan Chengda is assessing his own relationship with Buddhism. With these two points in mind, let us now consider the language and imagery in the final couplet. In the penultimate line Fan juxtaposes two key concepts in Buddhist writings, especially Chan texts: *shentong* 神通, rendered here as "divine perspicacity," and Fofa 佛法, or Buddhadharma (lit., "Buddha's teachings"). The first of these expressions, *shentong*, is a Chinese translation for the Sanskrit term *abhijñā*. Bodhisattvas and thaumaturges are said to be endowed with six *abhijñā*, or wonder-working powers (Skt. *ṛddhi* or *siddhi*). These include the ability to pass through obstacles, appear anywhere at will, fly through the air, perform magic transformations, and much more.[56] Earlier in the poem (line 17) the expression "Six Perspicacities" (*liutong* 六通) a synonym for *shentong*), is used precisely in this way. That is to say, Samantabhadra has employed superhuman powers to transform himself into an image that is visible to humans. In line 39, however, Fan Chengda seems to be using *shentong* in a different sense; namely, as a synonym for yet another Buddhist expression, *ganying* 感應 (lit., "stimulus and response"). *Ganying* does not involve magic or supernormal activity per se; it generally refers to a *manifestation* from an enlightened being that occurs in *response* to the purity of a pious believer. This reading is supported by the "response" Fan Chengda mentions in line 34. Samantabhadra has been "moved to respond" to the Song writer's devotion to the faith, which has been constant throughout his three previous lives. Juxtaposed with *shentong/ganying* is the Buddhadharma, the potential source to ultimate understanding. Now, with these glosses of *shentong/ganying* and Fofa in mind, the penultimate line of Fan Chengda's poem might be paraphrased something like this: one must (*xu* 需) carefully distinguish (*panduan* 判斷) between appearances/sightings of bodhisattvas that take place in response to the religious purity of the beholder and the truth-revealing teachings of the Buddha. The reason for making this distinction will become clear as our discussion proceeds.

Fan Chengda executes his *gong'an* in the final line of the poem. Here the author says nothing directly about his Emei shan experience. Instead, following the standard convention of a *gong'an*, he invites readers to ponder or meditate on a statement. By doing so readers might be able to discover the true meaning or main insight to be gained from Fan's Emei experience. Two images, mentioned earlier, are prominent here: "hot bowl" (*rewan* 熱椀 [椀 is an alternate written form of 碗]) and "spring thunder" (*chunlei* 春雷). Both expressions are used frequently in Buddhist texts, often as metaphors. The first term, "hot bowl," is an abbreviated form of the four-character expression *rewan mingsheng* 熱碗鳴聲, which describes the *sound* made by frothing bubbles when hot water is poured into a bowl. Although *rewan mingsheng* is sometimes used in a general sense to connote the teachings of Buddha,[57] in my view this reading does not fit well in the context of lines 39 and 40. I would argue that in line 40 Fan employs *rewan* [*mingsheng*] as a metaphor for the meaninglessness of verbal expression.[58] In other words, the sound of bubbles frothing in a bowl of hot water *means* nothing at all. Could this be the key to understanding the elusive final line in Fan Chengda's poem? Before attempting to address this question, there still remains one final expression to decipher: "spring thunder." This is also a Chan term. It denotes the booming sound of *falei* 法雷, or "Dharma Thunder," which can awaken sentient beings from their "stupor" and immediately stimulate knowledge of the Ultimate Truth. In some contexts "spring thunder"/"Dharma thunder" can also serve as a metaphor for the stentorian voice of Buddha (Foyin 佛音 or Fosheng 佛聲), which similarly can awaken misguided souls to the True Path.[59]

Explicating the various *individual* Buddhist terms and images in Fan Chengda's poem, including those in lines 39 and 40, is not an especially challenging task. The great difficulty lies in understanding how these various lexical items relate to each other in a definable context that yields a main point or "punch line." As for line 39, Fan Chengda appears to be making a very straightforward statement: while pursuing the correct Buddha path and ultimate truth one must be careful to distinguish between (1) manifestations of bodhisattvas that occur in response to the religious purity of the beholder; and (2) the sacred and truth-revealing teachings of the Buddha. That is to say, Fan sees a clear distinction between witnessing a brief appearance of a bodhisattva and serious study of the Buddhadharma over a lengthy period of time. The religious nature of his Emei experience(s) —especially the encounter with Samantabhadra—was an overwhelmingly positive one. The miraculous nature of this event notwithstanding, Fan reminds his readers that such sightings are not the same as pursuing the Buddhadharma through long-term study and lifelong devotion. Why make such a distinction? Earlier in the poem Fan emphasizes the fact that during the three previous reincarnations of his life he has been a devote follower of Buddha, consistently following "the same practices and vows," and that the "reward" for his piety was a "response" from Samantabhadra. Two key questions now emerge: first, did Fan Chengda experience some sort of enlightenment on Mount Emei? Second, if he did experience an "awakening," how—if at all—is this related to his sighting of the Foguang?

Fan Chengda does not provide any direct answers to these questions, but he does drop some hints. The best clue of all appears in the last three words of the poem: "spring thunder resounds" (chunlei ming 春雷鳴). If Fan Chengda is the subject-referent of this phrase—and this seems to be the case, then the author is saying that he has experienced awakening from his previous "stupor" and his knowledge of the Buddha Truth has been enhanced in some way. We are not provided any further details about this event, but expression of such an idea is consistent with the purpose of a gong'an. The author seems to go out of his way, however, to emphasize that his awakening was *stimulated* by his experience on Emei, but was not the *result* of his encounter with Samantabhadra. Rather, his revelation came about because of *long-term* devotion, piety, and faith. Note that Fan says nothing directly about "achieving enlightenment." The author's point is that he has been on the true path for a long time and his Emei experience has inspired him in such a way where he now sees his future journey more clearly. As for the "hot bowl," Fan Chengda seems to use this expression to humble himself as he makes a self-deprecating confession in line 40: "Since I am still a writer and poet, while visiting Emei I have completely indulged myself in the useless activity of literary production." In a Buddhist sense, literary works are meaningless because, like frothing bubbles in a hot bowl of water, they are impermanent and thus have no lasting spiritual value. Is Fan patronizing Buddhism here, perhaps because he feels guilty about engaging in so much "worthless" literary activity at a holy Buddhist site? I doubt it. Such behavior would not be consistent with Fan's character and personality; he is always honest and direct and never patronizes anyone. I suspect the comment about the "hot bowels" is simply a statement of humility or perhaps an attempt by the author to "lighten" the tone of the ultimate line, which of course deals with a serious religious matter. Using self-deprecating humor in such a way *does* accord with Fan's customary demeanor. He never seems to take himself too seriously. At the same time, Fan's use of the expression "hot bowl" is quite successful, perhaps even brilliant, because it immediately grabs the reader's attention and forces him/her to think more carefully about what is being said. These are some of the functions of a *huatou* 話頭, or "crucial phrase," in what scholars sometimes call "Gong'an Introspection Chan Buddhism." Authors employing this technique give readers a *huatou*, upon which they are to concentrate and eventually experience a breakthrough to enlightenment.[60] Did Fan Chengda intend his "hot bowl" as a *huatou* to help readers reach enlightenment? Probably not. As already mentioned, he uses the image of a "hot bowl" to startle readers into thinking more carefully about what is being said, to humble himself by "confessing" the uselessness of writing, and perhaps to inject a slight jocular tone into a very serious discussion.

In the final analysis, then, the main point of Fan's *gong'an* is actually quite simple: "I came to Mount Emei and wrote a travel diary and numerous poems, all of which—like bubbles in hot water—are devoid of serious meaning and spiritual significance. And yet, because I have been faithful and devoted to Buddhism throughout my three previous lifetimes, Samantabhadra has graced me with an appearance and the Dharma Thunder has boomed loudly to awaken me and help me to see the Way more clearly." Although it is impossible to determine just how "Buddhist" Fan Chengda became after he left Emei shan, there is no doubt that he maintained a strong interest in the religion throughout the remaining years of his life. We know this because numerous poems on Buddhist themes fill the pages of his collected works. As noted by Schmidt, however, Fan's interest in Buddhism was expressed mainly through piety and faith.[61] Philosophical and polemical issues did not interest him in the least.

Fan Chengda and his companions now begin their descent of the mountain. Perhaps one might expect the trip down to be easier than the climb up, but this was not the case. In fact, as we discover in the next entry, the descent can be more much more difficult:

Dingyou day (26 July): Started down the mountain. When we first made our ascent, although we clambered upward with difficulty and had ropes pulling us in front, it was dangerous but not perilous. When we started down the mountain, although ropes were again tied to our sedan chairs to lower us down the rungs of the ladders, the bearers found it difficult to keep their footing, and it was both dangerous and perilous. As we went down the mountain, gradually I began to feel the hot summer air, and so I peeled off my heavy winter garments one by one. During the wu *double-hour (11:00 AM–1:00 PM), when we reached the White Stream Monastery, I put on the light summer linens I had on before.*[62]

The Black Stream Monastery (Heishui si) is located to the northeast of the White Stream Monastery. The two mountain streams from which these temples derive their names, it will be recalled, join at Twin Streams Bridge, near the Ox Heart Monastery. Legend has it that during his travels on Mount Emei during the Tang dynasty the Chan monk Huitong wished to restore the Black Stream Monastery, built originally by one Master Zhao (Zhaogong) of the Wei-Jin period. During his travels Huitong encountered a torrential mountain stream, however, and this prevented him from reaching the original site of the temple. Fortunately, he chanced upon an accommodating tiger that helped him ford the torrent (see below). According to the *Mount Emei Gazetteer*, this miraculous event became known to the imperial Court and, as a result, Huitong received imperial patronage that supported his extensive temple renovation work in the late ninth century.[63] Note that in the next entry Fan Chengda identifies Huitong as the founding patriarch monk (*kaishan seng*) of the mountain. In his honor, a "Master Patriarch Hall" (Zushi tang) was once built upon Facing-the-Moon Peak, where Huitong's "flesh body" (or corpse, *roushen*) was reportedly preserved and stored:[64]

After eating I made a trip to the Black Stream {Monastery}. Crossed Tiger Creek Bridge (Huxi qiao). The turbulence and rush of the creek's swift current was somewhat like that at Twin Streams (Shuangxi), but less intense. Earlier, the patriarch monk of the mountain reached here from the White Stream {Monastery} while searching for a surpassing spot. The creek was swollen and he could not ferry across it. Since there was a tiger crouching beside the creek, he proceeded to straddle it through the reckless current in order to get across. Thus the creek is so named. The White and Black Streams get their names from the colors of their rocks. In front of Black Stream {Monastery} is the Facing-the-Moon Peak (Duiyue feng). The rooms {in the monastery} are quite clean. Spent the night in the monastery's eastern gallery.[65]

Autumn, Wuxu or First Day (27 July): I left Black Stream {Monastery} and again passed White Stream Monastery. Crossed Twin Streams Bridge and went into the Ox Heart Monastery. After a rainstorm the trail was cut off. The stream in White Cloud Gorge (Baiyun xia) was just now swelling. . . . The monastery faces Azure Lotus Peak (Qinglian feng). . . . My bamboo sedan chair proceeded down the shallow area of the gorge so we could get into the monastery. Spray and froth from flying billows soaked our lapels and the front of our garments. The scene here is so exceedingly clear that my hair stood completely on end. . . .[66] *This monastery was built by Tripiṭaka Jiye. Ye's family name was Wang, and he was a native of Yao county.*[67] *He was attached to the Celestial Longevity Cloister (Tianshou yuan) in the Eastern Capital.*[68] *In the second year of the Qiande reign (964) an imperial order sent three hundred monks to India in order to search for {Buddhist} relics and scriptures written on palm leaves. Ye traveled among them, and did not return to the monastery until the ninth year of the Kaibao reign (976). The Niepan jing (Nirvana-sūtra) housed in the monastery comprises forty-two chapters in one slipcase. At the end of each chapter Ye separately records his travel itinerary to the Western Regions. Although not very detailed, most of the geographical descriptions can be consulted. Since such descriptions are rarely seen in the world, I record them here so they make up for omissions in the National History.*[69]

I left Ox Heart and once again passed before the Central Peak. Entered the New Emei Abbey. From the mountain in front of the abbey a new trail has been opened up, which is extremely steep and abrupt in its descent. Braving the rain in order to travel to Dragon Gate (Longmen), I strained and stumbled along for several li and suddenly reached a place where a torrent gushed out from a stone gate between two mountains. This is Dragon Gate Gorge (Longmen xia). We plied a leaflike boat and rowed our way into the stone gate. The two banks here are one thousand zhang high. The color of the precipice walls is like cyan: carved and pared, shining and sleek. After passing ten-some zhang into the gorge, you see two waterfalls, each of which emerges from a precipice summit. They face one another as they fly downward. At the base of the cliff is a dishlike rock that collects the tumbling waterfalls, arouses the water, and makes a flying rain. Its splash and froth floods the gorge. When our boat passed before it, all of our clothes were sprinkled and became thoroughly soaked. Several zhang further on, there was a circular sacrarium halfway down the precipice {wall}. It is about two zhang from the water. I climbed up to it by means of a wooden ladder. In fact, this is the Dragon {Gate} Grotto (Long{men} dong). The deep violet and blue-green hue of the gorge is never ending. The rocks {here} are frigid; the water is clear. I am no longer in the human world. . . . I began to get goose bumps. My bones were startled and my spirit was frightened. I shivered from fear and could no longer remain there.[70]

Again, following his usual practice, Fan Chengda evaluates and categorizes the scene he has just visited.

One can probably say that of the surpassing gorges and springs in the world, those at Dragon Gate should be considered preeminent. In short, those who have traveled here know this; those who have yet to travel here will certainly take my words to be an exaggeration. However, the trail here is decidedly narrow, and there are scattered rocks on the trail. Just before reaching the gorge one must descend from his sedan chair and put on straw sandals. Measuring your gait in half-steps, you trudge amid "rafter teeth" (that is, rocks) that are loose and unsteady. Only then do you reach the mouth of the gorge. The summit of Big Emei is a superlative sight in the world, and yet natives of Shu rarely travel there. Dragon Gate is also a surpassing and superla-

tive place within the mountain itself. Those who travel to Emei are rarely able to get to it.[71]

Finally, some advice to readers who might entertain thoughts about visiting Emei and, in particular, Dragon Gate:

> *Those who are not fond of the remarkable, who cannot take pleasure in new experiences, who cannot disregard toiling and suffering, and who dread sickness and disease, can never reach here. . . . We found the main trail again and left the mountain. It was just after nightfall when we reach the prefecture (that is, Emei town).*[72]

CHAPTER 7

How and Why Did Mount Emei Become a "Famous Buddhist Mountain"?

As for the worshippers from the ten directions, no matter clergy or laity, from far or near, . . . some will see the white elephant traversing the sky, and Samantabhadra lowering his hand to touch their head. Straight away they will then swim across the Ocean of Vows and cross to the Other Shore, where they will dwell in a wonderful and fantastic land.[1]

—Fu Guangzhai (*jinshi* 1577)

BACKGROUND AND BEGINNINGS

Based on the sources we considered in the previous chapter, especially information preserved in the *Fozu tongji*, it is certain that Mount Emei received substantial amounts of imperial patronage in the late tenth century. The most important result of this support was that the mountain became described almost exclusively in Buddhist terms by writers in the early decades of the Northern Song. This new definition of the mountain's religious space was manifested primarily by the presence of a community of monks who occupied several temples, chief among which was the White Stream Monastery. Another important consequence of imperial patronage was that by the late tenth century the mountain was already sanctified, by imperial authority, as the *national* cult center of Samantabhadra. Later, Putuo joined Emei and Wutai to form the "Three Major [Buddhist] Manifestation Sites" (Sanda daochang) in China.[2] In this chapter, drawing on much of the material we have already considered, I will identify, describe, and explain just *how* and *why* this process took place.

Before our discussion begins, four key points need to be emphasized. First, Emei shan would never have become a major Buddhist center without imperial patronage and support. As we have seen, the first two Song emperors, Taizu and Taizong, played pivotal roles in this process. Although it seems likely that personal religious interest may have inspired the two monarchs to support Buddhist activities during their reigns, especially temple building, at the same time we must keep in mind that another important motivation for Northern Song imperial support of "Buddhist mountains" (that is, Wutai and Emei, and later Putuo) was *political*. These mountains, as we saw in chapter 6, were expected to perform functions for the state, for which they in turn received patronage. It was a mutually beneficial arrangement which, during the Song, seems to have worked quite well. The main reason this symbiotic relationship succeeded is because the Song monarchy was able to maintain control over the church. Of course, the promulgation of edicts and laws from Kaifeng was just one means of containing the spread and influence of Buddhism. Another key method of control was the creation, maintenance, and supervision of the "Three Major Manifestation Sites," each located in a different part of the empire (more on this below).

A second point to keep in mind is this: China's so-called sacred mountains or Buddhist mountains do not exist naturally. They are created by political and religious leaders through a process that sanctifies and reconfigures a particular mountain's place and space. This reordering of landscape is undertaken in order to serve the special needs and values of different groups of people and institutions. In the case of Mount Emei, no single individual was responsible for accomplishing the reordering process. Rather, it was a collective effort made by the local Buddhist community on Emei *and* its government and lay supporters. Moreover, the redefinition of the mountain's religious space took place slowly, over the course of several centuries, beginning in the early Northern Song and culminating in the late Ming, when Emei's development as a "Buddhist mountain" reached its height.

Third, the one challenge that most concerned individuals and institutions who sought to "make" Emei a "Buddhist mountain" was *legitimacy*. In other words, ways had to be found or created to explain and thereby legitimize the mountain's Buddhist religious identity. Of course, acts of imperial patronage, by their very nature, confer legitimacy. I would argue, however, that the legitimization process requires additional support mechanisms. If Emei's Buddhist community was to recruit new monks, attract significant numbers of pilgrims and visitors, and entice generous support from patrons—all necessary to sustain a flourishing religious community, it was essential to prove, in convincing fashion, that the mountain's Buddhist "credentials" were genuine. The methods employed to produce these credentials are discussed below.

And finally, we should be mindful that Mount Emei's Buddhist identity was not in place until well *after* the mountain became famous, and not the other way around. That is to say, Emei shan did not become well known in China because of its association with Buddhist religious activity. The presence of Buddhism on the mountain, as I argue in chapter 1, is one part of its identity as a *mingshan*. What distinguishes the Buddhism on Emei shan, however, is its longevity and the crucial role it has played in the Buddhist religious geography of China. This role was sanctified first during the Song, when Emei became one of the "Three Major [Buddhist] Manifestation Sites," and then *again* in the seventeenth century, when Emei, along with Wutai, Putuo, and Jiuhua, became identified as China's "Four Great Famous [Buddhist] Mountains" ([Fojiao] Sida mingshan). The more recent of these two crucial developments fixed the Buddhist geographical landscape of China and this configuration remains in place today.

Our discussion of how and why Emei shan became a "Buddhist mountain" begins with what is perhaps the most basic point of all: the physical and metaphysical conditions on the mountain are ideally suited for the creation of "sacred space." One theme that permeates virtually all sources on the mountain, traditional and modern, secular and religious, is that the Emei's physical environment is exceptional (*qi*). Surely one reason why the mountain's "patriarch monk" Huichi traveled to Emei around 400 AD was because he thought the mountain's isolated location and beautiful scenery would provide a favorable environment for study, meditation, temple building, and ultimately missionary work. In the centuries following Huichi's visit, as more information about the mountain was disseminated through the literary works of Li Bo, Fan Chengda, and others, selected aspects of the mountain's "exceptional" landscape became well known throughout China. Of special importance here is the dramatic nature of the mountain's topography and its remote location on the western border of China; the mountain's grotto system; the strange and unusual flora and fauna that populate Emei's landscape; and Buddha's Glory. Were it not for the presence of these extraordinary *environmental* phenomena, Emei shan would probably have never attracted the attention of Huichi, Li Bo, Fan Chengda, and others, and achieved long-term status as a "famous mountain." I would argue that the same may be said for Wutai, Putuo, and Jiuhua. All of these mountains host extraordinary physical environments of one sort or another, real or imagined.[3]

The Buddhist transformation of Mount Emei began during the Tang; specifically, in the mid-ninth century following the persecutions of 845.[4] Especially notable in this regard is the temple restoration efforts made by the monk Huitong. Reconstruction of the Black Stream Monastery, along with Huitong's rebuilding of the Samantabhadra, Extended Prosperity, Central Peak, and Avataṃsaka monasteries, are also significant, for the presence of these temples, all active in the latter half of the ninth century, strongly suggests that a modest-sized Buddhist community was already in place on the mountain in the late Tang. In addition to temples, it is likely some Buddhist shrines and rudimentary stūpas were also present as well. These monasteries and shrines, presumably built (or rebuilt) under the direction of Huitong, collectively constitute the first identifiable religious community on Emei shan. That one of these Tang monasteries was dedicated to Samantabhadra is especially noteworthy, for it means that by the ninth century Emei was already associated with the Indian deity.[5]

How did the Buddhist transformation of Emei's landscape relate to the mountain's earlier Daoist immortal, or *xian*, tradition, if at all? Huitong and his fellow monks were certainly familiar with the early tales concerning the Yellow Emperor, Madman of Chu, and others whose exploits and Daoist miracles on the mountain are documented in ancient literary sources. Huitong's task, as already mentioned, was to redefine the mountain's space in Buddhist terms. One example of how the redefinition process was carried out, at least in textual sources, is detectable in the story about the monk Mingguo and how he outwitted and killed the malevolent python that had been terrorizing Daoist adepts at the Celestial Illumination Abbey. According to tradition, the abbey's adepts were so impressed by Mingguo's heroic deed that they decided to convert their Daoist enclave into a Buddhist monastery. This incident, we are told, explains the founding of the Central Peak Monastery, one of Emei's earliest and most important Buddhist institutions. Although we cannot determine the authenticity of the snake-slayer tale, it seems almost certain the story was invented in order to help explain the Daoist-to-Buddhist conversion of Mount Emei's religious space.[6] While some modern scholars have argued that Daoists and Buddhists actively competed for space on the mountain as far back as the Jin period,[7] there is no evidence of this in the primary sources. In fact, aside from the python tale, the gazetteers say nothing about the so-called Daoist-to-Buddhist conversion of Mount Emei. I suspect this is because— to repeat an earlier point—there was no significant, organized Daoist community on the mountain in the ninth century with whom Huitong and his temple-building colleagues had to "contend" or "fight" for space. No doubt, there was *some* Daoist presence on the mountain during the Tang but, as I have already argued, this presence was probably limited to individual adepts practicing their arts alone in caves or remote locations. Emei shan is a huge place, and there was certainly more than enough room on the mountain in the Tang period to accommodate a handful of Daoist hermits and a modest-sized community of Buddhist monks.

Founding Myth

In order to convert Emei shan into a Buddhist mountain, there must be some explanation of how Buddhism "arrived" or was "discovered" there. One way to do this is to create a narrative, centered on a miraculous event that seemingly proves a *historical* connection between the mountain and Buddhism. This is precisely the function of the Master Pu story, and so we now need to take a closer look at this tale. Although there are several versions of the story, most follow the same narrative. Here I present the account preserved in Hu Shian's *Yi elai*, which is the oldest extant version of the tale:

> At the time of King Weilie of Zhou (r. 425–401 BC), there was a monk Baozhang who was named Thousand Years. At the time he was born there was some writing imprinted on the palm of his hand. He eventually came [to Sichuan?] to worship Samantabhadra, and devised an image (or statue of the bodhisattva) to which he made offerings. Once, exclaiming in admiration of Mount Emei, he remarked: "Loftier than the Five Cardinal Mounts, in elegance it ranks first in the Nine Regions."
>
> During the Yongping reign of the [Eastern] Han, Guihai year (63 AD), sixth month, first day, there was one Master Pu who was gathering herbs where clouds make their nests.[8] He encountered a deer, [the sight of] which amazed him.[9] He followed the deer to the summit, until its tracks disappeared. Then he saw a magnificent light blazing brilliantly, and a purple fog welling upward. The light and fog connected, meeting in glorious fashion, and formed into a Web of Luminous Brilliance (Guangming wang). Astonished, Master Pu exclaimed: "Such auspicious omens are quite rare. Is this not from Heaven?" He then went to see the monk from the West, Thousand Years, and told him what had happened. The monk replied: "This is an auspicious omen from Samantabhadra, who in the Final Dharma period guards and protects the Tathāgatas[10] and conveys teachings and manifest appearances at this place. His transformations convey benefit to all sentient beings. You can pay a visit to the two masters, Teng and Fa, to further investigate this matter.
>
> In the Jiazi year (64 AD) Master Pu scurried off to Luoyang and paid his respects to the two masters [Teng and Fa], telling them everything he had seen. One of the masters said: "Excellent! This is quite rare! You have been able to see Samantabhadra, a true friend and spiritual guide. Long ago our World Honored One (Shizun) was [lecturing] at a *Lotus-sūtra* Gathering (Fahua hui) and imparted the Four Teachings (Sifa) to Samantabhadra: first,

safeguard the various buddhas through [sūtra] recitation; second, plant and cultivate the roots of merit; third, enter a proper meditation assembly; and fourth, save the minds of all sentient beings.[11]

The bodhisattva [Samantabhadra], in accordance with his original vow, manifests his appearance at Mount Emei. It is named Emei because long ago, when Sudhana (Shancai) was paying respects to the mendicant monk Meghaśrī (Deyun), he stood for a while on Mount Sumeru (Miaogao feng) and observed that this mountain (or Emei) resembles the appearance of a crescent moon. Thus, it is called Emei.[12]

As noted in chapter 2, earliest mention of the Master Pu tale in Chinese letters occurs in the quatrain "First Hall," written sometime in the eleventh century by the Song poet Fan Zhen. The story was certainly in circulation well before Fan Zhen's visit to Emei, but no Tang writer references Master Pu. Moreover, although there are surviving Tang texts that describe Samantabhadra and his influential role in Buddhist religious history and doctrine,[13] none of these works even hints at a connection between the Indian bodhisattva and Emei shan. It would seem, then, that our founding myth probably dates from the early Song, at just about the same time Taizu and Taizong began to patronize Mount Emei. Although we will probably never know what person or persons devised the Master Pu legend, we can, with some confidence, discern the underlying purpose of the story: the creation of a three-way connection between Emei shan, Samantabhadra, and the Foguang (referred to in the Master Pu story as the *weiguang*, or "magnificent light"). This three-way association is the foundation of Emei shan's identity as a "Buddhist mountain."

In order to forge the critical Emei-Samantabhadra-Foguang link, the authors of the Master Pu tale crafted an account intended to "look historical" and thereby be convincing. On the surface, the narrative is quite simple. This is intentional, for the primary target audience of the story was probably lay followers of Buddhism, most of whom (in premodern times) were illiterate. Donations from this group traditionally served as one of the main means of financial support for Buddhist institutions in China (this is still the case today). What is fascinating is *how* the narrative is designed to be convincing. At the outset, the person who discovered the "magnificent light" on Emei is identified by name—Master Pu. Employing a local herb gatherer to fulfill this role works especially well, for it is general knowledge that Emei has long produced rare and efficacious herbs, with the choicest specimens available only in isolated spots at higher elevations. Moreover, who else but an herb gatherer (or hunter) would have been able to scale Emei's forbidding heights? The gazetteers even mention that there was once a village on the mountain comprised entirely of people who shared the family name Pu, all of whom were presumably clan descendents of our herb gatherer.[14]

Now, it is no historic coincidence that Master Pu's discovery is placed in an Eastern (or Later) Han context; specifically, 63 AD The timing here matches, almost to the exact year, the date of an embassy supposedly dispatched to India in 64 AD by Emperor Ming (r. 57–75) of the Han. Puzzled by a dream in which he saw a deity—with a golden body and emanating sunlight from its neck—flying before his palace, the emperor asked his ministers to identify the divine being. One of them, Fu Yi, replied that it was a sage from India called "Buddha." Emperor Ming thereupon dispatched an embassy to India, the purpose of which was to learn more about the sage "Buddha" and his teachings. The emperor's envoys returned after three (some versions say eleven) years, not only with a copy of the famous *Sūtra in Forty-Two Sections* (*Sishierzhang jing*), but also with India's first Buddhist missionaries to China: Shemoteng (Skt: Kāśyapa Mātaṅga?) and Zhufalan (Skt: *Dharmaratna). Several scholars have raised questions about the embassy and the names of the Indian monk(s) who supposedly returned with the Chinese envoys,[15] but these issues need not concern us here. What does interest us, however, is that Shemoteng and Zhufalan are the very same monks ("Teng" and "Fa") who in Luoyang explained to Master Pu the meaning and significance of his experience on Emei. The Master Pu tale, then, is crafted to connect Emei with the introduction of Buddhism to China in the first century.

Another reason for placing the Master Pu tale into a first-century historical context is perhaps less obvious. Those persons who sought to establish Mount Emei's Buddhist credentials were aware that Mount Wutai in the north had already been settled by monks by the late fifth century and, during the Tang, had received generous imperial support for temple construction.[16] Furthermore, by the mid-Tang period Wutai was already a major Buddhist center in China and each year eminent monks and pilgrims from China and abroad visited there. If those persons seeking to legitimize Emei aimed at creating a "Buddhist mountain" that equaled or rivaled Wutai—and this undoubtedly was one of their goals—then Emei shan would need a history that at least matched that of its prominent counterpart in north China. It is thus not surprising to discover that the two Buddhist masters in Luoyang mentioned in the Master Pu story also play a role in the lore of Mount Wutai. One account even reports that during the Yongping reign (57–75) of the Han, Teng and Fan together ascended Wutai and built the Great Faith and Numinous Vulture Monastery (Dafu lingjiu si), where they "expounded the Dharma and passed it on to the world."[17]

The monk Baozhang, or "Thousand Years," is also a semihistorical figure. Not much is known about his life, and what information we do have is sketchy and, in places, downright far-fetched. The earliest biographies for him relate that Baozhang was a native of central India who experienced reincarnation in the twelfth year in the reign of King Weilie of the Zhou dynasty, or 414 BC. Some six or seven hundred years later, during the Wei-Jin period, he supposedly traveled to China and visited Sichuan. Baozhang later left Sichuan and embarked on a tour of China, which included stops at Mount Wutai and Mount Lu. He eventually reached Zhejiang, where he passed away in 657 at the advanced age of 1,072 years.[18] What is interesting is that these accounts of the Indian monk's life say nothing that connects him to Mount Emei. Later sources, however, embellish lavishly on his earlier biographies. The most recent edition of the *Emei Town Gazetteer*, for instance, claims that while in residence on Emei shan, Baozhang lived on a peak bearing his name, situated just behind Giant Toon Tree Flat (Hongchun ping).[19] Even if we disregard the issue of Baozhang's amazing longevity, there is a glaring inconsistency between the Master Pu tale and the Indian monk's received biography: if Baozhang did not arrive in Sichuan until the Wei-Jin period, how was Master Pu able to consult with him (in Shu) in 63 AD? Although this inconsistency has led several modern scholars to question the historical reliability of the Master Pu tale, Baozhang has nevertheless retained his status in the gazetteers as the "first foreign monk on Emei shan." In other words, the accuracy of Baozhang's "embellished" biography has not been an issue, at least with most gazetteer editors. More importantly, no one has rejected Emei's Buddhist connection because of historical inconsistencies in the Master Pu yarn. Those who decided to include Baozhang as a main character in Emei's Buddhist origin myth probably did so because of the monk's alleged Sichuan connection. For the purposes of the Master Pu tale, his traditional role as Emei's first foreign monk qualified him to interpret the "magnificent light" and "purple fog" as a manifestation of Samantabhadra. But to enhance the credibility of Master Pu's auspicious sighting, the crafters of the origin story next dispatch our herbalist off to Luoyang for further consultations with Shemoteng and Zhufalan.

The conversation between the two Indian monks and Master Pu not only confirms Mount Emei as the *daochang* of Samantabhadra; the two missionaries also provide specific information about the bodhisattva and how he is connected to the mountain. Again, the goal here is to authenticate the link between the deity and Emei shan. This is accomplished by using selected expressions and allusions drawn from well-known Buddhist texts. For instance, Samantabhadra is identified as a "true friend and spiri-

tual guide" (*shan zhishi*; Skt. *kalyaṇa-mitra*). This expression, used prominently in the *Banruo boluomiduo xinjing* (*Prajñāpāramitā-sūtra*) and *Avataṃsaka-sūtra*, refers to intimates who are capable of teaching the proper road
to Buddhist enlightenment. In their conference with Master Pu, Shemoteng and Zhufalan relate that Buddha, or the World Honored One, while
lecturing at a *Lotus-sūtra* Gathering, transmitted the Four Teachings (Sifa)
to Samantabhadra. The last of these instructions—that Samantabhadra was
charged with saving "the minds of all sentient beings"—relates to the
"original vow" (*benyuan*) mentioned in the next line. The Buddha and all
bodhisattvas make this vow in order to save the people of the world from
their endless suffering and help them reach the "Other Shore." A direct
connection between Samantabhadra and Emei shan is made in the same
line: this is the place where the deity "manifests appearances." Onlookers,
then, can actually gaze upon a physical manifestation of Samantabhadra
on Mount Emei. Visions of resident bodhisattvas are also reported in the
gazetteers on Wutai, Putuo, and Jiuhua. This is no surprise, for the
promise of such visionary experiences is an essential feature shared by
China's "Four Famous [Buddhist] Mountains."[20] Indeed, it was this quality,
perhaps more than any other, which drew pilgrims to these numinous sites
in the first place.

The final topic addressed by the Master Pu tale concerns the origin
of the name "Emei." A connection to Buddhist scripture is established by
invoking the name Sudhana (Shancai), the youthful character who figures
prominently in the *Avataṃsaka-sūtra*.[21] The last section of this scripture,
known as the *Gaṇḍavyūha*, describes the young Sudhana's journey in search
of enlightenment, undertaken at the suggestion of Mañjuśrī. During his
long pilgrimage Sudhana calls upon fifty-three (some versions of the story
say fifty-five) "true friends and spiritual guides," all of whom mentor him
as he moves closer and closer to his spiritual goal. The young pilgrim's
ultimate "true friend and spiritual guide" is none other than Samantabhadra, who appears to him riding a white elephant. In Sudhana's final
vision, just before attaining enlightenment, the bodhisattva descends on
auspicious clouds, his body emanating all sorts of wondrous lights and
halos. Samantabhadra then extends his right hand and touches Sudhana
on the crown of his head. At that precise moment the young pilgrim
attains ultimate awakening.[22] Reference in our story to the mendicant
monk (*biqiu*) Meghasri alludes to an episode in the *Gaṇḍavyūha* in
which Sudhana takes time out from his studies and climbs Mount
Sumeru, a famous peak in the Kingdom of Rāmāvarānta (Shengle guo).
After mentioning these events, which are indeed chronicled in the
Gaṇḍavyūha,[23] the designers of the Master Pu tale then embellish the story

with a few additional details that are *not* found in any version of that text: gazing at Emei in the distance, Sudhana observes that the Chinese mountain "resembles the appearance of a crescent moon" (*ru chuyue xian* 如初 月現). Hence, we are told, the mountain came to be known as "Emei."

When Sudhana climbed Mount Sumeru he was in the early stages of his pilgrimage and still had not yet achieved enlightenment. So how, then, did the young pilgrim possess the superhuman physical ability to "observe" Emei shan all the way from Mount Sumeru in southern India? No explanation is provided and, like other inconsistencies in the Master Pu narrative, Sudhana's incredible eyesight has not been an issue of critical concern to most editors of the gazetteers. As for Mount Sumeru, I suspect the main purpose of associating the Indian mountain with Emei stems from the latter's physical location in southwestern China, which has always set it apart from China's other *mingshan*. In fact, among China's very large family of famous mountains—in particular, peaks associated with Buddhism, Emei is the geographically closest to India. If Emei stands in closer proximity to the land of Buddha's birth, one could reasonably conclude that its ties with the Indian religion are stronger.

What is especially significant in the final lines of the Master Pu story is the phrase "resembles the appearance of a crescent moon." The simile *ru chuyue* (lit., "like a crescent moon") appears frequently in the *Tripiṭaka*, most often in reference to the *physical characteristics* of a buddha or bodhisattva. A commentary to the *Avataṃsaka-sūtra*, written by the influential Tang dynasty monk Chengguan (738?–820?), includes a passage especially relevant to our discussion. The reference in these lines is to the World-Honored One, or Buddha: "His twin eyebrows are lofty and conspicuous, shiny and glossy, and shaped like crescent moons."[24] This and numerous other similar references in the *Buddhist Canon* reveal that the image of a crescent moon is often used to define the physical features of the World-Honored One and the various buddhas (*zhufo*); specifically, the shape of their eyebrows. But how does all this relate to Mount Emei? Keeping in mind that the main purpose of Emei shan's founding myth is to forge a three-way connection between the mountain, its resident deity, and the Buddha's Glory, I would argue that the formulation "resembles the appearance of a crescent moon" is designed intentionally to link the physical form of Mount Emei with the physical body of Samantabhadra. If we follow this argument a step further, the line mentioning "crescent eyebrows" in the Master Pu tale might also be paraphrased: "[Mount Emei] resembles the appearance of Samantabhadra [manifesting himself]." In other words, when Sudhana sees Mount Emei in the distance, the mountain itself seems to appear in the physical form of its Buddhist deity.[25]

A related question, of course, is this: how is the crescent moon representation of Emei/Samantabhadra related to the Foguang? Another passage in the *Canon* describes the physical appearance of buddhas or bodhisattvas in the following terms: "the face is like a full moon, while the eyebrows are like crescent moons; between the eyebrows white tufts of hair curl around to the right, soft and pliant."[26] The image of "white tufts of hair" is used to describe shafts of white light that dart through the sky during appearances of Buddha's Glory. Wang Zhiwang and Fan Chengda both drew on this image in their poems describing the Foguang (translated and discussed in chapter 6). Now, if we consider the crescent moon/eyebrows metaphor in the context of what is arguably the most prominent among the various physical signs (*xiang* 相) of buddhas and bodhisattvas, namely, the soft tufts of white hairs between the brows (these are said to produce brilliant light during auspicious moments), we have two, closely related images that are well documented in Buddhist scripture and, at the same time, describe and neatly link (via metaphor) the mountain, its deity, and Buddha's Glory. Finally, we note that the "crescent eyebrows" image fits perfectly with the more traditional "silkworm-moth eyebrows" etymology of Mount Emei's name, discussed in chapter 2. This is because the term "crescent moon" (*chuyue*), along with its synonym *xinyue*, or "new moon," are both common metaphors in Chinese poetry for "silkworm-moth eyebrows."[27]

Scriptural Authentication

> *What we call a mountain is thus in fact a collaboration of the physical forms of the world with the imagination of humans—a mountain of the mind.*[28]
> —Robert Macfarlane

Although the Master Pu tale no doubt served to disseminate the idea that Emei shan had a long-standing Buddhist connection, a founding myth cannot, on its own, establish a religious identity for a mountain. The legitimization process also requires *scriptural* authentication. In other words, references in the *Tripiṭaka* must be identified and explicated in such a way so as distinguish Emei shan as the place where the bodhisattva Samantabhadra manifests his body to the devout. According to the gazetteers, Buddhist scriptural authority that establishes Mount Emei as the *daochang* of Samantabhadra derives from exegesis of passages in three sūtras: the *Zahua jing* (Skt. *Malya-sūtra*), the *Lengyan jing* (*Śūraṅgama-sūtra*), and the *Huayan jing*. Interpretation of selected passages in these scriptures, undertaken by those supporting the Buddhist reorientation of Emei's space, seeks not only to provide a scriptural basis for the residence of Samantabhadra on Emei, but also establish the mountain as a key site in the "sacred" Buddhist geography of China.

The first of these three works, the *Zahua jing*, identified by title and cited in all the gazetteers (and quoted in numerous modern secondary sources), in fact appears to be an alternate name for the *Huayan jing*.[29] For our purposes, the most important passage attributed to the *Zahua jing* is cited in the *Yi elai*: "At his *daochang* Samantabhadra teaches and transforms men, devas, and the multitudes, manifests his image profusely on Mount Emei, and intimately guides the people of the world to thoroughly comprehend perfect wisdom, awakened nature, and fundamental perceptions."[30] On the surface, at least, this passage appears to be quite significant because it provides a scriptural reference identifying Emei shan as the *daochang* of Samantabhadra. These same lines are also invoked in the *Shuzhong guangji*, which also specifically identifies Emei shan as Samantabhadra's manifestation site.[31] At issue, however, is the source of this passage. As far as I have been able to determine, an independent scripture bearing the title *Zahua jing* does not appear in the current version of the *Tripiṭaka*. Of course, it is possible that Hu Shian got his information from a sūtra now lost. Without additional information or clarification, however, the source of our *Zahua jing* reference remains unknown. Thus it can only be dated with certainty to the seventeenth century, when Hu Shian copied it into the *Yi elai*. Scriptural authority for Emei most certainly was devised well before this date.

Our second scriptural reference, also provided by Hu Shian, is to the *Lengyan jing*. This scripture was first translated (into Chinese) in 443 by Gunabhadra (398–468), then in 513 by Bodhiruchi (d. 572), and again in 700 to 704 by Śikṣānanda (652–710).[32] The *Yi elai* quotes a lengthy section from the last of these translations.[33] Although the passage describes Samantabhadra riding a six-tusked elephant and mentions his power to "enlighten" with the touch of his hand, it says nothing directly about Mount Emei and hence does not (at least in my view) provide scriptural authority for Emei shan as the *daochang* of Samantabhadra. Hu Shian may have cited these lines simply because they reference Samantabhadra, whose association with Emei was of course already well established when Hu compiled his gazetteer in the late Ming. It is also possible that Hu Shian may have simply copied this passage from an earlier Mount Emei gazetteer that is now lost.

The most important source for Emei shan's scriptural authority as a "Buddhist mountain" is the *Huayan jing*, a Mahāyāna text that became popular in China and served as the basic scripture of the Huayan School of Buddhism. This work exists in several recensions. According to tradition, this was the first sūtra expounded upon by Buddha after he achieved enlightenment. It came to China in partial translation as early as the second century and by the late Eastern Jin the entire work (in sixty *juan*) had already been translated into Chinese by the Indian monk Buddhabhadra (359–429). This rendition was completed in 420. *Juan* 44 to 60 of Buddhabhadra's translation describes Sudhana's quest for the Ultimate Truth. A second version of *Avataṃsaka-sūtra*, in eighty *juan*, was translated by the Khotanese monk Śikṣānanda in Luoyang between 695 and 699. This text, like Buddhabhadra's earlier version, came to China from India via Khotan (or Hetian; an oasis city-state on the Silk Road in modern southwest Xinjiang), and also includes a section describing Sudhana's pilgrimage. About a century later, during the period 795 to 810, the monk Prajñā made a new translation of the Sanskrit manuscript, which was now in forty *juan* (Sudhana's quest in this translation is treated as a separate work). These different versions of the *Huayan jing* play an especially important role in the scriptural authentication process, for they identify various mountains as the dwelling places of particular bodhisattvas and their followers. Three of these peaks, mentioned first in the sixty-*juan* version, require our attention. The first is a mountain in the "northeast" called "Qingliang shan" (or "Mount Clear-and-Cool"), where dwells the bodhisattva Mañjuśrī. The second is (an island) "within the Four Great Seas" (Si dahai zhong) called Zhidan, where dwells the bodhisattva Tanwujie.[34] And the third is a place in the "southwest" called Shiny-and-Fiery Luminous Bright Mountain (Shuti Guangming shan),[35] where dwells the bodhisattva Xianshou (Skt. Bhadramukha). In the eighty-*juan* version of the sūtra there are some changes: the island-mountain in the sea is now designated Vajra Mountain (Jin'gang shan), and its bodhisattva is called Faqi, while the mountain in the southwest is shortened to Guangming and its resident deity is identified by the name Xiansheng (Skt. *Bhadraka).[36] Through exegeses and claims by those who sought scriptural support for establishing Buddhist mountain traditions in China, the three peaks just described came to be identified as *Chinese mountains*; namely, Wutai, Putuo, and Emei, each with its own bodhisattva: Mañjuśrī, Avalokiteśvara (or Guanyin), and Samantabhadra, respectively.[37] The association of Wutai, Putuo, and Emei with these deities finds its origin, then, in the *Huayan jing*. This work thus provides the primary scriptural authority for Emei shan's connection with Samantabhadra.

The section of the *Huayan jing* usually identified as the locus of Buddhist scriptural authority for Emei shan appears in chapter 45 of the eighty-*juan* version:

In the southwest region there is a place named Luminous and Bright Mountain (Guangming shan). Since long ago, various bodhisattvas and their followers have stopped and taken up residence there. Now a bodhisattva named Xiansheng is there with three thousand followers. He lectures to them on the Dharma.[38]

It should first be noted that the language in this passage is formulaic. The section of the *Huayan jing* from which these lines are quoted, titled "Dwelling Places of the Various Boddhisattvas" ("Zhu pusa zhuchu pin"), identifies numerous mountains that host bodhisattvas and in each case the text employs almost the same sentence formulations, illustrated by the passage just translated above (in such-and such region there is a place called such-and such mountain, and so on). As for the geographical identifications of the peaks described in these passages, all appear to be mountains in or near India. Mount Clear-and-Cool, however, by the seventh century was already understood in China as an alternate name for Wutai.[39] Since references to Qingliang shan (or Wutai) as the home of Mañjuśrī are consistent in *Avataṃsaka-sūtra*, while those for Putuo and Emei are not (the names of the mountains and their resident bodhisattvas change in different versions of the scripture), and the fact that the size of Mañjuśrī's retinue (ten thousand) is larger than almost all of the other mountains (note in the passage translated above that the resident bodhisattva of Guangming shan "only" had three thousand followers), it seems likely that Mañjuśrī references to Qingliang shan (or Wutai) as the abode of Mañjuśrī served as an exemplar or model in the scriptural authentication processes used for Emei and Putuo. This makes sense, especially since Wutai achieved prominence as a "Buddhist mountain" well before Emei and Putuo. Thus, those persons seeking Buddhist scriptural authentication for Emei (and Putuo) would naturally be drawn to the "Dwelling Places of the Various Bodhisattvas" section of the *Huayan jing* to seek a geographical "match." Since Emei shan is in "southwestern region" of China, it is logical to identify it as Guangming shan, which has the same directional orientation,[40] even though there is no evidence in Buddhist scriptures to support this correlation.[41] Moreover, and perhaps even more important, the very name "Guangming" itself (lit., "luminous and bright") is easily associated with one of Emei shan's most distinguished temples, the Luminous Light Monastery, whose name was directly inspired by the Foguang. But we should note that in two separate Tang dynasty commentaries on the *Huayan jing*, Guangming is identified as a mountain in India, not China.[42] This issue is never raised, however, in the influential gazetteers of Hu Shian and Jiang Chao, both of whom cite the passage translated above as a key scriptural source for Emei's identification as a holy Buddhist mountain.[43] Only Yinguang, who revised Jiang Chao's gazetteer (in 1934), questioned use of the passage.[44]

A second problem is the names of the bodhisattvas mentioned in our two *Avataṃsaka-sūtra* passages (that is, the eighty- and sixty-*juan* versions): Xianshou and Xiansheng. Both are figures related to the *Avataṃsaka-sūtra*, but neither has a connection to Emei. So how, then, do we get from either Bhadramukha or *Bhadraka to Samantabhadra? Jiang Chao provides an easy solution to the problem by simply declaring: "*Bhadraka is, in fact, Samantabhadra."[45] Undoubtedly, this exegesis is forced. And yet, even though the discerning and critical gazetteer compiler Yinguang dismisses the Guangming shan identification with Emei, at the same time he enthusiastically draws a clear *religious parallel* between Emei's "light and lamps" (*guangdeng*; referring to the Foguang and sage lamps) and appearances of Samantabhadra on the summit.[46] Yinguang did so because he knew the grand theme of the *Huayan jing* (more specifically, the *Gaṇḍavyūha*) is pilgrimage and ultimate enlightenment. In the accounts of Sudhana's experiences, light imagery is often used to describe visions of bodhisattvas, including Samantabhadra. If religious or lay followers of Buddhism hoped to witness an appearance of Samantabhadra, then, the ideal place for such a visionary experience was Emei shan. This is a persuasive argument and it certainly contributed powerful fuel to the legitimization process.[47]

Pilgrims, Diaries, and Gazetteers

> *Oh, the sights {on Emei} are perfect indeed!*[48]
> —Cao Xuequan (1574–1646)

Three additional topics related to the legitimization process that merit discussion are (1) the role of religious and lay pilgrims who traveled to Emei shan in order to worship and pay homage to Samantabhadra; (2) the role of travel writings about Emei penned by literate visitors to the mountain; and (3) the role of the gazetteers.

The earliest mention of visitors to Mount Emei occurs in Wang Zhiwang's poem (translated in chapter 6), who during his ascent of Emei remarks: "Sojourning laymen come from afar, travelers fill the trail" (*yuansu laiyou ke tianlu* 遠俗来遊客填路). Despite its brevity, this report, if we can call it that, is valuable because Wang Zhiwang is one of only a few pre-Ming writers to say *anything* about travelers to Mount Emei. Who were these visitors? The meaning of *su* in Wang's line is clear: this term is used often in writings about mountains in China to refer to "common men" (*suren*), meaning the laity in general. The precise reference of *ke* (lit., "guests"), however, is not clear. Wang Zhiwang could be referring to travelers in general (like himself), or to religious pilgrims in particular (or both). In any case, his poem does confirm there were substantial numbers of "laymen" (*su*) and "travelers" (*ke*) climbing the mountain's trails in the twelfth century. A twelfth-century geographical treatise, the *Yudi jisheng* (preface dated 1221) notes that the Luminous Light Monastery (on the summit) served as the ultimate destination of travelers.[49] The absence of additional written testimony notwithstanding, it is safe to assume that many travelers, both religious and lay, visited Emei shan over the centuries. While this activity may have begun as early as the fifth century (following Huichi's visit and temple-building efforts), by the Tang there was certainly some pilgrim activity on the mountain. After Huitong's renovations in the ninth century, we know that there were at least five active Buddhist temples on Emei, so visitations probably increased at this time. And most important, after Emei was established as the *daochang* of Samantabhadra in the late tenth century, and the huge bronze statue of the Indian deity astride his white elephant was installed in the White Stream Monastery, the number of visitors to the mountain surely increased. Unfortunately, there is no data available from the Tang or Song to tell us how many monks may have resided in Emei's temples and how many people might have visited the mountain during those dynasties. There are at least two reasons for this. First, most lay visitors were probably illiterate and hence left no written reports of their experiences. As for literate visitors to the mountain before the Ming, we only have Fan Chengda's diary entries and a few scattered poems by various Southern Song and Yuan writers, who say nothing about visitor/pilgrim activity. Second, most of the earliest written records on Emei, which probably included gazetteers dating from the Song dynasty, were already lost by the late Ming and early Qing.[50] Nevertheless, despite the lack of data, since we are sure that some level of visitor activity was present on Emei in the twelfth century, we may safely assume that at least some of these travelers were lay and religious followers of Buddhism. Moreover, the bronze statue of Samantabhadra and the Foguang must have been powerful attractions to pilgrims. I would argue the very act of devoted followers of Buddhism journeying to Emei reinforced the process leading to the religious reorientation of the mountain. Many of these visitors surely made financial contributions to Emei's Buddhist community, which in turn helped with the physical reconstruction of the mountain (the building and refurbishing of temples, the fashioning of new images, and so on). And finally, these pilgrims, after returning home, most certainly circulated stories about the sights they witnessed on Emei and their experiences there, which may well have inspired others to plan a pilgrimage to the mountain.

The prose travel accounts and verses left by literate visitors to Mount Emei also play a decisive role in the legitimization process. Since the influence of the prose diaries seems to have been much greater than the poems, our attention below will focus on these works. Without a doubt, the prose record of Fan Chengda's ascent to the summit and sighting of Buddha's Glory is the most important and influential literary work ever written about Mount Emei. The account of his 1177 climb is quoted, in full, in all the Emei gazetteers, and is cited or mentioned in most Emei scholarship written since, especially works concerning the mountain's geography and the development of Buddhism there. Virtually all the major *youji* authors and gazetteer compilers of the Ming, Qing, and Republican eras who either visited or climbed Mount Emei acknowledge their admiration of and indebtedness to Fan Chengda's travel journal. This is understandable because Fan's account is the earliest extended description of Emei shan in Chinese letters, his diary entries are detailed and based on firsthand observations, and finally, his diary can stand on its own as an admirable work of literature. As far as the legitimization process is concerned, we should pay particular attention to the fact that Fan Chengda's *youji* presents Emei shan in a context that is completely Buddhist. He says nothing about the mountain's earlier Daoist tradition, and this is because for personal reasons he approached, climbed, and experienced the mountain in a totally Buddhist "context" or "state of mind." His description of Buddha's Glory—the religious climax of his Emei experience—sends a very clear message to readers: if they visit the mountain, and if they are worthy, perhaps they too might have such a vision. This promise, along with Emei's sublime scenery, inspired many later writer-officials to visit the mountain and write of their experiences (discussed below). These writings, along with Fan's diary entries and poems, collectively served to spread the idea that Emei shan is a "Buddhist mountain" where visionary miracles can and did take place.

The surviving literary record concerning Emei shan during the Yuan dynasty is meager, to say the least. Only a handful of poems survive and these, for the most part, offer only general scenic descriptions. Following Fan Chengda's effort, the next important travel account on Emei does not appear until more than three hundred years later. The author of this text, Wang Shixing (1547–1598), was a prominent Ming dynasty official who for more than twenty years served in a variety of government posts in the capital (Beijing) and the provinces. His passion was climbing "famous mountains." Wang not only toured all of the Five Cardinal Mounts, but also scaled numerous other scenic peaks throughout China, including Mount Emei. Wang Shixing climbed Emei shan in 1588 and, along with a retinue of the more than one hundred people, observed an appearance of the Foguang. His description of Buddha's Glory is unmistakably modeled after Fan Chengda's account, and on one occasion Wang even quotes a line from the Song writer's travel journal. Interestingly, in the final lines of his journal the Ming writer cites and then questions the *Huayan jing* reference to "Guangming shan" (translated and discussed earlier) and its connection to Emei, but then seems to grudgingly acknowledge that "since ancient times it has been recorded that Emei is the *daochang* of Samantabhadra."[51]

The next important writer to be considered, Yuan Zirang (fl. ca. 1600), is unique in that he authored both an influential *youji* essay and compiled a gazetteer titled *Jiazhou ershan zhi* (*Gazetteer on the Two Mountains of Jia County*; preface dated 1605). Yuan assumed the post of Administrator in Jia county in 1601 and in the following year made his first ascent of Emei. The administrator's timing was perfect, for as soon as he reached the summit Yuan Zirang beheld an especially magnificent appearance of the Foguang. A monk on the summit remarked to him: "Since ancient times noble travelers have waited for the Light up to ten days with no result. Sir, [news of] your good government has reached all the way to Heaven. This is why you saw the Light as soon as you arrived."[52] Not only did Yuan Zirang witness an appearance of the Foguang, but that evening also spied the sage lamps, which "flew through the air like snowflakes." The magnificent sights the administrator saw on Emei led him to exclaim: "Alas! Buddha's Glory and the sage lamps are both present on this mountain; the Snow Mountains and India can be seen from this mountain. Among those who make the ascent to gaze upon them, however, not even one in ten succeeds. And yet, during this impromptu, hasty journey of mine, these wonders have all been present. What a wonderful journey this has been!"[53]

Several prominent Qing dynasty officials and writers also visited Emei and left prose accounts of their experiences. Among these, Jiang Gao (*jinshi* 1661) deserves special mention. When he was a boy, Jiang had heard stories about Emei from his grandfather. Later in life, while serving as a government official in Sichuan, he took advantage of the opportunity and made a journey to Mount Emei. His visit is documented in a number of poems and a travel diary titled "Record of a Trip to E[mei] in the Xinhai Year" ("Xinhai you E ji"). The opening line of Jiang Gao's essay reads: "Emei is the premier mountain in China. It is the place where the Celestial

Sovereign was conferred the Way, and where Samantabhadra manifests his appearance. It is divine and wondrous, numinous and extraordinary. I am no longer in the mortal world."[54] Jiang's *youji* is quite detailed and throughout the text the Qing author reveals an intimate familiarity with the history of Emei shan. At the end of the diary he even mentions some of the works he studied in preparation for the trip to Emei, which include Fan Chengda's diary and Hu Shian's gazetteer (for which, see below). It should also be mentioned that Jiang Gao authored the "Stele Inscription on Mount Emei's Crouching Tiger Monastery" ("Emei shan Fuhu si beiji"), an important source on one of Emei's oldest and most distinguished temples.[55]

After Fan Chengda, the most important writer we need to consider is arguably Hu Shian (1593–1663), author of the *Yi elai*, the earliest surviving "mountain gazetteer" on Emei. A native of Jingyan (just east of Emei shan), Hu passed the *jinshi* examination in 1628.[56] Thereafter he embarked on a career as an official, eventually rising to a distinguished post in the Household Administration of the Heir-Apparent (Zhanshi fu). After the fall of the Ming, Hu Shian switched dynastic loyalties and served the new Qing regime, thereby maintaining his status as a government official. Hu eventually reached the rank of Grand Academician in the Hall of Military Glory (Wuying dian daxue shi), one of the most powerful offices in the central government. After the ascension of the emperor Shengzu (or Kangxi; r. 1662–1723), Hu Shian was appointed Grand Academician in the Hanlin Academy (Hanlin yuan da xueshi). A short time later, however, he was forced to retire because of poor health. It was during his retirement that Hu Shian completed work on the *Yi elai*. The importance of his gazetteer cannot be overemphasized. Not only is it the earliest extant gazetteer on Emei; it also served the key source text for all subsequent Emei gazetteers, including Jiang Chao's 1672 edition, which in turn served as the main source of Yinguang's revised and expanded edition of 1934. Without the *Yi elai* material, virtually all of which is incorporated in the Jiang Chao and Yinguang versions of the *Emei shan zhi*, these later gazetteers would have far less material on the early history of the mountain.[57]

Hu Shian was interested in Daoism and for this reason the *Yi elai* contains numerous references to adepts and immortals associated with Emei shan. But it would be unfair, I think, to describe the *Yi elai* as a "Daoist oriented" gazetteer.[58] Indeed, the very organization of the text into nine topical chapters on subjects as diverse as astral geography (*xingye*), descriptive topography (*xingsheng*), sketches and paintings (*tuhui*), occult surveys (*xuanlan*), religious reflections (*zongjing*), poems and ballads (*shige*), and so on, indicates the balanced, nonpartisan nature of the text (this organization follows the traditional topical arrangement in gazetteers). Each chapter includes numerous quotations, many from works no longer extant. The eighth chapter of the *Yi elai*, titled "Daoli ji" ("Account of Trails and Distances"), is especially valuable because it presents a detailed, descriptive itinerary of Hu Shian's climb of Mount Emei, presumably based mainly on his final ascent in 1639. In the closing lines of his account the author notes that even within the relatively short period between his first (1619) and last (1639) climbs, Emei was "different" (that is to say, some of the sites he saw during his first ascent were abandoned or gone by the time of his third climb twenty years later), and if readers compared his descriptions with those of Fan Chengda, even more changes would be apparent.[59]

The second Emei gazetteer—Jiang Chao's *Emei shan zhi* of 1672—is also an essential source. Jiang Chao passed his *jinshi* examination in 1647 and thereafter served in a number of mid- and high-level posts in the Qing government. In 1672 he asked for a furlough from his official duties because of illness. His request was granted and Jiang Chao then took up residence in the Crouching Tiger Monastery at the foot of Mount Emei. Jiang's gazetteer (in eighteen *juan*) was completed in the autumn of 1672, just before he died. In 1689, a monk from the Crouching Tiger Temple named Haiyuan arranged for printing blocks to be cut and the gazetteer printed. Jiang Chao's text underwent two later revisions: first, by Cao Xiheng in 1687 (an associate of Cao's, Song Yizhang, actually finalized the project, reorganizing the text into twelve *juan*), and later in 1934 (lead type edition, now in eight *juan*) by Xu Zhijing, under the direction of the Buddhist monk Master Yinguang.

The travelogues of Fan Chengda, Yuan Ziran, and others, along with the gazetteers of Hu Shian, Jiang Chao, and Yinguang, collectively play a critical role in the legitimization process. With the exception of the *Yi elai*,[60] all of these texts enjoyed wide circulation in China. Since the Buddhist history of Emei shan receives prominent attention in the *youji* and gazetteers, one could argue that the works under discussion served to "historicize" Mount Emei. That is to say, these texts establish a chronology and historical context in which Emei shan developed and changed over time. Tales recounting the activities of the Yellow Emperor and various immortals, the many accounts of Daoist recluses who populated the mountain through the ages, the numerous references to Chinese and foreign monks, the histories of the many temples, terraces, and other sites on the mountain, and much more, are repeated over and over in these works. Almost all of these texts, in their presentation of the history and evolution of Emei shan as a "famous mountain" in China, stress the Daoist-to-Buddhist conversion of the mountain. Listen to the words of Cao Xiheng who, in his preface to the *Emei shan zhi*, presents a brief history of religious activity on the mountain:

> At first, Emei shan served as the place where the Sovereign of Celestial Perfection (Tianzhen huangren), or Guangchengzi, dwelled.[61] The Yellow Emperor, Xuanyuan, inquired about the Way there, and received the scriptures of the Three Unities and Five Sprouts (Sanyi wuya).[62] Subsequently, [Emei] became the *daochang* of the bodhisattva Samantabhadra, a Conjured City (Huacheng) was devised,[63] and there dwelled [Samantabhadra's] great assembly of three thousand followers. There were appearances of Buddha's Glory and the sage lamps; monasteries and cloisters expanded and flourished; in out-of-the-way places incense was burned; the "layered calluses" came from far and near.[64] [Emei shan] was thereupon transformed into Śākyamuni's realm.[65]

It is precisely summations like this that served to historize Mount Emei's religious tradition and legitimize its connection to Buddhism. Travel accounts and poems written by "elite" pilgrims like Fan Chengda, and gazetteers compiled by high government officials like Hu Shian and Jiang Chao, were powerful tools in communicating this message. In addition to establishing a historical context for the development of religious activities on the mountain, the rich descriptions and miracle tales recounted in these texts, though only accessible to the literate public, still must have inspired many readers to personally visit Emei. Furthermore, the *youji* and gazetteers convey very precise information on what one could expect to see and where to see it. As amazing as it may seem, Fan Chengda's diary and Hu Shian's chapter on "Trails and Distances," in which he intentionally retraces the same route followed by his Southern Song predecessor, can still serve as "travel guides" for hikers, for the main trail to the summit still follows the same route and many of the places mentioned by Fan and Hu are amazingly, still there.[66]

FOUR GREAT FAMOUS MOUNTAINS

As we have now seen, selected mountains in China, for a variety of reasons, came to be associated with Buddhism. For instance, a particular sect might develop and flourish at a specific location. The Tiantai sect (Tiantai zong), associated with Mount Tiantai in Zhejiang, is a good example. Or a particular mountain might attract attention because a famous monk is known to have lived and practiced asceticism there. Huiyuan's activities on Mount Lu certainly influenced that mountain's long association with

Buddhism. Although many mountains in China have traditionally been associated with Buddhism, in the seventeenth century four of these sites were selected and identified as the "Four Great Famous [Buddhist] Mountains." This is an extremely important development in the history of Buddhism in China for, as already mentioned, it fixed the Buddhist geography of China. In other words, the four locations in question—Wutai, Emei, Putuo, and Jiuhua—were now designated as China's premier Buddhist mountains. How was this designation formulated and why?

Although numerous secondary works (especially works in Chinese) mention the "Four Great Famous [Buddhist] Mountains," and there is even a monograph published on the subject,[67] the authors of these works say very little about when the grouping took place. To my knowledge, Chün-fang Yü and Pan Guiming are the only modern scholars to address this issue. Referring to the expressions Sanda daochang ("Three Major [Buddhist] Manifestation Sites") and Sida mingshan, Chün-fang Yü notes: "By the late Ming, both expressions became widely used by writers of the *Gazetteer of P'u-t'o*."[68] Yu's reference is the 1698 edition of the *Zengxiu Nanhai Putuo shan zhi*, compiled by the monk Qiulian (dates unknown). The earliest reference I have found to the term Sida mingshan (referring unquestionably to Wutai, Emei, Putuo, and Jiuhua) appears in Cao Xiheng's preface to the *Emei shan zhi*, dated 1687: "The Three E [Mountains] are loftier than the Five Cardinal Mounts, and in beauty rank first in the Nine Regions (or China). [Collectively] they are the premier mountains in China. They have never been part of the Five Cardinal Mounts, but are one of the Four Great Famous Mountains."[69] We can be certain, then, that by the end of the seventeenth century Wutai, Emei, Putuo, and Jiuhua had already been grouped together as China's "Four Great Famous [Buddhist] Mountains." Furthermore, we know that as late as 1605 the phrase "Three Major [Buddhist] Manifestation Sites" was still in general use,[70] meaning that Jiuhua had yet to be named as China's fourth primary Buddhist mountain. This strongly suggests that the formulation "Sida mingshan" was devised sometime in the seventeenth century.

It is not known what person or persons first formulated the expression "Four Great Famous [Buddhist] Mountains." As far as I have been able to determine, the grouping of the four mountains was not the result of a formal declaration made by either the Buddhist church or the Qing government. Rather, the expression seems to have come into general use in the seventeenth century because of the premier status of Wutai, Emei, Putuo, and Jiuhua as "Buddhist mountains" at that time. This premier status was the direct result of developments that took place during Ming. The leadership role of Wutai, Emei, Putuo, and Jiuhua was based mainly on their long histories (transmitted in gazetteers and *youji*), association with particular bodhisattvas, and scriptural exegeses. Temple-building activity thrived during the Ming, and this was directly related to imperial patronage and increased pilgrim visits. On Mount Emei, for instance, pilgrim activities increased so much that the old trails on the mountain had to be improved and new ones had to be made.[71] As for Jiuhua, although sources on the early history of the mountain are not abundant, we know the eighth-century activities of Kim Kyo Gak led to the construction of a Buddhist temple complex there. It is reported that after the Korean monk died, his mummified corpse did not decompose after three years. Moreover, the ridge where the mummy was enshrined produced many colored lights. For this reason Kim came to be regarded by many people in the region as the bodhisattva Dizang (Skt. Kṣitgarbha).[72] As a result, by the end of the eighth century a substantial monastic community was already in place on the mountain.[73] Jiuhua continued to develop as a "Buddhist mountain" after the Tang. Many famous Song literati, including Wang Anshi (1021–1086), Mei Yaochen (1002–1060), and Zhou Bida (1126–1204), visited and wrote poems about their experiences there. By the Ming and Qing periods Jiuhua reached the peak of its development, with more than one hundred large and small temples on its slopes, many of them built with generous support received from Ming and Qing emperors. We also know that pilgrim activity on the mountain was substantial by the Ming. One modern scholar has even argued that beginning in the Ming (and extending into the modern period), the influence of Jiuhua and Putuo as "Buddhist mountains" among the laity exceeded that of Wutai and Emei, and that pilgrim activity on Jiuhua surpassed that of Putuo.[74]

The expression Four Greats (Sida 四大) is significant in Buddhist contexts. It has numerous references, but two are especially relevant to our discussion. First, "Sida" is often used to designate the "Four Great Bodhisattvas" in the *Lotus-sūtra*; namely, Mañjuśrī, Samantabhadra, Maitreya, and Avalokiteśvara. Second, the same expression is used to denote the four elements of which everything is made: earth, water, fire, and air (or wind). Based on this Indian Buddhist typology, each member of our quartet of mountains was assigned an element: Wutai represents air/wind; Emei is fire; Jiuhua symbolizes earth; and Putuo stands for water. Although we do not know who assigned these elements, the purpose is clear: it provides the Sida mingshan with an organizational unity that collectively denote *the* key sites on China's Buddhist map. For pilgrims this was important, for it provided a blueprint of China's sacred Buddhist geography. They now also knew that the four designated mountains were *the* most numinous and efficacious Buddhist sites in China, all of which hosted major bodhisattvas who not only appeared to the most devout, but who could (and did) work miracles.

THE BIG PICTURE

In this chapter I have attempted to outline the process whereby the religious orientation of Mount Emei was molded into a Buddhist framework. In many ways, my findings echo previous published research on other "Buddhist mountains" in China. For instance, in his work on Mount Wutai, Raoul Birnbaum has called attention to the importance of geological factors, especially caves; the creation of a new "built environment" that includes monastery construction, carving new images, and the addition of funerary monuments; recognition as a "site of manifestation" (*daochang*); and how space on Wutai was "reordered" through a Buddhist "occupation."[75] Yü Chün-fang, in her study of Putuo shan as a national and international pilgrimage center, discusses geographic factors such as island location and proximity to Ningbo; sūtra exegeses that identifies Putuo as the Chinese Potalaka; the role of founding myths in establishing Guanyin pilgrimage sites; miracle tales in building Putuo's reputation as a sacred place; and the role of gazetteers and literary works in creating a Buddhist history of Putuo shan.[76]

It is certain that there are recurrent patterns in the process that established Buddhist identities for Wutai, Putuo, and Emei. My limited research and reading on Mount Jiuhua suggests that many of these same configurations of development are detectable in the history of that mountain as well. Now, although a serious comparative study of the "Four Great Famous [Buddhist] Mountains" would tell us much more about these patterns of development, based on the research of Birnbaum, Yü, myself, and others, it seems possible to sketch at least a preliminary outline of the process that resulted the "Buddhaization" of sacred space in China. Following is a list of the essential elements of that paradigm, presented roughly in the order they occur:

- Each mountain is identified as hosting an extraordinary (*qi*) physical environment conducive to retreat and asceticism.

- Each mountain initially attracts Daoist attention.

- Daoist space on each mountain is later reordered into a Buddhist configuration.

- Creation myths are fashioned to explain the Buddhist history of the mountain.

- Exegeses of Buddhist scriptures establish each mountain as the home of a major bodhisattva.

- Imperial patronage is conferred upon the mountain, which enhances its legitimacy as a state-sanctioned holy site.

- Sightings of the bodhisattva are reported in literary works and then documented in the gazetteers, thereby attracting lay and religious pilgrims.

- Continued imperial patronage and development during the Ming leads to the formulation of the "Four Great Famous [Buddhist] Mountains" in the seventeenth century.

Finally, a few additional remarks on a subject mentioned earlier: Mount Wutai and its role as an "exemplar Buddhist mountain" in China. Wutai's earliest historical connection with Buddhism probably dates from the Northern Wei dynasty (386–534)—roughly, the same time that Huichi reportedly built the first temple on Mount Emei.[77] Hence, the Buddhist history of Wutai is roughly the same as that of Emei shan. What is different, however, is that Buddhism *developed earlier* on Wutai. The reasons for this have yet to be fully addressed by scholars, but geography certainly plays a role. Not only does Wutai host an extraordinary physical environment, but the capital of the Northern Wei dynasty, which actively promoted Buddhism, was initially in Datong, not far from Wutai (in 494 the capital was moved to Luoyang). Whatever the reason(s), by the reign of Tang emperor Gaozong (r. 649–684) Buddhism was flourishing on the mountain. The scriptural authentication process, which interpreted Mount Clear-and-Cool as Wutai shan, is acknowledged in the very opening lines of Huixiang's (596–667) *Gu Qingliang zhuan*.[78] By the seventh century (and probably earlier), Wutai was already recognized as the *daochang* of Mañjuśrī. The diary entries of the Japanese pilgrim Ennin (794–864) confirm that the Tang imperial treasury made huge donations to monasteries dedicated to Mañjuśrī.[79] There is no doubt that Wutai was the most important and influential Buddhist mountain in China during the Tang dynasty.

Birnbaum has remarked: "A significant factor underlying the initial inspiration to establish a cultic center at P'u-t'o Shan may well have been the example of Wu'tai Shan."[80] I would advance this argument a step further and contend that Wutai first served as a model or exemplar mountain for Emei, then later for Putuo, and finally for Jiuhua. As for Emei, this is perhaps most evident in the scriptural authentication process, described earlier, which closely follows the one made for Wutai during the Tang. That Emei would "adopt" Samantabhadra as its own bodhisattva makes perfect sense, for in Buddhist history, iconography, and scripture Mañjuśrī and Samantabhadra are often paired in their roles as the right- and left-hand assistants of Buddha. Mañjuśrī is the personification of wisdom (*zhi*); Samantabhadra is the personification of practice (*xing*). The relationship between the two bodhisattvas is complementary in almost every respect. Together they symbolize two aspects of perfect enlightenment. But the development of this complementary relationship raises a fascinating question: since China already had a premier Buddhist mountain (Wutai) during the Tang, what need or reason was there to sanctify additional "Buddhist mountains," beginning with Emei in the early Song and then following with Putuo and Jiuhua later?

As already mentioned, the primary motivation for granting imperial patronage to Emei by the Song emperors Taizu and Taizong was political. Perhaps inspired by the many problems created by the Buddhist church during the Tang that led to the Huichang persecutions in 845, maintaining control of the saṃgha was a central issue underlying Song dynasty policies vis-à-vis Buddhism. In light of this concern, could one motivation behind imperial patronage for Emei shan in the early Song have been the creation of a *second*, or *alternate* center of Buddhism in China? In other words, could those early Song emperors, especially Taizong, have thought that by diffusing the power center of the religion (Wutai) and then carefully crafting the development of two (and later three) additional *daochang*, they could better control the church and its influence? This seems quite possible, even likely.

Now a brief, historical digression: During the Southern Song an imperially designated arrangement for the classification and control of important Buddhist holy sites and institutions was put into place. This system was called the "Five Mountains and Ten Monasteries" (Wushan shicha 五山十刹), or "Five Mountains" for short. As indicated by the title, it comprised ten monasteries that stood on five appointed mountains. With just a few exceptions, these mountains and monasteries were all located either in or near the Southern Song capital at Hangzhou. The "ten monasteries" were all classified by the government as Chan institutions, all had imperial plaques, and all had received generous donations and gifts from the imperial family. Emperors bestowed samples of their writing on these institutions, literati made visits and wrote poems that extolled their splendor and glory, and practitioners and visitors flocked to them on a daily basis. This system was confined to southeast China because the Jin invasions in the twelfth century had caused a huge population shift into the Jiangnan region. By the end of the twelfth century the southeast had become *the* political and commercial center of the Song empire, or what was left of it.

According to the prominent Ming writer and official Song Lian (1310–1381), the "Five Mountains" system had been devised by Shi Miyuan (1164–1233), a powerful Southern Song state minister active during the reign of emperor Ningzong (r. 1194–1224).[81] The "Ten Monasteries" were ranked like government offices and institutes in the Song bureaucracy. Ranks were also established for monks who, for meritorious service, could be promoted to higher positions in the "bureaucracy" that "governed" the Five Mountains and their various monasteries. Decisions regarding promotion were made by the Southern Song government. Although Song Lian and others viewed the creation of this system as an attempt to secularize Chan, one could also justifiably view the Five Mountains system as an instrument created by the Song government to control the saṃgha. After the founding of the Ming dynasty in 1368, a three-tier classification system for monasteries in the capital at Nanjing was put into place. This was done so chief monk-officials of the Ming, all recommended to the emperor by government ministers (later, after the 1606 regulations were promulgated, candidates for abbot had to take examinations given by the Ministry of Rites), could conveniently supervise all the monasteries in the realm, just as the central government supervised all the people.[82] The Ming three-tier system is explained in a government document, dating from 1606, titled "Rules and Regulations on Monks and Monasteries" ("Gesi senggui tiaoli"). In many ways, this classification scheme essentially was a renewed expression of the "Five Mountains" system of the Southern Song, but applied only to monasteries in Nanjing. Clearly, it reveals that government policy concerning Buddhist monasteries was primarily civil and administrative in nature.[83]

Michael J. Walsh has demonstrated that although the "ten monasteries" were powerful institutions with large landholdings, a given monastery's capital could be confiscated by the Song government at anytime and for just about any reason.[84] Of course, there were benefits derived from supporting these institutions. These came mainly in the form of rituals and ceremonies, performed by monks, on behalf of the emperor and the state. But the point here is that these institutions were always vulnerable to government authority. Moreover, since they were classified under the Song as "public monasteries" (shifang), abbots were appointed by the government. Surely one reason this system was created in the first place was to better monitor and control the activities of the Buddhist church.

Now, to return to our earlier discussion, is it a coincidence that in 980, the year Taizong mandated the casting in Chengdu of Mount Emei's famous bronze statue of Samantabhadra and his white elephant, the emperor also directed that a bronze image of Mañjuśrī, likewise gilded with gold dust, be cast and placed in the True Appearance Cloister (Zhen-rong yuan) on Wutai? Is it fortuitous circumstance that Taizong, in that *same year*, ordered that Wutai's "ten monasteries" *and* Emei's "five monas-teries" all be rebuilt?[85] Finally, is it simply a case of happenstance that during the Northern Song calligraphy samples from Taizong, Zhenzong, and Renzong were presented to and then housed in key temples on both Emei and Wutai, all at about the same time?[86] In Northern Song times, especially during the reigns of Taizong, Renzong, and Shenzong, although acts of imperial patronage were extended to many mountains throughout China, the focus of these efforts was undoubtedly on Wutai and Emei. Judging from the sources available, which are quite adequate, it was the intentional policy of the Northern Song government to promote *two* com-plementary centers of Buddhism, one in the north (Wutai), one far away in the distant southwest (Emei). Later, in the eleventh and twelfth centu-ries, when Putuo achieved status and legitimization as the cult site of Guanyin, a third premier "Buddhist mountain" was added, but this time in southeastern China—far away from the other two centers. Was geogra-phy a factor in this decision? In other words, was the idea to apportion the centers of Buddhism in different parts of the country so as to better control them? Again, this seems like a distinct possibility. In any case, the Jin invasions and subsequent "recentering" of China in the southeast in the twelfth century removed the need to "manage" Wutai and Emei any further. By the 1120s Mount Wutai was already in Jin-held territory in north China, while Emei was in faraway Sichuan, thousands of miles away from the exile capital in Hangzhou. Could the "Five Mountains and Ten Monasteries" system have been inspired by earlier efforts to balance the power and influence of Wutai and Emei? Perhaps, but again we'll probably never find an answer to this question. What we can be sure of is this: by the seventeenth century the power and influence of "ten monasteries" was confined to the southeast. They no longer served as *national* Buddhist centers. At the same time, Wutai, Emei, Putuo, and now Jiuhua had achieved status as the supreme "Buddhist mountains" in China. How and why Emei shan achieved this position during the Ming period is discussed in the next chapter.

CHAPTER 8

The Ming, Qing, Republican, and Modern Eras

This final chapter surveys developments on Mount Emei over an unusually long span of time—from the fall of the Southern Song in the late thirteenth century to the present. Given the chronological breadth of the period under consideration, at best I can only address highlights of major events related to the mountain and its development. Despite the obvious limitations of covering so much material in a single chapter, this overview is essential, for not only will it bring us up to date about what happened on Emei shan after Fan Chengda's visit, but more important, will provide additional insights concerning social, economic, and political forces and how they have continued to develop and shape the mountain's place and space and adapt it to new demands and circumstances.

A BLOODY INTERLUDE

> *In the eleventh year (or 1275), {the Mongol commander Wang Liangchen} advanced and attacked Jiading. . . . He advanced on the ramparts and besieged the city. {Zan} Wanshou and his troops emerged to fight. They suffered a major defeat. Corpses of {Song loyalists} filled the {Min} River.*[1]

In 1236, less than sixty years after Fan Chengda climbed Mount Emei, Mongol troops surrounded and attacked Chengdu. This military operation was part of a general campaign to conquer all of China, beginning in Sichuan and then moving eastward into the heartland of the country. By January 1237 "fifty-four counties in Sichuan had been plundered; only the Kuizhou circuit and Lu, Guo, and He counties remained."[2] The *History of the Yuan* reports specifically that in that same year Jia (now officially known as Jiading) and Emei town were both crushed by cavalry led by the Mongol commander Wang Shixian (1195–1243).[3] Despite these initial military successes, however, Mongol armies met stiff resistance from

Song forces in Shu. Fighting continued intermittently over the next forty years, during which time Jiading was attacked on at least ten occasions. Since the county and the mountainous regions surrounding it together served as a key resistance base against the Mongol conquerors, numerous battles were fought in and around Jiading in the 1250s, 1260s, and 1270s. Decades of fighting had a devastating effect on the county. Numerous people fled the area, agricultural production came to a standstill, and famine was common everywhere.

What effect did the tense military situation in Jiading during the final decades of the Southern Song have on the development of Mount Emei during the subsequent Yuan dynasty? The sources provide no answer to this question, mentioning only the construction of a few temples and visits by officials. The gazetteers and bibliographies cite only scant references to visits dating from the Yuan,[4] which suggests that sightseer activity on the mountain during the Mongol occupation was occasional at best. A handful of poems about Emei dating from the Yuan have survived,[5] but they only offer standard scenic descriptions and say nothing specific about the mountain. The general silence of the sources and paucity of surviving literary works lead to only one conclusion: little activity and development, if any, took place on Emei shan during the Yuan dynasty. This at first may seem surprising, especially since it is well known that the Mongol rulers patronized Buddhism. But their main interest was Lamaism (Lama jiao), a form of the religion practiced in Tibet. Support for Han (or Chinese) Buddhism was limited, and there is no evidence of imperial patronage of Emei shan during the Yuan.[6] Moreover, after the pacification of Sichuan in 1279, the three main sources of support upon which Emei's monastic community had previously relied—imperial patronage, pilgrim and sightseer donations, and local lay supporters—were all cut off. Most people in Sichuan at this time were simply trying to survive. Many did not. According to one estimate, seven or eight people out of ten in Sichuan died as a result of the Song-Yuan war.[7] Consider the following figures, which are astounding: in 1223 the total population of Sichuan was around 6.6 million,[8] but by 1290 that number had fallen to about 616,000.[9] Although these figures do not tell us how many people died in the fighting as opposed to how many fled to other areas for safety, it is certain that the Song-Yuan war took a severe toll on human life in Sichuan.

By the middle of the fourteenth century several rebellions broke out to challenge Yuan authority. These uprisings led to military clashes between rebel forces seeking to overthrow the dynasty and the Mongol armies hoping to maintain control of China. We know of at least one Emei temple—the Luminous Forest Monastery (Guanglin si)—that was destroyed during fighting in the late 1360s.[10] No doubt other temples on the mountain suffered a similar fate. In any case, monasteries, shrines, and other structures that survived the Song-Yuan transition were probably in a severe state of disrepair by the middle of the fourteenth century, for with sources of support cut off it seems highly likely that little or no maintenance was performed on these buildings during the Yuan. Conditions would not stabilize until 1368, when a rebel army led by a military commander named Zhu Yuanzhang (r. 1368–1398) defeated the Mongols and proclaimed the founding of the Ming dynasty.

FLORESCENCE IN THE MING

During the Wanli reign, the Samantabhadra Hall in the Myriad Years Monastery was constructed on command of the emperor's mother.[11]

Despite the generally unfavorable conditions on Mount Emei during the Yuan, the subsequent Ming period saw the mountain flourish as it had never done before. This is especially the case with respect to the number of Buddhist monasteries and shrines on Emei, which increased dramatically. The florescence of Buddhism on Emei shan during the Ming is directly attributable to one source: patronage. As we will see below, support for the mountain, which came from different sources and in various forms, was substantial. Indeed, patronage of Buddhism on Mount Emei during the Ming surpassed even that of the Song period.

Before turning to specific developments on Emei shan, it might be useful to mention briefly some general trends in Buddhism during the Ming and how these developments were similar to or different from our earlier discussions on the Song. First, the close relationship that existed between Buddhism and the state during the Song continued after Zhu Yuanzhang founded the Ming dynasty in 1368. Like their predecessors, Ming rulers considered it proper that the monastic community and its activities be subject to state supervision. Hence, ordination procedures, the construction of monasteries, and the activities of monks and nuns all came under close scrutiny. This posture closely parallels church-state relations in the Song, when support of Buddhism was predicated on the idea that the church, in return for patronage, would provide assistance and blessings to both state and emperor. A second important point is this: state sponsorship of Buddhism is probably best evidenced by direct imperial support for eminent monks and notable institutions, especially monasteries. Ming rulers and their relatives were especially generous in this regard. At the same time, however, Zhu Yuanzhang and his descendants, like their predecessors in the Song, on many occasions undertook measures to exert control over the saṃgha. One special concern was placing limits on the number of Buddhists allowed in society. Yet despite such government efforts, the number of ordinations of Buddhist and Daoist monks continued to increase in the Ming. In 1372, there were 57,200 Buddhist and Daoist ordinations. The following year the number jumped to 96,328. Thereafter age restrictions (20) were instituted, as were examinations to test the knowledge of monks. In 1418 further rules were imposed, limiting the number of annual ordinations in each county (*zhou*) to thirty, and each town (*xian*) to twenty. And yet, despite these restrictions, in 1486 about 200,000 Buddhist monks and nuns took ordination vows. If this figure is any indication, the effectiveness of Ming control measures to limit the size of the Buddhist Order is questionable.[12] In any case, it seems certain that efforts by Ming emperors and their administrations to control the power of the church did not in any significant way restrict the influence of Buddhism in Chinese society. On the contrary, the religion seems to permeate almost every level of Ming culture. One reason this happened was because of the strong desire among church leaders to make Buddhism more accessible to lay followers of the religion. The result was that Buddhism became an active force in society, especially in the lives of common people; much more so, it seems, than during the Song.[13] In short, Buddhism thrived during the Ming and, as we will see shortly, Mount Emei benefited directly as a result.

Zhu Yuanzhang became a novice at the age of seventeen and spent the next eight years of his life living in a Buddhist temple in Anhui. His early connections to Buddhism no doubt favorably disposed him toward the religion. Zhu supported Buddhism in a positive, active way, especially during his first decade of rule.[14] Since most monasteries in China were damaged or destroyed during the Yuan-Ming transition, the new emperor's initial support efforts focused on rebuilding damaged temples or erecting new ones. Some of these projects, especially those in large cities, were massive, requiring huge labor forces and extravagant budgets. Construction and rebuilding efforts supported by the emperor were also carried out in the provinces and on "famous Buddhist mountains," including Mount Emei. In 1369, just one year after assuming power, Zhu Yuanzhang dispatched Baotan (1334–1393), a former acquaintance and now eminent monk from the Heavenly Precincts Monastery (Tianjie si) in Nanjing, on a special mission to Mount Emei. The emperor instructed Baotan to take up residence on the mountain, where he would supervise construction of the Iron Tile Hall (Tiewa dian) and commission the casting of a gold image of Samantabhadra, to be placed inside the hall. All costs would be paid by the imperial treasury. Iron Tile Hall was part of a temple complex on the summit of Emei shan formerly known as the Luminous Light Monastery. This is the same temple visited by Fan Chengda two centuries earlier. Baotan had the roof of the new temple covered with iron tiles so as to protect it from the harsh weather conditions on the summit; hence the name Iron Tile Hall. The fact that the emperor, in the second year of his reign, would dispatch a renowned capital monk to distant Sichuan in order to supervise a construction project dedicated to Samantabhadra demonstrates that Zhu Yuanzhang regarded Emei shan as a key Buddhist religious site in China.

Baotan resided on Emei for about ten years, where he "refined the Rules of Buddha" (*jielü jingjin*) and "through noble deeds converted others to the Truth" (*daohua daxing*).[15] The actions and deeds of Baotan, funded and supported by the emperor, ignited resurgence in Buddhist activity on Emei shan.[16] After his work was completed Baotan returned to Nanjing, where he died in 1393. Zhu Yuanzhang personally wrote a funerary address for his old friend's burial ceremony and later conferred upon him the prestigious title State Preceptor (Guoshi).

Judging from reports in the gazetteers, virtually every Buddhist structure on Mount Emei experienced some level of restoration during the Ming. Several major new temples were built as well. Support for these efforts came from three sources: imperial patronage, regional supporters (most of whom were high government officials), and local benefactors. The results had a profound impact on the physical face of Emei shan. According to Hu Shian, at the end of the Ming there were more than seventy active Buddhist temples on the mountain, virtually all of which were dedicated to the worship of Samantabhadra.[17] This is more than double the number of Buddhist monasteries mentioned by Fan Chengda. One modern scholar estimates that there were over seventeen hundred Buddhist monks permanently living on Mount Emei during the Wanli reign (1573–1620).[18]

The history of temple restoration and construction on Emei during the Ming dynasty is long and complex. Details about the state of Emei's monastic community at the end of the Ming are provided by Hu Shian in the *Yi elai*. Based on a careful reading of this text and other gazetteers, I have compiled an inventory, arranged chronologically, of the major temple-building and restoration projects carried out on Mount Emei during the Ming. This list, which follows below, is not intended to serve as a complete history of monastic activity on the mountain from the fourteenth to seventeenth centuries. My aim is to provide a summary of some of the more important efforts and developments.[19]

- Early Ming: The monks Hongyi (fourteenth cent) and Yuandao (fourteenth cent) rebuild the Numinous Cliff Monastery, also known as the Luminous Forest Monastery (Guanglin si), which had been destroyed during the Yuan-Ming transition.

- Early Ming: The Clear Tones Gallery is built by the monk Guangji (fourteenth cent), a former acquaintance of the emperor Zhu Yuanzhang.

- 1369–1379: Baotan builds the Iron Tile Hall on the summit.

- ca. 1400: The monk Guangyuan (fl. ca. 1400) successfully petitions the throne for funds to refurbish the Huayan Monastery.

- 1465: The emperor Xianzong (or Zhu Jianshen; r. 1465–1488) presents the Numinous Cliff Monastery with a name plaque.

- 1465–1487: The Samantabhadra Hall (Puxian dian) is erected on the grounds of the Central Peak Monastery with funds provided by Prince Fan of Shu (Shu Fanwang), a member of the imperial family.[20]

- 1466: Zhu Huaiyuan, a member of the Ming imperial family, provides funds to refurbish the Universal Light Hall (Puguang dian). He pays all costs for the project, which is completed in 1469.[21]

- 1488–1505: The Numinous Cliff Monastery is expanded. At the height of its development the temple's grounds include forty-eight buildings.[22]

- 1508: "Master Wang (Wanggong) of Neijiang" provides funds to restore the Sagely Accumulation Monastery.[23]

- 1522–1566: The monastery complex on Giant Toon Tree Flat is rebuilt by the renowned Zen Master Chushan (Chushan chanshi).

- 1597: Wan Ren, Governor of Sichuan (Sichuan xunfu), and Yang Guoming, Provincial Administration Commissioner (Buzheng shi), provide funds to rebuild the Welcome Hall (Jieyin dian).[24]

- 1600: The Empress-Dowager Cisheng (Cisheng huang taihou; also known as Lady Li; 1546–1614) provides funds to reconstruct the Samantabhadra Hall, which in 1599 had been destroyed by fire.

- 1601–1602: The monk Fudeng (also known as Miaofeng; 1540–1613) oversees construction of the Brick Hall on the grounds of the White Steam Monastery, built specifically to house the famous statue of Samantabhadra cast in Chengdu in the 980s.

- 1603: Fudeng raises funds and completes construction on the Bronze Hall (Tongdian) on the summit.

- 1612: The abbot Mujiong constructs the Immortal Peak Monastery (Xianfeng si). The timbers of the monastery were covered with tin and its tiles were made of iron.

The highpoint of imperial patronage for Mount Emei occurs during the Wanli reign. This development coincides with the renewed interest or revival of Buddhism in the late Ming studied and described by Yü Chün-fang and Timothy Brook.[25] Although the reclusive emperor Zhu Yijun (Shenzong; r. 1573–1620) and his mother the Empress-Dowager Cisheng were both involved in the imperial patronage process, the emperor's mother was the most active. A fervent believer and supporter of Buddhism, she sponsored numerous activities related to the religion and even styled herself the "Nine-Lotus Bodhisattva" (Jiulian pusa). While serving as concubine to the emperor Zhu Zaihou (Muzong; r. 1567–1572) she bore him two sons and a daughter. Her first-born son, Yijun, became emperor at age nine. Posterity knows him as Shenzong or the "Wanli emperor." After Zhu Yijun ascended the Dragon Throne in 1573, his mother was designated empress-dowager and exercised supreme authority in state affairs. She was the driving force behind state support of Buddhist temple building and related endeavors in the late sixteenth and early seventeenth centuries.

Legend relates that the empress-dowager traveled to Mount Emei in 1562, when she was still serving as an imperial concubine. While visiting the mountain the empress-dowager reportedly made the following vow before an image of Samantabhadra: "If, in the future, I give birth to an heir apparent, I will then have a clay image of the bodhisattva made with its body covered with gold."[26] The following year (1563) she gave birth to Zhu Yijun. This event, tradition says, explains why Zhu and his mother were so supportive of Emei shan. While the origins of this story are dubious, the empress-dowager did indeed have a special interest in Mount Emei, but it was probably not directly related to birth of the heir apparent. Rather, it was a Chan monk named Fudeng, also known as Miaofeng (this was his *hao*, or nickname). This is the same monk mentioned in the chronology above, who was involved in various building projects on Emei shan in the early seventeenth century. Fudeng is one of the most fascinating Buddhist figures associated with Mount Emei. A closer look at his life and accomplishments will reveal some useful details on how the imperial patronage process actually worked during the Ming and how it benefited Mount Emei. What immediately distinguishes Fudeng is not so much his strong dedication to the faith, but the fact that he was also a skilled architect and civil engineer.

Fudeng hailed from Pingyang, Shanxi. Early in life he had the good fortune to meet Zhu Junzha (d. 1603), a member of the imperial Ming family who, because he was impressed with the young monk's potential to accomplish great deeds, became his protector, supporter, and advisor. The Ming prince not only financed Fudeng's early pilgrimage to Mount Putuo, but also once dispatched the monk to Beijing in order to locate copies of some rare Buddhist texts. While in the capital Fudeng met up with Deqing (also known as Hanshan Deqing; 1546–1623), a former acquaintance in Nanjing.[27] After their work in the Beijing was finished in 1573, the two monks traveled to Mount Wutai with the intent of settling there. While at Wutai, Fudeng and Deqing convened a huge gathering of monks and laymen to celebrate transcriptions each had completed of the *Huayan jing*. While copying out the scripture, Deqing had used ink made from his own blood mixed with a gold-based powder. When the empress-dowager heard about this deed she contributed gold paper for his use. The prayer assembly organized by Deqing and Fudeng took place in late 1581 and early 1582, in the Pagoda Cloister Monastery (Tayuan si) on Wutai. The temple had been restored a few years earlier with support from the empress-dowager. While the Wutai meeting was in progress the empress-dowager had sent messengers to several Buddhist and Daoist holy sites around the country, including Wutai, asking monks and adepts to pray for the birth of an heir apparent for her son, the emperor Shenzong. Her petition was included in the daily prayers at the Wutai meeting. Ten months later the emperor's first son was born, and Fudeng and Deqing's prayer assembly was credited as being responsible for this propitious event. Out of gratitude, the empress-dowager asked Fudeng to design and build the Avataṃsaka Monastery on Mount Luya (Luya shan) in Shanxi. From that moment forward, "the imperial treasury was open to any temple building that Fudeng might propose."[28]

Around 1599 Fudeng conceived an idea that he hoped would result in one of his life's greatest achievements: to erect bronze halls (*tongdian*) on each of China's three key Buddhist mountains: Wutai, Emei, and Putuo. This idea seems to have been inspired by another member of the imperial family, Zhu Xiaoyong (fl. late sixteenth cent), who in 1580 had been enfeoffed as Prince of Shen (Shenwang). When Fudeng visited Zhu Xiaoyong in Lu'an, Shanxi, probably in 1599, he discovered that the prince was in the process of casting a bronze, gilded image of Samantabhadra, which he intended to send to Emei shan. The monk then told Zhu Xiaoyong how he had dreamed about building bronze halls on Emei, Wutai, and Putuo. When Zhu asked about the costs involved, Fudeng said each hall would cost "10,000 gold" (*wanjin*). The prince immediately agreed to finance the project.[29] In addition to receiving generous support from the Prince of Shen and empress-dowager, Fudeng's various Emei projects were also supported by some high-ranking officials, including his good friend Wang Xiangqian (*jinshi* 1571; d. 1630), who served as governor of Sichuan province from 1601 to 1605.[30]

Judging from descriptions in the gazetteers, the bronze hall constructed by Fudeng on the summit of Mount Emei was magnificent. Known variously as the Eternally Bright Lotus Depository Monastery (Yongming Huazang si), the Samantabhadra Hall, or simply the "Bronze Hall," it was flanked by four bronze pagodas (two of these survive). The hall's tiles, posts, rafters, window lattice, and walls were all made of bronze and painted gold. A map was carved above and below the windows that portrayed the steep and precipitous trails leading to the summit of Emei. The hall stood approximately 9.5 m/32 ft high, about 4.1 m/14 ft across, and roughly 4.4 m/15 ft deep. The image of Samantabhadra in the hall was surrounded by "ten thousand Buddhas" (most likely, these were gilded relief panels). South of the hall was the Lotus Depository Tower (Huazang lou), which served as a library. On the main gate of the hall was engraved a map that highlighted scenic mountains and rivers in Shu.[31] It was said that on sunny days Fudeng's hall reflected a profusion of golden light. This, as it turns out, accounts for the name "Golden Summit."[32] Because of Fudeng's many accomplishments, in 1612 he was posthumously granted the prestigious title "True and Proper Son of Buddha" (Zhenzheng fozi).

The story of Fudeng's accomplishments on Mount Emei reveals a general pattern discernible in the experiences of other temple-building monks on Emei during the Ming. I refer here to a small group of extremely capable priests who, because of their great piety and admirable deeds, attracted the attention of capital, regional, and local supporters. This resulted in substantial support for the mountain. Another good example is the priest Biechuan. This is the same monk mentioned in chapter 5, who raised funds to cast the giant bronze bell originally housed in the Sagely Accumulation Monastery. In 1573, the first year of his reign, the emperor Shenzong (or, to be more precise, his mother the empress-dowager) heard about Biechuan's good deeds on Emei and summoned him to Nanjing for an audience. One of these accomplishments involved Biechuan's planting (in 1567) of azalea trees along the trail from the Clear Tones Gallery to the Forest of Ancient Virtue (Gude lin). As he planted each tree Biechuan and his followers would chant a line from the *Lotus-sūtra*, and for each character recited he would perform one bow or obeisance. Tan Zhongyue, a late Qing dynasty official who served as administrator of Jiading, claims to have counted the number of azalea trees along the trail, which number 69,707.[33] This figure, Tan says, matches precisely the total number of characters in the *Lotus-sūtra*. After Biechuan arrived in the capital he was lavished with numerous gifts, including a coveted purple robe (*ziyi*), a copy of the *Huayan jing*, and various Buddhist accoutrements. He was also

174

Fig. 8.1 *Flying Snow at Mt. O-mei* (Emei): Winter landscape with travelers (*Emei feixue tu* 峨眉飛雪圖); by Chang Ku (Zhang Gu) 章谷 (act. ca. 1640–1689), 1666. Hanging scroll: ink and colors on silk. University of California, Berkeley Art Museum; on extended loan from the Ching Yüan Chai Collection, CC. 21. Photographed for the University of California, Berkeley Art Museum by Benjamin Blackwell.

granted the prestigious title "Magnanimous and Beneficial Chan Master" (Hongji chanshi). A final example is Wuqiong (1536–1603). In 1591 Wuqiong left Mount Emei and embarked on a fund-raising tour of Hunan, Hubei, Guizhou, and Chengdu. Funds gathered during this trip were used to purchase bronze, which Wuqiong utilized to cast an image of Guanyin for Emei shan. The finished statue stood over 8.9 m/30 ft tall and was so heavy that workers could not transport it up the mountain. Wuqiong then went to Beijing to seek the empress-dowager's help. She immediately provided support to build a new monastery just outside Emei town, where the statue was housed. This structure was named the Great Buddha Monastery (Dafo si).[34]

It is perhaps worth noting that none of Emei's most famous monks during the Ming, including Baotan, Fudeng, Biechuan, and Wuqiong, were natives of Jiading and the surrounding region. All had either been dispatched there by the emperor (Baotan) or empress-dowager (Fudeng), or attracted by the mountain's reputation as a premier Buddhist holy site in China (Biechuan and Wuqiong). The success of their collective efforts, along with sustained patronage from the capital, served to attract even more eminent monks to the mountain, including at least one priest from Japan and another from Sri Lanka.[35] The presence of these monks on Emei further enhanced the domestic and international prestige and reputation of the mountain.

Another important form of imperial support during the Ming is the conferral of Buddhist texts, especially copies of the *Tripiṭaka*. Temples and individual monks on Emei shan both received such gifts. For instance, in 1460 the emperor Yingzong (r. 1436–1439; restored 1457–1464) sent a copy of the *Buddhist Canon* to the Numinous Cliff Monastery on Emei.[36] This temple, located on the summit next to the Beholding-the-Buddha Terrace, became one of the largest monastic complexes on Emei during the Ming.[37] Writing in the late nineteenth century, Tan Zhongyue notes that from front to back the temple grounds measured "over ten *li*," and that within the complex were "forty-eight towers and halls."[38] And in 1599, 1612, and 1614 additional copies of the *Tripiṭaka* were presented to the Myriad Years, Immortal Peak, and Eternally Bright Lotus Depository Treasury monasteries, respectively.[39] The person responsible for conferring these and other gifts (too numerous to mention here) was the empress-dowager Cisheng. In order to express gratitude, the monastic community on Emei erected the Compassionate Sagacity Tower (Cisheng lou) on the grounds of the White Steam Monastery, and the Compassionate Sagacity Retreat (Cisheng an), just outside the monastery. Wuqiong directed the construction. On some occasions copies of the *Buddhist Canon* were presented to individual monks. For instance, in 1573 Biechuan was presented with a copy of the *Huayan jing* in twenty-four sections. Mujiong was also conferred texts. The scriptures he received were lauded by the emperor himself as a complete version of the *Tripiṭaka*, in 678 cases (*han*), and intended to express his respect toward Heaven and the Buddhist patriarchs and hope for continued prosperity in the world.[40]

Another important form of imperial patronage and control we cannot overlook is the granting of name plaques (*ti'e*; also called *ci'e* or *biane*). Name plaques are essentially horizontal wooden signboards, displayed in front of a monastery to announce imperial recognition and confer status. Use of *ti'e* began in the Six Dynasties, and continued throughout the remainder of the imperial period. These signs were highly coveted, for they immediately legitimized and bestowed high rank on a monastery. Only a fraction of the empire's innumerable Buddhist sites enjoyed such favorable status. In general, name plaques were only granted to larger-sized monasteries, usually with thirty or more rooms.[41] Monks could petition the government for such plaques and did so with great enthusiasm. One government motivation behind establishing the plaque system was to require that larger monasteries register with the state. This of course helped the government to control them. Possession of a plaque not only meant legitimacy; it times of persecution against Buddhism it could mean survival. During the suppression of Buddhism by the Later Zhou in the 950s, for instance, all monasteries without an imperially bestowed name plaque were ordered to be destroyed.

Name plaques were conferred on Emei shan monasteries on several occasions during the Ming. For instance, in 1465 the emperor Xianzong presented a *ci'e* to the Numinous Cliff Monastery bearing the title Assembled Felicity Monastery (Huifu si), its new official title. This was done at the request of Baofeng (fifteenth cent), an eminent Emei monk.[42] The highpoint of name-plaque activity on Emei took place during the Wanli reign. In 1587 the emperor Shenzong presented a name plaque to a temple complex built below Heaven's Gate Rock (Tianmen shi) by Great Master Tongtian (1523–1598 or 1525–1601), another famous monk active on Emei during the Ming.[43] The name on the plaque read: "Protector of the Nation: Grass Retreat Gallery" (Huguo Caoan ge).[44] Tongtian's lectures on Buddhist scriptures attracted considerable attention in the capital because he sometimes drew audiences on Emei of up to one thousand people. Finally, in honor of his mother's seventy-first birthday in 1602, Shenzong bestowed upon the White Stream Monastery what is arguably the most famous *ti'e* in the history of Mount Emei. The plaque read: "Sagely Longevity Myriad Years Monastery" (Shengshou Wannian si). The emperor dispatched a special Imperial Commissioner (Zhongshi) to Emei, to oversee the construction of a commemorative stele with the new title written in the emperor's calligraphy (this stele survives today and is displayed in the Brick Hall). This act brought great honor and prestige to both the mountain and what was now its official, premier monastery.

Two final and related topics concerning Mount Emei's development during the Ming require attention: an increase in the number of pilgrims and visitors traveling to Emei; and the construction of new trails. If we look back at the history of Mount Emei before the Ming, it is apparent that very few people visited there. As we have already seen, this was largely the result of the mountain's remote location and daunting peaks. This situation changed in the Ming, when numerous temples and a large monastic community now thrived. In light of this development and Emei's official status (established earlier in the Northern Song) as the *daochang* of Samantabhadra, it is not surprising that more and more monks, lay Buddhists, officials, and educated travelers were journeying to Emei. Other factors during the Ming also contributed to the increase of religious and nonreligious visitors. First and foremost, in the latter part of the Ming there was an explosion in the size of the lay Buddhist population. Many educated and noneducated people actively embraced Buddhist principles and practiced them in their daily lives. Pilgrimages to Buddhist holy sites, especially Wutai, Emei, Putuo, and Jiuhua, were thus undertaken by monks and lay people with great enthusiasm. Many attempted to make a circuit of all four mountains. By far, the most popular dates for a visit were the eighth day of the fourth lunar month—the birthday of Buddha, and the birthdays of the respective bodhisattvas associated with each site.

There was also a surge in the popularity of tourism. The travel diaries of Xu Xiake (1587–1641), the most famous of all Ming sojourners, speak at length about the growth of the tourist industry in China, even in faraway Yunnan.[45] As for Mount Emei, although we do not have even approximate figures of just how many people may have journeyed there annually during the Ming, judging from comments such as "religious and lay worshippers from every direction come [to Emei] on a daily basis,"[46] and the many poems and *youji* about Emei that survive from the Ming, it is certain that the number was substantial. In fact, so many visitors were arriving at the mountain that new trails and hostels had to be built to accommodate them. A text surviving from the Ming, written by the official Fu Guangzhai and titled "Record of Repairs on the Twisting Trails of E[mei] shan," offers some fascinating insights into how and why new trails were constructed.[47] In the opening lines of his essay Fu first notes that the clergy and laity who flock to Emei shan experience great hardship in negotiating the steep and perilous trails leading to the summit. Some visitors, he notes, after gazing upon Emei's lofty heights, abandon their climb altogether. Government officials who are physically unable to make the climb sometimes ride up in bamboo chairs (*zhugan*) carried by local porters, but Fu remarks that this method of ascent is also difficult. Moreover, food and shelter were not conveniently available on the mountain trails. Given these circumstances, Fu Guangzhai reaches the conclusion that Emei's paths must be repaired or rebuilt. But who, he asks, would pay the tremendous cost of such a project? Fu then relates the following:

> There was one "Layman Jueyan" (Jueyan jushi)[48] who, after climbing Emei, made a solemn vow. In the Renyin year (1602) he chanced upon meeting Master Wang, the Governor-general and Minister of War (Zhifu Sima Wanggong 制府司馬王公), and Court of Imperial Sacrifices Master Qiu, the Palace Eunuch (Sili Taijian Qiugong 司禮太監丘公).[49] Both agreed to support Layman Jueyan's vow to adorn the mountain. They began by contributing funds and gathering workmen, then proceeded to the most hidden and remote places, and the most lofty and distant spots. Shortcuts were found and trails were widened.[50]

Repairs were first made on the old trail followed by Fan Chengda. This portion of the climb, as we have already seen, is especially difficult and dangerous. The new trail, sometimes called the "Ming road," bypassed most of this challenging route and instead followed an easterly direction from White Stream Monastery, then turned north, twisted behind Deer Path Ridge (Lujing gang) and Bow Back Mountain (Gongbei shan), and then up to Thunder Grotto Flat. Fu Guangzhai mentions that a public hostel (*gongguan*) was constructed along the trail. The new and old trails merged at Thunder Grotto Flat. According to Fu Guangzhai, the new trail, completed in the winter of 1603, made it possible for climbers to bypass the difficult ascent along the old trail.

The Qing (1644–1911) and Republican (1912–) Era to 1949

The transition period from the Ming to the Qing dynasties was similar to that following the fall of the Yuan and founding of the Ming in that large-scale peasant rebellions spread chaos throughout China, this time for about twenty years. And, as before, Jiading county and Emei town were directly involved in the fighting. The following comments, written by a native of Emei town named Zhang Hongfu, offers a vivid account of how the turmoil of the Ming-Qing transition affected the town and its residents:

> As for the district (that is, Emei town), following successive years of ravaging and pillaging by soldiers, animal husbandry and farming had stopped altogether, and the four directions were all overgrown with weeds. By the Dinghai year (1647) the area was a vast wasteland. Countless people died

of starvation daily. . . . Tigers [from Mount Emei] came down into the town and ate people.[51]

As is evident in this passage, the effects of the military campaign in Sichuan were devastating, even in remote towns like Emei. Zhang Hongfu also reports that "Below Mount Emei, for a hundred *li* in every direction, there was nothing but overgrown thorns and brushwood."[52] As for destruction on the mountain itself, the 1997 edition of the *Mount Emei Gazetteer* reports that the Central Peak Monastery was destroyed in the fighting and that some Song dynasty murals within the temple were lost as a result.[53]

After the political and military situation in Jiading finally stabilized in the early 1660s, development on the mountain resumed along the same lines it had followed in the early Ming. Monastery construction and expansion was especially vigorous. The Loyal-to-the-State Monastery, located at the base of the mountain, merits first mention. Today this temple serves as the initial itinerary stop for almost all visitors to the mountain. The monastery's history extends back to the Wanli era of the Ming, when the monk Mingguang erected a structure there he called the Assembled Ancestors Hall (Huizong tang). In 1655 the Chan Master Wenda, upon seeing the hall was in a severe state of disrepair, converted it into a monastery. Then later, in 1703, the temple was renamed Baoguo si, or Loyal-to-the-State Monastery.[54] A modern copy of the original name plaque bearing these characters, reportedly written by the Kangxi emperor himself, is still displayed above the main entrance to the temple. The monastery has been expanded several times since. Its current form, with five major halls ascending in a row up the slope of a mountain, dates from the 1860s. The Baoguo si also serves as the home of the Mount Emei Buddhist Association (Emei shan fojiao xiehui; more on this later).

One of the temples that suffered major damage as a result of fighting during the Ming-Qing transition was the Crouching Tiger Monastery.[55] In 1644 the monk Guanzhi, a native of nearby Qianwei, visited Emei and observed the damage. He then proceeded to raise funds and rebuild it. Guanzhi rebuilt the structure on the foundation of the Dragon Spirit Hall, which Fan Chengda visited in 1177. Guanzhi and his followers worked on the project for twenty years. When it was finished, the new monastery comprised thirteen halls (*dian*), making it Emei shan's largest Buddhist temple complex. The new monastery was first named Tiger Creek Purification Hall (Huxi jingshe). Sometime thereafter it acquired its current name, Crouching Tiger Monastery. One important function of the Crouching Tiger Monastery was to provide meals and lodging to pilgrims and travelers. According to one Qing dynasty source, the monastery had living quarters that could accommodate one thousand pilgrims (*xiangke*).[56] This strongly suggests that visitor activity on Emei shan was already quite vigorous in the early Qing period. Additional trail-building efforts undertaken later in the Qing suggests the mountain was hosting an ever-increasing number of visitors.[57]

Other notable construction projects of the Qing period include the bronze tower erected next to the Myriad Years Monastery's Brick Hall. This magnificent edifice stood about 5.9 m/20 ft tall and was adorned with no less than forty-seven hundred Buddhist images. The complete text of the *Huayan jing* was engraved on the face of the tower. Another major project on the mountain involved rebuilding the Welcome Hall in the mid-seventeenth century. This was made possible by the largesse of Li Zhuo, a military commander in Chengdu, who donated two thousand taels of silver to fund the construction. Li Zhuo engaged Kewen, a well-known monk associated with the Crouching Tiger Monastery, to supervise the project. Also, the Great Buddha Monastery, erected originally in the Ming, was completely rebuilt in the early Qing. During the Kangxi reign, Li Zhen, an Assistant Regional Commander from nearby Ebian, contributed funds to build two additional halls, and changed the name of the structure from Prosperity and Longevity Retreat (Fushou an) to Great Buddha Monastery. Additional towers and pavilions were added in the Guangxu reign (1875–1908). And finally, in 1700 the monk Xingneng built a new temple near the First Pleasure Pavilion (Chuxi ting). He also dug a pool, and on a nearby rock carved an elephant that seemed to be stepping right into the water. Xingneng's temple thus became known as the Bathing Elephant Pool. In the Qianlong reign the monk in charge of the Bathing Elephant Pool, Yuezheng, built stone steps up the cliff just below the temple. Since this section of the climb to the summit is especially steep and precipitous, it acquired a new name: Piercing Heaven Slope (Zuantian po). Xingneng also constructed an additional stretch of stone stairs above the Bathing Elephant Pool that became known as Arhat Slope (Luohan po). The temple was further expanded in 1899, when Abbot Langqing added two new structures to the monastery grounds: the Mountain Gate Gallery (Shanmen louge) and the Guanyin Hall (Guanyin tang). When I visited the temple in July 2003 a new and very attractive terrace was being built around the pool. Bathing Elephant Pool is an especially important site on the mountain because the two main trails to the summit—one from Giant Toon Tree Flat and the other from the Myriad Years Monastery, both pass by the temple. Many climbers still stop there to spend the night.

Imperial patronage for Emei shan continued during the Qing. While it is difficult to determine if support from Qing emperors equaled or surpassed that of the Ming, in any case it was substantial.[58] Of all Qing sovereigns, the Kangxi emperor was the most active in this regard. For

instance, in 1702 he bestowed gifts on the Emei monk Zhaoyu (fl. eigh-
teenth cent) of the Recumbent Clouds Retreat (Woyun an), including a
copy of the *Diamond-sūtra* and a name plaque. In that same year the
emperor dispatched four high-ranking capital officials to Emei shan bearing
additional gifts. Monks on the mountain specially built the Welcoming-
the-Princes Pavilion (Jiewang ting) to greet the high-ranking envoys from
the capital. Throughout his reign Kangxi conferred many other gifts on
distinguished monks from the mountain, all of whom were affiliated with
major monasteries.

In the Qianlong reign we see the first appearance of organized group
visits to Mount Emei. These groups were called *bang* 幫 or *hui* 會.[59] During
the Qing many individual towns in Sichuan had local organizations called
Brother-and-Elder Societies (Gelao hui), which in fact were secret societies
comprised mainly of workers in the handicraft industry. Although Gelao
hui are known mainly for their anti-Manchu attitudes and participation
in rebellions during the late Qing, there were organized subgroups within
these societies called Chaoshan jiahui, or Pilgrimage Assemblies. Many of
these assemblies made annual pilgrimages to Emei shan in order to offer
sacrifices in honor of a particular bodhisattva. These Pilgrim Assemblies
had several different names, depending on which bodhisattva they intended
to honor. For instance, there were Samantabhadra Assemblies (Puxian hui),
Guanyin Assemblies (Guanyin hui), and so on. The size of these groups
varied anywhere from thirty to one hundred people, probably because they
were usually organized on short notice. Before embarking on their pilgrimage, members would purchase pennants, streamers, bells, drums, wooden
fish (*muyu*),[60] and other Buddhist accoutrements. On the day of the pilgrimage they would then march along in procession style, displaying their
banners and playing bells and drums, while at the same time reciting
Buddhist sūtras. No doubt, such activity caused quite a bit of excitement
in Emei town. As a general rule, these groups only visited the larger monasteries on the mountain. Upon completing their worship activities, the
pilgrims would present their various Buddhist accoutrements to monastery heads and also make cash donations.

Reports also survive from the Qing that describe the ritual activities
of more serious lay pilgrims. Some of them, we are told, would make the
entire ascent and descent on foot. As they trekked along they would stop
after every five paces, kneel down and kowtow once, and then recite
"Nanwu Amituofo."[61] Since the round-trip journey to the summit and
back is some sixty miles, this would add up to more than one hundred
thousand kowtows, or knocks of the head on the ground. Some of these
devotees, we are told, even with bloodied knees and covered with mud,
never abandoned their mission. They engaged in this practice not only

because of their sincere devotion and piety, but also because they hoped the Buddha or Samantabhadra might be moved to make a response.[62]

Another development in the late Qing that merits mention involves the then Governor-general (Zongdu) of Sichuan, Ding Baozhen (1820–1886). In 1885 he submitted a memorial to the Guangxu emperor seeking to establish a semiannual sacrificial ceremony (*sidian*) on Mount Emei, to be performed every spring and fall.[63] This ceremony was needed, Ding argues in his petition, because the mountain spirit that controls floods, famine, and cholera could bring benefit to the people. The Governor-general's request was granted by imperial decree in 1886, and the Emei Spirit Temple (Eshen miao) was then built outside Emei town's south gate to host the sacrifices. This is the first and only time in the mountain's history when an emperor sanctioned state sacrifices on Emei shan.

During and after the Tongzhi reign (1862–1874), the number of pilgrims and sightseers visiting to the mountain decreased. This was probably related to the general instability of the Qing government in the second half of the nineteenth century, caused mainly by the Taiping Rebellion, local insurrections, and wars with foreign powers. Yet despite the difficulty of traveling in China at this time, the gazetteers still chronicle visits by several prominent persons in the late nineteenth and early twentieth centuries, including Liu Guangdi (1859–1898), former Secretary of the Board of Punishments, who visited Emei in 1885; Huang Shoufu and Tan Zhongyue, whose investigations on Emei in 1887 resulted in the compilation and publication of the *Illustrated Talks on Emei* (*Eshan tushuo*); A. E. Pratt and G. N. Patanin, well-known botanists from England and Russia, respectively, both of whom conducted field work on the mountain in the early 1890s; and the well-known calligrapher and painter Huang Yungu (fl. late Qing), who produced some superb calligraphy specimens at the Bathing Elephant Pool in 1908.

The number of pilgrims and sightseers coming to Emei decreased further in the years following the founding of the Republic of China in 1912. Yet, at the same time, foreign visitors continued to arrive. There are at least two reasons for this. First, Emei shan was a safe haven far removed from those areas in northern, central, and southern China that remained unstable in the decades following the formation of Sun Yatsen's Republican government. Second, unlike most "common" pilgrims and travelers, many foreign visitors had the resources and time to travel. To cite one example, several English, American, French, and Canadian nationals came to Emei in 1917, where they built seventeen summer villas.[64] In that same year the Abbot Renyu convened more than three hundred monks for a joint ordination ceremony in the Great Buddha Hall (Dafo dian).

This event supports the argument that Buddhism was still active on the mountain during the turbulent years of the second decade of the twentieth century. Scientific visits also continued. In 1922 the renowned Chinese geologist Li Chunyu (C. Y. Lee) conducted the first of his many scientific investigations of Mount Emei. One especially important event that occurred in 1927 was a new policy concerning Buddhism announced by the Republican government. This policy was outlined in a document titled "Regulations on the Management of Monasteries" ("Simiao guanli tiaoli"), which essentially sought to bring all matters regarding Buddhism and monasteries under strict government control. Shengqin, Abbot of the Welcome Hall on Emei, along with several other prominent Buddhist leaders in Sichuan, successfully led a fight to recall the "Regulations." A report in the *Mount Emei Gazetteer* concerning this event offers some useful information on the size of the saṃgha in Sichuan in the late 1920s: altogether there were 18,279 monasteries in the province, along with 39,930 monks and nuns.[65] These numbers provide further evidence that a sizeable Buddhist community was still in place in Sichuan in the 1920s.

As for Mount Emei, the modern scholar Wei Fuping reports that in the early Republican period Emei still had more than seventy monasteries and no less than three or four thousand monks. Wei also notes that the Buddhist community on the mountain at this time still maintained large-scale land holdings, and that half the peasants who lived at the base of the mountain worked as tenant farmers for the monasteries.[66] Based on information derived from interviews with elderly local farmers, Wei Fuping estimates the Loyal-to-the-State Monastery, Heir-to-the-Throne Flat (Taizi ping), and the Ancestral Hall together had more than two hundred monks in the early years of the Republic, who received a combined annual rice yield of over eight hundred piculs (*dan*). Figuring that one picul equaled 50 kg/110 lbs, this represents a sizeable harvest. Wei Fuping also mentions that the number of visitors to the mountain each year was "beyond calculation," but he provides no data to support this conclusion. Clearly, though, throughout the remainder of the Republican period to 1949, despite the turmoil caused by Japan's invasion and occupation of China and the civil war between the Nationalists and Communists following World War II, writers, scientists, calligraphers, zoologists, and even prominent leaders of the Nationalist government continued to visit Emei shan. Among them was Generalissimo Chiang Kai-shek (1887–1975), who came to the mountain in the summer 1935 to oversee military training operations in the area. He visited all the major temples on the mountain, and mobilized a work force of three thousand workers to build a two-kilometer stretch of road that led to the Loyal-to-the-State Monastery.

Yet despite the considerable size of the Buddhist church in Sichuan and the monastic community on Mount Emei, and the long list of prominent visitors to the mountain, there is hardly any mention in the sources of temple renovation or new monastery construction during the Republican period. The overall number of religious and lay visitors to the mountain surely decreased during the turbulent years of the 1920s, 1930s, and 1940s in China. The land holdings described earlier made it possible for the monastic community on the mountain to survive, but expansion and development came to a halt. Fires continued to plague monasteries on the mountain. To cite just one example, a devastating fire on the Golden Summit in 1931 destroyed most of the structures there, including the Lotus Depository Monastery. As support from visitors continued to fall off, many monasteries on the mountain encountered difficult times. Especially hard hit were temples that did not have land and the income it provided. As a result, many monks left the mountain. Aside from renovation work on the Welcome Hall, undertaken in 1929, temple construction on the mountain stopped altogether. In that same year there was also a terrible tragedy: sixty-four pilgrims perished in a natural gas explosion while participating in Buddhist ritual ceremonies in Three Nights Grotto (Sanxiao dong).[67]

In the late Qing and continuing into the Republican period, suicides became a serious problem on the summit. The 1934 edition of the *Mount Emei Gazetteer* reports that "many people have thrown themselves off the cliff at the Beholding-the-Buddha Terrace."[68] For this reason, the viewing terrace on the eastern edge of the summit acquired an ominous name: Sheshen yai, or "Suicide Cliff." Visitors fortunate enough to witness an appearance of Buddha's Glory usually do so from this outcrop. What makes the cliff unique is the sheer nature of the drop-off: about 1,500 m/4921 ft almost straight down to a misty river valley below. While most visitors understandably approach the brink of the precipice with great fear and trepidation, it is not difficult to imagine how a zealous pilgrim might, in a moment of ecstatic frenzy, attempt the leap directly to the "Pure Land." The sources give no indication when this practice may have begun, but it certainly predates the earliest extant reports from the late Qing. Writing about his visit to Emei in 1877, the British diplomat Edward Colborne Baber (1843–1890) noted "the edge is guarded by chains and posts, which for further precaution one is not allowed to touch."[69] Another Western traveler, L. Newton Hayes, provides a more detailed account: "[On the summit] a strong wall has had to be built along the edge and heavy chains fastened across to prevent fanatic worshippers from throwing themselves over to their death. . . . Scores of worshippers, unable to resist the impulse, have jumped to the edge and have flung themselves out into space to crash through the fog and down, down, down to a fearful death."[70] Judging by Hayes's report, the wall and chains intended to thwart jumpers had little or no effect. By the early Republican period the suicide problem on the summit became even more serious. One travel account reports that the Administrator of Emei town even threatened the monastic community on the mountain if they allowed any more leapers to make the plunge.[71] Official government proclamations aimed at reducing suicides were promulgated on other mountains in China as well, including Mount Wudang.[72] It is not known if these orders had an effect on stopping and reducing the practice. Unfortunately, there are still occasional leaps from Suicide Cliff today, but most of these appear to be motivated by nonreligious reasons. An article published in China in 1996 discusses the heightened vigilance of local police to prevent further suicide attempts on Mount Emei and cites some success stories. One of these was a young man surnamed Ding from Anhui province who, after a poor performance on the college entrance exams, traveled to Emei in May 1996 with the intention of leaping to his death.[73]

RECENT DEVELOPMENTS

In the first years after Liberation there were places in China where monasteries were destroyed, monks were beaten or killed, copies of the Buddhist Canon were burned, and sacred images were melted down for their metal.[74]
                                                              —Holmes Welch

After the communist government of Mao Zedong took control of Mainland China in 1949, the Buddhist church faced a formidable challenge. On a theoretical level, the new regime opposed Buddhism on the grounds that it was a "spiritual weapon used by the ruling class to keep the oppressed classes in subjugation."[75] At the same time, however, the leaders in Beijing were well aware of the pervasive force and long-standing influence of Buddhism in Chinese society. This is probably one reason the Constitution of the People's Republic, promulgated in 1950, provides for freedom of religious belief and the freedom not to believe.[76] Initially, at least, the new government did not formulate any overt or immediate policies designed to eradicate Buddhism. In that same year, however, the central government began issuing directives that indicated a clear intention to subjugate and control the church. As we have already seen, many emperors and states throughout Chinese history had promulgated laws designed to serve the very same purpose. But one could, I think, with the benefit of hindsight, argue that the ultimate aim of these particular orders was the eventual elimination of Buddhism in China. Consider the following: in 1951 the government launched the so-called Land Reform Movement. In one fell swoop, all land held by Buddhist temples throughout

China was confiscated. This action, in effect, deprived all land-holding monasteries of their income and, by extension, their livelihood. Numerous temples closed down as a result. With no source of income, large numbers of monks left the saṃgha and returned home, hoping to find jobs.

The next stage of government control appeared on May 30, 1953, with the creation of the Chinese Buddhist Association. This organization was created and supervised by national, provincial, and local units of government. Never before in Chinese history had Buddhism in China been organized into one, national-level administrative body. Delegates to the association, all hand-picked by the government, went so far as to reinterpret some of the basic tenets of Buddhism so they would more closely conform to communist ideology and Marxian principles. The basic Buddhist idea of "love and compassion for all" was now reformulated so as to reflect the "real spirit" of the religion: strife and conflict. With the founding of the Chinese Buddhist Association also came the creation of its official monthly publication: *Modern Buddhism* (*Xiandai fojiao*). Most issues comprised editorials and resolutions supporting government policies, and carried little serious scholarship. In 1955 the journal even passed a resolution that required all submissions to be "patriotic." In other words, no criticism of the regime and its policies toward Buddhism was permitted.[77]

One stated purpose of the Chinese Buddhist Association was extremely important: the association and its members were charged with identifying and protecting Buddhist cultural institutions and relics. As a result, some famous temples in China were actually restored at government expense. Among them were a few monasteries on Mount Wutai. At about the same time, despite the intended preservation policy of the association (and the central government), some zealous local communist leaders destroyed temples. The famous Huayan Monastery in Datong (Shaanxi), built during the Liao dynasty, fell victim to these extremes.

When Mount Emei was officially "liberated" on December 17, 1949, there were fifty-nine monasteries still standing on the mountain, populated by a community of over four hundred monks.[78] The most recent edition of the *Mount Emei Gazetteer* notes that fifteen monasteries were repaired in 1954.[79] This work was probably supervised and executed by special Cultural Relics Renovation Committees (Wenwu zhengxiu weiyuanhui), created on Wutai and Emei in the early 1950s. These committees were financed by the Shanxi and Sichuan provincial governments, respectively.[80] Several local Buddhist associations were created as well, including the Mount Emei Buddhist Association in 1956. Perhaps more important was the founding of the Emei County Cultural Relics Protection Management Office (Emei xian wenwu baohu guanlisuo) in 1954. This organization was charged with the protection of all artifacts and ancient sites on the mountain.

For reasons already explained, monks found it more difficult to travel around China after 1949 and hence fewer of them traveled to "famous Buddhist mountains." Pilgrimages and visits by laymen to Emei, however, continued. As reported in an article in *Modern Buddhism*, over thirty-seven thousand people visited Mount Emei in 1956.[81] Holmes Welch, author of *Buddhism under Mao*, reports that one of his informants mentioned that in August 1957 he saw "several thousand people a day" visiting Emei."[82] As noted by Welch, such estimates are of course casual and hence unreliable. Yet still, it is certain that visitors were flocking to Emei in the 1950s, especially during the warmer summer months. Reports from 1960 to 1962 indicate that throngs of devotees were also traveling to Wutai and Putuo as well.[83]

Then, in 1958, came the Great Leap Forward (1958–1960), a government program designed to propel China along the fast track to industrialization. The infamous "backyard furnaces" of this campaign, designed to produce steel, required fuel. In response to government directives, timber cut to fire these "backyard furnaces" destroyed almost ten hundred *mou* of forest land around the Crouching Tiger Monastery, Clear Tones Gallery, Dragon Gate, and the Big Emei Monastery. At the same time, a bronze pagoda cast in the Yuan dynasty, a Ming dynasty statue of Guanyin, and iron and tin tiles from structures on the Golden Summit were dismantled and shipped to Chongqing for smelting.[84]

By 1959 there were only 104 monks and nuns left on the mountain.[85] Several local organizations conducted a damage survey in 1962, presumably covering the years of the Great Leap Forward. The survey reported that twenty temples had been destroyed and three thousand trees removed.[86] Throughout the 1950s and first half of the 1960s, however, several notable persons visited the mountain, including the military hero and influential party leader Zhu De (1886–1976). During his stop at Emei in the spring of 1963 Zhu composed four poems while visiting the Loyal-to-the-State, Crouching Tiger, and Myriad Years monasteries.[87] Other visitors arrived during the 1950s and early 1960s as well, including several well-known painters, calligraphers, and scientists. One wonders if any of them took notice of the rundown physical condition of the mountain's temples. Zhu De probably only saw the three monasteries mentioned above, which were certainly "spruced up" before his arrival. In any case, the situation on the mountain was soon to deteriorate much, much further.

Scarcely four months after Mao Zedong proclaimed the start of the Great Proletarian Cultural Revolution in June 1966, thirteen hundred "Red

Guards" stormed Mount Emei. Their mission was to destroy all remnants of the "Four Olds" (Sijiu) on the mountain; specifically, *anything* related to traditional thought, culture, customs, and habits. According to the *Mount Emei Gazetteer*, up to one thousand images, stele, name plaques, paintings, calligraphic works, and various Buddhist implements were destroyed.[88] An elderly gentleman I interviewed in 1993, who witnessed these events, told me Red Guards "swept down on the monasteries like locusts, consumed everything that was 'old'." I asked him what he meant by "consumed" (*chidiao le* 吃掉了 in modern Chinese). He replied: "destroyed" (*pohuai le* 破壞了). In 1967 the situation deteriorated further: "Thought of Mao Zedong Worker Propaganda Teams" (Mao Zedong sixiang gongren xuanchuandui) took control of the mountain and occupied its monasteries. Those monks who still remained on the mountain were rounded up and taken to the Loyal-to-the-State Monastery, where the Red Guards conducted "struggle sessions" aimed at catching "monsters and demons" (*niugui sheshen*) among them. Many priests were found "guilty" of "antirevolutionary crimes" and, as a result, sent to an area near Ox Heart Monastery for "reform through manual labor" (*laodong gaizao*), a practice formerly used only to rehabilitate criminals. The monasteries of Mount Emei were now abandoned. The local Cultural Relics Bureau did manage to save a few treasures, such as the giant ceramic Buddha in the Porcelain Buddha Monastery (Cifo si). There is no published inventory of the irreplaceable artifacts on Emei shan lost to the madness of the Cultural Revolution, but it was certainly extensive. More "struggle sessions" against monks and nuns continued in 1968.

Emei shan was closed to tourists during the tumultuous years of the Cultural Revolution (1966–1976). It finally reopened in 1977, during the Chinese Lunar New Year holiday. Of the fifty-nine monasteries still standing in the early 1950s, only twenty-seven now remained. No doubt, some of the lost temples had fallen victim to fires and neglect. Many, however, were destroyed in various political campaigns culminating in the Cultural Revolution. Yet in that first year (1977) an estimated one hundred thousand tourists visited the mountain.[89] But in what direction would Emei now develop, if at all? Who would supply the necessary funds to restore the dilapidated infrastructure of Emei shan? What would now happen to the monasteries and surviving remnants of the monastic community?

THE TOURIST ERA EMERGES

Mount Emei should serve as a center for tourism, should use cultural artifacts and ancient sites as its main appeal, and should showcase the elegance of its physical environment.[90]

These are the words of Zhao Ziyang, spoken at Mount Emei on January 30, 1979, when he visited the mountain in his capacity as first secretary of the Communist Party in Sichuan. It is interesting to observe that Zhao's comments say nothing about of the mountain's long-standing Buddhist tradition. Clearly, the first secretary saw a new priority for Emei: it should now develop as a center for tourism. Remarks made by political leaders visiting famous places in China usually contain little or no substance. This occasion, however, was different. Zhao Ziyang's observation about Emei shan can be linked directly to the economic reform measures initiated by Deng Xiaoping (1904–1997) in 1978, which continue today. At the heart of the reforms is a far-reaching plan to restructure China's economic system. We can now see one important result of the reform program begun in the late 1970s. Simply put, China is now essentially driven by a market economy. Former state-controlled industries are being phased out, privatization is gaining speed, and entrepreneurial skills and M.B.A. degrees are now much more valued than the economic theories of Karl Marx and Chairman Mao. One aspect of this process especially relevant to our discussion is this: as China's economy becomes more and more market oriented and profit oriented, and as government support for state-run enterprises is proportionally reduced, provincial, municipal, and local government units must devise ways to raise their own revenue. Zhao Ziyang's comments are a reflection of this attitude and policy. In other words, since Emei shan is a top attraction that possesses cultural artifacts, ancient sites, and breathtaking scenery, it makes sense to mobilize or exploit its cultural resources for economic and social reasons. If successfully implemented, everyone involved will make money and, at the same time, the Chinese people will have an outstanding recreation facility to enjoy in their leisure. While there has been some private investment on Emei over the last two decades, the planning and development of its tourist industry has been undertaken exclusively by government officials in Chengdu, Leshan, and Emei City. Thus, once again in the long history of Emei shan, its place and space are being redefined. The results are profound.

On February 21, 1979, just three weeks after Zhao Ziyang's visit, the Sichuan Provincial Revolutionary Committee (Sichuansheng geming weiyuanhui) formally approved Mount Emei's "reopening" to the general public. Later in that same year a new local government office was established to oversee the mountain's development: the Leshan Area-Mount Emei Management Bureau (Leshan diqu Emei shan guanliju). Even Deng Xiaoping himself made a trip to Mount Emei in July 1980.[91] Two related developments that have taken place since Deng's visit that are especially important. First, Emei has now been secularized in the sense that the primary interest of the Management Bureau is development of Emei shan as a tourist site. The goal is to attract an ever-increasing number of annual visitors, thereby earning an ever-increasing level of revenue. Local party officials are tight-lipped about exactly how tourist industry profits are used. Clearly, however, much of it has been reinvested into the mountain to further develop infrastructure. Here I refer especially to new roads, hotels, restaurants, and various "mountain attractions" (discussed below). A second important issue concerns Emei shan's Buddhist legacy and how this relates to the new tourism industry.

Many monasteries have survived or have been rebuilt. The Loyal-to-the-State Monastery and the Myriad Years Monastery, for instance, are both in top form today, as are most facilities on the Golden Summit. No surprise here, for these are popular stops for sightseers. The two monasteries just mentioned certainly earn substantial income from tourists.[92] Do religious and lay Buddhists still make pilgrimages to Emei? Indeed they do. Each summer, during the popular travel season, busloads of lay pilgrims roll into Emei City. Most of these pilgrims are elderly women. While some devotees either hike the trails or ride up the mountain in bamboo litters, my distinct impression is that most of them bus to the Myriad Years Monastery and Welcome Hall, and then from there ride a cable car to the summit. This trip is easily accomplished in less than three hours. Having noted the continuing presence of lay pilgrims on the mountain, we should realize that today the overwhelming number of people who journey to Emei do so for recreational purposes. At the same time, the developers are certainly aware that the mountain's Buddhist tradition serves to attract many of these fun-seeking tourists. After all, virtually everyone in China knows that Emei shan is a "famous Buddhist mountain." The presence of the Colossal Buddha in nearby Leshan, which also attracts substantial numbers of tourists annually, reinforces that status. Were the monasteries, monks, and nuns to disappear, the mountain would lose a major part of its identity, resulting in smaller tourist numbers. And so, by developing the recreational aspect of the mountain (better trails, hotels, roads, recreating areas, and so on) *and* supporting a continued Buddhist presence on the mountain,[93] Emei's appeal to potential visitors or pilgrims is maximized.

Development of the tourist industry on Emei shan over the last two decades has been successful in that the overall number of annual visitors has been almost steadily on the rise. In 1979, the first year of the mountain's official "opening," 282,000 domestic and foreign visitors—more than double the number in 1977—paid the admission fee at the mountain entrance near the Crouching Tiger Monastery.[94] By 1984 this figure rose to about 1,000,000. Four years later, in 1988, the annual visitor number climbed to more than 1,570,000, but the fell to 1,250,000 in 1989.[95]

Average figures for the years 1989 to 1993 dipped slightly to 1,400,000, but in recent years the numbers have begun to rise again. In 2002, for instance, Emei hosted 1,746,200 paying visitors.[96] The mountain admission fee in 2002 was RMB 80—roughly, US $10.00. This means that gate receipts alone for 2002 came to almost US $11 million. If one factors in additional income made by monasteries, hotels, restaurants, curio shops, and local transportation outlets, it is clear that the economic base of Mount Emei is substantial.

Little development took place on Mount Emei in the way of tourist-related construction during the 1980s and early 1990s. Numerous committees and bureaus concerned with the development and preservation of the mountain were created during these years, but their main concern seems to have been planning. Funds available for construction were still quite limited at this time, though electricity, running water, and telephone service was introduced to all temples. By early 1993, however, the actual reconstruction of the mountain's infrastructure had begun in full force. There has been a steady stream of construction ever since, aimed at enhancing the appeal of Emei as a recreation site. These projects include the building of numerous hotels and restaurants. While most of these businesses are located at the base of mountain, two new hotels were also built on the Golden Summit. A narrow-gauge train has been installed there, which transports visitors to the "Thousand Buddha's Summit" and "Ten Thousand Buddha's Summit," the highest elevation points on the mountain. In 1993 a cableway, covering a distance of 1,168 m/3,854 ft, was completed, connecting the Welcome Hall with the Golden Summit. The following year construction on the new Mount Emei Museum was completed. This is an attractive, modern structure and very visitor friendly. Adjacent to the museum, the Mount Emei Tourist Center includes educational and tourist information facilities. Patrons can now access the internet or send postcards home from the post office in the lobby. And there is modest-sized ski slope now operating on the mountain. Finally, in 1996 both Emei shan and the Colossal Buddha in Leshan were both awarded "World Heritage Site" status by UNESCO, which significantly enhanced their prestige and undoubtedly have served to attract even more tourists.

More projects are planned for the immediate future. One of these involves the installation of two new cable cars: one from Nine Elders Grotto to the Myriad Years Monastery, and another from the Myriad Years Monastery to the Clear Tones Gallery. These efforts are designed to move visitors up and down the mountain more efficiently. Cable car access to Nine Elders Grotto will bring in additional tourist dollars from the steeper, relatively inaccessible southern route up the mountain. There is also talk of creating a "Daoist Center" near Nine Elders Grotto, but the planners seem to have not yet figured out what exactly constitutes a "Daoist Center." By far, the most ambitious current plan is to make Emei the "Number One Mountain in China" (Zhongguo diyi shan) by the end of 2005. "Number One" here means the top mountain tourist center in all China. This is a major endeavor, involving twenty-four major projects and sixty-two smaller-scale ones, with a combined projected budget of RMB 2.7 billion/US $3.3 million. The highlight of the project will be the construction of forty-one hundred square meters "Natural Scenic Observation Terrace" (Tianran guanjing tai) and "Buddhist Pilgrimage Center" (Fojiao chaosheng zhongxin) on the summit. In connection with the latter, a massive four-faced statue of Samantabhadra is now being erected on the summit, near the Lotus Depository Monastery. The image will be built on a scale comparable to the Colossal Buddha in Leshan.[97] When this statue is completed, it will certainly qualify Mount Emei as having the "biggest Buddha" among China's Buddhist mountains, a distinction the developers eagerly seek. "Bigger" is always "better" in China.

Now, it is undeniable that government efforts to develop Mount Emei have concentrated on tourism and not Buddhism. Having said that, it is fascinating to observe that government and tourist industry leaders on Emei now plan to erect two very different structures on the summit, one largely intended for sightseers and other designed more for religiously minded people. Again, this approach will offer the greatest tourist appeal and will likely draw the largest crowds.[98] While I am not informed about the possible religious intentions or motivations of the developers, if they exist at all, this is not a key issue in the context of our discussion here. What ultimately is most important is that an essential component of Mount Emei's identity—Buddhism—has again apparently survived a very difficult time. Its place on the mountain is now being redefined in the context of a modern, market-driven society. As far as I have been able to tell, the modest Buddhist community on the mountain has not raised any objections to its new supporting role (they have no choice, really). In any case, the Buddhist community now has a source of steady income and all indications are that its annual revenue will rise as more tourists and pilgrims come to the mountain. The monks still rise every morning at 4:00 AM for chanting and prayers; various Buddhist ceremonies and rituals are still performed on a regular basis. Monks still attend class every morning, and study, meditate, and chant sūtras throughout the rest of the day. In some respects, then, things seem to be "getting back to normal" in the monasteries on Mount Emei.

Closing Thoughts

The magistrate of Emei xian, Zhao Mingsong, writing in his preface to Dryden Linsley Phelps's *Omei Illustrated Guide Book,* mentions that he visited Mount Emei twice. In preparation for each ascent the magistrate looked over various "writings of the past." Here is how he describes his reaction to those texts:

> Before each ascent I invariably glanced over the pure and fragrant writings of former authors, as well as the polished and assorted writings of modern scholars. They merely praise and exaggerate Mount Emei's peaks, grottoes, springs and rocks, precipices and ravines, purification halls, Buddhist enlightenment sites, the bright luster of icy snows, the strange illusions of mists and clouds, the majestic manifestations of Tathāgata, and the great arhats who meditate cross-legged and are at peace with the world. These are the divine wonders that met the eyes of these writers, which they assembled together. They just saw what everyone else saw, described what everyone else described, and that is all. Upon close examination, all of their accounts are contradictory and bear no resemblance to the facts. . . . The reason Emei's fame is second to [Mounts] Song and Hua is due to the fanciful tales told by mountain monks, and to those men of letters who, fond of crafting compositions, append to them numinous vestiges of the past in order to show off their talent. And yet, they do not know a single name or single artifact of the mountain. Although the names and artifacts are slight in number, they must be utilized to the full extent.[1]

Within the space of a single paragraph, Zhao Mingsong dismisses virtually all the written sources upon which this book is based. The problem with these texts, he argues, is that the authors failed to probe deeply enough into the names (*ming* 名) and artifacts (*wu* 物) associated with the mountain. Later in his preface Zhao Mingsong extols the *Omei Illustrated Guide Book* because, he says, it reveals Mount Emei's "true appearance" (*zhen mianmu* 真面目; lit., "true face and eyes"), "true facts" (*zhen yuanli* 真原理), and "true function" (*zhen gongyong* 真功用).[2]

Since Zhao's purpose in writing the preface was to heap praise on the *Guide Book*, and also because he admits to never having seen the original Chinese text on which Phelp's based his English translation (that is, the *Eshan tushuo*), we need not take his indictment of past and present sources too seriously. The magistrate does, however, raise a fascinating issue. If the writings of the past and present fail to reveal the genuine "appearance, facts, and function" of Emei shan, then where should we look for these truths? Zhao Mingsong provides no satisfying answer to the question.

Of course, one of the best ways to gain knowledge about a particular place is to go there and experience it first hand. But this is not always possible; hence there are many books in circulation (like this one) that attempt to describe places for people who will probably never have a chance to visit them. To be sure, the sources upon which this study is based are all biased to some degree. But isn't all writing informed first by the predisposed perspective of its author? A related problem of course is how does a writer deal with sources that are far removed from him or her in time, history, and culture? The best anyone can do is to try to understand and interpret the biases of the old authors and one's own "predisposed perspective." My ultimate goal, as outlined in the introduction, has been to demonstrate how human interaction has impacted the place and space of Mount Emei over the course of its long history as a "famous mountain." Whether my findings would satisfy Zhao Mingsong's demand for the "true appearance" of Mount Emei I cannot say. In my view, the magistrate's demand is impossible to achieve for the simple reason that no single "reality" of Mount Emei exists. I take this position for the same reason mentioned in chapter 1: the lengthy history of human activity on Emei shan has always maintained a dynamic quality. This is one of the main themes to emerge from my research. There is no single "true reality" of Mount Emei because over the centuries many people with varied backgrounds and views have traveled or lived there and interacted with the mountain's place and space in different ways. If you were to ask a Buddhist monk and a China Travel Service tour guide to describe the "true appearance, significance, or function" of Mount Emei, you would get very different answers. Neither answer would be right, nor would it be wrong. They would just be different. With all due respect to Magistrate Zhao, he missed this point altogether.

Without a doubt, Emei shan's remote location and unique environment have played the greatest roles in determining what has happened there over the centuries. Among the five imprints I describe in the introduction—myths about the mountain's religious origins; legends of Daoist immortals; the arrival and development of Buddhism; poems and prose works about Emei written through the dynasties; and recent developments in the tourism industry—two have dominated the history of the mountain. These are the long-term influence of Buddhism and the rich literary legacy left by Fan Chengda and countless other writers. Throughout this book I have attempted to demonstrate how these two imprints function as an indelible part of the mountain's heritage and identity. As for the gazetteers and large corpus of poetry and prose that constitute the written history of Mount Emei, collectively these works helped to define how the mountain has been understood since the Southern Song. Fan Chengda's diary, along with Hu Shian and Jiang Chao's gazetteers, have played the most influential role in this process.

Another important theme that has emerged from my research is Mount Emei's "ability" to adapt, change, and reinvent itself, especially when faced with difficult times and circumstances. This happened often. Just three examples would be threats and attacks by non-Chinese "tribes" during the Period of Disunion and Tang, the wars of the Yuan-Ming and Ming-Qing transitions, and the destruction resulting from the Maoist political campaigns of the 1950s and 1960s. After each of these setbacks the mountain was able to adapt, change, and survive adverse conditions. What accounts for the Emei's ability to cope with difficult times? I have attempted to demonstrate how imperial, provincial, and local patronage played the greatest role in the mountain's survival and development as a Buddhist center, as did the individual efforts of some very capable monks. Until quite recently, almost all patronage for Emei shan was related to its Buddhist heritage. For this reason, I would argue that Emei shan's ability to recover from adversity is intimately tied to its long-standing reputation and function as a major Buddhist holy site in China. My distinct impression is that this same pattern is also detectable in the histories of Wutai, Putuo, and Jiuhua. The persistent religious beliefs of individuals and communities on Emei, along with local peoples' deep connection to Samantabhadra's holy *daochang*, are the driving force behind the preservation of religious space on Mount Emei. I suspect future research will reveal the same pattern on China's other "Buddhist mountains" as well.

The introduction also mentioned the importance of *interaction*—the different ways in which humans have either reacted to and/or modified Mount Emei's place and space over time—in assessing the history and place of Mount Emei in Chinese culture. Another key point to emerge from this study is the crucial role the mountain's distinct location and physical environment played in this process. Virtually everyone mentioned in this book (and many others not mentioned) who traveled to or lived on Emei shan did so, in part at least, because they were attracted to the mountain's beautiful landscape. Once there, they reacted to the scenic environment in very different ways. Some took up residence in caves or huts and practiced alchemy; others built monasteries; still others executed paintings or undertook scientific investigations. It is this diversity of interaction that makes the history of Emei shan so fascinating. The dominant role of Buddhism on the mountain is undeniable. Yet, as I argue in the introduction, there is much more to the history and role of the mountain in Chinese culture than "just" religion.

Looking back over the long history of Mount Emei since Huichi's visit around 400 AD, developments over the last century have pushed the mountain into directions it has never experienced before. During the Republican period, Emei no doubt "lost" many monks because of the unstable political and military situation in China at that time. And yet, in the 1920s there were still seventy monasteries and no less than three or four thousand monks on the mountain. These numbers roughly match those of the late Ming, when Emei reached the height of its development as a "Buddhist mountain." In 1949, when Mao Zedong assumed political control of Mainland China, there were fifty-nine monasteries still standing on Emei, but the size of the monastic community had fallen dramatically to about four hundred monks. Most of the surviving temples were probably in terrible physical condition at the time, but their sites or locations were preserved. The years of the Great Leap Forward and Cultural Revolution are quite another story. That *any* monasteries and monks survived the ravages of this period is truly remarkable.

As for the rise of the modern tourist industry on Emei shan, this is really no surprise. China's "famous mountains" are all being developed along similar lines, though some are receiving more attention than others. Regional and local developers are modifying Emei's space and place to serve the needs of new "self-sufficient" regional and local governments in China. This means government and party planners are seeking to take advantage of the burgeoning consumer market in China and earn as much revenue from scenic sites as possible. The current campaign to make Emei China's "Number One Mountain" by the end of 2005 is designed to achieve this purpose.

There are a few dozen temples on the mountain today. Among these, the Loyal-to-the-State and Myriad Years monasteries receive the most attention and hence the most tourist and pilgrim traffic. Other monasteries are not as well kept up (they get less income from tourist activity), but none of them are run-down. A community of about 240 monks and nuns occupy these institutions. Nuns on Mount Emei (around 60, altogether) reside mainly in the Crouching Tiger Monastery.[3] As far as I know, demographic figures on the monk and nun populations on Mount Emei have not been published. My impression, however, is that most of the monks and nuns on Emei are quite young, perhaps around twenty-five years old.[4] This brings two questions to mind: (1) What is the role of Buddhism in the future of Mount Emei? and (2) What role, if any, will the mountain's current crop of young monks and nuns play in the future of Buddhism on the mountain?

As for the first question, some answers have already been suggested in chapter 8. It is clear that government leaders and planners see a place for Emei's rich Buddhist tradition in the future of the mountain. That role, however, is restricted to the religion's *legacy* on Emei. In other words, party leaders view the mountain's Buddhist tradition as an "attraction," which they can use and manipulate to draw more tourists. I see no indication of active government interest in developing Buddhism *as a religion* on Emei (that is, building new monasteries and religious academies, recruiting new monks and nuns, and so on). Is it even possible, then, that Buddhism might one day again thrive as a religion on Emei, with patrons coming forward to sponsor new monastery construction and related activities? Will we see increased ordinations of monks and nuns in the future? Of course, government leaders will ultimately decide on all these issues. The "glory days" of the late Ming dynasty, when powerful monastic communities and influential monks could circumvent or disregard government control measures, seem gone forever. The government in China today exercises almost complete control over the saṃgha. Having said that, the religion still attracts some young converts, but the numbers are meager. I doubt highly that the monastic communities on Emei and other Buddhist mountains in China will grow in any appreciable way in the near future. Some scholars in the West have spoken of a "revival" of Buddhism in China in the late twentieth century. A better word, I think, is "adjustment." The young monks and nuns of contemporary China, many of whom were born after Deng Xiaoping initiated his reforms in the late 1970s, in many ways represent a new kind of Buddhist in China. Their piety and devotion seem genuine, but they have been forced to make "adjustments" in a society that has probably changed more in the last twenty-five years than it has in the last two millennia. As an example, consider a young monk I met on Emei a few years ago. He studies English passionately, prefers to be called by the name "Jeffrey," commands formidable computer skills, and sends me emails about how he looks forward to visiting the United States and perhaps investing in the stock market. We have had numerous conversations, but Jeffrey has never once mentioned anything about "restoring Buddhism to it rightful and proper place on Mount Emei." In thirty or forty years from now, Jeffrey and his generation will be the leaders of the Buddhist community in China. In what direction will they lead the young monks and nuns of the future? I suspect they will blaze new trails never even dreamed of by their predecessors. Just how "traditionally Buddhist" those trails will be no one knows. Buddhism has always provided answers about the ultimate purpose of life and death—issues that transcend politics and history. Perhaps China's emerging middle class of conspicuous consumers will one day turn to Buddhism (or some other religion) when they need answers to these questions. This does not seem likely right now, but China has always been a land of changes and surprises.

Abbreviations

EMSZ (1934 ed.)	*Emei shan zhi*, compiled by Xu Zhijing, in collaboration with Yinguang (1861–1940).
EMSZ (1997 ed.)	*Emei shan zhi*, edited by *Emei shan zhi* bianzuan weiyuanhui.
FCDBJ	*Fan Chengda biji liuzhong*, edited and with collations by Kong Fanli.
FSHJ	*Fan Shihu ji*, by Fan Chengda (1126–1193).
HYGZ	*Huayang guozhi jiaozhu*, by Chang Qu (fourth cent), with notes and commentary by Liu Lin.
HYJ	*Taiping huanyu ji*, by Yue Shi (930–1007).
LBJ	*Li Bo ji jiaozhu*, with collations and commentary by Qu Shuiyuan and Zhu Jincheng.
MSJ	*Shuzhong mingsheng ji*, by Cao Xuequan (1571–1664).
QTS	*Quan Tangshi*. 1960 Zhonghua shuju ed.
SCTZ	*Sichuan tongzhi*, edited by Chang Ming and Yang Fangcan (1754–1816).
SJZ	*Shuijing zhu*, compiled by Li Daoyuan (d. 527).
SKQS	*Siku quanshu*. *Wenyuan ge* ed.
SS	*Songshi*, edited by Togto [Tuotuo] (1314–1355) et al.
SSJZS	*Shisan jing zhushu*, edited by Ruan Yuan (1764–1849).
Taishō	*Taishō shinshū daizōkyō*, edited by Takakusu Junjirō et al.
WCL	*Wuchuan lu* (*Zhibuzu zhai congshu* ed.), by Fan Chengda.

Notes

Chapter 1. Introduction

1. "Medical Problems of High Altitude," cited in Winifred Gallagher, *The Power of Place: How Our Surroundings Shape Our Thoughts, Emotions, and Actions* (New York: Poseidon, 1993), 73.
2. "The Polymorphous Space of the Southern Marchmount," 222.
3. *The Oxford English Dictionary, Second Edition* (Compact Edition; Oxford: Clarendon Press, 1991), 1123.3.
4. One recent example of this practice is evident in the title of Kiyohiko Munakata's book *Sacred Mountains in Chinese Art* (Urbana and Chicago: University of Illinois Press, 1991).
5. "Marchmount," as a translation for the Chinese word *yue* 岳 (or 嶽), was devised by Edward H. Schafer. See his *Pacing the Void: T'ang Approaches to the Stars* (Berkeley and Los Angeles: University of California Press, 1977), 6.
6. The closest Chinese equivalents to the English word "sacred" are *sheng* 聖 and *ling* 靈. Originally, *sheng* meant "to hear" or "to listen" (readers who know Chinese will note that *sheng* has an "ear" classifier), referring specifically to someone whose sense of hearing and, by extension, ability to comprehend and gain wisdom, exceeds that of ordinary people. Later, *sheng* was used to denote superior persons ("sages") whose talent, wisdom, and moral attributes exceeded all others. Hence, *Shuowen jiezi* 說文解字 (Beijing: Zhonghua shuju, 1963), 250a, defines *sheng* as "*tong*" 通, or "all knowing."

    The character *ling* originally referred in a generic sense to gods, spirits, or deities (*shen* 神 or *shenling* 神靈), and thus came to be associated with words related to "spirit," "spiritual," "the soul," and even deceased persons. Later its meaning expanded to include various human traits originally associated with *shen*, such as clever, sharp, keen, sensitive, wondrous, and so on. The term *lingshan* 靈山 does appear often in Chinese letters, referring to mountains (*shan*) where spirits (*ling*) dwell. See also the comments on "sacred" in n. 8 below.

7. Eliade sees the "sacred" and the "profane" as the "two modes of being in the world, two existential situations assumed by man in the course of his history." *Myths, Rites, Symbols: A Mircea Eliade Reader*, Wendell C. Beane and William G. Doty, eds. (New York: Harper and Row, 1976), 1:143. See also Eliade's *The Sacred and the Profane* (New York: Harper and Row, 1959).

8. Cf. the following observation from Susan Naquin and Chün-fang Yü: "While we use the term *sacred*, we are keenly aware of its associated meaning of *transcendent* and its implied opposition to *profane*, terms derived from Western religious traditions. Such implications are natural in the three related religions (Christianity, Judaism, and Islam) that affirm the existence of a transcendent god, but they cannot be extended to other cultures, including those of East Asia, *where the religious object is not separated from but located within nature* (italics mine)." *Pilgrims and Sacred Sites in China*, 2. The following comment, once made to me by a monk who lives on Mount Emei, punctuates the main point here very succinctly: "For me, Mount Emei *is* the Buddha, and the Buddha *is* Mount Emei. I do not distinguish between the two."

     It might also be mentioned that, as far as I have been able to determine, the original meaning of *yue* (the most often-mentioned "sacred Chinese mountain" in Western scholarship) had nothing to do with things "sacred" or "transcendent." As used in the *Classic of History* (*Shujing*), *yue* is an office title, referring to leaders who "counseled the Four Yue" (*zi siyue* 咨四岳); that is to say, officials who managed the feudal lords (*zhuhou*) stationed by the emperor in the "four *yue*" or "four directions." See *Shangshu zhengyi* 尚書正義 (*SSJZS* ed), 1:122a. The places in the four directions where these hereditary feudal lords resided and performed sacrifices to assist the emperor in maintaining control over the empire were called *yue*. The sage-emperor Shun is reported to have traveled once every five years to the *yue* and performed sacrifices for the purpose of delimiting the boundaries of his rule. See *SSJZS*, 1:127c. It was the responsibility of the four *yue* officials to protect the four quarters and accept the homage of other feudal lords who lived therein. Some scholars believe that since the *zhuhou* resided in mountainous areas for protection, the word *yue* eventually came to denote "mountain." See, for instance, the comments on this in Gu Jiegang 顧頡剛, "Siyue yu Wuyue" 四嶽與五嶽, in *Shilin zashi, chubian* 史林雜識, 初編 (Beijing: Zhonghua shuju, 1963), esp. 34.

9. These various functions of monasteries are discussed in Kenneth K. S. Chen, "The Role of Buddhist Monasteries in T'ang Society."

10. For a useful discussion of these changes see Xie Ninggao 謝凝高, *Zhongguo de mingshan* 中國的名山 (Shanghai: Shanghai jiaoyu chubanshe, 1987), 5 ff.

11. *Wenxuan*, 4.17b.

12. The opening lines of the "Shudu fu" suggest that the state of Wu had already been defeated by Shu when Zuo Si composed his rhapsody. The Shu pacification of Wu took place in 280.

13. Some scholars identify the following line, which appears in a fragmentary work (in several versions) attributed to the Han dynasty writer Yang Xiong (53 BC–AD 18) titled "Shu Capital Rhapsody" ("Shudu fu"), as the earliest textual reference to Mount Emei: "To the south is Qian, Zang, Qianyi, Kunming, and Emei." The longest extant version of this *fu* is preserved in the *Guwen yuan* 古文苑 (*Sibu congkan* ed.), 4.4b–10b (the line mentioning Mount Emei appears on 4.6a). There is some question, however, as to the authorship of this work. David Knechtges accepts the traditional attribution to Yang Xiong. See his *The Han Rhapsody: A Study of the Fu of Yang Hsiung, 53 BC–AD 18* (Cambridge: Cambridge University Press, 1976), 117–18, and 139, n. 8. Some contemporary Chinese scholars, however, have convincingly argued that Yang Xiong's *fu* is a forgery that dates *after* Zuo Si's work. See, for instance, Luo Mengting, "Emei shan kaituo shilue," 2. Since the attribution and dating issues of Yang Xiong's rhapsody are not yet resolved, I identify Zuo Si's *fu* as the earliest reliable reference to Emei shan in Chinese letters.

14. This pattern is certainly evident in James Robson's excellent study of the Southern Yue (or Hengshan), "The Polymorphous Space of the Southern Marchmount."

15. "Chronicle of Taoist Studies in the West: 1950–1990," 307.

16. Among these scholars, those whose work has been most influential on my own include Raoul Birnbaum, Patricia Buckley Ebrey, Peter N. Gregory, Thomas Hahn, Susan Naquin, James Robson, Anna Seidel, Michel Soymié, Franciscus Verellen, and Chün-fang Yü. I have also consulted the work of Allan G. Grapard on mountain traditions in Japan. Refer to the selected bibliography for details on the various works of these authors.

17. "The Collision Between India and Eurasia," *Scientific American* 236.4 (Apr. 1977): 30.

18. Wegener, *The Origin of Continents and Oceans*, John Biram, trans. (London: Mithuen, 1924).

19. For a more detailed account of the tectonics that created these mountains, including Emei, see Luo Zhili et al., "The Emei Taphrogenesis of the Upper Yangtze Platform in South China," *Geological Magazine* 127.5 (Sept. 1990): 393–405.

20. Verellen, "The Beyond Within," 276.

21. Ge Hong 葛洪 (283–343), *Baopuzi neipian jiaoshi* 抱朴子內篇校釋 (expanded ed., with collations and commentary by Wang Ming 王明; Beijing: Zhonghua shuju, 1985), 17.299.

22. *Shuowen jiezi*, 190a.

23. *Liji zhengyi* 禮記正議 (*SSJZS* ed.), 2:1425c.

24. "Zone of terror" is adapted from Paul Demiéville's "zone d'horreur sacréed" ("region of sacred horror"). See his "La montagne dans l'art littéraire chinois," 15.

25. *Baopuzi neipian jiaoshi*, 17.299.

26. *Baopuzi neipian jiaoshi*, 17.299.

27. There is considerable debate among scholars as to when the grouping of the Wuyue took place. The estimates I have seen range from about the sixth century BC to the reign of Emperor Wu of the Han (r. 141–87 BC). I will not attempt to resolve this issue here.

28. It should also be acknowledged that these mountains were likely important local cult sites that developed transregional importance over time.

29. The author of these lines, Dagui 大圭, lived during the Yuan dynasty. His collected works, titled *Mengguan ji* 夢觀集, survive in the *SKQS*, but the verse translated here is not included therein. My translation is based on the text of the poem preserved in *Shicang lidai shixuan* 石倉歷代詩選 (*SKQS* ed.), 366.8b–9a.

30. *EMSZ* (1997 ed.), 1. The contemporary "tourist area" of Mount Emei, which is largely confined to the main section of the mountain, measures 154 sq km/92 sq mi.

31. The direction of the anticline also explains why Emei town (now Emei *shi*, or Emei City), an essential way-stop for all travelers to the mountain, was built below the eastern slope.

32. *Su Shi shiji*, 18.927–28.

33. Figures on temperature, rainfall, and fog provided here are drawn from *EMSZ* (1997 ed.), 96, 98; and Feng Ling, *Emei jingguan tanyuan*, 22.

34. *People's Daily* (*Overseas Edition*), Nov. 7, 1992.

35. *EMSZ* (1934 ed.), 8.3b.

36. The figures here concerning flora are taken from *EMSZ* (1997 ed.), 125.

37. Zhang Shiliang 張士良, "Emei shan yaoyong zhiwu ziyuan gaikuang" 峨眉山藥用植物資源概況, *Emei wenshi* 1:105.

38. *HYGZ*, 3.282.

39. *QTS*, 198.2046.

40. According to Qikun Zhao, "Macaques and Tourists at Mt. Emei, China," *Folia Primatologica* 58 (1992): 116–17, "at least 10 [tourists] have died as a result of trying to get away [from the monkeys] and falling down the mountainside."

41. *QTS*, 849.9611 ("Tonghua niao").

42. *LBJ*, 12.808 ("Zeng Huang Shanhu gong qiu baixian, bing xu").

43. *EMSZ* (1934 ed.), 8.1a; *EMSZ* (1997 ed.), 641.

44. *EMSZ* (1934 ed.), 4.8a.

45. *WCL*, 1.17b; *FCDBJ*, 202. Fan Chengda's observation of the Precious Light and other experiences on the summit of Mount Emei are discussed in chapter 6.

CHAPTER 2. LAND OF SHU

1. *LBJ*, 3.199 ("Shudao nan").
2. At the time of this writing (June, 2005), China is organized administratively into twenty-three provinces (*sheng*), five autonomous regions (*zizhi qu*), and four cities (*shi*) under central government control. If we discount the Xinjiang and Tibet autonomous regions, in land area Sichuan is second only to Qinghai province (721,000 sq km/447,020 sq mi). As for population, Henan province now has the most people in China (96.1 million), followed closely by Shandong (94.3 million). It should be mentioned that the large industrial city of Chongqing (or "Chungking") is no longer part of Sichuan province. In 1997 it became China's fourth (after Beijing, Tianjin, and Shanghai) largest city (or municipality), with a land area covering 82,366 sq km/51,067 sq mi and population of 32.1 million.
3. Michael Nyland, "The Legacies of the Chengdu Plain," in Bagley, *Ancient Sichuan*, 310.
4. Chinese historians usually cite one of two conflicting dates to mark the Qin conquest of Shu: 329 BC and 316 BC Here I follow the latter date, provided in *Shiji*, 5.207. As noted by Sage, *Ancient Sichuan*, 199, the *Shiji* date has a strong claim to authority.
5. In 1001, what was previously called the Chuanxia circuit (Chuanxia lu) in Sichuan was reorganized into four separate circuits: Yi (this later became the Chengdu fu lu, or Chengdu municipal circuit), Zi, Li, and Kui. See Bi Yuan 畢沅 (1730–1797). *Xu Zizhi tongjian* 續資治通鑒 (Beijing: Zhonghua shuju, 1957), 48.1052. Many modern scholars believe this administrative reorganization to be the source of the name "Sichuan."
6. Sage, *Ancient Sichuan*, 9; 219, n. 1.
7. In 1985 it was discovered that the "Three Star Mounds" are actually three surviving sections of a single, man-made wall.
8. The first Sanxing dui discovery was made in 1929, after a local farmer came upon a cache of several hundred jade and stone disks, blades, and other implements at the bottom of an irrigation ditch. Several generations of archaeologists have since worked at the site. The most significant finds to date were made in 1986. The second chapter of Sage's *Ancient Sichuan*, 9–46, describes and summarizes the most important discoveries at Sanxing dui up to the early 1990s; more recent developments are discussed by Jay Xu in "Sichuan Before the Warring States Period," in Bagley, *Ancient Sichuan*, 24–27. Among the most important of these developments was the discovery, since 1995, of five walled settlements. Centered in the Chengdu Plain, these sites date to the second half of the third millennium BC, and are products of a Bronze Age civilization with a distinctive Neolithic culture. Taking its name from the site of the first of these discoveries, the "Baodun culture" of Shu was the foundation on which civilization was to later arise in Sichuan.

The Sanxing dui culture, described below, had its foundations in the Baodun culture.

9. These dates are based on carbon-14 tests of strata at Sanxing dui. See Jay Xu, "Sichuan Before the Warring States Period," in Bagley, *Ancient Sichuan*, 24.

10. On the various contributions of Shu culture in general, and Chengdu in particular, to the development of Chinese culture and civilization, especially during the Qin and Han unification periods, see Michael Nylan's excellent essay "The Legacies of the Chengdu Plain," in Bagley, *Ancient Sichuan*, 309–25.

11. Sage, *Ancient Sichuan*, 44.

12. On orders from King Hui of Qin, an alpine road traversing the Qinling and Daba mountains was once constructed between the Qin capital in Xianyang and Chengdu. Legend has it that the road was built as a ruse to dupe the Shu king (Kaiming XII) into accepting some stone cattle (that supposedly excreted gold!) as gifts. The real purpose of this mountain road was to prepare an invasion route into Shu (the old narrow paths across the mountains could not accommodate heavy military transport wagons).

13. A general description of Li Bing's irrigation system is provided in Joseph Needham et al., *Science and Civilisation in China*, 4.3: 288–96.

14. Sage, *Ancient Sichuan*, 126–27.

15. This is only one possible explanation concerning the origin of the city's name. There are several others, which are summarized in Cui Rongchang, *Sichuan fangyan yu Ba-Shu wenhua*, 299–302.

16. *HYGZ*, 3.182. "Xionger" refers to Xionger Gorge (Xionger xia) on the Min River in modern Qingshen *xian*; "Lingguan" is south of modern Baoxing *xian*; "Yulei [shan]" (or Jade Citadel [Mountain]) fell within the boundaries of modern Dujiang yan *shi* (near Li Bing's "Partition Mound"). *EMSZ* (1997 ed.), 8–9, 636.

17. Luo Mengting, *Emei shan kaituo shihlue*, 3. As mentioned by Luo, Chang Qu was a native of Shu and served as an official there for many years. Thus, it seems reasonable to assume that he was familiar with available sources on the region and their reliability.

18. For a detailed discussion of the connection between Mount Yamen and Emei shan, see my article "Where Are the Moth Eyebrows?", 345 ff.

19. *Shuijing zhu*, 36.1b, quoting from a (lost) work titled *Yizhou ji* 益州記.

20. Proponents of the "moth-eyebrows" interpretation of Mount Emei's name never mention when the *e* character with the "insect" classifier (蛾) changed to the *e* character with the "mountain" classifier (峨).

21. Several examples are cited in *EMSZ* (1997 ed.), 636.

22. *Shanhai jing jiaozhu*, 5.157.

23. *Quan Shanggu Sandai Qin Han Sanguo Liuchao wen* 全上古三代秦漢三國六朝文 (Beijing: Zhonghua shuju, 1958), 2:22.4b ("Yu Xie An shu").

24. *LBJ*, 14.863 ("Lushan yao ji Lu Shiyu xuzhou").

25. One ancient method used to calculate seasonal change involved placing reed ashes (*jiahui*) into each of the twelve bamboo (tube) pitch-pipes (*lülü*) used in traditional music, which were then locked away in a closet. With the arrival of each season, the ashes in their pipes would supposedly be "blown away." The point in this opening couplet of Taizong's poem is that although autumn's shadows (or "arrows") are starting to move on the sundial, some reed ashes still remain in the "summer's pipes."

26. *QTS*, 1.9 ("Duqiu"). As I understand the last line of this verse, Li Shimin is trying to sound humble: "I nibble at my brush tip in search of the right words, but I really have not found them; this is because the passage of time is controlled by laws that are too subtle to be grasped by my mind."

27. *QTS*, 83.894 ("Ganyu," no. 36). Mount Wu (Wushan), paired here with Mount Sui, is located in eastern Sichuan, near the border with Hubei.

28. Tales of immortals associated with Mount Emei are discussed in chapter 4.

29. *Lunyu zhushu* 論語注疏 (*SSJZS* ed.) 2:2529a.

30. See, for instance, Jieyu's biography in *Gaoshi zhuan*, 1.13b–14b

31. This is another name for Second Emei; it stands about 40 *li*/13 mi south of the main section of the mountain.

32. Most of the comments on Li Bo that follow are drawn from my article "Li Bo (701–762) and Mount Emei."

33. *LBJ*, 8.566 ("Emei shan yue ge"). "Pingqiang" is an alternate name for the Green Robe River (Qingyi jiang) in Sichuan; "Clear Creek" (Qingxi) was a post station (*yi*) during the Tang and Song, located about 40 *li* north of Jia county, in what is now called Suping.

34. The Han dynasty writer Sima Xiangru supposedly once owned a zither known as "Green Tracery" (Lüqi). This is mentioned in the preface to Fu Xuan's (217–278) "Zither Rhapsody" ("Qinfu"), in *Quan Shanggu Sandai Qin Han Sanguo Liuchao wen*, 2:1716.

35. This line alludes to a passage in the *Mountains and Seas Classic*, which tells of nine bells on Mount Feng that would sound whenever there was a frost. *Shanhai jing jiaozhu*, 5.165.

36. *LBJ*, 24.1416 ("Ting Shuseng Jun tanqin").

37. Li Bo's biographers agree that he left the Sichuan area (or Shu) in the mid 720s, at which time he traveled down the Yangzi River Valley to points east. See, for instance, Wang Qi 王琦 (1696–1774), *Li Taibo nianpu* 李太白年譜, rpt. in *LBJ*, "Nianpu," 2: 1749.

38. These figures are based on information in Hanabusa Hidecki 花房英樹, comp., *Ri Haku kashi sakuin* 李白歌詩索引 (Kyoto: Jimbun kagaku kenkyūshō, 1957), 137–38.

39. *LBJ*, 8.543–44 ("Dangtu Zhao Yan shaofu fentu shanshui ge"). "Wuling" refers to the utopia described by Tao Qian in the prose preface to his famous "Poem of the Peach Blossom Font" ("Taohua yuan shi").

40. In some editions of Li Bo's *Works*, the first two characters in this line, *zhenxian* 真仙 ("perfected immortality") instead read *zhenshan* 真山

("perfected mountain"). See *LBJ*, 8.544. If we follow this reading, my translation would then read "Perfected mountains (like Emei and those depicted on Zhao's mural) could complete my body, [thus turning me into an immortal]."

41. See, for instance, *LBJ*, 13.837–38 ("Wen Danqiuzi yu Chengbei shan . . ."), and 3.199 ("Shudao nan")

42. Chao refers to Chaofu, a well-known hermit of remote antiquity who supposedly was once offered the throne by the legendary emperor Yao. Boyi was also a famous recluse who, along with his younger brother Shuqi, preferred suffering from cold and hunger in the mountains to serving an alien dynasty.

43. *LBJ*, 18.1076 ("Jiangxi: song youren zhi Luofu").

44. The term *fangzhi* 芳枝 ("fragrant branches") is interchangeable with *zizhi* 紫芝, the "purple mushroom." This efficacious vegetable, along with other varieties of *zhi*, was considered by many to be the "food of immortality."

45. See, for instance, the comments in Wong Siu-kit, *The Genius of Li Po*, AD *701–762* (Hong Kong: University of Hong Kong, Centre of Asian Studies, 1974), 12–22.

46. This line might be paraphrased: "When you get to the capital you will be appointed to the highest position." The so-called Lion Throne is where the Buddha himself sits. The character *shi* 師 here is used for *shi* 獅, or "lion."

47. *LBJ*, 8.568 ("Emei shan yuege: song Shu Seng Yan ru Zhongjing").

48. Ruo of the Sea (Hairuo) is a sea god that appears in the "Autumn Floods" ("Qiushui") chapter of the *Zhuangzi* 莊子 (*Sibu beiyao* ed.), 6.7a ff.. The Black Dragon (Lilong), mentioned in the next line, also appears in the *Zhuangzi*, 10.11a. It supposedly kept a pearl tucked under its chin.

49. The parallel structure of this couplet suggests that "Sandalwood Gallery" (Zhantan ge) is used as a proper noun. Since this was a common name for galleries in Buddhist temples, it is difficult to tell which "Sandalwood Gallery" Li Bo has in mind. "Parrot Isle" (Yingwu zhou), however, refers to an island of that name in the Yangzi River within sight of the famous Yellow Crane Tower (Huanghe lou) in modern Wuhan. If Monk Xingrong was traveling by boat from Shu to the "great sea," he would certainly have passed by these well-known landmarks.

50. *LBJ*, 12.807–08 ("Zeng Seng Xingrong"). The famous White Tower (or White Tower Pavilion [Bailou ting]), was located in what is now Shaoxing, Zhejiang.

51. A check of Bao Zhao's *Works* turned up two poems addressed to Huixiu. See *Bao Canjun shizhu* 鮑參軍詩注 (Taibei: Heluo tushu chubanshe, 1985), 91–92. These verses say nothing about Huixiu accompanying Bao Zhao on his travels.

52. Their friendship is mentioned in Lu Zangyong 陸藏用, *Chen Ziang biezhuan* 陳子昂別傳, quoted in *LBJ*, 12.807. A verse by the Tang poet Cui Hao

(d. 754), addressed to Shi Huaiyi, mentions that Shi "recited sūtras" on Mount Emei. See *QTS*, 130.1322.

53. *LBJ*, 21.1212–13 ("Deng Emei shan"). The last line of this verse is taken almost verbatim from Chen Ziang's famous "Long Bamboo" ("Xiuzhu") poem, which describes how the "Ying Terrace Maiden" (Yingtai nü) and her lover "Hand in hand climbed to the bright sun" and later "Forever followed companies of immortals." See *QTS*, 83.895–96.

54. *Zhuangzi*, 1.4b.

55. *Wenxuan*, 31.28a. The line to which Li Zhouhan's gloss is appended appears in one of Jiang Yan's (444–505) famous "Thirty Poems in Miscellaneous Styles" ("Zati shi sanshi shou"); specifically, the nineteenth of these verses, which includes the line "Rising lightly on the wind, I enjoy the void." Li Bo's "Rising lightly on the wind, I enjoy the purple auroras" is modeled directly after Jiang Yan's line.

56. One of the earliest appearances of the term "purple auroras" is recorded in a Lu Ji (261–303) poem. The subject of this verse is a gathering of "traveling immortals." See *Wenxuan*, 28.13b.

57. *Wudi neizhuan* 武帝內傳 (*Daozang* ed.), 22a.

58. This seems a fitting place to discuss two questions suggested earlier; namely, first, did Li Bo ever visit Mount Emei?; and second, if so, did he actually climb the mountain? We can be reasonably certain that Li Bo visited the Emei shan area sometime between the time when he left Chengdu in 720 and when he traveled down the Great River in 725. This period of his life, however, is not well documented. Except for the poems considered in this chapter, there is no other evidence to confirm his visit to the mountain. Still, it seems unlikely that Li Bo would have written verses with titles such as "Climbing Mount Emei" and then later in life nostalgically recall the mountain if he had not personally visited Emei shan. The Min River, which passes within about twenty five miles of Mount Emei, likely served as the poet's transportation route from Chengdu south to the Yangzi. So, there is no reason to doubt that Li Bo paid a visit the general environs of Mount Emei sometime between 720 and 725. The second question—whether he actually climbed Emei—is an entirely different matter. Again, aside from the verses discussed earlier, there is no evidence to confirm the poet's ascent of Mount Emei. As we have seen, the content of the poems themselves are of little help; none of them even suggest a physical ascent. Not only do they fail to mention specific landmarks; they say nothing about the difficulties of scaling the mountain. The only clue that might help us solve this puzzle is the allusion to the immortal Ge You that appears in line 15 of "Climbing Mount Emei." As it turns out, Ge You is *not* traditionally associated with what we today identify as the main section of Mount Emei ("Big Emei"). Rather, he is identified with a completely different part of the mountain, mentioned earlier, known individually as Mount Sui (also called "Middle Emei" and "Second Emei"). According to a passage in the *Liexian zhuan*,

1.11a–b, Ge You's association with Mount Sui extends back to the reign of King Cheng (r. 1115–1078 BC) of the Zhou. This same text also mentions that "all of those who followed Ge You to Mount Sui discovered the immortal Way and never returned." The history of "Second Emei" actually predates that of Big Emei, or the main part of the mountain. This is easily explained: Mount Sui was much more accessible than the lofty peaks of "Big Emei." The land around "Second Emei," as opposed to the towering, almost impassable crags found in the main part of the mountain, is flat and cultivated. Is it possible that Mount Sui was Li Bo's Mount Emei? Could this have been the place he visited in the 720s? This seems quite possible. The modern scholar Li Jiajun 李家俊 argues that this, in fact, is what happened. See his "Er'e shan" 二峨山, in *Emei wenshi* 5:69. The area around Mount Sui was accessible, had a long history, and was rich in Daoist hagiography and topographical features, including a grotto system. It certainly would not have been unusual for Li Bo to refer to this mountain as "Emei shan," nor would it have been wrong. As far as I can tell, the practice of referring to various parts of Emei as "Big Emei," "Second Emei," "Third Emei," and so on, did not begin until the Song dynasty. Finally, the fact that there is no evidence to prove that *any* Tang figure ever climbed the peaks of Big Emei makes it all the more likely that Li Bo's "Emei experience" took place at Mount Sui.

59. On Du Fu's association of Emei shan with immortals, see especially his "Twelve Rhymes Sent to Sima Shier," where the Han dynasty *xian* Jizi Xun is heard making "a long whistle north of Mount Emei." *Dushi yinde*, 403/2/9 ("Ji Sima shanren shier yun").

60. *QTS*, 198.2046 ("Emei dongjiao: linjiang tingyuan huai ershi jiu lu").

61. *HYJ*, 74.577.

62. The history of the Lao people (or Laozi 獠子) in the Emei shan area is discussed in chapter 4.

63. *QTS*, 293.3335. The precise topographical reference of "Celestial Pillar" (Tianzhu), mentioned in the opening line of the poem, is not clear.

64. *WCL*, 1.15a; *FCDBJ*, 199.

65. *EMSZ* (1934 ed.), 4.2a, mentions that during the Southern Song "tigers and wolves were doing harm" near the Crouching Tiger Monastery (Fuhu si), at the base of the mountain.

66. See, for instance, Bao Rong's (ninth cent) poem "I Had a Meeting Scheduled with a Gentleman of the Way from Mount Emei, But He Never Arrived the Whole Day Long," in *QTS*, 485.5510 ("Yu Emei shan daoshi qi jinri buzhi").

67. A good example is Bao Rong's verse "Sent to Refined Master Yang on Mount Emei," *QTS*, 486.5530 ("Ji Emei shan Yang Lianshi"), which mentions how the "Gentleman of the Way" (that is, Refined Master Yang) mounts a "white crane" and rides an "immortal wind" into the "dark and gloomy" autumn night.

68. *QTS*, 717.8238 ("Songseng ru Shu guoxia").

69. For instance, the famous monk Qiji (fl. 881) has left a verse titled "Longing to Make a Trip to Mount Emei: Sent to All My Retired Friends in the Country." See *QTS*, 839.9463 ("Si you Emei: ji linxia zhuyou").

70. *QTS*, 561.6510 ("Wang deng").

71. The possible origins of Mount Emei's "sage lamps" are discussed in chapter 6.

72. Luo Mengting contends that Xue Neng's verse has nothing to do Mount Emei's "sage lamps." The basis of his argument is traced to the title of the poem as it appears in the *QTS*, 561.6510, which reads: "Gazing at the Lamp(s)" ("Wang deng" 望燈). Jiang Chao, editor of the *Mount Emei Gazetteer*, later changed the title of Xue Neng's poem to read "The Sage Lamps of Mount Emei" ("Emei shengdeng" 峨眉聖燈). See *EMSZ* (1934 ed.), 7.9a. Without these alterations in the title, Luo Mengting contends, Xue Neng's poem could easily be read as a description of a simple oil lamp (*youdeng* 油燈). To bolster his argument, Luo cites mention of "fire" and "smoke" in line 3 which, he says, are unmistakable references to an ordinary (oil) lamp. See *Emei shan kaituo shilue*, 25. On the other hand, in his recent M.A. thesis Justin O'Jack cites Xue Neng's poem as evidence that "a high-ranking [Tang] official was able to reach the Golden Summit." O'Jack, "Auspicious Lights," 49. Although Luo makes a convincing argument, the vague language in the poem makes it impossible to determine, one way or the other, if Xue Neng's verse concerns Emei's sage lamps and whether or not he ever saw them.

73. Only a fraction of Fan Zhen's *wenji*, or collected works, has survived, and is preserved in *juan* 39 of *Liang Song mingxian xiaoji* 兩宋名賢小集 (*SKQS* ed.). The "First Hall" ("Chudian") poem translated here is not found among Fan Zhen's works preserved in that collection. My source is the *Jiading fu zhi* (1986 ed.), 756. Although the title of Fan Zhen's poem is always rendered Chudian ("First Hall" 初殿), it should instead read "First Way-stop" (Chudian 初店). During the Song dynasty, such rest stops (*dian* 店) on Emei were one-room structures built along the mountain trail where travelers could stop, rest, and have a hot meal (provided by monks). The name "First Hall" was not used until the Ming period, when Chan Master Xuen built a temple on the site of the original "First Rest Stop." Clearly, some later editor tampered with the title of Fan Zhen's poem.

74. See, for instance, *Su Shi shiji*, 34.1844 ("Song Yunpan Zhu chaofeng ru Shu"), in which Su Shi remarks: "Beautiful and elegant is the moon above Mount Emei."

75. *Su Shi shiji*, 28.1479–80 ("Song Yang Mengrong").

76. *Su Shi shiji*, 38.2049–50 ("Wang Huting").

77. *Yuanhe junxian tuzhi*, 32.3b; *HYJ*, 74.572.

78. *Su Shi shiji*, 9.426 ("Fahui si Hengcui ge").

CHAPTER 3. A JOURNEY OF TEN THOUSAND MILES

1. *Wenxuan*, 4.83 ("Shudu fu"); Knechtges, *Wen xuan*, 1:343.
2. The estimated population figure here is based on the report of "76,256 households" given in *Hanshu*, 28A.1598.
3. In traditional China, resin from lac trees was melted, strained, and formed into irregular thin plates called shell-lac (or shellac), which was used to produce lacquer ware.
4. Nyland, "The Legacies of the Chengdu Plain," 311.
5. *Shiji*, 123.3166.
6. Jeannette L. Faurot, *Ancient Chengdu* (San Francisco: Chinese Materials Center, 1992), 43.
7. *QTS*, 382.4290.
8. *SS*, 42.2211, gives a population of 567,930 persons, dated to 1102–1107, which includes Chengdu and its nine surrounding towns. As far as I know, no accurate population figures for Chengdu during the Southern Song are available. We do know, however, that during the Southern Song the population of Sichuan exceeded six million for the first time in history. See Cui Rongchang, *Sichuan fangyan yu Ba-Shu wenhua*, 39.
9. Fan Chengda's Chengdu poems, many of which celebrate scenic sites around the city, are found in *juan* 17 of *FSHJ*. On the many verses Lu You penned in Chengdu, see Wei Jiongruo 魏炯若, "Lu You shizhong de Chengdu" 陸游詩中的成都, *Sichuan shiyuan xuebao* 3 (1980): 55–58 (Part 1); and 4 (1980): 60–64 (Part 2).
10. Fan Chengda maintained a lifelong interest in Buddhism. One expression of this interest is evident in his self-chosen *hao* 號, or nickname, translated here as "Layman of Rocky Lake." In its most general sense, the term *jushi* 居士, or "layman" (lit., "resident scholar") refers to an individual who studies and practices Buddhism at home, as opposed to someone who takes formal vows and enters a monastery.
11. Yongkang command (Yongkang jun) corresponds to modern Guan *xian*, Sichuan.
12. The two commanderies mentioned here are actually the names of counties. Peng county (Pengzhou) corresponds to modern Peng *xian*, Sichuan. Shu county (Shuzhou) is modern Chongqing *xian*, Sichuan. The name "Shu county" was actually abandoned in the 1140s in favor of Chongqing Command for Order and Rule (Chongqing jun jiedu). Later, in 1177, Chongqing was elevated to the status of a *fu*, or municipality. See *SS*, 89.2211.
13. Modern Xinjin *xian*, Sichuan.
14. My translations from the *WCL* are based on the text in the *Zhibuzu zhai congshu*, collection no. 18, edited by Bao Tingbo (1728–1814) and published in 1805. This is still the best edition of the diary available. The modern scholar Kong Fanli has recently produced a useful recension of this text, with punctuation and collation notes. This appears in his *Fan Chengda biji*

liuzhong (FCDBJ), 181–242. References to the *WCL* will contain two citations, the first to the *Zhibuzu zhai congshu* text, the second to Kong Fanli's recension. The references for this opening passage from Fan's diary are: *WCL*, 1.1a; *FCDBJ*, 187.

15. Although I have followed the common practice of translating the botanical term *mei* 梅 as "plum," in fact it is a variety of apricot; specifically, the *Prunus mume*, or "Japanese apricot."

16. *WCL*, 1.1a; *FCDBJ*, 187.

17. Wang Wencai 王文才, *Chengdu chengfang kao* 成都城坊考 (Chengdu: Bashu shushe, 1986), 47.

18. The standard sources on the history of Myriad Mile Bridge, conveniently assembled in *SCTZ*, 31.7b–10b, say nothing about it being built for "the benefit of natives of Wu."

19. "Board their boats" (*dengzhou*) is another way of saying "began their journeys."

20. A. D. Syrokomla-Stefanowska, in her article "Fan Cheng-ta's Wu-Boat Journey of 1177," 67, n. 5, points out that although this line is often attributed to Zhuge Liang, at least one source assigns it instead to Fei Yi. See also *Yuanhe junxian tuzhi*, 31.428.

21. *Dushi yinde*, 409/26/26c ("Jueju sishou"); translated in William Hung, *Tu Fu*, 184. The title of Fan Chengda's diary, then, is adapted from this line in Du Fu's poem.

22. *WCL*, 1.1a–b; *FCDBJ*, 187.

23. Modern Pengshan *xian*, Sichuan; Mei county corresponds to Meishan *xian*, Sichuan.

24. Government officials in traditional China did not consider their subordinates and servants as "true" members of their traveling party. Since his family had already gone downriver to Pengshan, Fan thus remarks that he rode his horse "alone" around the city wall. In fact, however, he was still traveling with a large support staff.

25. This dike, also known as the Attendant Esquire Weir (Shilang yan), was eighteen *li* east of Yongkang. *HYJ*, 73.570. "Attendant Esquire" is an office title, and probably refers to the official who was responsible for constructing the dike.

26. The graph *qin* 秦 in this line seems superfluous and so I have not translated it. Cf. the comments by Kong Fanli in *FCDBJ*, 208, n. 1.

27. *WCL*, 1.2a; *FCDBJ*, 187.

28. Modern Pi *xian*, Sichuan. *HYGZ*, 3.240, marks the town sixty *li* northwest of Chengdu.

29. The canopies mentioned here were probably tents of some sort, erected to protect onlookers from the hot summer sun in Sichuan.

30. Fan Chengda is referring to himself. "Regulation Marshal" (Zhishuai) is not a bureaucratic title, but rather another way of saying "a high-ranking official."

31. Pi district (Pi yi) was two *li* north of Pi town. According to tradition, it was once known as Hawk-Cuckoo City (Dujuan cheng), where the ancient ruler of Shu, Duyu, had his capital. *HYGZ*, 3.183, n. 3.

32. *WCL*, 1b–2a; *FCDBJ*, 187–88.

33. The phrase "fertile countryside below the Min Mountains" is quoted from the *Shiji*, 129.3277.

34. According to a passage preserved in *MSJ*, 84, this temple was situated two *li* west of Yongkang command. The poem Fan Chengda composed to commemorate his visit to the temple is found in *FSHJ*, 18.248 ("Chongde miao").

35. *WCL*, 1.2b; *FCDBJ*, 188. Tradition says that Li Bing's son, Li Erlang, succeeded him as overseer of the Partition Mound engineering project.

36. *WCL*, 1.2b; *FCDBJ*, 188.

37. Li Fan was a native of Sichuan and served for many years there as a government official. Fan Chengda held him in high regard because Li's administrative efforts brought tax relief to the people of Sichuan. See the remarks on this in Li Fan's biography in *SS*, 398.12118–19.

38. *Dushi yinde*, 353/21/42 ("Denglou"). The poem is translated in Hung, *Tu Fu*, 207.

39. *WCL*, 1.2b; *FCDBJ*, 188.

40. On the Exalted Virtue Temple, see n. 34 above.

41. *WCL*, 1.3a; *FCDBJ*, 189.

42. *MSJ*, 83, mentions that the bridge was one *zhang* in width, and stood five *chi* above the Min River. Further details on the bridge are provided in Needham, *Science and Civilisation in China*, 4.3: 192–93. Fan also composed a poem about the bridge. See *FSHJ*, 18.248 ("Xi ti Suoqiao").

43. *WCL*, 1.3b–4a; *FCDBJ*, 189.

44. The events described here concerning the Feifu Monastery are drawn from the account in *MSJ*, 6.21b.

45. See *Liexian zhuan*, 1.1a.

46. *Qingcheng zhinan*, 5b.

47. Mount Qian is northwest of modern Qianshan *xian*, Anhui; Mount Lu stands in the very northern part of modern Jiangxi province.

48. Fan's petition has not survived, but a poem commemorating the event is preserved in *FSHJ*, 18.248–49 ("Qingcheng shan Huiqing jianfu gong").

49. The Jiao Ceremony is a ritual of renewal, performed by a Daoist adept with assistance from a company of spirits and deities. On the use of the *jiao* ritual ceremony during the Song, see Robert Hymes, "A *Jiao* Is a *Jiao* Is a?: Thoughts on the Meaning of a Ritual," in *Culture and State in Chinese History: Conventions, Accommodations, and Critiques*, Theodore Huters, R. Bin Wong, and Pauline Yu, eds. (Stanford: Stanford University Press, 1997), 129–60.

50. The rhyming expression *huifei* 翬飛, rendered loosely here as "like a pheasant in flight," is drawn from the *Classic of Poetry* (*Shijing* [*Maoshi* no.189]).

Fan Chengda's reference is probably to the colorful appearance of the tower's eaves.

51. Sun Zhiwei (*style* Taigu) is a well-known painter from Sichuan who once lived as a recluse on Mount Qingcheng. Sun is especially well known for his paintings of Buddhist and Daoist clergy.

52. Zhangguo is a famous recluse of the Tang who is said to have had supernatural powers. The emperor Xuanzong once persuaded Zhang to leave his hermitage and come to the capital, where the recluse supposedly performed several magic feats for his royal patron. Zhangguo, however, eventually lost interest in Chang'an and returned to his mountain retreat. Several references to accounts of his life and exploits are provided in *Tang Wudai renwu zhuanji ziliao zonghe suoyin*, 163. See also *Taiping guangji*, 30.192–94.

53. Sun Simiao, also known as "Sun the Realized One" (Sun Zhenren), was a Daoist adept supposedly born during the Sui and active during the seventh century. Like Zhangguo (see n. 52), Sun refused several lucrative offers of government employment in the capital, preferring instead to pass his days on Mount Emei. Information on Sun's life and activities is assembled in Zhang Xiaomei et al., *Emei shan*, 80–81. The death date of 682 used here is taken from Sun's biography in the *Jiu Tangshu*, 191.5096.

54. *WCL*, 1.4a–b; *FCDBJ*, 190.

55. Use of the verb "moor" (*bo* 泊) here indicates that at some earlier point (not mentioned in the *WCL*) Fan Chengda boarded a boat (on the Min River) to take him to Mount Qingcheng.

56. "Minor City" is another name for the western section of Chengdu, where the (circuit-level) governmental offices were located.

57. This is an esoteric Daoist ritual in which an initiate ceremoniously paces through "the barren wastes of space, beyond even the stars, where subjective and objective are indistinguishable." Schafer, *Pacing the Void*, 1.

58. On the "great flare of light" described here, see the discussion below.

59. Here I follow the gloss in Ogawa Tamaki, *Gosen Roku*, 18, n. 9, and read *jingzang* 經藏 (lit., "sūtra depository") to mean *lunzang* 輪藏, or "revolving scriptures." The reference here is to Buddhist scriptures arranged on a revolving stand or wheel with eight faces, each representing a direction and holding a section of the *Buddhist Canon*.

60. One source dates this palace (or Daoist temple) from the eighth century; another says it was built during the Jin dynasty (265–420). See *MSJ*, 89. Fan Chengda wrote a poem to commemorate his visit to the Supreme Clarity Palace. See *FSHJ*, 18.250.

61. In other words, the hall, supported by timbers inserted into the rocky face of a cliff, seemingly stood suspended in midair.

62. Although the expression *yishang* 一上 is sometimes used in Song texts to mean "for a short while" or "immediately thereafter," these glosses do not seem to match the implied conditional aspect of Fan's line here. On the other hand, in this context it does make sense to read *shang* as a verb

("to go up," "to ascend"). Perhaps the character *yi* is being used in an adverbial sense, meaning something like "directly" ("If you go straight up the mountain for another 60 *li* . . ."). In any case, I have not attempted to translate it. None of the translators and commentators of the *WCL* have addressed this textual question.

63. Hemlock parsley (*xiong* or *Chuanxiong*; *Conioselinum uymbelliferae*) is an herb indigenous to Sichuan and Gansu.

64. "Feathered robes" (*yuyi*) is another name for Daoist adepts.

65. The Snow Mountains, also known as the Big Snow Mountain Range (Daxue shanmai), stretch north to south along the west side of the Great Ford River in extreme west-central Sichuan. Gongga Mountain (Gongga shan) is the highest peak in this range. The "three peaks" mentioned here may be part of Gongga shan. But if this is the case, then Fan Chengda was viewing a mountain some 200 km/124 mi southwest of his current position on Mount Qingcheng. Cf. the comments on this question in Chen Cheng-Siang, *Zhongguo youji xuanzhu*, 1:17–18, n. 31. See also Fan's poem, "Gazing at the Snow Mountains from [Mount Qingcheng's] Highest Peak" ("Zui gaofeng wang Xueshan"), in *FSHJ*, 18.250.

66. During the Southern Song, the term Western Regions (Xiyu) was applied generally to areas west of about 103 degrees longitude. It referred to those regions to the west of and beyond the control of the Southern Song empire.

67. *WCL*, 1.5b–6a; *FCDBJ*, 191.

68. *Huainanzi*, 13.20b.

69. See, for example, Chen Cheng-Siang, *Zhongguo youji xuanzhu*, 1:17, n. 28.

70. Fan Changsheng (or "Long-Life Fan") is Fan Ji (*style* Wuwei), a Daoist adept who lived during the third century. As reported here, Fan Ji supposedly "found the Way"—that is to say, he discovered the secret to eternal life, on Mount Qingcheng. Hence, the nickname "Long-Life Fan." His retreat on the mountain was later converted into the Long-Life Abbey.

71. Sun's dragon and tiger were probably serving as ceremonial "guards" of the audience hall.

72. The *SKQS* ed. of the *WCL* has a different title for Sun's painting: "Longwei cheng" 龍未成 ("[Painting of a] Dragon Still Incomplete"). Kong Fanli, *FCDBJ*, 209, n. 7, suspects this is the correct title of the painting, but provides no evidence to support such a reading.

73. Referring to Kaifeng, the Eastern Capital of the Northern Sung.

74. *WCL*, 1.6a; *FCDBJ*, 191–92. Manors, or *zhuangyuan*, are large private estates. Fan Chengda composed a quatrain to mark the occasion of his visit to the Fan Clan Manor. See *FSHJ*, 18.250.

75. Qingcheng town (Qingcheng xian) was forty *li* southwest of Yongkang command. *HYJ*, 73.570. The town took its name from nearby Mount Qingcheng.

76. *WCL*, 1.6a–b; *FCDBJ*, 192.

77. In other words, there have been no upheavals in the area since the founding of the Song dynasty in 960.

78. Chen Xin, *Songren Changjiang youji*, 202, n. 1, points out that "continuous tranquility" (*chengping*) was a term used during the Southern Song to refer to the Northern Song (that is to say, the era of "continuous tranquility" that preceded the Jin invasions of the 1120s).

79. *WCL*, 1.7a–b; *FCDBJ*, 192–93.

80. *WCL*, 1.7b; *FCDBJ*, 193.

81. This was another name for the section of the Min River below Frog Chin Hill, which stands seven *li* east of Meishan.

82. *WCL*, 1.8a; *FCDBJ*, 193. Wang Yangying served in several posts in the Song government, both at the national and local levels, including Administrator of Mei county. For additional information on his life and career, see *Songren zhuanji ziliao suoyin*, 1:344–45.

83. "Grand Protector" (Taishou) refers to the chief administrative officer of the county.

84. *WCL*, 1.8b; *FCDBJ*, 194.

85. *WCL*, 1.8b–9a; *FCDBJ*, 194.

86. The Central Precipice was located ten *li* east Qingshen town. Fan composed a poem on the Central Precipice. See *FSHJ*, 18.252 ("Zhongyan").

87. "Enlightenment site" (*daochang*) originally referred to the spot under the famous Bodhi Tree in India where the Buddha found enlightenment. Here it means Central Precipice was the place where Nuojuna (Skt. Nakula; Tang dynasty), the Fifth Luohan, became "awakened" and found enlightenment.

88. *WCL*, 1.9a–b; *FCDBJ*, 194.

89. The *WCL* text here reads Qingyi 青衣. Ogawa, *Gosen roku*, 27, identifies Qingyi as the name of a river. There indeed is a Qingyi (or "Green Robe") River in this part of Sichuan, but it was not on Fan Chengda's present itinerary (it is located *south* of Jia county, which Fan has yet to reach). I suspect that Qingyi here is a mistake for Qingshen 青神. Qingshen town is located 65 *li* south of Mei county, on the western bank of the Min River, just a short distance from Jia county.

90. Chen Xin, *Songren Changjiang youji*, 211, n. 2, argues that Fan is referring here to a water passageway through the mountains (Hu Rang Gorge) that allowed our traveler to take a direct route from Qingshen town to Jia county, thus by-passing a large bend in the Min River. Chen's argument is based on a gloss of the word *rang* 瀼 provided by Lu You in the *Ru Shu ji*: "Local (Sichuan) folks refer to waterways flowing through mountains to the [Yangzi] River as '*rang*'." See *Ru Shu ji*, 6.298; Chun-shu Chang and Joan Smythe, trans., *South China in the Twelfth Century: A Translation of Lu Yu's Travel Diaries, July 3–December 6, 1170* (Hong Kong: The Chinese University Press, 1981), 172.

91. The "old town of Pingqiang," which takes its name from a river of the same name, was 40 *li* north of Jia county. *SCTZ*, 55.2043. Pingqiang was first

established as a town during the Northern Zhou. In Tang and Northern Song times it fell under the jurisdiction of Jia county, but in 1072 the town was abolished and became part of Longyou town. See *SS*, 89.2212.

92. Modern Leshan *shi*, Sichuan.

93. *WCL*, 1.10b; *FCDBJ*, 195.

94. Guo Yundao 郭允蹈 (fl. ca. 1200), *Shujian* 蜀鑒 (Chengdu: Ba Shu shushe, 1985), 1.5b.

95. For a useful overview of the history of the boat-building industry in Jia county, see Yang Bingkun, *Leshan gushi xintan*, 117–20.

96. *Ru Shu ji*, 3.279; Chang and Smythe, *South China in the Twelfth Century*, 95. Lu You nearly lost his boat near Kuizhou, Sichuan, when its bottom hit a sharp rock. The craft apparently was overloaded with chinaware his boatmen hoped to sell in Shu.

97. For additional details on dimensions and nomenclature, see Wang Guanzhuo 王冠倬, "Cong wenwu ziliao kan Zhongguo gudai zaochuan jishu de fazhan" 從文物資料看中國古代造船技術的發展, *Zhongguo lishi bowuguan guankan* 5 (1983): 25–26.

98. "Seal and striker" (*fengchuang* 封樁) funds are surplus tax revenues, unused by the various commands in Sichuan (*jun* 軍; "commands" here probably refers to the various administrative areas formerly under Fan's control), which eventually would be delivered to the central government in Lin'an.

99. *WCL*, 1.10b; *FCDBJ*, 196. Government officials like Fan Chengda were exempt from paying taxes on goods transported on boats. For this reason, businessmen sometimes tried to arrange special "deals," especially with crew members on boats transporting government officials, for "tax-free shipping."

100. This hall was located within the walled confines of Jia county and served as a popular traveler's lodge during the Song. See *Sichuan tongzhi*, 55.2045. Also see Fan's poem "A Wine Toast at Parting at Query the Moon Hall" ("Wenyue tang zhuo bie"), *FSHJ*, 18.255.

CHAPTER 4. WITHIN SIGHT OF MOUNT EMEI

1. Ma Duanlin 馬端臨 (1254–ca. 1325), *Wenxian tongkao* 文獻通考 (Taibei: Xinxing shuju, 1965), 328.2579. Huan Wen (312–373) was a military figure who in 347 recovered Sichuan for the Eastern Jin dynasty.

2. According to Liang Fangzhong, *Zhongguo lidai hukou*, 27, the territory of Qianwei in 140 AD encompassed 129,930 sq km/80,557 sq mi, making it in land area the third largest commandery in China.

3. Historically there are two Emei towns, in three different places. During the Northern Zhou dynasty (557–581), the first Emei town was built on the site of what is now Qingshen *xian*, north of Mount Emei. Later, in 593, a second Emei *xian* was established at the foot of the mountain. In 760, because of uprisings by local non-Chinese people who presumably lived on

Emei, the town seat was moved further east, away from the mountain. *HYJ*, 74.10b.

4. "Mei commandery" refers to Mei county, the hometown of Su Shi (or Su Dongpo).

5. "Jia" was probably adopted from the name of an old Han dynasty commandery known as Hanjia, which was located nearby in the general vicinity of modern Ya'an.

6. *SS*, 89.2212.

7. Leshan City (Leshan *shi*) was created in 1978. The name "Leshan" is adopted from a Qing dynasty *xian* and mountain of the same name situated five *li* south of the city.

8. *Hanshu*, 28A.1599.

9. That is, $489,486 \div 12 = 40,790$.

10. According to the *Hou Hanshu*, 23.3509, the population of Qianwei commandery in the year 140 AD was 411,378. The commandery now comprised nine *xian* (instead of twelve, as it was under the Former Han), so the average population in each *xian* was $411,378 \div 9 = 45,708$.

11. Essentially, Nan'an comprised Jia county (modern Leshan City), Emei town (modern Emei City), and Mount Emei itself.

12. According to Liang Fangzhong, the population density for Qianwei commandery in 140 AD was 3.2 people per sq km, which made it one of the most sparsely populated areas in China at that time. See his *Zhongguo lidai hukou*, 27.

13. Tang Changshou, *Jia Mei jigu lu*, 2–3.

14. Since at least the late third century, Emei shan has been identified as a place that produces outstanding tea and efficacious herbs. See the comments, for instance, in *HYGZ*, 3.281. Mount Emei also has a long-standing reputation for producing rare medicinal herbs (*yao*). See *EMSZ* (1997 ed.), 169–82, and *Emei xian zhi* (1991 ed.), 372–78.

15. The best summary of these finds appears in *EMSZ* (1997 ed.), 324 ff.

16. The bronzes were discovered in underground tombs at Qinglong *chang* in June, 1972. Excavation work yielded about forty pieces, which included porcelain ware (*taozi qi*) and stone and bronze implements.

17. Chen Liqing 陳黎清, in her article "Emei xian chutu de Zhanguo shiqi qingtong qi" 峨眉縣出土的戰國時期青銅器, *Emei wenshi* 1:45, dates the Emei finds to the "middle and late Warring States period."

18. According to a passage in the *HYJ*, 74.12a, King Hui of Qin relocated "ten thousand families" to Shu. We can be sure that at least some of these immigrants settled in the Qianwei area, because following their arrival the settlers renamed a local waterway after the Jing River (Jingshui) in Qin.

19. *Liji zhengyi* (*SSJZS* ed.), 1:1342b. The term "Western Quarters" (Xifang) includes Shu.

20. *Shuowen jiezi*, 167a.

21. Zhou Cong, "Emei diqu guzu shu shikao," 123–24.

22. These farming implements are described in *EMSZ* (1997 ed.), 325–27.

23. *Hanshu*, 57B.2581. This thoroughfare was most commonly known as the "Five-Foot Road" (Wuchi dao).

24. Zhou Cong, "Emei diqu guzu shu shikao,"126–27.

25. Zhou Cong, 127.

26. Zhou Cong, 129. The Yi people, because of their origins in Yunnan, are sometimes called Kunming yi. During the Tang and Song they were also known as the Mahu yi.

27. Liang Fangzhong, *Zhongguo lidai hukou*, 4; Hans Bielenstein, "Chinese Historical Demography AD 2–1982," 12.

28. *Jinshu*, 14.415, gives a total population of 16,163,863 for the year 280. Bielenstein, 17, argues this figure is "unsupported and therefore suspect." The source for my "under ten million" figure for the year 370 is *Jinshu*, 113.2893.

29. According to the *Jinshu*, 40.439, Qianwei commandery in 280 comprised five towns with a total population of ten thousand households (*hu*). Nan'an was one of these towns. If we follow Bielenstein's suggestion ("Chinese Historical Demography AD 2–1982," 7) that the average number of members per household (the so-called m/h value) in traditional China was around five, this would mean that the population of Qianwei was somewhere near 5 × 10,000 = 50,000 persons. Liang Fangzhong, *Zhongguo lidai hukou*, 54, lists the population figure for Qianwei in 464 at 4,057. If we divide this number by five—the number of *xian* in Qianwei at that time—then the population of Nan'an would have been well under one thousand.

30. *Shujian*, 4.13b, quoting Li Ying 李膺, *Yizhou ji* 益州記.

31. Zhou Cong, "Emei diqu guzu shu shikao,"128.

32. *EMSZ* (1997 ed.), 82.

33. See *Jiading fu zhi* (1986 ed.), 82, and *Jinshu*, 121.3047.

34. *Jiading fu zhi* (1864 ed.), 2.20b, 2.21b, 2.22a–b.

35. *Jiading fu zhi* (1864 ed.), 2.22b.

36. "On the Alchemy of T'ao Hung-ching," in *Facets of Taoism: Essays in Chinese Religion*, Holmes Welch, and Anna Seidel, eds. (New Haven: Yale University Press, 1979), 168.

37. Thomas H. Hahn, "Daoist Sacred Sites," 684.

38. Barbara Hendrichke, "Early Daoist Movements," in *Daoism Handbook*, 141.

39. Peter Nickerson, "The Southern Celestial Masters," in *Daoism Handbook*, 256.

40. *Shuzhong guangji*, 72.10b. Luo Mengting argues that the Emei travel parish was established in 198 AD. See "Emei shan kaituo shilue," 16.

41. Wang Xiangzhi 王象之 (*jinshi* 1196), *Yudi beiji mu* 輿地碑記目 (*SKQS* ed.), 4.6a.

42. Piet van der Loon, *Taoist Books in the Libraries of the Sung Period* (London: Ithaca Press, 1984), 126.

43. Hahn, "Daoist Sacred Sites," 686.

44. Luo Mengting, "Emei shan kaituo shilue," 17.

45. *Quan Tangwen*, 608.6145.

46. The Master Pu story will be discussed in detail in chapter 7.

47. To cite just one egregious example of textual tampering, what reads as "Seventh Grotto Heaven" (Diqi dongtian 第七洞天) in Hu Shian's *Yi elai* is changed by Jiang Chao to read "Samantabhadra, King of Vows" (Puxian yuanwang 普賢願王). *EMSZ* (1934 ed.), 1.19a.

48. Benjamin Penny cites some useful examples in his "Immortality and Transcendence," in *Daoism Handbook*, 119 ff.

49. Penny, 109.

50. Verellen, "The Beyond Within," 268.

51. Verellen, 271.

52. *Baopuzi neipian jiaoshi*, 18.324.

53. Zhang Junfang 張君房 (fl. 1008–1029), ed., *Yunji qiqian* 雲笈七籤 (*Daozang* ed.), 3.2b.

54. According to a work titled *Xuanpin lu* 玄品錄 (*Daozang* ed.), 3.12a, Lu Xiujing once visited Emei during his travels, where he made inquires about the "'high prancing' (*gaozhu*) technique of Qingxu [or Wang Bao]").

55. *Yunji qiqian*, 3.14c ("Tianzun Laojun minghao . . .").

56. For example, in the official history of the Wei dynasty we find the following: "The Daoist School originated with Laozi. . . . [Laozi] conferred teachings on Xuanyuan (that is, the Yellow Emperor) on Mount Emei." *Weishu*, 114.3048. Tradition says that the Yellow Emperor was born at a place called Xuanyuan; hence, he is sometimes called Xuanyuan.

57. *Quan Tangwen*, 250.2548b ("Tianchang jieshi . . .").

58. *Shuzhong guangji*, 11.12a, notes that Taizong's calligraphy was displayed in the Samantabhadra Hall (Puxian dian).

59. *EMSZ* (1997 ed.), 314.

60. Verellen, "The Beyond Within," 271.

61. "Dongtian fudi yuedu mingshan ji" 洞天福地嶽瀆名山記 (*Daozang* ed.), 3b–4b; 6b–8b.

62. "Dongtian fudi yuedu mingshan ji," 3b–4b.

63. *Yunji qiqian*, 27.159c. No other information is available on Tang Lan.

64. *EMSZ* (1997 ed.), 316.

65. *Liexian zhuan*, 1.10b–11a.

66. Gan Bao 干寶 (fl. 320), ed., *Soushen ji* 搜神記 (Beijing: Zhonghua shuju, 1979), 1.4.

67. *Liexian zhuan*, 1. 10b–11a.

68. *Gaoshi zhuan*, 1.14b.

69. *Youyang zazu* 酉陽雜俎 (Beijing: Zhonghua shuju, 1981), 2.19.

70. *Su Shi shiji*, 24.1257 ("Ti Sun Simiao zhen").

71. An informative study of Sun Simiao's connection to Mount Emei appears in Liu Xiaochun 劉曉春 and Wu Jialin 鄔家林, "Sun Simiao yu Emei shan" 孫思邈與峨眉山, *Emei wenshi* 5:91–96.

72. *EMSZ* (1934 ed.), 4.2b. It is worth noting that Hu Shian does not say anything about the so-called Jin dynasty origins of the Celestial Illumination Abbey, but only mentions that it still existed in the Northern Song and the famous poet and calligrapher Huang Tingjian (1045–1105) once practiced meditation (*xijing*) there. See *Yi elai*, 18.

73. Liu Junze, *Emei qielan ji*, 21–22.

74. *EMSZ* (1934 ed.), 4.2.

75. *Yi elai*, 17.

76. *QTS*, 486.5530 ("Ji Emei shan Yang Lianshi"). The title mentioned in line one (*Ruizhu jing* 蕊珠經) is otherwise unknown.

77. In addition to "Refined Master Zhang" and "Refined Master Yang," a verse by Shi Jianwu (*jinshi* 815) in *QTS*, 494.5591, refers to an Emei adept named "Tian," while a poem by Wei Zhuang (ca. 836–910) in *QTS*, 700.8053, mentions a "Secluded Gentleman Li" (Li Chushi).

78. *EMSZ* (1934 ed.), 3.5a–b.

79. "Four Sichuan Buddhist Steles and the Beginnings of Pure Land Imagery in China," 77.

80. Useful descriptions and discussions of images of Buddha discovered in Sichuan during and after the Han dynasty are found in Wu Zhuo 吳焯, "Sichuan zaoqi fojiao yiwu ji qi niandai yu chuanbo tujing de kaocha" 四川早期佛教遺物及其年代與傳播途徑的考察, *Dongnan wenhua* 5 (1991): 40–50, and in Ruan Rongchun 阮榮春 and Kida Tomoo 木田知生, "'Zaoqi fojiao zaoxiang nanchuan xitong' diaocha ziliao" 早期佛教造像南傳系統調查資料, *Wenwu* 5 (1991): 49–54.

81. Edwards' two-part article, "The Cave Reliefs at Ma Hao," appeared in *Artibus Asiae* 17.1 (1954): 5–28 (Part 1), and 17.2 (1954): 103–29 (Part 2).

82. Edwards, "The Cave Reliefs at Ma Hao," Part 2, 103, identifies the right-hand gesture as *abhaya-mudrā* (Chin.: *shuo fayin* 說法印), the purpose of which was the dispel fear and communicate protection and benevolence.

83. "The Cave Reliefs at Ma Hao," Part 2, 129.

84. See the remarks on Yu's dating in Wu Hung, "Buddhist Elements in Early Chinese Art," 266, n. 17.

85. Wu Hung, 266.

86. The provenance of the Mahao and other early images of Buddha discovered in Sichuan is still being debated by scholars.

87. Li Zhichun 李之純 (eleventh cent), "Da Shengci si huaji" 大聖慈寺畫記, in *Chengdu wenlei* 成都文類 (*SKQS* ed.), 45.7a.

88. The histories of these various Chengdu monasteries are reported in great detail in chapter 38 of the *SCTZ*.

89. Images on the four Sichuan steles studied by Dorothy Wong in her article "Four Sichuan Buddhist Steles" attest to Daoan and Huiyuan's influence in Shu during this period.

90. The best expression of this idea is found in Huiyuan's "Preface to the Poems on an Outing to Stone Gate by the Laymen of Mount Lu," in *Quan Shanggu Sandai Qin Han Sanguo Liuchao wen*, 3:2437.

91. On the relationship between Buddhism and Chinese landscape poetry, see especially Francis A. Westbrook, "Landscape Transformation in the Poetry of Hsieh Ling-yün," *Journal of the American Oriental Society* 100.3 (July–Oct. 1980): 237–54. On the development of landscape painting, see Michael Sullivan, *The Birth of Landscape Painting in China* (Berkeley: University of California Press, 1961), and Hubert Delahaye, *Les Premières Peintures De Paysage En Chine: Aspects Religieux* (Paris: École Française d'Éxtrême-Orient, 1981).

92. *Gaoseng zhuan*, 6.230.

93. *Gaoseng zhuan*, 6.230. The expression *zhenxi* 振錫, translated here as "make a trip," literally means "roust one's staff or walking stick."

94. *Gaoseng zhuan*, 6.230. Here I read *xibing* 棲病 to mean 棲炳; lit., "nestle in luminosity."

95. Gan Shude 干樹德, "Huichi yu Emei shan de Puxian chongbai" 慧持與峨眉山的普賢崇拜, *Zhonghua wenhua luntan* 3 (1998): 111.

96. Mao Qu's brief biography in the *Jinshu*, 81.2126–28, says nothing about Huichi or support for Buddhist-related activities. Some modern scholars believe that Mao Qu supported Huichi's temple-building activity on Mount Emei. See, for instance, Gan Shude, "Huichi yu Emei shan de Puxian chong-bai," 110.

97. The earliest reference I have found to a "Samantabhadra Monastery" (Puxian si) appears in the Song dynasty geographical work *Yudi jisheng*, 146.9b, which says that "during the former era there were six Buddhist monasteries on Emei shan." The third of these temples is identified by the name "Samantabhadra." The *Yudi jisheng* also mentions that the Samantabhadra Monastery on Mount Emei was formerly known as the Puguang si, or "Universal Light Monastery." Since Song authors customarily used the expression "former era" (*qiandai* 前代) to refer to the Tang dynasty, the *Yudi jisheng* reference confirms the presence of a temple dedicated to Samantabhadra on Mount Emei during the Tang. Cf. the biography of Chengguan (b. 738) in the *Song Gaoseng zhuan*, 5.105, which mentions he traveled to Emei in 776 to "seek out an appearance of Samantabhadra." No doubt, worship to Samantabhadra took place on Emei in the eighth century and perhaps even earlier. But how this relates, if at all, to Huichi's earlier temple-building efforts is unclear.

98. These temples are mentioned in *EMSZ* (1997 ed.), 243–44.

99. *Gaoseng zhuan*, 5.189.

100. Luo Kunqi, *Emei shan fojiao shihua*, 16. The monk mentioned here, Baozhang, is a historical figure of the late Sui or early Tang period and should be distinguished from the priest with the same name who figures prominently in the Master Pu legend discussed in chapter 7.

101. *Emei shan fojiao shihua*, 16.
102. *Emei shan fojiao shihua*, 17.
103. *EMSZ* (1997 ed.), 244.
104. *QTS*, 717.8238.
105. Imperial support for Buddhism during the Tang is a complicated subject and thus well beyond my space limitations here. It is essential to realize that imperial support for the religion took many forms, some inspired by political motivations, some by genuine religious interest. For additional information on these matters I refer readers to Stanley Weinstein's article "Imperial Patronage in the Formation of T'ang Buddhism" and especially his seminal study *Buddhism under the T'ang*.
106. Pan Guiming 潘桂明, *Zhongguo jushi fojiao shi* 中國居士佛教史 (Beijing: Zhongguo shehui kexue chubanshe, 2000), 1:297–98.
107. *EMSZ* (1934 ed.), 4.2a; see also Liu Junze, *Emei qielan ji*, 7.
108. *EMSZ* (1934 ed.), 4.2a.
109. *EMSZ* (1997 ed.), 273.
110. *EMSZ* (1934 ed.), 4.2b. Huitong renovated the Samantabhadra Monastery in 887 and renamed it "White Stream Monastery."
111. *QTS*, 130.1322. In chapter 2 we considered a Li Bo poem that mentions Shi Huaiyi and his relationship with Chen Ziang, another well-known Tang writer.
112. Shao Bo 邵博 (d. 1158), *Shaoshi wenjian houlou* 邵氏聞見後錄 (Beijing: Zhonghua shuju, 1983), 28.220.
113. This is confirmed by Wang Xiangzhi who, writing in the early thirteenth century, says: "stone steps were in place for twenty *li* beyond the White Stream (or Samantabhadra) Monastery, but [after that] for the most part there was no trail." He also mentions that ladders fashioned out of timbers were in place at higher elevations to help climbers reach the summit. See his "Shushan kao" 蜀山考, quoted in *Quan Shu yiwen zhi* 全蜀藝文志 (*SKQS* ed.), 48.37a–38b.
114. Shao Bo (d. 1158), "Record of the Clear Tones Pavilion" ("Qingyin ting ji" 清音亭記), quoted in Li Zhongyi 李中毅, ed., *Leshan difang wenhua zuopin jingxuan* 樂山地方文化作品精選 (Leshan: Leshan jiaoyu xueyuan zhongwen ke, 1992), 4.
115. *SCTZ*, 41.1a.
116. See the prose preface to Fan's poem "Lingyun jiuding" in *FSHJ*, 18.255. There was widespread, government-sponsored persecution of Buddhism throughout China from 842 to 845, resulting in destruction of temples, reclamation of Buddhist lands, and even slaughter of monks and nuns. The monasteries on the "Nine Crests" were probably destroyed during these persecutions. The *Fangyu shenglan*, 52.9a, says that the nine crests of Jiuding shan each had monasteries prior to the Huichang reign of the Tang (841–847).
117. Cancong is the legendary first king of Shu. Tradition says that he taught the art of sericulture to his subjects.

118. The Dao is a tributary that branches off from the Min River near the Partition Mound and then rejoins it in Pengshan town. It did not "join below [Lingyun] Hill and then flow south down to Qianwei [town]." Fan Chengda is mistaken here. "Mo River" is an alternate name for Green Robe River.
119. *WCL*, 1.11a; *FCDBJ*, 196.
120. Although the statue was repaired and restored several times since the Tang dynasty, the current dimensions of the statue, as provided here, are not very different from the figures given by Fan Chengda.
121. By comparison, the taller of the two giant images of Buddha at Bamiyan, Afghanistan, carved from a cliff in the third century and destroyed by Taliban in February 2001, stood 175 feet or 53 meters tall.
122. This thirteen-storied superstructure, in place when Fan Chengda visited Jia county in 1177, is no longer standing.
123. *WCL*, 1.11a–b; *FCDBJ*, 196.
124. The events described here are based on Wei Gao, "Jiazhou Lingyun si Dafo ji" 嘉州凌雲寺大佛記, reproduced in Li Zhongyi, *Leshan difang wenhua zuopin jingxuan*, 1–3.
125. See "Jiazhou Lingyun si Dafo ji," 2.
126. *Jiading fu zhi* (1864 ed.), 5.2b, says Lü built the tower during the Xuanhe reign, 1119–1126.
127. This is mentioned in the prose preface to his poem "Myriad Prospects Tower," in *FSHJ*, 18.254 ("Wanjing lou").
128. Qianwei (commandery), Rong (or Xu 敍county), and Lu (county) are all downriver from Jia county.
129. Since at least the Northern Song dynasty, Mount Emei has often been described as comprising three parts or sections: the main portion of the mountain (Big Emei) and two foothills: "Second Emei" (or Mount Sui), thirteen miles to the southeast, and "Third Emei," southeast of there. Hence, the expression "Three E[mei]" (San'e).
130. *WCL*, 1.11b–12a; *FCDBJ*, 197. The reference in the last line of this diary entry is to Fan's poem "Myriad Prospects Tower," in *FSHJ*, 18.254 ("Wanjing lou").

CHAPTER 5. THE ASCENT

1. L. Newton Hayes, "A Trip to Sacred Mount Omei," in *Valiant But Gentle: Selected Writings of L. Newton Hayes* (Santa Fe, N.M.: Vergara, 1979), 211.
2. *WCL*, 1.12b; *FCDBJ*, 197.
3. *FSHJ*, 18.256 ("Guo Yandu wang Da'e . . .").
4. *WCL*, 1.12b–13a; *FCDBJ*, 197–98.
5. The modern scholar Jia Daquan 賈大泉, basing his research on data culled from Song dynasty historical and geographical records, calculates the population of Jia county as follows: (1) for the years 976–997: 28,898; (2) for

the year 1080: 70,546; and (3) for the years 1102–1107: 71,652. *Songdai Sichuan jingji shulun* 宋代四川經濟述論 (Chengdu: Sichuan sheng shehui kexue yuan chubanshe, 1985), 10. Jia's figures represent the county's population in terms of the number of individuals (*kou*). Unfortunately, no other population figures are available for Jia county during the Southern Song, so we cannot be sure exactly how many people might have been living in Emei town when Fan Chengda visited there in 1177. Clearly, however, the population of Jia county increased dramatically between the tenth and eleventh centuries, a development which closely parallels the surge in Sichuan's overall population during the Northern Song. It seems quite likely, then, that by the mid or late twelfth century the population of Emei town could have been well over 70,000, perhaps even approaching 100,000.

6. These discoveries, made in nearby Luomu *zhen* in 1985, are outlined and described in Chen Liqing 陳黎清, "Emei xian Luomu zhen chutu Songdai jiaocang" 峨眉縣羅目鎮出土宋代窖藏, *Emei wenshi* 3:173–75.

7. *FSHJ*, 18.256 ("Emei xian").

8. *Song huiyao jigao*, "Daoshi" 道釋, 1.1–3, 1–4, 7861. Figures for Buddhist and Daoist clergy throughout the Song are conveniently summarized, with reliable source citations, in Huang Minzhi 黃敏枝, *Songdai fojiao shehui jingji shi lunji* 宋代佛教社會經濟史論集 (Taibei: Xuesheng shuju, 1989), 350–52.

9. Chen Shisong 陳世松, ed., *Sichuan jianshi* 四川簡史 (Chengdu: Sichuan sheng shehui kexue yuan chubanshe, 1986), 164.

10. Gu Jichen, *Songdai fojiao shigao*, 17.

11. The history of Buddhism and its development during the Song dynasty has been studied by several modern scholars in China and Japan. As for works in Chinese, see Gu Jichen, *Songdai fojiao shigao*; Pan Guiming, *Zhongguo jushi fojiao shi*; Huang Minzhi, *Songdai fojiao shehui jingji shi lunji*; and Huang Chi-chiang, *Bei Song fojiao shi lungao*. Important works in Japanese include Takao Giken, *Sōdai bukkyōshi no kenkyū*, Satō Seijun, *Sōdai bukkyō no kenkyū*, and especially Chikusa Massaki, *Chūgoku bukkyō shakaishi kenkyū*. As for titles in English, consult Robert M. Gimello, "Imperial Patronage of Buddhism During the Northern Sung," and especially the various essays in Peter N. Gregory and Daniel A. Getz, Jr., eds., *Buddhism in the Sung* (Honolulu: University of Hawaii Press, 2002). The discussion that follows is not intended as a history of Buddhism from the tenth to the twelfth century, but rather as an introduction to how some developments in Buddhism during those centuries relate to Mount Emei's new status in the Northern Song as a "Buddhist mountain."

12. "Pieties and Responsibilities: Buddhism and the Chinese Literati, 780–1280" (Ph.D. diss., University of California, Berkeley, 1997), 187–88.

13. According to Chikusa Massaki, *Chūgoku bukkyō shakaishi kenkyū*, 84, during the Later Zhou suppression of Buddhism 30,336 monasteries were destroyed, and only 2,694 survived.

14. *Song da zhaoling ji* 宋大詔令集 (Beijing: Zhonghua shuju, 1997), 223.860 ("Cunliu tongxiang zhao").
15. *Xu Zizhi tongjian changbian*, 3.67.
16. *Xu Zizhi tongjian changbian*, 7.168. Taizu's edict supporting the mission is preserved in the *Fozu tongji*, 49.395b.
17. Although its printing blocks were carved in Chengdu, the *Tripiṭaka* itself was printed in Kaifeng.
18. *Jinshi cuibian* 金石萃編, Wang Chang 王昶 (1725–1806), comp. (Beijing: Zhongguo shudian, 1985), 125.1a–b ("Chongxiu Longxing si dongta ji" 重修龍興寺東塔記).
19. *Fozu lidai tongzai*, 49.659c.
20. Construction work on the stūpa, which took eight years, was completed in 989. *SS*, 5.84.
21. These control efforts are summarized in Gu Jichen, *Songdai fojiao shigao*, 6–7.
22. Emperor Wu's experiences are outlined in Kamata Shigeo 鎌田茂夫, *Chūgoku bukkyōshi* 中國佛教史 (Tokyo: Tōkyō daigaku shuppankai, 1984), 3:204–18, and in Kenneth Ch'en, *Buddhism in China: A Historical Survey*, 124–28. Several modern scholars have argued that the vast wealth acquired by monasteries in the Tang was a chief factor behind the widespread suppression of Buddhism ordered in 845 and the chaos that followed. See, for instance, Kenneth Ch'en, "Economic Background of the Hui-ch'ang Persecution," *Harvard Journal of Asiatic Studies* 19 (1956): 67–105.
23. *Song huiyao jigao*, "Daoshi" 2.1, 7:7875.
24. *Fozu tongji*, 44.402a.
25. *SS*, 299.9933.
26. *Song da zhaoling ji*, 224.868 ("Fohao dajue Jinxian Yuwei xianren . . .").
27. *Song huiyao jigao*, "Daoshi," 1.34, 7871.
28. *Song huiyao jigao*, "Daoshi," 1.34, 7871.
29. Here I follow the variant reading *neng* 能, or "was able to." In the context of Wang's memorial, this makes much more sense than *jie* 皆. *Fozu tongji*, 49.398, n. 1.
30. *Fozu tongji*, 49.398a.
31. *Fozu tongji*, 49.397c. This image survives today and stands in the Myriad Years Monastery (Wannian si), formerly known as the White Stream Monastery. See fig. 5.1.
32. During the Song, 1 *zhang* was equal to about 3.6 m/12 ft. "1.6 *zhang*," then, would be roughly 5.8 m/19.2 ft. This supposedly was the size of the Buddha's body when he was living on earth as a mortal being.
33. Although it is possible to observe Buddha's Glory from the western side of the summit (with the rising sun at one's back), the overwhelming majority of Foguang sightings on Mount Emei are made on the *eastern* side of the mountain.

34. Cf. the following comment from the Southern Song writer Wang Zhiwang (*jinshi* 1139), who witnessed an appearance of Buddha's Glory on Emei sometime in the mid twelfth century (before Fan Chengda): "This auspicious realm (that is, Mount Emei's Foguang) adjoins and links with Mount Wawu." See chapter 6 for a translation and discussion of this verse. We should also note, however, that appearances of a Buddha's Glory have been reported on Wawu shan. In fact, Fan Chengda remarks later in the *WCL* (chapter 6, p. 124) that the mountain had its very own Foguang. This is confirmed in Wang Haoyin 王好音 (Qing) et al., eds., *Hongya xian zhi* 洪雅縣志 (1813 ed.), 2.14b.

35. Various events related to Mount Emei, described throughout the entry for "980" in *Fozu tongji*, 43.397–98, make this very clear.

36. The list that follows is not intended to be complete, but rather representative of the types of imperial support received by Emei shan in the Northern Song. Some of the information on this list appears in *EMSZ* (1997 ed.), 636; O'Jack also translates and discusses some of this material in "Auspicious Lights," 84 ff.

37. The main source for information on the 964 expedition to India is the *WCL*, 1.19b ff; *FCDBJ*, 204 ff.

38. *Fozu tongji*, 49.395c. Zhang Zhong is otherwise unknown. As far as I know, except for Wang Gun's memorial, no other communication concerning Mount Emei, sent to the capital by officials in Jia county, has survived.

39. *WCL*, 1.22a; *FCDBJ*, 204.

40. *Fozu tongji*, 49.397c; *EMSZ* (1934 ed.), 5.6a. No additional information survives on Zhang Renzan. The precise year when the bronze image of Samantabhadra was completed in Chengdu is unknown. Some modern scholars have argued that it was probably cast in 987. See Hu Zhaoxi 胡昭曦, et al., "Emei shan Songdai Puxian tongxiang" 峨眉山宋代普賢銅像, in *Songdai Shuxue yanjiu* 宋代蜀學研究 (Chengdu: Ba-Shu shushe, 1997), 365. According to Huang Ch'i-chiang, the emperor Taizong "only allowed images to be cast when he himself undertook state projects." See his "Imperial Rulership and Buddhism in the Early Sung," 148. If this is the case, then Taizong himself was directly involved in the project that produced a statue of Samantabhadra for the White Stream Monastery.

41. *Fozu tongji*, 49.397c.

42. *Fozu tongji*, 49.398c.

43. *Fozu tongji*, 49.400a.

44. *Fozu tongji*, 49.400b.

45. *Fozu tongji*, 49.404b. 3,000 taels is about 150 kg, or roughly 330 pounds of gold.

46. *Fozu tongji*, 49.404c. Maozhen supposedly predicted the imminent birth of an heir apparent, who later became the emperor Renzong. There are some questions regarding the chronology of Maozhen's prediction and Renzong's

subsequent birth, which are discussed in Hu Zhaoxi, et al., "Emei shan Songdai Puxian tongxiang," 365–66.

47. *WCL*, 1.14a; *FCDBJ*, 199. Fan Chengda describes these gifts below.

48. *EMSZ* (1997 ed.), 273. "Cash pennants" were decorated with coins; "streamers" were hung from the roofs of Buddhist temples.

49. Here I follow the *SKQS* edition of Xu Xuan's collected works, *Qisheng ji* 騎省集 (25.13a), and read *zhu* 鑄 ("to cast") rather than *chou* 疇 (or 酬). The Chinese character *chou* is certainly misplaced here. I understand the personal pronoun *wo* 我 in this couplet to mean "we" in the sense of "the present dynasty."

50. That is to say, based on descriptions of him in the Buddhist sūtras, Samantabhadra's "divine brilliance" is now "fashioned" in the form of an image or statue.

51. The expressions "auspicious image" (*ruixiang* 瑞相) and "Globe of Light" (*yuanguang* 圓光) both relate to the Buddha. *Ruixiang* alludes to the legendary first image of Śākyamuni, made of sandalwood and carved by the King of Kauśāmbī. "Globe of Light," on the other hand, denotes the circular halo that emits from the head of the Buddha or from a bodhisattva. In lines 27–30 Xu Xuan is describing an imagined appearance of Samantabhadra in the form of Buddha's Glory. Swift moving clouds on the summit of Emei shan sometimes temporarily block out the Foguang. Hence, the remark in line 27 about the "auspicious image—now manifest, now obscure."

52. *Quan Songwen*, 19.523 ("Da Song chongxiu Emei shan Puxian si beiming").

53. This is the same line in Zuo Si's rhapsody discussed in chapter 1.

54. Xu Xuan may be alluding here to the tale of Master Pu, the Han dynasty herbalist who "discovered" Samantabhadra on Mount Emei in the first century (roughly, a thousand years earlier).

55. Yang Tianhui 楊天惠 (fl. early twelfth cent), "Zhengfa yuan changzhu tian ji" 正法院常住田記, in *Chengdu wenlei*, 39.7b.

56. *WCL*, 1.15a; *FCDBJ*, 199.

57. *FSHJ*, 18.257 ("Chu ru Da'e").

58. The Benevolent Fortune Cloister, just south of Emei town, was rebuilt in 1508 and renamed Sagely Accumulation Monastery (Shengji si). The Sagely Accumulation Evening Bell was housed in this temple during the Ming dynasty.

59. *WCL*, 1.13a; *FCDBJ*, 198.

60. This is mentioned in the opening lines of Jiang Gao 江皋 (*jinshi* 1661), "Stele Record of Mount Emei's Crouching Tiger Monastery" ("Emei shan Fuhu si beiji" 峨眉山伏虎寺碑記), preserved in *EMSZ* (1934 ed.), 6.11a–12a.

61. The trail followed by Fan Chengda in his ascent of the mountain is the same route taken by most travelers to Emei during the Song and subsequent periods. In one of his poems Fan describes the trail as "a single thread"

(*yixian*). See *FSHJ*, 18.257 ("Huayan si"). This same trail, with some modifications, is still in use today.

62. *EMSZ* (1934 ed.), 4.2a. This mile marker dates from the Shaoxing reign (1131–1163) of the Southern Song. See *Emei xian xuzhi*, 1.17b, 10.3b; and *Yi elai*, 17. The Ming dynasty official Yuan Zirang (fl. 1600) saw the stone mile marker in 1602, when it was on display in the Huayan Monastery. He also mentions that monks from the monastery had excavated the mile marker earlier. See *Emei shan youji xuanzhu*, 34.

63. Liu Junze, *Emei qielan ji*, 17.

64. Emei's New Abbey is the only structure with a Daoist name on Mount Emei mentioned by Fan Chengda. In the Ming period it functioned as a worship site to the immortal Lü Dongbin and acquired the name by which it is known today: Pure Solarity Hall (Chunyang dian). In the early Qing period, however, it was converted into a Buddhist temple. *EMSZ* (1997 ed.), 261.

65. There is an alternate reading for the name of this hall: Yulong tang 雨龍堂 ("Rain Dragon Hall"). *WCL*, 1.13a; *FCDBJ*, 210, n. 18.

66. Now the Central Peak Monastery (Zhongfeng si). See *Emei shan youji xuanzhu*, p. 12, n. 15. This structure was initially Daoist, but was later converted into a Buddhist monastery. It survives today.

67. *WCL*, 1.13a (*FCDBJ*, 210, n. 18), gives an alternate reading here of "twelve peaks" (*shier feng* 十二峰). In his preface to the poem "Central Peak" Fan says the Samantabhadra Gallery was wreathed by seventy peaks. See *FSHJ*, 18.257.

68. *WCL*, 1.13a–b; *FCDBJ*, 198.

69. *EMSZ* (1934 ed.), 3.9b, 4.2b.

70. *WCL*, 1.13b; *FCDBJ*, 198.

71. *WCL*, 1.14a; *FCDBJ*, 198.

72. Today the situation is much different. It is now possible to take a bus from the base of the mountain to a cable car station near the top, which then transports visitors directly to the Golden Summit. This trip can be accomplished within a few hours' time.

73. The Ming author Wang Shixing 王士性 (1547–1598), writing in his travelogue "Record of a Trip to Mount Emei" ("You Emei shan ji" 游峨眉山記), mentions seeing a "monk's raiment" and "gemmy necklace," which were probably the same items Fan Chengda observed in the monastery four hundred years earlier. See *Emei shan youji xuanzhu*, 23.

74. *WCL*, 1.14a–b; *FCDBJ*, 199.

75. The monk Maozhen arranged for the casting of these small, iron statues. Of the original 3,000, only 304 survive today.

76. *WCL*, 1.14b–15a; *FCDBJ*, 199.

77. *FSHJ*, 18.258–59 ("Da Fuyu").

78. *FSHJ*, 18.259 ("Xiao Fuyu").

79. *WCL*, 1.15a; *FCDBJ*, 299–300.

80. *FSHJ*, 18.258 ("Dianxin shan").
81. *WCL*, 1.15a; *FCDBJ*, 300.
82. *FSHJ*, 18.259 ("Bashisi pan").
83. *FSHJ*, 18.260 ("Suoluo ping").
84. *FSHJ*, 18.260 ("Guangxiang si"). This poem is translated in chapter 6.
85. In his poem "Monkey's Ladder" ("Husun ti"), *FSHJ*, 18.259, Fan mentions that the "ladder" was covered with mud and was very slippery.
86. The mention of stone steps here is puzzling for two reasons. First, earlier Fan Chengda stated that there were no stone steps above White Stream Monastery. Second, the area around Thunder Grotto Flat is, as the name indicates, quite flat. Perhaps Fan is referring to some natural formation of rocks between the trail and the cliff (?).
87. *WCL*, 1.15a–b; *FCDBJ*, 200.
88. *EMSZ* (1997 ed.), 136–41.
89. In the seventeenth century a monastery was built on this site called the Welcome Hall (Jieyin dian). It has been rebuilt twice since and still stands today.
90. *WCL*, 1.15b; *FCDBJ*, 200.
91. Fan Chengda's time reference is the lunar calendar. The Chinese term *jixia* literally means "the last part of summer" or "late summer," and refers to the sixth lunar month. This roughly corresponds to July on the Western calendar.
92. "Eight Immortals" is a general name for hydrangeas. "Oxherd" is a reference to *Ipomcea hederacea*, a vegetable plant that produces blue flowers and seeds used for medicinal purposes. Liao, or knotweed, is a generic term for various species of *Polygonum*.
93. *WCL*, 1.16a; *FCDBJ*, 200.
94. *EMSZ* (1934 ed.), 4.1a, says the renaming took place in the Tang or Song.
95. *WCL*, 1.16a–b; *FCDBJ*, 201.
96. *FSHJ*, 18. 260–61 ("Qibao yan").

CHAPTER 6. THE SUMMIT

1. Edwin Bernbaum, *Sacred Mountains of the World* (Berkeley: University of California Press, 1997), 35.
2. The Buddhist expression *xukong* 虛空 (Skt. *śūnya*), or "vacuous void," refers broadly to sky, space, and the heavens—a realm without shape, substance, or resistance.
3. *FSHJ*, 18.260 ("Guangxiang si").
4. The water would not boil because of the high air pressure on the summit. Presumably, the water Fan had delivered from the lower reaches of the mountain would not boil either.

5. *WCL*, 1.16b; *FCDBJ*, 201.

6. According to his biography in *SS*, 372.11538, Wang Zhiwang once served as Deputy Fiscal Commissioner (Zhuanyun fushi) and Supervisor of Horse Trading (Tiju chama) in Sichuan.

7. *WCL*, 1.16b; *FCDBJ*, 201.

8. *Jiading fu zhi* (1864 ed.), 5.11b. Gaopiao is also known as Myriad Prospects Hill (Wanjing shan).

9. "Celestial pillar(s)" (*tianzhu*) is a common metaphor for lofty heights; "eight tethers" (*bahong*), indicating the eight cardinal points on a compass, is a synecdoche for "the world."

10. "Mighty citadel" (*xiongzhen*) refers to Mount Emei. The term *kunwei*, rendered here as "protector of earth," is associated with the direction of southwest. It can also mean "a great landmass."

11. "Sixty *li*" probably refers to the distance from White Stream Monastery to the summit.

12. Mount Emei is associated with a constellation of stars called the Well Net (Jingluo), which designates the direction of southwest. Chengdu is sometimes called the "well bottom" (*jingdi*) because of its location in the center of the Chengdu Plain, surrounded by mountains, and also because the city was thought to sit directly below the "Well Net" constellation.

13. This line probably refers to the grottoes below Thunder Grotto Flat, which legend says hosts a rain- and thunder-producing "divine dragon" (mentioned in line 20). This is the same "divine dragon" (*shenlong*) described earlier by Fan Chengda. Wang Zhiwang's point here is that although he hears the rumbling of thunder, it "harbors its anger." In other words, the weather remains favorable.

14. Tentative translation. "Lengjia" 楞伽 in this line seems to be a reference to the *Lengjia jing* (*Laṅkāvatāra-sūtra* 楞伽經), but I have not been able to locate any mention of "melodious voices" or "wondrous birds" in that text. It is possible that Wang Zhiwang's intended reference was instead the *Lengyan jing* (*Śūraṅgama-sūtra* 楞嚴經), the first chapter of which describes "the Kalaviṅka bird's melodious voice" (*jialing xianyin* 伽陵仙音) and how it spreads to the "worlds in the ten directions" (*shifang [shi]jie* 十方[世]界). See *Taishō*, 19.106b. This same source also notes that the expression "melodious voice" (*xianyin* 仙音; lit., "immortal voice") is used to describe the voice of the Buddha.

15. "White tufts" (*baihao*) is a synecdoche for the Buddha, referring to the white hairs between his brows. From these hairs Buddha can emit a special light which, if seen by sentient beings, can "reveal all worlds."

16. The "inky reflection" (*danmo*; lit., "light ink") mentioned here was probably the shadow of Wang Zhiwang's own reflection on the clouds below the summit. Cf. Fan Chengda's description below, where he mentions a "watery, inky reflection that looks like the Immortal Sage."

17. The referent of "arhat" (*yingzhen*) here is unclear.

18. In other words, Wang is now seeing the outline of his body reflected inside the "globe of light" positioned on the clouds below the summit.

19. For instance, see *Taishō*, 85.1365c.

20. According to ancient folklore, a "fiery-red raven with three feet" (*sanzu chiwu*) represents the essence of the sun. This creature is the subject of Edward H. Schafer's book *The Vermilion Bird: T'ang Images of the South* (Berkeley and Los Angeles: University of California Press, 1967). As noted by Schafer, 261, the vermilion bird flew down from the sun with messages for human paragons and to confirm meritorious rule. Here in Wang Zhiwang's poem, however, the reference is Buddha's Glory, the brilliance of which the poet likens to the sun.

21. The referents of the similes in this couplet have Buddhist connections. Lapis lazuli (*liuli*) is one of the "Seven Treasures" (*qibao*) of Buddhism. The udumbara plant (*youtan*) is said to produce flowers only once every three thousand years and hence is a symbol of the rare appearance of a buddha.

22. The sage lamps have appeared to pay homage to Samantabhadra.

23. "Immortal wind" (*xianfeng*) in this context might also be translated "Buddha wind." Buddhist literature describes various types of *xian*, some of whom can fly to deva heavens and transform their physical appearance at will. Winnowing Basket (Ji) and Tail (Wei) usually denote Sagittarius and Scorpio, respectively.

24. Fu Yue was a minister of King Wuding (Wuding wang) of the Shang dynasty. According to legend, after finding the Way he ascended to the heavens and became a star. See *Zhuangzi*, 3.6a–b.

25. Junping is the *style* of Yan Zun (first century BC and AD), a famous fortune teller and native of Sichuan. Tradition says that he was especially knowledgeable about matters related to stars and astrology. "Dipper-Ox Ferry" (Douniu du) refers to the starry bridge that once each year allows a brief reunion between the "Herdboy" (Niulang) and "Weaving Maid" (Zhinü) stars in Chinese legend. According to a story preserved in the *Shuzhong guangji*, 41.3a–b, Junping once explained to Zhang Qian, the famous Han general and envoy, how Zhang had encountered the Weaving Maid and Herdboy during his travels in Central Asia. Wang Zhiwang's point here is that since he plans to seek out Fu Yue, there is no need to ask Junping for directions to the stars.

26. Tentative translation. "Lofty orb" (*gaoyuan* 高圓) probably refers to Buddha's Glory.

27. *Hanbin ji*, 1.21a–b ("Deng Da'e jueding du yuanxiang Foguang cheng changju ershi yun").

28. Wang Gun's sighting is discussed in chapter 5, pp. 97–98.

29. The "inky reflection" described here was actually a reflection of Fan Chengda himself. He will see himself more clearly in a second appearance of the Foguang, described below.

30. *WCL*, 1.16b–17a; *FCDBJ*, 201.

31. Feng Ling, *Emei jingguan tanyuan*, 29–30.

32. Although Fan Chengda clearly distinguishes between a "[Little] Mount Wawu" and a "Big Mount Wawu" (in the next line), traditional sources do not make this distinction. Instead, they identify a single peak (elevation: 2,834 m/9,296 ft) as Mount Wawu. It is located on the boundary of modern Hongya *xian* and Xingjing *xian*.

33. Nanzhao is a Tang dynasty name for a state ruled by a confederation of ethnically Tibeto-Burman tribal groups. From about 650 to 900 they controlled most of what is now Yunnan, as well as parts of modern Sichuan and Guizhou provinces. By Southern Song times, roughly the same area was ruled by another state called Dali.

34. *WCL*, 1.17a–b; *FCDBJ*, 201–02.

35. It is rare to see a triple-ring Buddha's Glory, as described here by Fan Chengda (most are of the single or double varieties).

36. *WCL*, 1.17b–18a; *FCDBJ*, 202.

37. As is evident from Fan Chengda's marvelous description, Buddha's Glory on Mount Emei can move about, seemingly at will. These movements are the result of changes in light refraction occurring when there are shifts in wind, temperature, and humidity.

38. Fan is referring to the famous Suspended Rainbow Bridge (Chuihong qiao), built in 1048 in Wujiang town. It spans the Wusong River (Wusong jiang), not far from Fan Chengda's villa at Rocky Lake.

39. *WCL*, 1.17b–18a; *FCDBJ*, 202. Also translated in Strassberg, *Inscribed Landscapes*, 215–18, and O'Jack, "Auspicious Lights," 88–95.

40. "Superior Peak [Mountain]" (Shengfeng [shan]) is an alternate designation for Mount Emei. The origin of this name is unknown.

41. These are the same "Seven Treasures" mentioned earlier. Here the idea is that Buddha's Glory is so bright, it sparkles like precious metals and gems.

42. Devas (*tian*) and Nāgas (*long*) are protectors of the Buddha Law, or Dharma.

43. "Nighttime spirits" (*yeshen*) are the "sage lamps" described earlier. The expression I translate as "become Buddhas" literally means to "receive a prediction from a Buddha to become a Buddha" (*shouji* 受記).

44. The "lights" mentioned here also refer to "sage lamps." Lines 1–16 of Fan's poem describe events that took place late in the afternoon and early evening of 24 July 1177. The "Silvery World" mentioned in line 13 is a dense fog that usually blankets the mountain just before a "Great Manifestation" (described earlier in the *WCL* and below in lines 23 to 26; this "manifestation" took place in the early morning hours of 25 July).

45. The term "Six Perspicacities" (*liutong*) is discussed below.

46. Following the *SKQS* ed. of *Fan Shihu ji*, 18.16a, and reading *diecai* 疊采(彩) ("layered colors") instead of *sangcai* 桑采 ("mulberry colors").

47. Although the term *huaren* (lit., "transformed being") is often used in Daoist contexts when referring to immortals, here it denotes Samantabhadra.

48. "Ocean Treasury" (*haizang*; lit., "the sea of precious things") is the *Tripiṭaka*.

49. The expression *yinian* 一念 ("a single instant of consciousness") refers to a single moment in which "everything is understood and all distinctions disappear, in a vision of complete and immediate enlightenment." Halperin, "Pieties and Responsibilities," 153, n. 134.

50. Here I read *yin* 印 to mean "gain confirmation" or "obtain approval." The idea is that since Samantabhadra has made an "appearance," Fan Chengda has thus received confirmation that his "mental ground" (or mind) has been following the correct spiritual path.

51. Mani pearls (*baozhu*) are globe-shaped and to be effective in warding off sickness and evil and in purifying water. Here, however, the term is used in a much wider sense. Fan now realizes the experience he has just had on the summit of Emei can fulfill all his spiritual and religious needs, so there is no need for him to seek anything else.

52. In Buddhist scriptures, a *gāthā* (*jie*) is a verse relating a teaching or praising a buddha or bodhisattva.

53. *FSHJ*, 18.261 ("Chunxi sinian liuyue ershiqi ri . . . ").

54. "Conjured City" (*huacheng*), as it is described in the *Fahua jing* (or *Lotus-sūtra*), represents temporary or incomplete nirvana. In the opening couplet of his poem Fan uses the expression as an alternate name for the summit of Emei shan.

55. J.D. Schmidt's translation of the final couplet reads: "I must examine the spiritual powers and teachings of the Buddha— / Let my cup of boiling tea rumble forth like the thunder of spring." Schmidt also adds a footnote to his translation of the second of these lines: "Fan seems to be saying that he is going to enjoy boiling a cup of tea to show his indifference to the material world. *Stone Lake*, 146 (and n. 8). Justin O'Jack offers this translation: "The spiritual powers of the Buddhadharma are certainly admirable; / I have complete faith the hot bowl will ring with peels of spring thunder." "Auspicious Lights," 103 (and n. 469).

56. My description here only deals with the first of the six *abhijñā*. The remaining five are outlined and discussed in Faure, *The Rhetoric of Immediacy: A Cultural Critique of Chan/Zen Buddhism*. (Stanford: Stanford University Press, 1991), 102, n. 11.

57. For examples see, for instance, *Taishō*, 48.109b and 48.166c.

58. *Zengaku daijiten* 禪學大辭典 (Tokyo: Taishukan shoten, 1978), 1001.

59. *Taishō*, 85.443b.

60. For additional information on Gong'an Introspection Chan Buddhism and *huatou*, see Morten Schlütter, "Silent Illumination, Introspection, and Competition," in *Buddhism in the Sung*, 115–16.

61. Schmidt, *Stone Lake*, 62.
62. *WCL*, 1.18b; *FCDBJ*, 202–03.
63. *EMSZ* (1934 ed.), 5.5a.
64. *EMSZ* (1997 ed.), 212. Beginning in the eighth century, Chan monks in China began saving the mummified corpses of enlightened teachers, to which other monks would come and pay respects and make offerings. For additional information on Chan "flesh bodies" in China, see Bernard Faure, "Relics and Flesh Bodies: The Creation of Ch'an Pilgrimage Sites," in *Pilgrims and Sacred Sites in China*, esp. 166 ff.
65. *WCL*, 1.19a; *FCDBJ*, 203.
66. *WCL*, 1.19a–b; *FCDBJ*, 203.
67. Modern Yao *xian*, Shaanxi.
68. That is, Kaifeng.
69. *WCL*, 1.19b–20a; *FCDBJ*, 204.
70. *WCL*, 1.22a–b; *FCDBJ*, 207.
71. *WCL*, 1.22b–23a; *FCDBJ*, 207. Unfortunately, most of Dragon Gate was destroyed in 1958 to build a road. A portion of the area around the grotto has since been restored.
72. *WCL*, 1.23a; *FCDBJ*, 207.

CHAPTER 7. HOW AND WHY DID MOUNT EMEI BECOME A "FAMOUS BUDDHIST MOUNTAIN"?

1. *EMSZ* (1934 ed.), 6.8a ("Emei shan Jindian ji"). The author of this passage, Fu Guangzhai (*style* Bojun), was a high government official in Sichuan. He climbed Emei shan in 1601.
2. Chün-fang Yü, "Pu-t'o shan," in *Pilgrims and Sacred Sites in China*, 190, identifies "an early fourteenth-century gazetteer of Ningpo" as marking the earliest use of the expression "Sanda daochang." Her reference (confirmed with Prof. Yü through email communication) is the *Yanyou Siming zhi* 延祐四明志 (1320 ed.), 16.8b.
3. For an introduction to the various *qi* qualities of Mount Wutai's physical environment, see *Qingliang shan zhi*, esp. 1a–b (pp. 9–10 in the rpt. pagination). Certainly one extraordinary aspect of Wutai's geology—its grottoes— is discussed in Raoul Birnbaum's article "Secret Halls of the Mountain Lords: The Caves of Wu-tai shan." As for Putuo, its geography is unique because, unlike all other "Buddhist mountains" in China, it is an ocean island. It is precisely for this reason that Putuo was claimed to be the Potalaka, or the island home of the Bodhisattva Guanyin mentioned in the *Avataṃsaka-sūtra*. Finally, compared with Wutai and Putuo, Mount Jiuhua's physical environment is more similar to that of Emei shan. In addition to its "unusual" flora and fauna, the mountain comprises numerous peaks, grottoes, strange rock formations, bizarre-shaped trees, and even occasional sightings of a Buddha's Glory. See *Jiuhua shan zhi*, 36 ff.

4. Following his ascension in 846, the Tang emperor Xuanzong (r. 846–859) immediately took measures aimed at restoring the Buddhist church to a status similar to that which it had before the persecutions. In this regard the emperor issued a proclamation saying that "famous monks" (*mingseng*) would be permitted to restore old or build new monasteries, and would have complete control over and responsibility for construction activities. Local officials were ordered to not interfere with these efforts. See *Quan Tangwen*, 81.844 ("Fufei si chi").

5. Having noted the presence of a Samantabhadra Monastery on Emei in the late ninth century, it should also be mentioned that Huitong was concerned about the possibility of further persecutions against Buddhism. Probably in an effort to safeguard the monasteries on Emei from such danger, Huitong changed the names of the temples he renovated to "safer" (read "non-Buddhist") designations. For instance, what was formerly the "Avataṃsaka Monastery" now bore the name "Returning Clouds Monastery" (Guiyun si). *EMSZ* (1991 ed.), 244–45.

6. Hisayuki Miyakawa 宮穿尚志 has collected folklore stories about pythons and shown how some of them are told from a Buddhist perspective in order "to explain—or explain away—the lore of Taoist [Daoist] immortality." See his essay "Local Cults Around Mount Lu," in *Facets of Taoism*, esp. 96–98.

7. Examples can be found, for instance, in Wei Fuping, *Emei congtan*, 111–12, and Luo Kunqi, "Emei shan zongjiao lishi chutan," esp. 31.

8. In other words, Master Pu gathered herbs at higher elevations on the mountain.

9. Deer are considered propitious in both Daoist and Buddhist folklore.

10. Buddha's presence on earth is customarily described as passing through four periods. The last of these, the Final Dharma (Mofa 末法) period, is a time of decay and termination of Buddha's teachings, and is scheduled to last ten thousand years. Tathāgata (Rulai) is the highest of Buddha's titles and means "one who has arrived according to the norm," or "one who has attained the goal of enlightenment."

11. Buddha's "imparting" of the Four Teachings occurs in the *Lotus-sūtra*. See *Taishō*, 9.61a. The character *jiu* 究 in the verb form *fajiu* 發究, describing the last of the Four Teachings, appears to be corrupt. Here I follow the variant reading *fajiu* 發救 ("to save"), noted in the *Yi elai*, 44, n. 7.

12. *Yi elai*, 12–13.

13. Just one example is Daoshi's 道世 *Fayuan zhulin* 法苑珠琳, compiled in 668. This work includes numerous references to Samantabhadra, but says nothing about the bodhisattva's connection to Emei.

14. *Yi elai*, 19.

15. See, for instance, H. Maspero, "Le songe et l'ambassade de l'empereur Ming, etude critique des sources," *Bulletin de l'École Française d'Éxtrême-Orient* 10 (1910): 95–130.

16. Imperial patronage to Mount Wutai during the Tang is outlined in the *Qingliang shan zhi*, 126–28.

17. *Qingliang shan zhi*, 54–55.

18. *Jiatai Guiji zhi* 嘉泰會稽志 (1808 ed.), 15.38b–39a; *Wudeng huiyuan* 五燈會元 (Beijing: Zhonghua shuju, 1984), 2.124–25.

19. *Emei xian zhi* (1991 ed.), 621.

20. Cf. the remarks concerning appearances by Mañjuśrī (and other deities) on Wutai in Birnbaum, "Secret Halls of the Mountain Lords," esp. 134–40. On manifestations of Guanyin on Mount Putuo, see Chün-fang Yü's chapter "P'u-t'o shan: Pilgrimage and the Creation of the Chinese Potalaka," in *Kuan-yin*, 353–406, which describes how Guanyin appeared to pilgrims at the Tidal Sounds Grotto (Chaoyin dong) and how she sometimes would perform miracles there. As for Jiuhua, see the remarks later in this chapter regarding a monk from the kingdom of Silla named Kim Kyo Gak (d. 794).

21. This scripture is discussed below.

22. *Taishō*, 9.795c (60 *juan* version); *Taishō*, 10.441a (80 *juan* version).

23. *Taishō*, 10.334a.

24. *Taishō*, 36.387c. The description here is the forty-first of the eighty notable physical characteristics (*bashi suixing hao* 八十隨形好) of buddhas and bodhisattvas.

25. The idea that "Buddhist mountains" can (and do) embody deities is not unusual at all; in fact, it is quite common.

26. *Taishō*, 17.661b; cf. O'Jack, "Auspicious Lights," 99, n. 446.

27. As an example, consider the following line from the Tang poet Wang Ya (fl. ca. 900): "I only see the new moon spitting out moth eyebrows." *QTS*, 346.3877 ("Qiusi zeng yuan, er shou").

28. *Mountains of the Mind*, 17.

29. This is made very clear in the *Da Huayan jing luece* 大華嚴經略策, in *Taishō*, 36.709a. There are a few references in the *Canon* to the title *Zahua jing* (see, for instance, *Taishō*, 35.397b, and 35.494a), but these appear to be citations from or references to the *Huayan jing*.

30. *Yi elai*, 12.

31. *Shuzhong guangji*, 11.12b; translated in O'Jack, "Auspicious Lights," 118–19.

32. These translations are in four, ten, and seven *juan*, respectively.

33. *Yi elai*, 12; *Taishō*, 19.126c.

34. *Taishō*, 9.590a. In addition to the island-mountain "within the Four Great Seas," a second mountain "within the seas" is also mentioned.

35. My translation of *shuti*, or more properly *shutijia* 樹提伽 (Skt: Jyotiṣka), is tentative. This term has a wide range of meanings, including "shiny and fiery"; "heavenly body"; and so on. It is not clear to me which meaning applies in this context.

36. *Taishō*, 10.241b–c.

37. On interpretations of Buddhist scripture passages that link Putuo shan with Mount Potalaka, the mythological home of the bodhisattva Guanyin, see Yü, *Kuan-yin*, esp. 371 ff. As for Wutai, references to the mountain in various versions of the *Huayan jing*, especially as they relate to issues concerning scriptural authority, have been studied in detail by Étienne Lamotte, "Mañjuśrī," *T'oung Pao* 48 (1960); 1–96.

38. *Taishō*, 10.241c. The name Guangming shan, here translated as "Luminous and Bright Mountain," is also customarily used as a name for Potalaka, the mythological home of Guanyin in India.

39. I should mention here that there are different opinions in the scholarly community about when the name "Clear-and-Cool" became identified with Wutai. See the discussion of this issue by Chen Yangjiong and Feng Qiaoying in *Gu Qingliang zhuan*, 6. "Clear-and-Cool" as an alternate name for Mount Wutai extends at least back to the seventh century. In fact, one of the earliest monographs on Wutai, compiled by the monk Huixiang (who visited Wutai in 667), uses this name in its title. See *Gu Qingliang zhuan*, in *Taishō*, 51.1092c.

40. For instance, see Zhang Xiaomei et al., *Emei shan*, 4.

41. In fact, Yinguang, editor of the 1934 edition of the *Mount Emei Gazetteer* and himself a strong promoter of Emei's Buddhist tradition, dismisses the identification altogether, saying it was made by novices who know nothing about Buddhism. Yinguang, "Preface," 2.

42. See Fazang 法藏 (Tang), "*Huayan jing* tanxuan ji" 華嚴經探玄記, in *Taishō*, 35. 471c, and Chengguan 澄觀 (738?–820?), "*Dafang guangfo Huayan jing shu*" 大方廣佛華嚴經疏), in *Taishō*, 35.860b. Fazang specifically locates Guangming shan in southern India.

43. See *Yi elai*, 12, and *EMSZ* (1934 ed.), 2.26.

44. Yinguang, "Preface," 2.

45. *EMSZ* (1934 ed.), 2.26.

46. See the third of his "New Guiding Rules of Compilation" ("Xinding fanli"), in *EMSZ* (1934 ed.), 8b–9a.

47. This same argument is articulated in Justin O'Jack's "Auspicious Lights."

48. *Emei youji xuanzhu*, 51.

49. *Yudi jisheng*, 146.9b.

50. Writing in his preface (dated 1834), Hu Linxiu 胡林秀 notes that Jiang Chao's *Emei shan zhi* was based on Hu Shian's *Yi elai*, and that following the "warfare" (presumably, this is a reference to fighting during the Ming-Qing transition) nothing remained of the earlier written records on the mountain.

51. A useful, punctuated version of Wang Shixing's travel account is included in *Emei shan youji xuanzhu*, 22–32. The quotation from Fan Chengda's *WCL* and Wang's comments about Guangming shan and Puxian appear on p. 26. It might be mentioned here that several Ming and Qing dynasty *youji* on Emei shan, including Wang Shixing's account, are not included in the Jiang

Chao and subsequent editions of the *Mount Emei Gazetteer*, presumably because they express negative, critical attitudes about the cult of Samantabhadra on the mountain.

52. "You Da'e shan ji," in *Emei shan youji xuanzhu*, 41.

53. *Emei shan youji xuanzhu*, 41.

54. In *Emei shan youji xuanzhu*, 79–90; the line quoted here appears on p. 79. Jiang Gao's trip to Emei was undertaken during the Kangxi reign of the Qing. Since there was only one "Xinhai year" during this period, we thus know that his trip was made in 1671.

55. In *EMSZ* (1934 ed.), 6.11a.

56. The biographical information on Hu Shian that follows is drawn mainly from his biography and epitaph (*muzhi ming*) in the *Jingyan Gazetteer* (*Jingyan zhi* 井研志), which are reproduced in the 1988 edition of the *Yi elai*, 69–71.

57. Several additional factors make Hu Shian's gazetteer an especially valuable text. Hu was meticulous and critical in his collection of information, which was gathered over a period of twenty years during three separate visits to Emei in 1619, 1624, and 1639. His gazetteer is thus based both on personal observation and on "assorted works" concerning the mountain, which he checked for accuracy. Hu Shian also collected the poems and travelogues of various writers since the Tang and Song, added to these the verses and prose accounts that he himself had composed, and assembled all of these works into a single collection supplemented with illustrations (the pictures have not survived). The *Yi elai* was completed and printed during the Shunzhi reign period (1644–1662).

58. Xiong Feng has convincingly argued that Hu Shian went out of his way to be fair and balanced vis-à-vis Buddhism and Daoism on Mount Emei. See his "Shilun Mingdai Emei shan fojiao."

59. *Yi elai*, 22; also in *Emei shan youji xuanzhu*, 69.

60. The *Yi elai* was "lost" for many years until an original edition was discovered in the Beijing Municipal Library. Luo Kunqi and some of his colleagues at Emei shan prepared a reprint, with notes and collations, which was published in Leshan in 1988.

61. This line refers to the traditional Daoist sage and commentator who reportedly explained the basic Lingbao talismans to the Yellow Emperor.

62. According to the *Five Talismans Scripture* (*Wufu jing* 五符經), quoted in *EMSZ* (1991 ed.), 313, the Yellow Emperor received the "techniques of the Three Unities and Five Sprouts" from the "Sovereign" (Huangren 皇人) on Mount Emei. The precise identity of the "Sovereign" here is unclear.

63. The expression *huacheng* 化城, rendered here as "Conjured City," most often alludes to a famous parable in the *Lotus-sūtra* in which the leader of a group of pilgrims devises a "conjured" or "mirage" city where his charges can rest on the difficult road to enlightenment. Here the idea seems to be that Samantabhadra, after locating his *daochang* on Emei, devised a temporary

"conjured city" there for his followers (buildings, temples, rest stops, and so on), where they could find food and shelter during the exhausting pilgrimage to ultimate awakening.

64. "Layered calluses" (*chongjian* 重繭) refers to travelers or pilgrims.

65. Cao Xiheng's preface is reproduced in *EMSZ* (1991 ed.), 629.

66. In July, 2003, I visited Emei shan and retraced the travel itinerary in Fan Chengda's diary. All of the *topographical* sites mentioned by him are of course still there (some have different names now). As for the monasteries mentioned by Fan, none have survived from the Song. But some, such as the White Stream Monastery and Central Peak Monastery, have been rebuilt and are still active today.

67. Zheng Shiping 鄭石平 et al., eds., *Zhongguo sida foshan* 中國四大佛山 (Shanghai: Shanghai wenhua chubanshe, 1985).

68. *Pilgrims and Sacred Sites in China*, 190.

69. *EMSZ* (1687 ed.), Cao Xiheng, "Preface," 1b.

70. See the remarks by Li Changchun 李長春 in his preface to "Emei Dafo si Luocheng song bingxu" 峨眉大佛寺落成頌並序, rpt. in Xu Zhijing, *Emei shan zhi*, 6.16b. The preface is dated 1605.

71. This and related developments on Emei shan during the Ming are discussed in chapter 8.

72. According to one Tang account, three years after his death, the face of the monk's mummified corpse still remained as it was when he was alive, and his bones emitted sounds like "clanking, golden goblets." Resident monks on the mountain regarded this as an appearance of the bodhisattva Kṣitgarbha (Dizang) and, on the very spot where the monk's body had manifested a "globular light like a fire," erected a stone pagoda to house his mummified corpse. See Fei Guanqing 費冠卿 (Tang), "Jiuhua shan Huacheng si ji" 九華山化成寺記, in *Wenyuan yinghua*, 817.4313.

73. William F. Powell, "Literary Diversions on Jiuhua Mountain," 5.

74. Pan Guiming, *Zhongguo jushi fojiao shi*, 2:834.

75. See his "Thoughts on T'ang Buddhist Mountain Traditions and Their Context," and "Secret Halls of the Mountain Lords," esp. 116–18.

76. See Yü's chapter "P'u-t'o Shan," in *Pilgrims and Sacred Sites in China*," 190–245, and *Kuan-yin*, 353–406.

77. *Gu Qingliang zhuan*, preface by Chen Yangjiong and Feng Qiaoying, 3.

78. *Gu Qingliang zhuan*, 11.

79. Edwin O. Reischauer, trans., *Enmin's Diary: The Record of a Pilgrimage to China in Search of the Law* (New York: Ronald Press, 1955), 258–59. Birnbaum, in "Thoughts on T'ang Buddhist Mountain Traditions and Their Context," 8, acknowledges imperial patronage as "an important factor in the rise of the [Mañjuśrī] cult [on Wutai]," and identifies the Tang emperor Daizong as "perhaps the greatest of the Tang patrons."

80. "Secret Halls of the Mountain Lords," 136.

81. See Song Lian, "Zhuchi Jingci chansi Gufeng Degong taming xu" 住持淨
    慈禪寺孤峰德公塔銘序, cited in Chikusa, *Chūgoku bukkyō shakaishi
    kenkyū*, 108, n. 22.
82. Yü Chün-fang, "Ming Buddhism," 928–29.
83. Yü Chün-fang, "Ming Buddhism," 928.
84. Michael J. Walsh, "Profiting the Treasure House," 79.
85. *Fozu tongji*, in *Taishō*, 49.397c. See also *Guang Qingliang zhuan*, 63, which
    provides further details on this massive project.
86. On the imperial calligraphy specimens on display in Emei's White Stream
    Monastery, see chapter 6; on those presented to Wutai, see *Guang Qingliang
    zhuan*, 63.

CHAPTER 8. THE MING, QING, REPUBLICAN, AND MODERN ERAS

1. *Yuanshi*, 155.3654. Wang Liangchen (1231–1281) was a key Mongol commander in the military campaign to conquer Sichuan. Zan Wanshou (thirteenth cent) led the Song defense of Jiading in his capacity as Pacification
   Commissioner (Anfu shi) of the county.
2. *Songji sanchao zhengyao* 宋季三朝政要 (*Congshi jicheng chubian* ed.), 1.13.
3. *Yuanshi*, 155.3649.
4. *Emei shan zhi* (1997 ed.), 14.
5. These verses are scattered in different sources. See, for instance, *Emei xian
   zhi* (1997 ed.), 704; *EMSZ* (1997 ed.), 376.
6. On the other hand, Wutai was *the* Lamaist site in China most revered by
   the Mongols and received patronage from at least three Yuan emperors:
   Khubilai Khan (r. 1260–1294); Temür (r. 1294–1307; he personally visited
   Wutai in 1296, where he witnessed a "numinous appearance" [*lingxian* 靈
   現]); and Shidebala (r. 1321–1323; he also journeyed to Wutai, where in
   1322 he saw a manifestation of Mañjuśrī). The visits of Temür and Shidebala
   both resulted in new temple construction. *Qingliang shan zhi*, 5.3b–4a.
   There is also evidence that Putuo received imperial patronage during the
   Yuan. See Xue Dong 薛冬 and Cheng Dong 程東, *Putuo shan* 普陀山
   (Beijing: Yanshan chubanshe, 1993), 11.
7. Wu Changyi 吳昌裔 (1183–1240), "Lun jiu Shu sishi shu" 論救蜀
   四事書, in *Songdai Shuwen jicun* 宋代蜀文輯存, Fu Zengxiang
   傅增湘 (1872–1950), ed. (Hong Kong: Longmen shudian, 1971),
   84.17b.
8. My source for this figure is Jia Daquan, *Songdai Sichuan jingji shulun*, 17.
   Jia's computation includes the combined populations of four circuits: Yi,
   Zi, Li, and Kui.
9. Yang Bingkun, *Leshan gushi xintan*, 134. Yang's figure includes the population of the Chengdu and six other circuits created during the Yuan.
10. *EMSZ* (1997 ed.), 14; 260.
11. *Yi elai*, 19.

12. Yü, "Ming Buddhism," 894–95. Timothy Brook, in his article "At the Margin of Public Authority: The Ming State and Buddhism," discusses state regulations promulgated by the Ming government between 1381 and 1394, the aim of which was "to subordinate monks and monasteries to the complete authority of the state" (161). Brook also notes that the Buddhist church "would spend the rest of the Ming dynasty adjusting to, and growing out from under, the burden of these regulations" (161). Later in his essay, however, Brook acknowledges that emperors of the late Ming "turned their backs on the (later) regulations of the founder" (that is, Zhu Yuanzhang) and became "patrons of Buddhism" (177). This conclusion is supported by the substantial imperial patronage received by Mount Emei in the late fifteenth and early sixteenth centuries (discussed below).

13. "Ming Buddhism," 894.

14. For an overview and discussion of Zhu Yuanzhang's early policies in support of Buddhism see Brook, "At the Margin of Public Authority: The Ming State and Buddhism," 163–65.

15. *EMSZ* (1997 ed.), 246.

16. Xiong Feng, "Shilun Mingdai Emei shan fojiao," 1.

17. The figure "more than seventy" is based on my counting of monasteries and associated Buddhist structures (towers, galleries, and so on) mentioned in the "Daoli ji" chapter of the *Yi elai*.

18. Luo Kunqi, *Emei shan fojiao shihua*, 48. Luo does not cite his source(s) for this figure.

19. The list that follows is based mainly on information culled from chapter 6 of the *EMSZ* (1934 ed.).

20. I have not been able to establish the identity of Prince Fan of Shu (Shu Fanwang).

21. Zhu Huaiyuan, "Emei shan Puguang dian ji" 峨眉山普光殿記, in Cheng Dong 程東 and Xue Dong 薛冬, *Emei shan* 峨眉山 (Beijing: Beijing Yanshan chubanshe, 1993), 173–74.

22. *EMSZ* (1997 ed.), 261.

23. Zhang Xiaomei, *Emei shan*, 122. The precise identity of "Master Wang of Neijiang" (Neijiang Wanggong) is unknown.

24. *Eshan tushuo*, 1.14b.

25. This important development in Buddhism during the late Ming is discussed at length in Yü's *The Renewal of Buddhism in China* and Brook's *Praying for Power*.

26. This legend is recounted in Luo Kunqi, *Emei shan fojiao shihua*, 44.

27. Deqing is a great Buddhist master of the late Ming. For more information on his life and deeds, see especially Sung-peng Hsu, *A Buddhist Leader in Ming China: The Life and Thought of Han-shan Te-Ch'ing* (University Park and London: Pennsylvania State University Press, 1979), and Pei-yi Wu, "Te-ch'ing," in *Dictionary of Ming Biography*, 2:1272–75.

28. Else Glahn, "Fu-teng," in *Dictionary of Ming Biography*, 1:463.

29. Deqing, *Hanshan laoren mengyou ji* 憨山老人夢遊集 (*SKQS* ed.), 30.27a.
30. Else Glahn, 2:464.
31. Liu Junze, *Emei qielan ji*, 36b. Fudeng also completed construction of bronze halls for both Wutai and Putuo.
32. *EMSZ* (1997 ed.), 274.
33. *Eshan tushuo*, 1.8b; translated in Phelps, *Omei Illustrated Guide Book*, 27. Also mentioned in *EMSZ* (1934 ed.), 5.11b.
34. Luo Kunqi, *Emei shan fojiao shihua*, 43–44.; Xiong Feng, "Shilun Mingdai Emei shan fojiao" 3. This monastery is being rebuilt today, but in a different location in Emei City.
35. The Japanese priest's name was Tokushi 德始. He visited Emei in the late fourteenth century. The monk from Sri Lanka arrived during the Jiajing reign (1522–1566), bearing a "Buddha tooth" gift for the mountain.
36. Presumably, this was a copy of the Northern Ming edition of the *Tripiṭaka*, published in Beijing during the Yongle reign (1403–1424).
37. Liu Junze, *Emei qielan ji*, 55.
38. *Emei tushuo*, 1.11a; translated in Phelps, *Omei Illustrated Guide Book*, 47.
39. Judging from comments in the *EMSZ* (1934 ed.), 6.1b, these were the so-called Wanli edition of the *Tripiṭaka*.
40. *EMSZ* (1934 ed.), 6.2b.
41. On the thirty-room requirement for larger monasteries, see Chikusa, *Chūgoku bukkyō shakaishi kenkyū*, esp. 98 ff.
42. *EMSZ* (1997 ed.), 274.
43. *EMSZ* (1997 ed.), 17. See also Wang Zaigong 王在公 (d. 1627), "Tongtian dashi taming" 通天大師塔銘, in *EMSZ* (1934 ed.), 5.17b–19b.
44. *EMSZ* (1997) ed., 274.
45. Julian Ward, *Xu Xiake (1587–1641): The Art of Travel Writing* (Richmond, Surrey: Curzon, 2001), 21. In 1620 Xu Xiake expressed a desire to visit Mount Emei. This trip was never realized, he explains, because his "mother was aged and the road there was too far." See *Xu Xiake youji* 徐霞客遊記, Chu Shaotang 褚紹唐 et al., eds. (Shanghai: Shanghai Guji chubanshe, 1980), 1:33.
46. Fu Guangzhai, "Eshan xiugai panlu ji" 峨山修改盤路記, in *EMSZ* (1934 ed.), 6.9a.
47. This is the same text ("Eshan xiugai panlu ji") cited in n. 46 above. See *EMSZ* (1934 ed.), 6.9a–10a.
48. At the end of his essay (10a) Fu Guangzhai identifies the "Layman Jueyan" as one Wang Li. Fu also mentions that Wang Li had taken layman vows from "Daguan, the Honored One" (Daguan zunzhe). Wang Li is otherwise unknown.
49. "Master Wang" was in fact, Wang Xiangqian, Fudeng's friend and governor of Sichuan in the early seventeenth century. The identity of "Master Qiu" is unknown.
50. *EMSZ* (1934 ed.), 6.9b.

51. *Emei xian zhi* (Kangxi ed.), cited in Wei Fuping, *Emei congtan*, 145.

52. *Emei congtan*, 145.

53. *EMSZ* (1997 ed.), 19.

54. *EMSZ* (1997 ed.), 260. The editors of this gazetteer note that the new name is drawn from a passage in a Buddhist text titled *Shishi yaolan* 釋氏要覽 (*Taishō*, 54.0290a–b), which describes the "Four Graces" (*sien* 四恩) one receives from parents, teachers, emperors, and patrons, and the four ways in which one can demonstrate gratitude or loyalty (*bao* 報) for receiving their graces. Specifically, the term *baoguo* 報國 in this context means "show loyalty to the state/emperor for his grace or kindness" (*bao guozhu en* 報國主恩).

55. Jiang Gao 江皋 (*jinshi* 1661), "Emei shan Fuhu si beiji" 峨眉山伏虎寺碑記, in Cheng Dong and Xue Dong, *Emei shan*, 191.

56. *Eshan tushuo*, 1.7b.

57. To cite just one example, in 1745 the monk Xinglin built a new trail near the Sagely Accumulation Monastery. *Eshan tushuo*, 1.14b. All major trails on the mountain were in place by the Qing period. Most of the newer trails were actually side trails, leading to various off-trail sites.

58. Imperial support for Mount Emei during the Qing is better documented than in previous dynasties. For a detailed chronological outline of this support, see *Emei xian zhi* (1997 ed.), 19–26.

59. The information here and following on organized pilgrim group activity in the Qing relies heavily on He Zhiyu's 何志愚 useful article "Emei shan lishi qianshu" 峨眉山歷史淺述, in *Emei wenshi* 1: esp. 8–10.

60. There are two kinds of "wooden fish": a round one used for keeping time during chanting, and a longer one used for summoning monks to meals.

61. This incantation, popular with followers of Pure Land Buddhism, might be loosely translated: "I devote myself completely to Amitabha Buddha."

62. Luo Kunqi, *Emei shan fojiao shihua*, 57.

63. *Eshan tushuo*, 1.4b (following illustration #2).

64. These villas were located roughly 7 km/4 mi from the Loyal-to-the-State Monastery. This heavily forested area was isolated and provided cool temperatures during the hot summer months in Sichuan.

65. *EMSZ* (1997 ed.), 27.

66. Wei Fuping, *Emei congtan*, 146.

67. *EMSZ* (1997), 27. Apparently, the explosion was ignited by pilgrims burning incense in the grotto. See Nian Xianchun 年先春 and Li Xianding 李先定, "Sanxiao dong shijian shimo" 三霄洞事件始末, in *Emei wenshi* 1: 111–16, and Yi Ruilong 衣瑞龍, "Emei shan Sanxiao dong shijian tanyuan" 峨眉山三霄洞事件探源, in *Emei wenshi* 3:122–28.

68. EMSZ (1934 ed.), 8.11b.

69. *Travels and Researches in Western China* (1882; rpt., Taibei: Ch'eng-wen, 1971), 28.

70. Hayes, *Valiant But Gentle*, 212–13.

71. Harry A. Franck, *Roving through Southern China* (New York and London: Century, 1925), 577. On p. 575 Franck reports that "the iron big chains of other years having broken and fallen into disrepair." Virgil C. Hart, a Western missionary, reports seeing a proclamation on one of the old temples on Emei forbidding people from throwing themselves over the edge of the cliff. See Virgil C. Hart, *Western China: A Journey to the Great Buddhist Centre of Mount Omei* (Boston: Ticknor, 1888), 248–49.

72. As for suicides on Mount Tai, see Chavannes, *Le T'ai chan*, 63–64, and Paul Demiéville, "Le T'ai Chan ou la montagne du suicide," rpt. in *Choix d'études sinologiques (1921–1970)* (Leiden: Brill, 1973), 1–7. Chavannes notes that the "contagion of suicide" on Mount Tai extends back to the Ming period, when a wall was erected on the summit to prevent the practice. In his essay "The Pilgrimage to Wu-tang Shan" John Lagerwey discusses suicide on Mount Wudang in Hubei and translates an inscription forbidding its practice. See *Pilgrims and Sacred Sites in China*, esp. 319–20.

73. Xiao Xingwen 肖興文, "'Sheshen yai' qian de baohu shen" 舍身崖前的保護神, *Renmin gongan* 23 (1996): 16–18. My thanks to Justin O'Jack for bringing this report to my attention.

74. *Buddhism under Mao*, 10.

75. Kenneth Ch'en, *Buddhism in China*, 461.

76. "Religious freedom" in contemporary China is restricted to a community of five government-sanctioned "official religions": Buddhism, Islam, Daoism, Catholicism, and Protestantism. According to a white paper issued by the Chinese government in 2002, there are about sixteen thousand Buddhist monasteries and more than thirty-two hundred thousand Buddhists monks and nuns in China today. See the "International Religious Freedom Report; 2002," prepared by the U.S. Department of State (http://www.state.gov/g/drl/rls/irf/2002/13870.htm).

77. Welch, *Buddhism under Mao*, 14.

78. *EMSZ* (1997), 307.

79. *EMSZ* (1997), 36.

80. *Xiandai fojiao* (June 1953): 57.

81. *Xiandai fojiao* (May 1957): 16.

82. Holmes Welch, *Buddhism under Mao*, 310.

83. Welch, 310.

84. *EMSZ* (1997 ed.), 38.

85. *EMSZ* (1997 ed.), 39.

86. *EMSZ* (1997 ed.), 40. Presumably, destruction of the twenty temples mentioned here was the result of all metal on their premises being stripped and taken away for melting and industrial purposes.

87. These verses are anthologized in *EMSZ* (1997 ed.), 412.

88. *EMSZ* (1997 ed.), 42.

89. *EMSZ* (1997 ed.), 45.

90. *EMSZ* (1997 ed.), 46.

91. Shu Hun 蜀魂 and Lian Xiaofang 連曉仿, "Emei shan lüyou ye de fazhan" 峨眉山旅遊業的發展, in *Emei wenshi* 5:192.

92. Not surprisingly, my efforts to gather data on investment and profits earned from the tourist industry have failed. Local leaders will simply not divulge such information.

93. A fascinating issue, but one I cannot address properly here because of space limitations, concerns the tension that exists between the resident Buddhist community on Emei and provincial and local developers of the tourist industry. Surely the monasteries benefit from the presence of large numbers of tourists who visit and patronize their temples and commercial enterprises (hostels, gift shops, and so on). But how much financial support do the monasteries and monks receive, if any, from the party leaders who head the tourist industry? In other words, what is the nature of the relationship between the mountain's monastic community and the developing tourist industry? How will this relationship develop and change in the future? These are questions that, alas, must be addressed in a future study.

94. With the exception of 2002 (see below), the figures here and following are based on information in the *EMSZ* (1997 ed.), 533.

95. I suspect the attendance drop in 1989 was the result of the Tian'anmen incident, which had an especially negative impact on the overseas tourist industry in China.

96. This figure was provided to me by Mr. Xiong Feng, chief historian at the Mount Emei Museum.

97. One unconfirmed report I have heard says the Samantabhadra statue on the Golden Summit will rise to a height of 69 m/233 ft.

98. Cf. the following comment by Wen-jie Qin: "The sacred mountain (that is, Mount Emei) was made sacred again because sacredness could now sell." "The Buddhist Revival in Post-Mao China: Women Reconstruct Buddhism on Mt. Emei" (Ph.D. diss., Harvard University, 2000), 133.

CLOSING THOUGHTS

1. "Preface" (undated), in *Illustrated Omei Guide Book*. Zhao Mingsong served as magistrate of Emei xian from December 1934 until September 1937. He wrote his preface in response to an invitation from Dr. Phelps.

2. The phrase "'true appearance" alludes to Su Shi's famous couplet: "I do not know Mount Lu's true appearance; / This is because I am in the very midst of the mountain itself." *Su Shi shiji*, 23.1219 ("Ti Xilin bi").

3. Nuns first appeared on Mount Emei in 1956, as a result of a government effort to reform Buddhism on the mountain.

4. Wen-jie Qin has studied the nun population at Crouching Tiger Monastery. She notes the nuns observed there "seemed young as high school students." See her "The Buddhist Revival in Post-Mao China," 9.

Selected Bibliography

Primary Sources on Mount Emei and Surrounding Administrative Areas

Emei shan zhi 峨眉山志 (*Mount Emei Gazetteer*). Compiled by Jiang Chao 蔣超 (1623–1672). 1672.

Emei shan zhi 峨眉山志 (*Mount Emei Gazetteer*). Compiled by Cao Xiheng 曹熙衡 (fl. late seventeenth cent). Preface dated 1687.

Emei shan zhi 峨眉山志 (*Mount Emei Gazetteer*). Compiled by Xu Zhijing 許止淨, in collaboration with Yinguang 印光 (1861–1940). 1934.

Emei shan zhi 峨眉山志 (*Mount Emei Gazetteer*). Edited by *Emei shan zhi* bianzuan weiyuanhui. Chengdu: Sichuan kexue jishu chubanshe, 1997.

Emei shan zhi bu 峨眉山志補 (*Supplement to the Mount Emei Gazetteer*). Compiled by Zhang Yujia 張玉甲. 1713; rpt., Taibei: Mingwen shuju, 1980.

Emei xian zhi 峨眉縣志 (*Emei Town Gazetteer*). Preface by Yin Zongji 尹宗吉 dated 1541; rpt., Haikou: Hainan chubanshe, 2001.

Emei xian zhi 峨眉縣志 (*Emei Town Gazetteer*). Compiled by Wang Xie 王燮, Zhang Xijin 張希縉, and Zhang Xixu 張希珝. 1813.

Emei xian zhi 峨眉縣志 (*Emei Town Gazetteer*). Edited by Sichuan sheng *Emei xian zhi* bianzuan weiyuanhui. Chengdu: Sichuan renmin chubanshe, 1991.

Emei xian xuzhi 峨眉縣續志 (*Continuation of the Emei Town Gazetteer*). Compiled by Li Jincheng 李錦成 and Zhu Rongbang 朱榮邦. 1911; rev. ed. 1935; rpt., Taibei: Xuesheng shuju, 1971.

Eshan tushuo 峨山圖說 (*Illustrated Talks on Mount Emei*). Edited by Huang Xitao 黃錫濤, Huang Shoufu 黃綬芙 (d. 1886), and Tan Zhongyue 譚鐘嶽. 1887–1891; rpt. Chengdu: Sichuan renmin chubanshe, 1984.

Jiading fu zhi 嘉定府志 (*Jiading Municipality Gazetteer*). Compiled by Zhu Qingyong 朱慶鏞 et al. 1864.

Jiading fu zhi 嘉定府志 (*Jiading Municipality Gazetteer*). Edited by Sichuan sheng Leshan shi shizhongqu bianshi xiuzhi bangongshi. Leshan, 1986.

Jiazhou ershan zhi 嘉州二山志 (*Gazetteer on the Two Mountains of Jia County*). Compiled by Yuan Zirang 袁子讓 (fl. ca. 1600). 1605.

Yi elai 譯峨籟 (*Translating the Sounds of E[mei]*). Compiled by Hu Shian 胡世安 (1593–1663). Compiled between 1639 and 1644; preface dated 1639. Rpt. in 1988 by Sichuan sheng Leshan shi shizhongqu bianshi xiuzhi bangongshi, with punctuation by Luo Kunqi 駱坤琪 and collations by Mao Xipang 毛西旁.

Yi elai huilu 譯峨籟彙錄 (*Classified Notes on Translating the Sounds of E[mei]*). Compiled by Hu Shian 胡世安 (1593–1663). N.d.; rpt., Leshan: Leshan shi shizhongqu bianshi xiuzhi bangongshi, 1988.

OTHER PRIMARY SOURCES

Cao Xuequan 曹學佺 (1574–1646). *Shuzhong guangji* 蜀中廣記 (*Extensive Records on Shu*). *SKQS* ed.

———. *Shuzhong mingsheng ji* 蜀中名勝記 (*Records of Famous and Surpassing Sights in Shu*). Punctuation and collations by Liu Zhijian 劉知漸. Chongqing: Chongqing chubanshe, 1984.

Fan Chengda 范成大 (1126–1193). *Fan Shihu ji* 范石湖集 (*Fan Shihu's Collected Works*). Beijing: Zhonghua shuju, 1962.

———. *Wuchuan lu* 吳船錄 (*Diary of a Boat Trip to Wu*). *Zhibuzu zhai congshu* ed.

Fangyu shenglan 方輿勝覽 (*Scenic Sights of the World*). Compiled by Zhu Mu 祝穆 (fl. thirteenth cent); addenda and revisions by Zhu Zhu 祝洙 (*jinshi* 1256). Beijing: Zhonghua shuju, 2003.

Fozu lidai tongzai 佛祖歷代通載 (*Comprehensive Materials on Buddha and the Patriarchs through the Successive Eras*). Compiled by Nianchang 念常 (1282–1341). *Taishō* ed.

Fozu tongji 佛祖統紀 (*Comprehensive Chronicle of Buddha and the Patriarchs*). Compiled by Zhipan 志磐 (1220–1275). *Taishō* ed.

Gaoseng zhuan 高僧傳 (*Biographies of Eminent Monks*). Compiled by Huijiao 慧皎 (497–544); collation and notes by Tang Yongtong 湯用彤 (1893–1964); textual organization by Tang Yixuan 湯一玄. Beijing: Zhonghua shuju, 1992.

Gaoshi zhuan 高士傳 (*Biographies of Eminent Figures*). Compiled by Huangfu Mi 皇甫謐 (215–282). *SKQS* ed.

Gu Qingliang zhuan 古清涼傳 (*Ancient Records on {Mount} Clear-and-Cool*). Compiled by Huixiang 慧祥 (seventh cent). *Taishō* ed.

Gu Qingliang zhuan, Guang Qingliang zhuan, Xu Qingliang zhuan 古清涼傳, 廣清涼傳, 續清涼傳 (*Ancient Records on {Mount} Clear-and-Cool; Expanded Records on {Mount} Clear-and-Cool; Continuing Records on {Mount} Clear-and-Cool*). Collations and commentary by Chen Yangjiong 陳揚炯 and Feng Qiaoying 馮巧英. Taiyuan: Shanxi renmin chubanshe, 1989.

Hanshu 漢書 (*History of the Han*). Edited by Ban Gu 班固 (AD 32–92) et al. Beijing: Zhonghua shuju, 1962.

Hou Hanshu 後漢書 (*History of the Later Han*). Edited by Fan Ye 范曄 (398–445) et al. Beijing: Zhonghua shuju, 1965.

Huayang guozhi jiaozhu 華陽國志校注 (*Collations and Commentary on the Monograph on the Land South of {Mount} Hua*). Compiled by Chang Qu 常璩 (fourth cent); notes and commentary by Liu Lin 劉琳. Chengdu: Ba Shu shushe, 1984.

Jinshu 晉書 (*History of the Jin*). Edited by Fang Xuanling 房玄齡 (578–648) et al. Beijing: Zhonghua shuju, 1974.

Jiuhua shan zhi 九華山志 (*Mount Jiuhua Gazetteer*). Edited by *Jiuhua shan zhi* bianzuan weiyuanhui. Hefei, Anhui: Huangshan shushe, 1990.

Jiu Tangshu 舊唐書 (*Old Tang History*). Edited by Liu Xu 劉昫 (887–946) et al. Beijing: Zhonghua shuju, 1975.

Li Bo 李白 (701–762). *Li Bo ji jiaozhu* 李白集校注 (*Li Bo's Collected Works, with Collations and Commentary*). Collations and commentary by Qu Shuiyuan 瞿蛻園 and Zhu Jincheng 朱金城. Shanghai: Shanghai Guji chubanshe, 1980.

Lu You 陸游 (1125–1210). *Ru Shu ji* 入蜀記 (*Record of a Trip to Shu*). In *Lu Fangweng quanji* 陸放翁全集: *Weinan wenji* 渭南文集 43.265–48.298. Taibei: Heluo tushu chubanshe, 1975.

———. *Laoxue an biji* 老學庵筆記 (*Notes from the Venerable Learner's Retreat*). Beijing: Zhonghua shuju, 1979.

Qingliang shan zhi 清涼山志 (*Mount Clear-and-Cool Gazetteer*). Compiled by Zhencheng 鎮澄 (Ming). Preface dated 1596. Yangzhou: Jiangsu guangling guji keyinshe, 1993.

Quan Songwen 全宋文 (*Complete Song Prose*). Edited by Zeng Zaozhuang 曾棗莊, Liu Lin 劉琳, et al. Chengdu: Ba Shu shushe, 1988–.

Quan Tangwen 全唐文 (*Complete Tang Prose*). Compiled by Dong Hao 董浩 (1740–1818). Beijing: Zhonghua shuju, 1983.

Shanhai jing jiaozhu 山海經校注 (*Collations and Commentary on the Mountains and Seas Classic*). Collations and commentary by Yuan Ke 袁珂. Shanghai: Shanghai Guji chubanshe, 1980.

Shenxian zhuan 神仙傳 (*Biographies of Immortals*). Compiled by Ge Hong 葛洪 (283–343). *SKQS* ed.

Shiji 史記 (*Records of the Historian*). Edited by Sima Qian 司馬遷 (ca. 145–ca. 86 BC). Beijing: Zhonghua shuju, 1959.

Shisan jing zhushu 十三經注疏 (*Commentaries and Sub-Commentaries on the Thirteen Classics*). Edited by Ruan Yuan 阮元 (1764–1849). Beijing: Zhonghua shuju, 1980.

Shuijing zhu 水經注 (*Commentary on the Waterways Classic*). Compiled by Li Daoyuan 酈道元 (d. 527). 1897 ed.; rpt. Chengdu: Ba-Shu shushe, 1985.

Sichuan tongzhi 四川通志 (*Comprehensive Gazetteer of Sichuan*). Compiled by Chang Ming 常明 (Qing), Yang Fangcan 楊芳燦 (1754–1816), et al. 1816; rpt., Chengdu: Ba Shu shushe, 1984.

Song Gaoseng zhuan 宋高僧傳 (*Biographies of Eminent Song Monks*). Compiled by Zanning 贊寧 (919–1022). Beijing: Zhonghua shuju, 1987.

Song huiyao jigao 宋會要輯稿 (*Edited Draft of the Assembled Essential {Documents} on the Song*). Compiled by Xu Song 徐松 (1781–1848) et al. 1936; rpt., Taibei: Xinwenfeng chuban gongsi, 1976.

Songshi 宋史 (*History of the Song*). Edited by Togto [Tuotuo 脫脫] (1314–1355). Beijing: Zhonghua shuju, 1977.

Su Shi 蘇軾 (1037–1101). *Su Shi shiji* 蘇軾詩集 (*Collected Poems of Su Shi*). Commentary by Wang Wengao 王文誥 (1764–?). Beijing: Zhonghua shuju, 1982.

Taiping huanyu ji 太平寰宇記 (*Records Encompassing the Universe from the Taiping [Reign]*). Compiled by Yue Shi 樂史 (930–1007). Rpt., Yonghe: Wenhai chubanshe, 1963.

Taishō shinshū daizōkyō 大正新修大藏經 (*The Tripiṭaka: With Major Corrections and New Revisions*). Edited by Takakusu Junjirō 高楠順次郎 et al. Tokyo: Daizō, 1924–1932.

Weishu 魏書 (*History of Wei*). Edited by Wei Shou 魏收 (506–572). Beijing: Zhonghua shuju, 1974.

Wenxuan 文選 (*Choice Literary Selections*). Compiled by Xiao Tong 蕭統 (501–531); commentary by Li Shan 李善 (?–689). Hong Kong: Shangwu yinshuguan, 1973.

Xin Tangshu 新唐書 (*New Tang History*). Edited by Ouyang Xiu 歐陽修 (1007–1072) et al. Beijing: Zhonghua shuju, 1975.

Yudi jisheng 輿地紀勝 (*Chronicle of Scenic Spots in the World*). Compiled by Wang Xiangzhi 王象之 (*jinshi* 1196). 1849 ed.; rpt., Yangzhou: Jiangsu guangling guji yinshe, 1991.

Yuanhe junxian tuzhi 元和郡縣圖志 (*Maps and Gazetteer of the Commanderies and Townships of the Yuanhe [Reign]*). Compiled by Li Jifu 李吉甫 (758–814). *Congshu jicheng* ed.

Yuanshi 元史 (*History of the Yuan*). Edited by Song Lian 宋濂 (1310–1381) et al. Beijing: Zhonghua shuju, 1995.

Zhibuzu zhai congshu 知不足齋叢書 (*Collectaneum from the Knowledge-Is-Insufficient Studio*). Compiled by Bao Tingbo 鮑廷博 (1728–1814). 1805; rpt. 1921.

Reference Works

A Dictionary of Chinese Buddhist Terms: With Sanskrit and English Equivalents and a Sanskrit-Pali Index. (*Zhong-Ying foxue cidian* 中英佛學辭典). Compiled by William Edward Soothill and Lewis Hodous. 1937; rpt., Gaoxiong: Buddhist Culture Service, 1971.

A Dictionary of Official Titles in Imperial China. Compiled by Charles O. Hucker. Stanford: Stanford University Press, 1985.

A Sung Bibliography (*Bibliographie des Sung*). Edited by Yves Hervouet. Hong Kong: The Chinese University Press, 1978.

Alphabetical List of Geographical Names in Sung China. Compiled by Hope Wright. Paris: École Practique Des Hautes Études Centre De Recherches Historiques, 1956.

Boltz, Judith M. *A Survey of Taoist Literature: Tenth to Seventeenth Centuries.* Berkeley: Institute of East Asian Studies, University of California, 1987.

Daoism Handbook. Edited by Livia Kohn. Leiden: Brill, 2000.

Dictionary of Ming Biography. Edited by L. Carrington Goodrich and Chaoying Fang. New York and London: Columbia University Press, 1976.

Dushi yinde 杜詩引得 (*A Concordance to the Poems of Tu Fu*). Compiled by William Hung (Hong Ye 洪業) et al. Harvard-Yenching Institute Sinological Index Series, Supp. No. 20. 1947; rpt., Cambridge: Harvard University Press, 1966.

Foguang da cidian 佛光大辭典 (*Great Dictionary of Buddhism*). Compiled by Xingyun 星雲. 5th ed., Gaoxiong: Foguang chubanshe, 1989; electronic version, 1997.

Foxue da cidian 佛學大辭典 (*The Great Dictionary on Buddhism*). Edited by Ding Fubao 丁福保 (1874–1952). 1922; rpt., Beijing: Wenwu chubanshe, 1984.

Read, Bernard E. *Chinese Medicinal Plants from the Pen Ts'ao Gang Mu* AD *1596*. 1936; rpt. Taibei: Southern Materials Center, 1982.

Songdai guanzhi cidian 宋代官制辭典 (*Dictionary of the Civil Service System in the Song Period*). Compiled by Gong Yanming 龔延明. Beijing: Zhonghua shuju, 1997.

Songren zhuanji ziliao suoyin 宋人傳記資料索引 (*Index to Biographical Materials on Song Figures*). Compiled by Wang Teh-yi [Wang Deyi] 王德毅 et al. Taibei: Dingwen shuju, 1974–1976.

Songren zhuanji ziliao suoyin bubian 宋人傳記資料索引補編 (*Supplement to Index to Biographical Materials on Song Figures*). Compiled by Li Guoling 李國玲 et al. Chengdu: Sichuan daxue chubanshe, 1994.

Stuart, G. A. Chinese *Materia Medica*: *Vegetable Kingdom*. 1911; rpt., Taibei: Southern Materials Center, 1987.

Sung Biographies. Edited by Herbert Franke. Wiesbaden: Franz Steiner, 1976.

Tang Wudai renwu zhuanji ziliao zonghe suoyin 唐五代人物傳記資料綜合索引 (*Comprehensive Index to Biographical Materials on Personages of the Tang and Five Dynasties*). Compiled by Fu Xuancong 傅璇琮 et al. Beijing: Zhonghua shuju, 1982.

SECONDARY SOURCES: CHINESE AND JAPANESE

Chen Cheng-Siang (Chen Zhengxiang) 陳正祥, trans. *Wuchuan lu de zhushi* 吳船錄的注釋 (*Commentary and Explanations to Diary of a Boat Trip to Wu*). 1976; rpt. in Chen Cheng-siang, *Zhongguo youji xuan zhu* 中國遊記選注. Hong Kong: Commercial Press, 1979, 1:11–53.

Chen Shuzhou 陳述舟. *Emei shan shi xuanzhu* 峨眉山詩選注 (*Selected Poems on Mount Emei with Notes*). Chengdu: Sichuan renmin chubanshe, 1986.

Chikusa Massaki 竺沙雅章. *Chūgoku bukkyō shakaishi kenkyū* 中國佛教社會史研究 (*Studies in the Social History of Chinese Buddhism*). Kyoto: Dōhōsha, 1982.

Cui Rongchang 崔榮昌. *Sichuan fangyan yu Ba-Shu wenhua* 四川方言與巴蜀文化 (*Sichuan Dialect and Ba and Shu Culture*). Chengdu: Sichuan daxue chubanshe, 1996.

Cui Zhengsen 崔正森. *Wutai shan fojiao shi* 五臺山佛教史 (*History of Buddhism on Mount Wutai*). Taiyuan: Shanxi renmin chubanshe, 2000.

Emei shan shiwen xuanzhu 峨眉山詩文選注 (*Selected and Annotated Poetry and Prose on Mount Emei*). Edited by Wei Yixiong 魏奕雄. Chengdu: Xi'nan jiaotong daxue chubanshe, 1995.

Emei shan youji xuanzhu 峨眉山游記選注 (*Selected and Annotated Travel Records on Mount Emei*). Commentary by Gu Ren 顧刃 and Zhang Longgao 張隆高. Chengdu: Sichuan renmin chubanshe, 1986.

Emei shan yu Ba Shu fojiao 峨眉山與巴蜀佛教 (*Mount Emei and Buddhism in Ba and Shu*). Edited by Yongshou 永壽. Beijing: Zongjiao wenhua chubanshe, 2004.

Emei wenshi 峨眉文史 (*Culture and History of Emei*). 1985?–.

Fan Chengda biji liuzhong 范成大筆記六種 (*Six Occasional Works by Fan Chengda*). Edited by Kong Fanli 孔凡禮. Beijing: Zhonghua shuju, 2002.

Fan Chengda nianpu 范成大年譜 (*Chronological Biography of Fan Chengda*). Compiled by Kong Fanli 孔凡禮. Ji'nan: Qi Lu shushe, 1985.

Fan Chengda nianpu 范成大年譜 (*Chronological Biography of Fan Chengda*). Compiled by Yu Beishan 于北山. Shanghai: Shanghai Guji chubanshe, 1987.

Feng Ling 馮陵. *Emei jingguan tanyuan* 峨眉景觀探源 (*Tracing the Sources of Emei's Landscape*). Chengdu: Chengdu keji daxue chubanshe, 1992.

Gu Jichen 顧吉辰. *Songdai fojiao shigao* 宋代佛教史稿 (*Draft History of Buddhism during the Song Period*). Zhengzhou: Zhongzhou guji chuban she, 1993.

Huang Ch'i-chiang (Huang Qijiang) 黃啟江. *Bei Song fojiao shi lungao* 北宋佛教史論稿 (*Draft Essay on the History of Buddhism in the Northern Song*). Taibei: Taiwan Shangwu yinshuguan, 1997.

Liang Fangzhong 梁方仲 (1908–1970). *Zhongguo lidai hukou, tiandi, tianfu tongji* 中國歷代戶口田地田賦統計 (*Statistics on China's Population, Land, and Land Taxes through the Successive Eras*). Shanghai: Renmin chubanshe, 1980.

Liu Junze 劉君澤. *Emei qielan ji* 峨眉伽藍記 (*Notes on Emei's Monasteries*). Leshan: Leshan chengbao yinshuabu, 1947.

Luo Kunqi 駱坤琪. "Emei shan fojiao yu daojiao" 峨眉山佛教與道教 ("Buddhism and Daoism on Mount Emei"). *Emei wenshi* 1:21–36.

———. *Emei shan fojiao shihua* 峨眉山佛教史話 (*Historical Talks on Buddhism on Mount Emei*). Edited by Luo Kunqi. Chengdu: Sichuan renmin chubanshe, 1992.

———. "Emei shan zongjiao lishi chutan" 峨眉山宗教歷史初探 ("Preliminary Investigation of Mount Emei's Religious History"). *Zongjiaoxue yanjiu* 宗教學研究 5 (Apr. 1984): 27–34, 14.

Luo Mengting 羅孟汀. *Emei shan kaituo shilue* 峨眉山開拓史略 (*Outline History of the Emergence of Mount Emei*). Unpublished manuscript, dated 1990; revised, 2000.

Ogawa Tamaki 小川環樹, trans. *Gosen roku, Ranpi roku, Sanran roku* 吳船錄, 攬轡錄, 驂鸞錄 (*Diary of a Boat Trip to Wu, Diary of Grasping the Carriage Reins, Diary of Mounting a Simurgh*). Tokyo: Heibonsha, 2001.

Qingcheng shan zhi 青城山志 (*Mount Qingcheng Gazetteer*). Edited by Wang Wencai 王文才. 1887; rev. and expanded ed., Chengdu: Sichuan renmin chubanshe, 1982.

Qingcheng zhinan 青城指南 (*Guide to [Mount] Qingcheng*). Qingcheng Tianshidong, 1939.

Satake Yasuhiko 佐竹靖彦. "Tōsō henkakuki ni okeru Shisen Seitofuro chiiki shakai no hembō ni tsuite" 唐宋變革期における四川成都府路地域社會の變貌について ("On the Transformation of Local Society on Sichuan's Chengdu *fu* Circuit in Relation to the Tang-Song Transition"). *Tōyōshi kenkyū* 東洋史研究 35.2 (1976): 103–36.

Satō Seijun 佐藤成順. *Sōdai bukkyō no kenkyū* 宋代佛教の研究 (*Studies on Buddhism During the Song Period*). Tokyo: Sankibō Busshorin, 2001.

Song Liao Jin huajia shiliao 宋遼金畫家史料 (*Historical Materials on Painters of the Song, Liao, and Jin*). Edited by Chen Gaohua 陳高華. Beijing: Wenwu chubanshe, 1984.

Takao Giken 高雄義堅. *Sōdai bukkyōshi no kenkyū* 宋代佛教史の研究 (*Studies on the History of Buddhism during the Song Period*). Kyoto: Hyakkuen, 1975.

Tang Changshou 唐長壽. *Jia Mei jigu lu* 嘉眉稽古錄 (*Investigation of Ancient Sources on Jia and Mei*). Leshan: N.p., 2001.

Wang Zhiping 王志平. *Diwang yu fojiao* 帝王與佛教 (*[China's] Emperors and Buddhism*). Beijing: Huawen chubanshe, 1997.

Wei Fuping 魏福平. *Emei congtan* 峨眉叢談 (*Collected Talks on Emei*). Chengdu: Xi'nan jiaotong daxue chubanshe, 1986.

Yang Bingkun 楊炳昆. *Leshan gushi xintan* 樂山古史新探 (*New Investigations into the Ancient History of Leshan*). Chengdu: Sichuan daxue chubanshe, 1991.

Zhang Xiaomei 張肖梅 et al. *Emei shan* 峨眉山 (*Mount Emei*). 1936; rpt. Taibei: Xinwenfeng chuban gongsi, 1978.

Zhou Cong 周聰. "Emei diqu guzu shu shikao" 峨眉地區古族屬試考 (*Preliminary Study of the Ancient Ethnic Groups in the Emei Area*). *Emei wenshi* 7: 123–30.

WESTERN LANGUAGES

Bagley, Robert, ed. *Ancient Sichuan: Treasures from a Lost Civilization*. Princeton: Princeton University Press, 2001.

Bielenstein, Hans. "Chinese Historical Demography AD 2–1982." *Bulletin of the Museum of Far Eastern Antiquities* 59 (1987): 1–288.

Birnbaum, Raoul. *Studies on the Mysteries of Mañjuśrī: A Group of East Asian Mandalas and Their Traditional Symbolism*. Boulder: Society for the Study of Chinese Religions, Monograph No. 2, 1983.

———. "Thoughts on T'ang Buddhist Mountain Traditions and their Context." *T'ang Studies* 2 (Winter 1984): 5–23.

———. "Secret Halls of the Mountain Lords: The Caves of Wu-t'ai Shan." *Cahiers d' Éxtreme-Asie* 5 (1989) 115–40.

Bowring, Richard. "Buddhist Translations in the Northern Sung." *Asia Major*, Series 3, 5.2 (1992): 79–93.

Brook, Timothy. "At the Margin of Public Authority: The Ming State and Buddhism." In *Culture and State in Chinese History: Conventions, Accommodations, and Critiques*, edited by Theodore Huters et al. Stanford: Stanford University Press, 1997, 161–81.

———. *Praying for Power: Buddhism and the Formation of Gentry Society in Late Ming China*. Cambridge: Council on East Asian Studies and the Harvard-Yenching Institute, 1993.

Buddhism in the Sung. Edited by Peter N. Gregory and Daniel A. Getz, Jr. Honolulu: University of Hawaii Press, 1999.

Chapman, Beryl. "Travel Diaries of the Southern Sung Dynasty with Particular Reference to Fan Ch'eng-ta's *Wu-ch'uan lu*." Unpublished M.A. thesis, University of Sydney, 1983.

Chavannes, Édouard. *Le Tai chan: Essai du monographie d'un culte chinois*. Paris: Leroux, 1910.

Ch'en, Kenneth K. S. *Buddhism in China: A Historical Survey*. Princeton: Princeton University Press, 1964.

———. "The Role of Buddhist Monasteries in T'ang Society." *History of Religions* 15.3 (1976): 209–30.

Demiéville, Paul. "La Montagna dans l'art littéraire chinois." *France-Asie* 183 (1965): 7–32.

Faure, Bernard. "Space and Place in Chinese Religious Traditions." *History of Religions* 26 (1987): 337–56.

Gimello, Robert M. "Imperial Patronage of Buddhism in the Northern Song Dynasty." In *Proceedings of the First International Symposium on Church and State in China*, edited by John E. Geddes. Taibei: Tamkang University, 1987, 73–85.

———. "Chang Shang-ying on Wu-t'ai Shan." In *Pilgrims and Sacred Sites in China*, 89–149.

Grapard, Allan G. "Geotyping Sacred Space: The Case of Mount Hiko in Japan." In *Sacred Space: Shrine, City, Land*, edited by Benjamin Z. Kedar et al. New York: New York University Press, 1998, 215–24.

Gregory, Peter N., and Patricia Buckley Ebrey. "The Religious and Historical Landscape." In *Religion and Society in T'ang and Sung China*, 1–44.

Hahn, Thomas. "The Standard Taoist Mountain." *Cahiers d'Extreme-Asie* 4 (1988): 145–56.

———. "Daoist Sacred Sites." In *Daoism Handbook*, 683–708.

Hargett, James M. *On the Road in Twelfth Century China: The Travel Diaries of Fan Chengda, 1126–1193.* Wiesbaden: Franz Steiner, 1989.

———. "Where Are the Moth-Eyebrows? On the Origins of the Toponym 'Omeishan' 峨眉山." *Hanxue Yanjiu (Chinese Studies)* 12.1 (1994): 335–48.

———. "Li Bo (701–762) and Mount Emei." *Cahiers d' Extrême-Asie* 8 (1995): 67–85.

Huang, Chi-chiang (Huang Qijiang 黃啟江). "Experiment in Syncretism: Ch'i-sung (1007–1072) and Eleventh-Century Buddhism." Ph.D. diss., University of Arizona, 1986.

———. "Imperial Rulership and Buddhism in the Northern Sung." In *Imperial Rulership and Cultural Change in Traditional China*, edited by Frederick P. Brandauer and Huang, Chun-chieh. Seattle: University of Washington Press, 1994, 144–87.

Hung, William. *Tu Fu, China's Greatest Poet.* Cambridge: Harvard University Press, 1952.

Jan, Yün-hua. "Buddhist Relations between India and Song China." *History of Religions* 6.1 (Aug. 1966): 24–42 (Part 1); 6.2 (Nov. 1966): 135–68 (Part 2).

Knechtges, David. R., trans. *Wen xuan, or Selections of Refined Literature, Volume 1: Rhapsodies on Metropolises and Capitals.* Princeton: Princeton University Press, 1982.

Mizuno, Kōgen. *Buddhist Sutras: Origin, Development, Transmission*. Tokyo: Kōsei, 1982.

Needham, Joseph et al. *Science and Civilisation in China, Volume 4, Physics and Physical Technology: Part III: Civil Engineering and Nautics*. Cambridge: Cambridge University Press, 1971.

O'Jack, Justin. "Auspicious Lights of the Golden Summit: Transforming the Religious Identity of a Sacred Mountain in Southwest China." M.A. thesis, University of California, Santa Barbara, 2002.

Phelps, Dryden Linsley. *A New Edition of the Omei Illustrated Guide Book*. Chengdu: Western China Union University, 1936.

———. "A Sung Dynasty Document of Mount Omei." *Journal of the West China Border Research Society* 11 (1939): 66–77.

Pilgrim and Sacred Sites in China, edited by Susan Naquin and Chün-fang Yü. Berkeley: University of California Press, 1992.

Powell, William F. "Mt. Jiuhua: The Nine-Floriate Realm of Dicang Pusa." *Ajia bunka kenkyū (Asian Culture Studies)* (International Christian University Tokyo) 16: 55–69.

———. "Literati Diversions on Jiuhua Mountain: The Buddhist Realm of Dizang Bodhisattva." Paper presented at the conference "Mountains and Cultures of Landscape in China," University of California, Santa Barbara, January 1993.

Religion and Society in T'ang and Sung China, edited by Peter N. Gregory and Patricia Buckley Ebrey. Honolulu: University of Hawaii Press, 1993.

Robson, James. "The Polymorphous Space of the Southern Marchmount (Nanyue): An Introduction to Nanyue's Religious History and Preliminary Notes on Buddhist-Daoist Interaction." *Cahiers d'Extrême-Asie* 8 (1995): 221–64.

Sage, Steven F. *Ancient Sichuan and the Unification of China*. Albany: State University of New York Press, 1992.

Schafer, Edward H. *Mao Shan in T'ang Times*. 2nd edition, revised. Boulder: Society for the Study of Chinese Religions, Monograph No. 1, 1989.

Schmidt, J. D. *Stone Lake: The Poetry of Fan Chengda, 1126–1193*. Cambridge: Cambridge University Press, 1992.

Seidel, Anna. "Chronicle of Taoist Studies in the West 1950–1990." *Cahiers d'Extrême-Asie* 5 (1989–90): 223–347.

Shi, Mingfei. "Li Po's Ascent of Mount Omei: A Daoist Vision of the Mythology of a Sacred Mountain." *Taoist Resources* 4.1 (Jan. 1993): 31–45.

Soymié, Michel. "Le Lo-feou chan, étude de géographie religieuse." *Bulletin de l'École Française d'Éxtrême-Orient* 48 (1956): 1–139.

Strassberg, Richard E. *Inscribed Landscapes: Travel Writings from Imperial China.* Berkeley: University of California Press, 1994.

Syrokomla-Stefanowska, A. D. "Fan Ch'eng-ta's Wu-Boat Journey of 1177." *Journal of the Oriental Society of Australia* 10.1–2 (June 1975): 65–80.

The Cambridge History of China, Vol. 6: Alien Regimes and Border States, 907–1368, edited by Herbert Franke and Denis Twitchett. Cambridge: Cambridge University Press, 1995.

Verellen, Franciscus. "Liturgy and Sovereignty: The Role of Taoist Ritual in the Foundation of the Shu Kingdom (907–925)." *Asia Major* 3rd ser., 2, pt. 1 (1989): 59–78.

―――. "The Beyond Within: Grotto-Heavens (Dongtian) in Taoist Ritual and Cosmology." *Cahiers d'Extrême-Asie* 8 (1995): 265–90.

Vervoon, Aat. "Cultural Strata of Hua Shan, the Holy Peak of the West." *Monumenta Serica* 39 (1990–91): 1–30.

Walsh, Michael J. "Profiting the Treasure House: Monasteries and Land in Thirteenth-Century China." Ph.d. diss., University of California, Santa Barbara, 2000.

Weinstein, Stanley. *Buddhism under the T'ang.* Cambridge, New York: Cambridge University Press, 1987.

―――. "Imperial Patronage in the Formation of T'ang Buddhism." In *Perspectives on the T'ang,* edited by Arthur F. Wright and Denis Twitchett. New Haven: Yale University Press, 1973, 265–306.

Welch, Holmes. *Buddhism under Mao.* Cambridge: Harvard University Press, 1972.

Wong, Dorothy C. "Four Sichuan Buddhist Steles and the Beginnings of Pure Land Imagery in China." *Archives of Asian Art* 51 (1999): 56–79.

Wright, Arthur F. "T'ang Tai-tsung and Buddhism." In *Perspectives on the T'ang,* 239–63.

Wu, Hung. "Buddhist Elements in Early Chinese Art (second and third centuries AD)." *Artibus Asiae* 47.3–4 (1986): 263–352.

Yü, Chün-fang (Yu Junfang 于君方). *The Renewal of Buddhism in China: Chu-hung and the Late Ming Synthesis.* New York: Columbia University Press, 1981.

―――. "Ming Buddhism." In *Cambridge History of China: The Ming Dynasty, 1368–1644.* edited by Frederick Mote and Denis Twitchett. Cambridge: Cambridge University Press, 1998, 893–952.

———. *Kuan-yin: The Chinese Transformation of Avalokiteśvara.* New York: Columbia University Press, 2001.

Zhang Cong 張聰. "The Culure of Travel in Song China (960–1276)." Ph.D. diss., University of Washington, Seattle, 2003.

Zürcher, Erik. *The Buddhist Conquest of China.* Leiden. Brill, 1959.

Glossary-Index

Tongzhi 同治 reign (1862–1874), 182
tongzhong 銅鐘. *See* bronze bell
transformed body (*huashen* 化身), 98
Transformed One (Huaren 化人), 127, 128, 235n47
Transparent Glass River (Boli jiang 玻璃江), 58, 217n81
Transverse Mountain (Hengshan 衡山), 33
"traveling to the lands of immortals" (*youxian* 游仙), 37
travel parishes (*youzhi* 游治), 69
Traversing-the-Clouds Hill (Lingyun shan 凌雲山), 63, 85, 86, 88, 122, 225n118
Traversing-the-Clouds Monastery (Lingyun si 凌雲寺), 85
Tree Bark Hall (Mupi dian 木皮殿), 82, 114
Tree Bark Village (Mupi li 木皮里), 114
Tripitika (*Sanzang jing* 三藏經), 93, 94, 146, 147, 148, 175, 176, 215n59, 227n17, 235n48, 238n29, 244n36, 244n39
True and Proper Son of Buddha (Zhenzheng fozi 真正佛子), 173
true appearance (*zhen mianmu* 真面目), 193–94
True Appearance Cloister (Zhenrong yuan 真容院), 164
true facts (*zhen yuanli* 真原理), 194
true friend and spiritual guide (*shan zhishi* 善知識), 141, 144–45
true function (*zhen gongyong* 真功用), 194
tuhui 圖繪. *See* sketches and paintings
tūla-clouds (*douluo yun* 兜羅雲; *douluo mianyun* 兜羅綿雲), 18, 90, 114, 115, 121, 123, 125, 126
Tūla-Cloud World (Douluo mian shijie 兜羅綿世界), 125
tuofo 陀佛, 16
tutan 土壇. *See* altars of earth
tuzhu minzu 土著民族. *See* aboriginal people
twin-shoulder stone hoes (*shuangjian shichu* 雙肩石鋤), 65
Twin Streams (Shuangxi 雙溪), 106, 133
Twin Streams Bridge (Shuangxi qiao 雙溪橋), 106, 107, 133
two sages (*ersheng* 二聖), 101

udumbara flower (*youtan* 優曇), 122, 233n21
uncultivated and abandoned (*huangfei* 荒廢), 67
UNESCO (United Nations Educational, Scientific, and Cultural Organization), 191
Universal Light Hall (Puguang dian 普光殿), 116, 170
Universal Light Monastery (Puguang si 普光寺), 223n97

Universal Light Radiance (Pu guangming 普光明), 127
Universal Security Cloister (Pu'an yuan 普安院), 104

vacuous void (*xukong* 虛空), 119, 231n2
Vajra Mountain (Jin'gang shan 金剛山), 149
van der Loon, Piet, 220n42
various Buddhas (*zhufo* 諸佛), 146
Verellen, Franciscus, 203n16, 203n20, 221n50, 221n51, 221n60
Vice Grand Councilor (Can[zhi] zheng[shi] 參 [知] 政 [事]), 120
Vietnam, 46
virtuous acolytes (*detong* 德童), 95
virtuous adepts (*deshi* 德士), 95

Walsh, Michael J., 163, 242n84
Wang 王 (surname), 134
Wang Anshi 王安石 (1021–1086), 159
Wang Bao 王褒, 221n54
Wang Chang 王昶 (1725–1806), 227n18
Wangdi 望帝, 25
Wang Guanzhuo 王冠倬, 218n97
Wang Gun 王袞 (tenth cent), 97, 98, 123, 228n38, 233n28
Wang Haoyin 王好音 (Qing), 228n34
Wang Jian (847–918), Grave of (Wang Jian mu 王建墓), 48
Wang Li 王禮, 244n48
Wang Liangchen 汪良臣 (1231–1281), 165, 242n1
Wang, Master (Wanggong 王公), 178, 244n49
Wang, Master, of Neijiang (Neijiang Wanggong 內江王公), 170, 243n23
Wang Ming 王明, 203n21
Wang Qi 王琦 (1696–1774), 207n37
Wang Shixian 汪世顯 (1195–1243), 165
Wang Shixing 王士性 (1547–1598), 153, 230n73, 239n51; "Record of a Trip to Mount Emei" ("You Emei shan ji" 游峨眉山記), 230n73
Wang Wencai 王文才, 213n17
Wang Xiangqian 王象乾 (*jinshi* 1571; d. 1630), 173, 244n49
Wang Xiangzhi 王象之 (*jinshi* 1196), 220n41, 224n113
Wang Xizhi 王羲之 (321–379; alt. 303–361), 26, 27, 102
Wang Ya 王涯 (fl. ca. 900), 238n27
Wang Yangying 王陽英 (*style* Zhaozu 昭祖; *jinshi* 1124; d. 1159), 58, 217n82
Wang Zaigong 王在公 (d. 1627), 244n43